Finding Billy

Diana J. Dale

Finding Billy

AN
INTERNET
ODYSSEY

by

Diana Thompson Dale

GOLDEN SLIPPER PRESS

—— DENVER ——

For information, contact
Golden Slipper Press
15 Corona Street
Denver, CO 80218-3803
www.goldenslipperpress.com

Publisher's Cataloging-in-Publication Data

Dale, Diana Thompson.
    Finding Billy: an Internet odyssey by Diana Thompson Dale.
    p.   cm.
    Includes bibliographical references.
    LCCN: 2003107551
    ISBN: 0-9741596-3-8

    1. Wisner, Billy. 2. World War, 1939-1945—Aerial
operations, American. 3. World War, 1939-1945—Missing
in action—Italy. 4. World War, 1939-1945—Missing in
action—United States. 5. Air pilots, Military—United States
—Biography. 6. Missing persons—Investigation. I. Title.

D790.D24 2003   940.54'4973
                                 QBI03-200499

Production Management by
Paros Press
1551 Larimer Street, Suite 1301   Denver, CO 80202
303-893-3332   www.parospress.com

BOOK DESIGN BY SCOTT JOHNSON

Printed in the United States of America
1   3   5   7   9   10   8   6   4   2

TABLE OF CONTENTS

In Memory of Matthias Hosp

FOREWORD

Denver, Colorado
August 1, 2000

This would have been Billy's 76th birthday, so it's fitting I start telling his story today.

I've wanted to all my life, but until now I didn't know how it ended. I credit the Freedom of Information Act and the Internet for changing that. I thank the strangers, now good friends, whom I met along the way for making it a reality.

Had he lived, what Billy would have become is a mystery. But because of who he was when he died, he will remain forever a beautiful young man at the top of his game.

This book is written as a tribute to all the boys like Billy, not heroes but ordinary guys doing a job that makes the world safe.

May they never be forgotten.

PROLOGUE

Dallas, Texas
November 4, 1944

My darling,
*   Yesterday we received a telegram telling [us] you were missing,*
and we can't and won't believe it. I know you are safe somewhere. We are
so upset and have written eight letters trying to get some information,
also went to the Red Cross. Dad went all to pieces, but everybody is trying
to tell us you will get out somehow, wherever you are. I know you will let
us know if you can possibly do it. I just can't think, honey, and certainly
can't write. Maybe somebody will open this and can give me some
information. God bless and keep you, darling. I just can't stand it if I
don't hear. Your mom loves you. I will write every day. Maybe you will
come back in the meantime, and I want you to have your letters.

Mom

* * *

Billy was always a part of our lives. Whenever we visited our grand-parents in Dallas my sister and I slept in what had been his room. A print of an Indian and his pony still hung on one wall, a relic of Billy's cowboys-and-Indians phase. On another wall Billy and his sister smiled at us from a black-and-white portrait. He was 10, and his dimpled grin betrayed an impish quality. His sister, our mother at 16, looked far more sophisticated than her years.

A cardboard box in one of Billy's dresser drawers held the last of his belongings—a couple of flight scarves, his aviator sunglasses, a hunting knife, a wallet. Once or twice I opened the box to finger the fringe on the scarves and smell the hand-tooled leather wallet that still held a photo of his dad. Knowing they were treasures, I always put them back exactly as I found them.

On the closet shelf in the back bedroom was a tin breadbox full of documents and letters relating to Billy's wartime service and his disappearance. And a large, hand-made cedar chest held even more of his things. Mixed in with turn-of-the-century photo albums were Billy's baby book, his high-school, college, and flight-school yearbooks, report cards, an autograph book, and a scrapbook, whose cover bore the symbol of a son in the service, a single blue star on a field of white surrounded by a red border.

There was no shrine, but Billy's presence filled the little house on Melbourne Street. I can still picture my favorite photo of him on the shelf in the living room. Billy is hunkered down in his Army Air Corps uniform, relaxed and smiling broadly. His face is lean, but the dimples still show. Between his knees sits a little brown-and-white mutt, just like the ones in the "Our Gang" comedies of Billy's era. Next to the photo Billy's medals shine on a blue velvet background in a round gold frame. The Purple Heart holds center stage.

One person's whole life, tied up in boxes and bundles, scattered through three rooms in a tiny house.

My grandmother loved to talk about Billy. She rarely volunteered information, but if something I would do or say triggered a memory, she'd tell me a story about him. She wore her grief like a birthmark, never calling attention to it but not hiding it, either. Without meaning to, she imprinted her loss on me.

When I was old enough to understand, I shared her frustration at not knowing where Billy was. All she knew was that his plane had gone down over a place called Bolzano, Italy. It sounded exotic, and I dreamed of the day I might go there and look for him.

I knew there had to be more to Billy than some pictures, his belongings, and my family's memories. But over the years we'd lost touch with nearly everyone outside the family who had known him. I knew there must have been others, strangers to us, who were Billy's friends.

I wondered what he was like when he went to war. I wondered about Billy, the grown-up—Billy, the soldier.

When I started asking questions, I never expected to uncover a clue that might lead to finding Billy.

1

IS ANYBODY OUT THERE?

http://wae.com/messages/msgs
305th Fighter Wing, 1st Fighter Group,
71st Fighter Sqdn, Foggia Italy
Message posted by Diana Dale on Friday, May 01 [1998]:

Message:
Looking for anyone who might have known my uncle, Lt. William
O. Wisner, who flew P-38s out of Foggia starting 9/14/44. He flew
ten missions (Budapest, Munich, Athens, Vienna, Blackheimer,
Brussels, Regensburg). Was MIA over Bolzano … on 10/20/44. I
know he was short-lived over there, but would love to hear from
anyone who knew him or remembered how he went down. His
mother was never able to resolve his loss due to incomplete info on
his disappearance. Thanks.

* * *

In 1998 I hadn't used the Internet for much of anything. I was just
learning to trust e-mail, but I thought surfing the 'Net was a waste of
time. What little I had done, not looking for anything specific, had
yielded wasted time and few results. It never occurred to me it might be
useful in finding a person, especially one who had been dead for 54 years.

Besides, I knew my grandmother had exhausted every resource in her search for her son back in the '40s. She never could accept Billy's official, "missing presumed killed" status, and she agonized for years before finally giving up. We all trusted that if new information had come to light we would have been told.

Billy was gone, no one knew where he was, and that was that.

Still, I wanted to know more about him. It took changing my mind about the Internet to make that possible.

Nineteen-ninety-eight was the year my mother received a donation request from the American Battlefield Monuments Commission for a World War II memorial in Washington, D.C. She asked me if I knew anything about the project. We were both skeptical, assuming there was already a WWII memorial, so I told her I would check the Internet to find out if it was legitimate.

It was. I printed out the Web pages and mailed them to her, and Mama sent her donation in Billy's memory. But the Commission needed his service information for the dedication, and I had Billy's records in my grandparents' cedar chest, which I inherited in 1983 when Papa, my grandfather, moved into a nursing home. Even though it was big and rather ugly, that cedar chest held a lot of memories. To me it was the most important item in Idy and Papa's house.

When I opened the chest to get the information for Mama, the smell of old cedar, Papa's stale cigar smoke, and musty papers took me back to my last trip to Dallas. I'd flown down to help my parents ready Papa's house for sale. At 92 he had been a widower for nine years, and although he had remained active until he broke his hip, the house needed work. It fell to Mama and me to organize things while Daddy made repairs. Not much had changed since the death of my grandmother, whom I called Idy. So we knew what to expect when we opened the cedar chest: photographs, scrapbooks, a box of fleece marked "from my grandfather's sheep" in Idy's hand, and a moth-eaten coverlet made from the same wool.

We took an old breadbox down from the closet shelf and started to go through it. Idy had kept Billy's military files in there, including his pilot logbook and the crumpled telegram announcing his disappearance. Underneath the folders was a bundle of letters to him from Idy, Papa, and my mother that he never received. Each envelope had been marked "Missing" and was sent back by the War Department after his plane went down. Most were still sealed, so out of curiosity we opened one and started to read it.

But neither of us could finish. It happened to be the first letter Idy had written Billy after they'd received the telegram saying he was missing, and it broke our hearts. In tears, we tucked it back among the files and other letters, added the box and Billy's belongings to the chest, and packed it up for the move.

There was a lot representing Billy's life, but I remember thinking it just wasn't enough. Billy was so loved, so loving, so full of life, his spirit filled that little house.

I was born three years after he disappeared, but I have vivid second-hand memories of him. Until I was older and had learned to be uncomfortable about the loss of a loved one, I would ask Idy about Billy. Her face would beam as she told me how sweet and loving he was and how much I looked like him. My sister, Billie, bore his name, but I carried his coloring, eyes, and dimples, even his hands. Sister and I knew we were special because of legacies we had inherited from a young man we knew so well but had never met.

I felt such a strong kinship with him, in fact, there was a time I thought I was Billy. For a high school English composition assignment, we had to describe our philosophy of life. I knew at 17 mine was unformed, but I gave it my best effort, hoping some research would provide enlightenment. Transmigration of souls, an Eastern belief, caught my interest. If it were true that a soul could choose who to be in its next life, I was sure Billy's would have chosen someone in his own family. Because Sister was born only three months after Billy died, I reasoned her soul would have been in place already. I would have been his next logical choice. I have moved on in my beliefs since then, but I can't entirely discount the theory because I still feel his presence. At the very least it would explain my love of Glenn Miller and pre-'50s antiques.

Whenever Idy spoke of Billy, it was always with a note of hope. Had she accepted his death completely, she knew he would be lost to her forever. So a part of her continued to believe he was alive somewhere, lost, or perhaps a victim of amnesia. When I was little I shared those hopes, and I would envision Billy walking through the front door. Idy and Papa never moved away from the house Billy left when he went off to fight the Nazis, so I knew he'd be able to find his way home. And there they would be, waiting for him.

As an adult, that fantasy came back to me at the end of the film *Close Encounters of the Third Kind,* when the mother space ship releases its cargo of captured humans. Among them is a squadron of WWII fighter pilots, and I found myself peering into the faces of the dazed men as they emerge from the ship, hoping to see someone who looked like Billy. I knew it was only a movie, but still I wondered.

And so did my grandmother, all her life. About three years before Idy passed away, during one of our family visits my sister's name kept coming up. Idy sat and listened quietly as one person mentioned that Billie was teaching in Michigan and another remarked that Billie and her husband Harold had had a wonderful time in Florence. Sister told me later that Idy had looked at her with tears in her eyes, a pained expression on her face, and asked, "But where's my Billy?"

In later years, whenever Idy would start to talk about him we'd switch to another topic, thinking we would spare her the sadness. But once, frustrated and exasperated at having been pushed aside yet again, she said, "No one will ever let me talk about Billy. You don't realize how good it makes me feel to talk about him, and everyone keeps changing the subject." I realized then that while Idy was trying to deal with her grief, we were trying to avoid ours.

But I can't remember a time when Papa even mentioned his name. One time, after Idy passed away, Mama's cousin Cecil came to see us when we were in Dallas. He had on Billy's flight jacket, which Papa had given him years before, and he modeled it proudly for all of us. Getting no reaction from Papa, Cecil reminded him whose jacket it was, but all Papa could do was puff on his cigar and nod gravely. I knew Cecil had grown up with Billy and loved him, too, and Papa wanted him to have that jacket, but I wished he had put it away. It didn't seem right that anyone but Billy should be wearing it.

And so it was in 1998 that all these thoughts of Billy came flooding back because of the WWII memorial. I sent Mama Billy's service information for her dedication, and then I started wondering. Could the Internet help me find anyone who remembered him? Maybe someone could tell me what Billy had been like as a buddy, a grown-up person in his own right, instead of Mama's little brother or Idy's baby boy. Perhaps I could learn something the government couldn't or wouldn't reveal.

I decided to find out.

I wasn't sure where to start, so in one of the Internet search engines, I typed "71st Fighter Squadron." Not too many sites came up, but one looked promising. WAE, a CD-ROM re-seller "specializing in history, military history, military interest and aviation CD-ROM publications," had a message board with hundreds of postings from servicemen looking for buddies, war memorabilia, and related information. I posted a message that included Billy's unit and the missions he'd flown, and I asked if there was anyone out there who remembered him. I left the rest to chance.

I knew it was a long shot, and putting a message on an Internet bulletin board can be a gamble if you don't monitor the site, because someone might post a response on the board but not contact you directly. Novice that I was, after I posted my message I forgot about it.

But Billy was still in the back of my mind. The following month Sister and I were leaving for Italy with her daughter, Katie, and we decided to go see Billy's name on the Wall of the Missing at the Florence American Cemetery. I checked out the cemetery's Web site and learned it was on a main bus route seven miles south of Florence, easy to get to. This Internet thing was beginning to come in handy.

And just before I left for Europe I got a response from the WAE posting. A Polish war historian, Michal Mucha, had seen "Blackheimer" in the list of missions Billy flew and asked for more details. Blackheimer, he told me, was the English version of Blechhammer, the German name for Kedzierzyn, a city that was in Poland before the war. Michal was researching Allied raids over Polish territory and wanted to add Billy's Blackheimer mission to his research. I told him what I knew—only the date and results from Billy's logbook—and I sent him Billy's photograph and told him the details of his disappearance.

Michal promised to let me know if he came across anything pertinent to Billy in his research and asked for a copy of Billy's Missing Aircrew Report (MACR). I didn't know what he was talking about. When I checked Billy's files in the cedar chest, nothing fit that description so I let it go.

Besides his offer of help, Michal had some trivia to pass along. "By the way," he wrote, "one of my close friends met a Pole in south Poland some years ago. He saw a pair of Lightnings [P-38s] over Poland at WW2. The P-38s had black spinners and black waists. The black markings were carried usually by the 71st Fighter Squadron/1st Fighter Group. It seems the Pole saw a pair of Lightnings from your uncle's squadron." Small world, I thought.

I set Michal's e-mail aside and left for Florence. It was late June and the city was hot, crowded, noisy, and jammed with tourists and conventioneers. Before our trip to the cemetery, which would get us out of town on one of the hottest days, we visited an artists' supply shop. I wanted to take a rubbing of Billy's name for Mama, and the shop owner not only sold us the graphite and a piece of paper, he also told us which bus to take to the cemetery.

It's a good thing he did, too, because the Web site directions didn't specify a bus route, and the posted schedules were confusing. With our picnic lunch packed, we boarded the air-conditioned bus and asked the driver if he could stop at the cemetery. He nodded, and we were on our way.

A half-hour later, as the noise and fumes of the departing bus faded, we took in the vista in front of us. Beyond a lovely stream lay a broad expanse of green dotted with white, stretching up the hillside as far as our eyes could take us.

Besides the caretaker and a groundskeeper mowing the grass, we were the cemetery's only living souls. The caretaker looked up Billy's name in his computer and, as we expected, told us that Billy had no grave. He pointed us toward the Wall of the Missing, far at the back, nestled against a hillside at the end of a long, broad path.

As we made our way, the gravel path crunching under our feet, the only other sounds we could hear were birdsong, the distant drone of the lawnmower, and the whoosh-whoosh-whoosh of the sprinklers. That was a welcome relief from the constant, irritating drone of those omnipresent Italian motor scooters we had learned to dodge but come to hate.

We gazed over acres of perfectly arranged white marble crosses and Stars of David, dazzling in the bright Tuscan sun. As our perspective changed, the patterns transformed from straight rows into smooth, graceful arcs; then into a checkerboard, then back again. The effect was hypnotic.

Finally we reached the wall. It was huge. Thirty granite tablets, each nearly 10 feet wide and inscribed with 24 names, stretched from one end to the other. As we got closer and our eyes adjusted to the shade, we could see that the names were arranged alphabetically. We found the tablets bearing the W's. At last there was Billy's name, on the next-to-last panel, fifth from the bottom:

But it was far above our heads, over 20 feet up. We couldn't reach it for the rubbing, and I toyed with the idea of asking for a ladder. But even if I could get high enough, it was obvious my 24x30-inch piece of paper wouldn't get even a third of the inscription.

Pondering the problem, we explored the two atria flanking the wall. One housed a chapel; the other a fountain surrounded by spectacular inlaid onyx, lapis and multicolor marble maps detailing the Allied campaigns in Italy after the D-Day invasion.

On an adjacent wall an inscription declared: "Their bodies are buried in peace, their name [sic] liveth for evermore." But only half that sentiment applied to Billy, I thought. His name surely would endure, carved as it was into a massive granite slab, but we didn't know whether Billy's body was buried in peace. We didn't know where it was or even if it existed anymore. As far as we knew it had vanished.

We sat down in the shade to eat lunch and take in the view. Beyond the cemetery lay the hills of Tuscany. Vineyards, lines of poplars, olive trees, and villas blanketed the panorama in a patchwork of greens and grays, stuccoes and red roofs. Except for a highway in the foreground, the tableau looked like the landscape in every Renaissance painting we'd ever seen.

We lingered as long as we could, drinking in the coolness and the quiet, before we started back down the hill. I had abandoned the idea of scaling the wall, but I needed to take a rubbing of something so I chose a headstone, one of many with the same inscription. I fought back tears as I read it: HERE RESTS IN HONORED GLORY, A COMRADE KNOWN BUT TO GOD. Sister and Katie held the paper still on the smooth marble face while I knelt and rubbed the graphite over the letters. Slowly they emerged, and I carefully rolled up the paper, so I wouldn't smudge the image.

As I stood up, I thought maybe, just maybe, that was the grave that held Billy.

2

THE CLUE

From: Michal Mucha
Sent: Wednesday, July 22, 1998
To: Dale, Diana
Subject: Italy, 20-Oct-44

Poznan, Poland

Dear Diana,
What [sic] are you doing? Well I hope.
I just received an e-mail message from an Italian researcher and
author Ferdinando D'Amico on the events of October 20, 1944.
His reply–attached.
I hope it will be of some interest.
Regards, Mike

* * *

I'd been back from Europe less than a month when I received another
message from my Polish e-mail friend, Michal Mucha. He had been in
touch with an Italian researcher and author about the events on the
day Billy disappeared, and he forwarded the man's reply.

Ferdinando D'Amico had told Michal, "It is really difficult for me to
be of some help in your search for a main reason: the area where the accident should have taken place is well into the Alps, so that to find something is an almost impossible task!" Then he quoted the circumstances of

the crash from a book I hadn't heard about, *An Escort of P-38s–The 1st Fighter Group in World War II*, by John D. Mullins*.

What a coincidence. I remembered John Mullins from 1994 when Mama, Daddy, and I attended the 1st Fighter Group Association reunion banquet in Colorado Springs. Billy's boyhood friend, John Chopelas, had told me that the reunion would be in my vicinity at a time when Mama and Daddy would be with me in Colorado, so I signed us up in the hope that we might meet someone there who remembered Billy.

But no one did, not even John Mullins, even though he'd flown the same mission in a different squadron when Billy went down. Only Sidney Howell, a man sitting at the table next to us, remembered Billy's name from his flight notes. He promised to send me copies of them when he got home.

Mullins had given us a copy of the October 20, 1944, mission report. It was the first time I had seen the complete report, and I scanned it for new information.

> Lts Olson and Twedt collided in mid-air near
> Bolzano, Italy and Lt Wisner spun in at Bolzano,
> Captain Elliott crashlanded at Duress, Italy;
> pilot ok. All this was due to intense, accurate
> heavy flak over Bolzano at 1115 to 1120 hours.

This was interesting. I never knew there was a fourth pilot involved in the incident. It went on:

> When Red Flight was about 5 miles northeast
> of town, Red #1 and 3 were hit and #1 called Pet
> Dog and told him he had two men on single engine
> and that he was going to take squadron back to
> base. About this time over "B" channel came the
> words: "Go down", repeated several times and then
> Red #1 and White #4 collided in mid-air. The
> flying debris from this collision apparently hit
> Red #2 and in a few seconds he went into a spin
> and went in. No chutes were observed.

---

*Mullins, John D., *An Escort of P-38s, The 1st Fighter Group in World War II*. Oxford: Phalanx Publishing Co., Ltd., 1995.

Billy was Red #2; that dovetailed with the story we'd always heard—that Billy's plane had been hit by falling debris. But, just like all the others, this report didn't pinpoint where Billy ended up.

When Howell got home from the reunion he sent me his notes, as promised. They coincided with the short time Billy was there, but Sid had to stop keeping them when he learned it was against Army regulations to track such sensitive information. He had flown four missions with Billy, each time in a different squadron. Interesting, but not helpful. But he did enclose an undated squadron photograph taken at Foggia. Howell apologized for its quality, saying it had been enlarged from a 2x2 $1/2$-inch photo. I peered at the faces. The typical southern Italian sun was high and bright, so the pilots' eyes were in deep shadow. Finding Billy eluded me. He could have been any one of the men–or none of them.

I bought a copy of Mullins's book. Billy was in the index, page 143, mentioned in the passage detailing the events of October 20. I saw that an error in the 1944 report had made its way into the text of Mullins's book, where the clerk had typed "Bologna," instead of Bolzano in one paragraph. I knew that was wrong and overlooked it, but Fernando D'Amico didn't and had told Michal Mucha he couldn't help me, because searching for a crash with a 250-mile discrepancy would be impossible.

I turned to the pilot roster in the book's appendix. Their names were not in alphabetical order, so it took me a while to find the men involved in Billy's crash. After Lt. Lowell Twedt, KIA 20 Oct 44, comes Lt. William Wisner, KIA 20 Oct 44. In another column, Lt. Virgil Olson was also listed KIA 20 Oct 44.

Mullins's history of the 1st Fighter Group gave an interesting snapshot of life at the Foggia base but held no clue to where Billy was. Grateful for the reference, though, I asked Michal to thank Mr. D'Amico for taking the time to help a stranger.

On February 15, 1999, nearly 10 months after I'd posted my Internet message, a man named Steve Duncan e-mailed me. His message said, "Did you get any responses on Wisner from any 71st F.S. people? I responded to your query on the 'Net today, even though it was an old query. You can contact me for more as I'm reluctant to provide more info on the web on my friend Jim Graham. He may have already responded to you and I believe he may be the best source for information on Wisner. Let me know if you had any success."

I hadn't checked the Web site since I first posted my message and sure enough, there was Steve's reply with Jim Graham's e-mail address. I answered Steve, gave him more information on Billy, and thanked him for the referral.

Before I could write Mr. Graham, Duncan wrote again, saying he was in the 71st but didn't remember Billy and couldn't give me any more details about his disappearance. He, too, recommended Mullins's book and warned me that it might not have any answers. "Bear in mind," he said, "that it is a big sky and no one is standing still and the discipline of flying the formation, maintaining a watchful eye and following the flight leader's lead is the number one priority." He told me his friend Jim Graham, who was also in the 71st, was compiling the archival record for the squadron's 2000 reunion.

His next statement gave me hope. "The 71st has as recently as June 1, 1998, been involved in locating a crash site in [Bulgaria] that we hope is the site of a pilot lost on June 10, 1944, the only one unaccounted for of many losses that day on that mission. The lady searching for her uncle has met with the U.S. Government Agency having the responsibility to do the search and she has the means to travel and has been to the site on two occasions. This search was led by a non-military man and conducted mostly by e-mail, including people in the Balkans that gave their time. I believe the e-mail search lasted about six months. Much of the details helping the search had [their] origin in the 1st Fighter Group's and 71st's mission reports and the 1st Fighter Group history by John Mullins. So give it a go with your objective and try to contact Jim Graham."

It was ironic that another niece had been looking for her uncle, also more than 50 years later. I didn't dare hope we'd have the same success in finding Billy, but just knowing they were making progress got my juices flowing. I wanted to see where this might lead.

So I wrote Jim Graham that day. He replied the next, saying he was heartened that the loved ones of the 71st guys are still thinking of them and looking for "new news."

He elaborated on the search Steve had mentioned, saying, "I became interested in digging out the records for the outfit after participating in an e-mail search for the crash site of Lt. Carl Hoenshell who crashed in Bulgaria on June 10, 1944 after a mission to Ploesti. We think we located the specific site after a request from his niece for help. I imagine that if you have a copy of the mission report… you have just about as much as I do. I presume you know that your uncle's name is on the 'Wall of the Missing' at the American military cemetery in Florence, Italy."

So far, nothing new and, yes, I did know that.

Graham re-stated the circumstances of Billy's crash and cited an eye-witness account in the Missing Aircrew Report (MACR), the second time that document had popped up. I wasn't sure what I was missing, but Jim enlightened me.

"I do have a copy of the Missing Aircrew Report (MACR) which reports on the circumstances of your uncle's loss very close to Bolzano, Italy. It reports that two P-38s flown by Lt.'s Twedt and Olson collided after Lt. Olson's plane was hit by flak. The witness reporting was Lt. Jack Anderson who was in the same flight. He was observing the colliding planes go down when he also noticed another plane going down with the right engine smoking. It looked damaged more from falling debris than due to collision or flak. He did not see a parachute and thought the cockpit was still closed. He could not identify the plane with certainty, but assumed it was that of your uncle, Lt. Wisner."

Jim said he would keep my name and e-mail address in case he came up with any more information and added, "There is a chance that there are some data entries in the German Luftwaffe records which were meticulously kept to record every American aircraft downed in German-held territory. The National Archives hold a considerable number of those captured records. In a couple other cases there were some Italian air war historians that held local news accounts of aircraft downings in their areas. Who knows, maybe the Bolzano city archives have such accounts. You have the date, and the location was shown in the MACR to be just immediately north of the town."

He thanked me for getting in touch with him when I should have been thanking him. But Billy had been Jim's squadron mate, and even though they had never met, the brotherhood forged by combat was strong and far-reaching.

Jim and Michal Mucha had both mentioned the MACR. I had never seen a copy of it, and except for the mission report John Mullins had given me and Billy's logbook, I was only vaguely familiar with Billy's service record. His files were buried in the cedar chest, and I'd never read them all. Each time I dug them out for a specific bit of information I would put them back, not expecting to need them again.

As president of the 71st Fighter Squadron of the 1st Fighter Group Association, Jim Graham would have access to a lot more information than I, and it looked like he was willing to help. I hadn't found anyone yet who remembered Billy, but it seemed I was now making progress.

Steve Duncan wrote the following day saying he had found an active member of the 1st Fighter Group Association who was on Billy's last flight as leader of the Blue Squadron (Billy's was the Red Squadron). His name was Myron J. Hutchins, and Steve gave me an address for him in Colorado Springs. After reading the mission report, Steve added that "Wisner was flying on the wing of the squadron leader Red #1 (Olson). Olson and Elliott were hit with flak northeast of the town. Olson and Twedt collided, it seems, when Olson opted to return to base with the squadron. Unfortunately, Red #2, Wisner, could not avoid the debris and it is likely that he [was] seriously injured by the debris. I believe this would have been the consensus of the returning pilots and summarized in the report by the Intelligence Officer. Here's hoping you and your family have found some comfort in what little you gathered from the report to overcome the tragic loss so many years ago."

It was sweet of him to care, but I wasn't looking for comfort; I was looking for answers. And the more tidbits that came my way, the hungrier I got.

Steve's interpretation of the accident mirrored what I'd heard all my life and gave me a first-hand a taste of what my grandmother had gone through. She had written countless letters only to get the same official account, lots of condolences, but no answers. I wrote Mr. Hutchins in Colorado Springs that same day.

Jim Graham wrote again February 28, saying his wheels began turning while he was searching the National Archives for information on another pilot, MIA on a mission to Germany. That pilot's MACR didn't give any conclusive evidence of his fate, so an archivist had suggested Jim try an agency in Alexandria, Virginia, that keeps records on servicemen who died on active duty. He'd called the number and told me the woman he spoke with verified that the man he was researching was listed, but that's all she could give him over the phone.

She said he had to write a letter requesting a copy of the file and to state that the request was under the Freedom of Information Act. Jim wrote me he had just received the file and, "There were nearly 100 pages of various letters, forms, reports, etc., on the pilot."

He summarized the case for me. "This pilot was lost on a mission near Munich on June 13, 1944. The Missing Aircrew Report indicated that witnesses only heard him on the radio a few miles southeast of Munich saying he was on fire and going down. No sightings, but there was an estimate of his location.

"In June of 1950, the American Graves Registration people went voluntarily to that area to investigate the possibility of identifying the crash site and to gather further evidence of the pilot's fate. They located the crash site and the owner of the property and excavated the remains of the pilot and his gear as well as parts of the plane. They buried his remains in a military cemetery in Belgium and then started trying to find the next of kin. Although his family had moved, they located them. The family then was informed as to their son's fate and location of the burial. The family had his remains shipped to the hometown and buried locally."

Just as I was wondering how this applied to me, Jim answered my question. "The point of this message to you is that you might contact that agency and request information about your uncle. There may be a remote possibility that they might have further information about him if the Graves Registration service actually followed up on the crash site years after the crash occurrence. If there was no actual verification of his death, they would not likely have his name in their files."

Jim's account boosted, then quickly diminished my hopes. I'd always trusted that if the government had ever learned anything about Billy after the war they would have told us. What Jim described had taken place in 1950, when memories were fresh and evidence was still undisturbed. We, on the other hand, were trying to solve a mystery now 55 years old.

I sent for the file, anyway, expecting little more than duplicate information. My grandmother had kept every letter she received and copies of many she wrote. They filled one end of the cedar chest, so I was sure she had exhausted every lead. But just to be safe, I mentioned the Freedom of Information Act when I composed my letter. I didn't want a simple oversight to ruin my chances of learning anything new.

Steve Duncan wrote again asking if I had heard from Blue Squadron Leader Myron Hutchins on Billy's last mission. Duncan encouraged me not to give up hope. He told me more about the search for the pilot found in Bulgaria, and added that often reports and recollections differ. "It would be great if you managed to contact Hutchins...hopefully he could provide you with more than what is contained in the mission report."

I, too, hoped Hutchins would remember something no one else had, but I still hadn't heard from him.

In mid-March, about a week after Steve's message, a form letter from the Department of the Army informed me that my request for IDPF (Individual Deceased Personnel File) had been received. But they added a caveat stating they didn't specialize in historical information, couldn't speculate, didn't evaluate documents or circumstances, and wouldn't draw conclusions in order to answer questions. I would have to go elsewhere if I had questions, but I didn't see that as a problem. I was willing to go anywhere and do anything, now that there was the slightest chance we might learn something new. And I was prepared to wait as long as it took.

But the file arrived on April 22, 1999, less than six weeks after I ordered it. It was thick—140 pages—and some things were immediately familiar. There were letters in my grandmother's handwriting; typewritten letters from Fritz Wencker, her brother-in-law and lawyer, and carbon copies of the government's responses. I'd seen those in my own files.

Others were not so familiar: Billy's health and dental records, an inventory of his personal effects sent home in 1944 and signed for by my grandfather, and, at last, a copy of the Missing Aircrew Report. The CONFIDENTIAL at the top of the MACR had been crossed out, and above it someone had written "Restricted" on 22 August 1949. I didn't know what that meant.

From what I could tell, the file was out of order, so before going any farther I rearranged it chronologically.

About half the documents fell between 1944 and 1946. Nothing happened in 1947, the year I was born, but a report dated 1948 caught my attention. Its attachments related to the proceedings of a Board of Officers that had convened at Rome, Italy, on 3 June 1948. The purpose of the report was "(a) To review and act upon all cases pertaining to the identity of unknown remains referred to the Board by Headquarters...(b) To review and determine in all cases, from evidence presented, the non-recoverability of remains referred to the Board by Headquarters...(c) If approved, these cases will be removed from the Agenda for further search and attempts to identify and no further search or investigation will be made unless additional information is forthcoming or orders are received from the OQMG to the contrary." It went on:

> The following case was brought before the
> Board:

William O Wisner, 2nd Lt., O-708778, 71st
Fighter Squadron, 1st Fighter Group, reported
Killed in Action 20 October 1944. The identifiable
remains of the above named deceased have not been
recovered by this Headquarters. (Exhibit B., OQMG
Form 371.)

FINDINGS

The Board having carefully considered the
evidence presented finds that:

(a) The above named deceased was the pilot of
a P-38J, AAF Serial Number 43-28379, which was
last seen in an uncontrolled spin while five miles
northeast of Bolzano, Italy, having been damaged
by falling debris from another plane, during a
Bomber Escort Mission. (Exhibit C, MACR Report.)
(b) A search of Bolzano and its surrounding area was
made by an AGRS/MZ [American Graves Registration
Service/Mediterranean Zone] Searching Team in August
1947, failing to recover the identifiable remains of
2nd Lt. William O. Wisner. …

Exhibit C was a copy of Jack Anderson's eyewitness report, which Jim
Graham had summarized but I'd never seen. I read it carefully.

> 71st Fighter Squadron
> 1st Fighter Group
> APO 520,
> 21 October 1944

STATEMENT

On the 20th of October, 1944, I was flying
with a squadron of fifteen (15) airplanes, on an
escort mission to a target at Regensburg, Germany.
The Red Flight consisted of Lt. Olson, flying

number one position, Lt. Wisner in number two,
Capt. Elliott element leader in number three, and
I was flying number four.

We had penetrated as far as Bolzano, Italy,
when we first encountered flak. Evasive action was
taken, and no one was hit. We continued on around
the east side of the town and more flak was
encountered from the N/E section of Bolzano. Lt.
Olson and Capt Elliott were hit almost
simultaneously in the right engine. They both
feathered their flak hit engines and continued
their flight on single-engine.

Lt. Olson immediately started losing altitude
and I throttled back to stay with the flight. A
few seconds later, I heard someone call, "Go down,
go down" on the radio. No flight designation was
given in this exclamation, so I started looking
around to see what was happening.

Before I could determine the reason, Lt.
Twedt, who was flying number four position in
White Flight, came in from slightly low and from
the left, and collided almost broadside with Lt.
Olson. The two aircraft exploded and disintegrated
into many pieces. I pulled up sharply to avoid the
accident.

Upon recovering from the pull-up, I looked
back and saw several pieces falling in flames. One
of the larger pieces, which I took to be the
remains of Lt. Twedt's airplane, appeared to have
the cockpit still intact. However, I did not see
the man get out and use his parachute. I did not
see the two aircraft hit the ground, but I do not
believe either pilot survived the accident.

Several seconds later, I discovered another
airplane going down in a stable attitude, but with
the right engine smoking and in flames. I flew
closer and saw that the nose and right engine were
badly smashed. I assumed that this was Lt.

Wisner's aircraft because the damage looked as though it had been caused by falling debris, and not from actual collision with another airplane.

The cockpit seemed undamaged, and still closed, so I called on the radio and told the pilot to bail out. I received no answer, and the plane then went into a steep dive, followed by a spin. I lost sight of the airplane very close to the ground, and did not see it crash. I did not see a parachute come from the airplane.

I do not understand why Lt. Twedt did not see Lt. Olson's aircraft in time to avoid it, but there is a possibility that he was wounded by the flak, and was unable to control his airplane.

Although there is a slight possibility that one or more of these pilots could have gotten clear of the wreckage and parachuted to safety unseen by me, it is my belief that this did not happen.

                         Jack C. Anderson
                         0-821114
                         2nd Lt., Air Corps

This eyewitness account was never shared with my family; only portions of it had been paraphrased in government letters.

Exhibit D was a search report [Appendix B]. That was big news. No one had ever told our family there had been a search for Billy, and just knowing they had been looking for him would have been reassuring.

The search report had a hand-drawn map with Bolzano roughly in the middle and an "X" marking the spot somewhat north of the city where Billy's plane was last sighted. Fortezza was indicated northeast of Bolzano and Trento to the southwest. I checked an atlas and saw that the area they described encompasses about 1,500 square miles, most of it mountains. No wonder they didn't find Billy; he was a tiny needle in a very big haystack.

But it did say they had recovered 14 American personnel from a U.S. cemetery at Mirandola. That name was familiar to me, but I couldn't find it in the atlas. I looked it up on the Internet, but the only results I got were about Giovanni Pico della Mirandola, an Italian Renaissance humanist philosopher (1463-94), whom I remembered from my Western Civilization course in college. But where was this village he was named after? Did a cemetery still exist there? Had Billy been found and buried there with no identification? Were his remains among those removed, and were they taken to the Florence cemetery? Too many questions and not one answer.*

Next, a memorandum dated 11 April re-stated the circumstances of the crashes of two of the planes, Billy's and Lowell Twedt's, and concluded they could not have survived the collision. Therefore, "The casualty report and official report of death will include the following statement: Finding of Death has been issued previously...showing presumed date of death as 21 October 1945," officially one year after he disappeared.

It referred to the statute that defined presumption of death, military-speak for crossing the t's and dotting the i's. Billy Wisner and Lowell Twedt were dead because their circumstances fit the legal code. A letter to that effect went to my grandparents on April 18, 1949, and on August 29 the Memorial Division wrote to tell them Billy's remains were "non-recoverable." Neither letter had told my grandparents that those findings were made as the result of a physical search for Billy.

I flipped a few more pages and found a form entitled "Memorialization of Non-Recoverable Remains of World War II." The photocopied handwriting was too faint to read, but it was stamped May 18, 1951. Another form, "Non-Recoverable Remains Reexamination of Records" dated September 6, 1951, had a hand-written note at the bottom, "Memorialized Florence ABMC [American Battlefield Monuments Cemetery]."

They never told the family about the memorial, either, and we didn't learn about the Wall of the Missing until nearly 40 years later, when John Chopelas, Billy's childhood friend, visited the cemetery and sent Mama a photograph of Billy's name there. I'm sure knowing Billy had been honored somewhere would have given my grandparents something to hold on to, but they were both dead by that time.

I turned the page and read the next memo. It was dated 1 December 1952 from the Memorial Division to the Quartermaster Mortuary Service Detachment, referring to the board findings of non-recoverability "for Unknown X-70035 Grieshiem/Main Maus[oleum] (Med[iterranean]

---

*I learned later that the Florence American Cemetery is at Mirandola. At least that was one mystery solved.

Zone), identified by your headquarters as 2/Lt William O. Wisner, 0-708 778." It reiterated the circumstances of the crash, saying two of the casualties, Wisner and Twedt, were approved non-recoverable and the third pilot [Olson] was captured and later repatriated. I knew all that, but who was this Unknown X-70035, and why was he identified as Billy, when all official reports said Billy was still missing?

There was more:

> 3. Due to the fragmentary condition of the remains designated Unknown X-70035; the anthropological findings indicating that it was impossible to make any definite association with 2/Lt Wisner with the exception of age and weight, and because there are two casualties from the same area to be accounted for, it is requested that Unknown X-70035 be assigned a CIL designation and that the status of Lt. Wisner remain non-recoverable.

> 4. It is further requested that CIL Number and Open Grave Report be forwarded for completion of records. Board Findings for X-70035 have been cancelled in this office.

Whose remains? Found where? If Billy had never been found, why was this memo in his file? What does it mean when they "cancel the board findings of non-recoverability"? I read the memo again. The answers weren't there.

I went to the next one, dated two weeks later. This one was from the Graves Registration Branch to the Memorial Division in Washington. It cited compliance with their request to assign a CIL number (whatever that was) and confirmed that "Subject Unknown remains has [sic] been redesignated CIL Remains 5034…The applicable CIL Remains Form with skeletal chart is attached hereto and grave 37 is now declared open." Huh? Nothing was attached, and none of this made sense. I tried not to hope for miracles, but I caught my breath when I read the next paragraph.

> 4. Also, attached hereto for appropriate

disposition, identification bracelet for William
O. Wisner. The status of 2nd Lt William O. Wisner,
O-708778 will remain Non-Recoverable.

His bracelet! How could they have had Billy's bracelet since 1952? Where did they find it, and where was it now? Wouldn't it be proof of the body's identity? And most frustrating of all, why wasn't the family ever told?

I looked for the skeletal chart they mentioned, but it wasn't there, so I went on to the next memo, 9 January 1953, from the Memorial Division to the Army Effects Agency in Kansas City, Mo. It said the bracelet was enclosed, and "due to the nature of this case, it is requested that [it] be held by you without disposition until further notice from this Office."

What did they mean by "the nature of this case"? It was all so mysterious. And ironic. In 1953, when the bracelet was at the Army Effects Agency in Kansas City, my family lived in Topeka, Kansas, just 60 miles west.

I looked for other clues. In the "Request for Information" dated 2 March 1953 from the Identification Branch, the writer had asked for "copies of all correspondence to and from NOK [next of kin] of above deceased." Someone had been on the case and wanted to find out how much the family knew. But there was no answer to his request. Did he forget to follow up?

Next was a memo from Army Effects to the Quartermaster General in Washington dated July 30, 1954, a year and a half after the first memo that mentioned Billy's bracelet. "In view of the lapse of time since instructions in preceding indorsement [sic] were furnished, request advice as to whether Lt Wisner's identification bracelet should be retained in a suspended status or whether it may be released to his next of kin...If the property may be released, request the inclosed [sic] copy of Form 129 be completed and returned to this Agency so that sufficient information will be of record to enable appropriate disposition."

A typewritten note added to the bottom of that memo reads, "Does correspondence of record in your office indicate whether decedent was married?" Again, someone wanted to contact Billy's family, but that question, too, went unanswered.

Then, on August 10, 1954, a memo from the Quartermaster General Memorial Division to the Army Effects Agency said the bracelet "will be designated CIL #5034...and forwarded to this office for further disposition. The effects case file at your Agency will be closed." The Quartermaster General in Washington signed for it on August 18, 1954.

The last piece of correspondence in the file is dated August 20, 1954, written on behalf of the chief, Memorial Division. It said, in part:

SUBJECT: Identification Bracelet

    1. It is requested that the attached envelope containing an identification bracelet be retained with the case file for Unknown CIL-5034, Griesheim, Main/Mausoleum (formerly Unknown X-70035) until the case is resolved.

    2. When this case is finally identified, the file and bracelet are to be forwarded to Memorial Division for further action in connection with the disposition of the bracelet. It is requested that the approval of the Chief, Memorial Division, be secured before the reference bracelet is detached from this file.

And there the file ended. From what I could see, the chief of the Memorial Division never gave his approval to detach the bracelet from the file so it must still be there. But where was that file, the one numbered CIL-5034?

I resolved to find out.

But first I had to process the astounding news that Billy may not have vanished, after all. Then I had to control my anger. I was furious to learn that they had found Billy's identification bracelet but had never told his family. Were they afraid of the questions my grandmother would ask, or was it just a bureaucratic snafu? They had a pretty good clue to where he was, and no one had ever followed up.

When they set that file aside I was seven; my grandparents were in their sixties and still living in the house Billy left when he went overseas.

But where did that bracelet go? And, more important, where was Billy?

3

BILLY
1924-41

October 1, 1940

Mom,
Have gone ice skating. Ate a sandwich. Will be home about 11:00.

Love,
Bill

* * *

Growing up, I had what can only be described as a crush on Billy. He was so handsome I idolized him the same way a little girl would admire her best friend's big brother. But now that I'm approaching the age my grandmother was when Billy disappeared, I've outgrown my crush. I'm protective, even maternal toward the young man who was barely past his teens when he died. Billy is frozen in time, a small part of a bigger history. But it's his own history that made him who he was.

He was the light of his parents' eyes, the only son in a loving family of four. His father, Ralph, was a tall, handsome, devil-may-care sort. Ralph had been pampered by his mother, Luella Owen Steele Wisner, whom everyone called Lula, but he didn't know much about his biological father, William Mell Wisner, who died in 1898, killed, according to family lore, by a trunk that fell from a second-story window.

Lula married E. D. Haight and moved to Ardmore, Oklahoma, when Ralph was still a boy. Mr. Haight abetted Lula in spoiling Ralph and even bought him a car when he thought Ralph was old enough. A little careless and always impractical, Ralph promptly ran it into a tree and demolished it. That was the last car he ever owned or drove.

A charmer, Ralph loved being the center of attention and would entertain his friends by writing poems, singing songs, and telling stories. As a youth he performed in minstrel shows and later said he regretted not having stayed in show business. "Oh, Dem Golden Slippers!" was his favorite song, and if you asked him he'd perform it for you, complete with a soft-shoe routine, even late into his 80s. Always well dressed, he never went out without a flower in the lapel of his neatly tailored suit, and as a result he would often be mistaken for the floorwalker whenever he was in a department store. Shoppers would ask him for directions, and he'd politely point the way, whether he knew the right answer or not.

Billy's mother, Ida Josephine McCue, was a tiny, lovely, homespun girl from Waxahachie, Texas, with black hair, blue eyes, and a beguiling smile. She was shy, industrious, self-effacing, and came from a big family— the exact opposite of Ralph. Ida's father, John Marshall McCue, was a proud farmer named for his distant cousin-twice-removed, the fourth chief justice of the Supreme Court. In 1879 John married Sallie Keesee, and Ida, born in 1888, was the fifth of their seven children, including Willie, Frank, Sadie, Howard, John, and "the baby that died," whose name and gender is lost to history. Ida's brother John took a job in Ardmore, where he became friendly with Ralph. When he introduced Ralph to Ida on a visit to Dallas, Ida was 27. On the rebound from a relationship that had been broken up by her parents, it didn't take her long to fall in love with the charming visitor, even though he was three years her junior.

After their marriage in 1916 Ida and Ralph settled in Ardmore, and in 1918, just shy of her 30th birthday, Ida went home to Dallas for her confinement. She gave birth to a red-headed daughter in the bedroom of her parents' house at 705 W. Ninth Street and named her Maxine Eleanor, after actress Maxine Elliott, who had invented the name to boost her stage career, and Ida's beloved big sister, Willie Eleanor.

The Wisners moved back to Dallas when Maxine was five, and a year later, on August 1, 1924, William Ormand Wisner came along. Billy was the first of his family to be born in a hospital, Mrs. F.C. Smith's Sanitarium, a converted house four blocks down from the McCue home. Billy inherited

Ida and Ralph Wisner 1917

both parents' dark hair and blue eyes and his mother's dimples and widow's peak. As the "baby" and a boy, he was the darling of the family.

Maxine and Billy grew up among the offspring of Ida's sisters Willie and Sadie. They all lived within a few blocks of their grandparents' house, and the gaggle of first cousins spanned Maxine and Billy's six-and-a-half-year age difference. Marshall, Maxine, Jean, Cecil, Peggy, Betty, and Billy spent every day playing under the watchful eye of "Mama" McCue. It was a "Little Rascals" existence, except these rascals were all blood kin.

Ida doted on her children. Their baby books, so full of cards and memorabilia, barely close. And they both adored Ida. Billy called her "Munny" and would bring her a flower every time he found one he could pick. Sweet-natured like his mother, but with his father's devilish streak, he often got into trouble. Ida was swift with a spanking the day his new red wagon got stuck in the door and Billy exclaimed, "Oh, this damned old wagon!"

When he was four Billy's face broke out with impetigo, a common skin condition that was difficult to cure in those days. Though uncomfortable through the ordeal, Billy was pragmatic. Ida wrote in Billy's baby book, "When I said you were finally well, you replied, 'Well, I prayed every night, and I thank God my sores are gone. Now I am going to pray for a pony.' "

Ida worried too much and resisted letting her children stray too far from the house. When Billy pestered Ida to let him play at a neighbor's house across the street, Ida acquiesced and stood on the porch to watch him go. Before he had made it to the other side a streetcar turned the corner and, even though it was too far away to be a threat, Ida fainted.

As the older sibling, Maxine had to be responsible for her little brother. She remembers one day when she kept going to the store because Ida was out of ingredients she needed for something she was making. The store was just two blocks away, so on the fourth request, Maxine asked her mother if Billy could go, instead. Ida said he could, but only if Maxine watched him the whole time. Maxine watched him, but only as he crossed the street–she didn't go with him. When her dad found out she hadn't minded her mother, he spanked her for the first and only time in her life.

After that, she kept a closer eye on him. "One day we were playing in Sadie's back yard," she remembers, "and Billy was walking on a wooden fence. He jumped off and landed on a nail sticking up, and I had to pull him off it. I took him home, and Mama soaked his foot in kerosene." No tetanus shots in those days, but Billy survived.

The Depression was hard on the working class, and the Wisner children could always tell when their father had lost another job, because they would pack up and move to a lower-rent house. Ida worked whenever she could, usually as a typist or shop girl at stores like Woolworth's, and Ralph was never out of a job long, so when he was employed again they'd move to a nicer house. But in spite of the moves, they always stayed in the neighborhood so the children could go to the same schools and play with their cousins.

In spite of the Depression, they never felt poor. A close friend and neighbor would give Maxine and Billy dimes for movies and treats. According to Maxine's diary they went to 45 movies in 1931. Once, at the Texas Theater*, they had enough money for admission but none for a snack. Someone had dropped his popcorn in the lobby, and Billy pounced on it and scooped it back into the bag. Embarrassed, Maxine made him throw it

---

*Known after the Kennedy assassination in 1963 as the place where Lee Harvey Oswald hid after allegedly shooting Officer J.D. Tippett.

away before he could eat any. They weren't starving, Billy just didn't want to pass up free popcorn.

Billy's John H. Reagan Elementary School report card showed good grades but a need for improvement in courtesy and conduct. The broad grin in all his photographs betrays a fun-loving, boisterous nature, so he must have been a handful. His grade-school playmate, John Chopelas, remembers the "gang" they belonged to, made up of Billy, John, Charles Day, and Roger Godwin. "But," adds John, "[It was] nothing like the gangs of today. We were perfect angels compared to them." About the worst damage they ever caused was breaking a pot of flowers on someone's front porch on Halloween. "It sounds mild, I know, but we relished the challenge, and membership actually did create a bond while we were fellow students.

"Billy always carried a most friendly grin and he was very sports-minded," John remembers, "which reminds me of the weekend I spent at

his house…[when we] were batting baseballs to each other, with every successful catch worth a point. Naturally, he had fewer misses than I did, [and]
I remember how exuberant he was when he reported to his dad that the
home team won. I think I muttered something like, 'Wait'll you come to
my house.' But my feelings were appeased by the delightful chop suey that
Ida prepared for supper. He and I had a continuous, friendly competition
going on, each of us trying to out[do] the other. If all this sounds like we
had fun, we surely did."

Billy had a gentle side, too. Playing mumbly-peg one day, a game that
involves throwing a knife in complicated ways to make it stick in the
ground, a caterpillar wandered into the playing field. One of Billy's friends
started to chop it in half, but Billy shouted, "No!" and put out his hand to
protect it. The result was a pretty serious cut on his index finger, and he
carried the scar into adulthood.

As Billy grew, so did his athletic abilities. Four of his closest friends in
high school were Jack, Dalton, Paul, and Bobby Tarver. Jack was Billy's
age, Dalton was two years younger, Paul a year behind Dalton, and Bobby
was the youngest. To them Billy was like another brother. Jack and Billy
played football for the Oak Cliff Mavericks, a merchant-sponsored team,
and Paul remembers the game against the Highland Park Scotties. But this
time the home team lost miserably. It's no wonder, though–two of the
Scotties were Bobbie Lane and Doak Walker. Lane went on to quarterback
for the Texas Longhorns, and Walker won the Heisman Trophy twice at
SMU. After college both went on to play pro ball for the Detroit Lions.

To Maxine's boyfriends, Billy was just that little kid who hung around
his pretty sister. When Maxine narrowed her choice of beaus to Fannon
Thompson, Billy was disappointed. He liked Fannon, all right, but he was
hoping she'd pick the boy with the motorcycle. "But I rode on it once,"
Maxine recalls, "and it scared the bejabbers out of me."

She married Fannon on October 8, 1940. Stepping up to the altar,
Maxine's maid of honor, her cousin and best friend Jean Wencker, tripped
on her dress. True to his nature, 16-year-old Billy laughed out loud.

Early in high school Billy excelled in English, history, and ROTC and
scored above average in everything else. But in his senior year C's in typing
and biology, and D's in accounting and algebra indicated a lack of interest.
Distracted by the oncoming war, Billy wasn't applying himself. He was so
focused on getting into the fight, in fact, his grade even dropped in ROTC,
so if he thought being an officer was in his future he was on the wrong

track. He pestered his parents to let him enlist early, but they refused to give their permission, insisting he graduate and go on to college.

Once Billy left home, Ida discovered why he had finally agreed to their plan. Cleaning his room one day, she came across a well-thumbed paperback novel he'd been reading about a combat pilot. Inside the cover Billy had written, "This is exactly what I want to do."

He had figured out how he would get into the war.

4

COLLEGE MAN
1942-43

Arlington, Tex.
Feb. 3, 1942

Dear Mom and Dad,

[...] I went to classes today and everything went along just as usual. That's just the trouble with this place. Everything always goes as usual. I sure am tired of waiting around for something to happen. But I suppose I'll just go on waiting and trying to learn something new.

I went downtown today and got a haircut. Boy, did I need one. I either had to get a haircut or get a fiddle. [...] Nothing else has happened to speak of. I guess I'll close and get to studying. Please Write Soon.

Love,
Bill

P.S. Still am tired of waiting around. Mom, please write my draft board and find out all you can about my status with them. Thanks a million

Bill

* * *

Billy was barely a teenager when Maxine enrolled at North Texas Agricultural College (NTAC) in 1935. Her tuition was paid by Oswald Fritz Wencker, Ida's brother-in-law. Fritz had lost his wife Willie in the influenza epidemic of 1918, and was left to raise their infant daughter, Jean Eleanor, with the help of Mama McCue. Because Fritz was a lawyer, he was wealthy by the standards of the day, and he took special interest in the welfare of all the cousins.

When it was Billy's turn for college, Fritz paid his tuition, too, and to help with the costs Billy worked part-time at Sears. He was the darling of his female co-workers and often went ice-skating with them, the only boy in a group of six or seven. "The girls" were all older than Billy, but he had an older sister, a loving mother, and three female cousins, so he felt right at home in a doting "harem."

Skating with the girls (Ruth Peck pictured second from right)

When Billy enrolled at NTAC in fall of 1941, the U.S. was still out of the war, but that soon changed. Maxine and Fannon remember sitting in the parlor with Ida and Ralph in the house on Sunday, December 7. Billy was home for the weekend, visiting a neighbor when he heard about the bombing of Pearl Harbor on the radio. He ran home and shouted the news through the window, telling his folks to turn on the radio and hear it for themselves. At last the U.S. was involved. Now there was no question Billy would go.

But he had some schooling to complete first. In high school he had written a paper about his hopes to become a lawyer, but when he got to college he signed up for engineering courses and joined the ROTC to improve his chances for a commission and acceptance into officers' training and flight school. Uncle Fritz, while complimented by Billy's first choice, thought Billy's new career choice was preferable.

NTAC was in Arlington, now part of the sprawling conglomeration of Dallas-Ft. Worth suburbs. But in the '40s Arlington was a separate city, far from home. But back then many things were different—a dollar bought something substantial, a long-distance phone call was a luxury, and the U.S. Postal Service was efficient, often delivering mail twice a day. Billy wrote home two or three times a week without fail. He missed his family and loved getting letters back.

Ida saved Billy's letters, and they form a diary of his college years, complete with homesickness, frustration, girl trouble, and the anxieties shared by all young men facing uncertain futures.

One of his letters, postmarked Monday morning, September 28, 1942, announced his safe arrival back at school after a weekend home. But he was depressed. "I'm trying to forget all about getting homesick although it is really hard. Every time I think of home, I think of how I didn't want to leave last nite and of how cozy it was in the sitting room with you and Dad. But I am coming home next weekend so I have something to look forward to…Mom, I never knew how much I could love anyone like I do you and Dad until last night when you and Dad made me pick up my spirits like you did. This morning I looked back on it and saw what a dope I was and it was then that I made up my mind to go ahead and do the best I can which is 'all a mule could do,' as Dad says."

He enclosed two dollars, one to pay his mother back for what he had borrowed, and the other for her to spend. "Please buy yourself something," he urged, knowing she would probably use it to buy food or pay a bill.

He told them was going to apply for another furlough and asked if Ida had written his excuse for it to the commandant. He wondered if anyone had called or written to him since he left, even though he'd been gone barely one day, and asked his mother to persuade his father to write a long letter, too, because he'd never gotten one from him.

Billy closed his letter with, "I love you and Dad more than anything (mushy, isn't it? Ha-Ha.)" It was mushy, but he loved his family and wasn't ashamed to show it.

His homesickness must have been compounded by some rough treatment he'd been getting. Although his October 8 letter said things looked good for the future, he added that he had been running back and forth to the bathroom all day. "It's not because I am sick," he explained, "but for another reason. Last nite was freshman initiation nite and that's where it all started. We formed at the quadrangle at 6:30 last nite and started down to the well in the middle of town. We would duck-walk for about a hundred yards at a time hanging onto each other's belts and yelling quack-quack-quack at the top of our voice. Boy, the guy behind me almost pulled me in two.

"After duck-walking that way we would then get up and run about four hundred yards in a swerving line, still hanging onto each other's belts. Some of the boys were thrown down and stepped on, but I kept my feet and hung on. When we got down to the well, the sophomores all made us drink about two quarts of that mineral water (ugh). After I drank all I could hold I bent over to throw it up so I wouldn't get sick, but evidently I didn't get it all up from the way I have been running today.

"After a while the sophomore in our house came over to me and tried to make me drink some more of the stuff. When I told him I wouldn't do it, he threw it in my face. I caught some of in my mouth and spit it all over him. Boy, was he mad. I laughed so much my sides hurt. He gave me five licks when we got home for doing this, but I didn't mind. It wasn't so hard duck-walking and running down there but it sure was hard doing it going back when I had all that nasty stuff in me and with the guy in back of me trying to pull me in two. When we got back we had to run around the quadrangle again and then get down on our hands and knees and pray for rain. Then they made us all get together and wrestle each other. Some of the guys on the bottom of the piles were nearly killed but I managed to stay on top."

He said that now everyone in the group were official members of "that great Organization, N.T.A.C.," and he looked forward to the next year when he could be on the other side of the "ceremony." He was proud he had lasted.

He asked his mother to send all his sports gear, because intramural sports would start the following week. He had signed up for football, baseball, basketball, tennis, fencing, track, and possibly boxing. And he was going to join the rifle team as soon as he finished the letter. He closed by congratulating Maxine and Fannon on their second anniversary.

The hazing he'd undergone was good practice for the military, so Billy took it in stride. But it didn't keep him from having girls on his mind.

On October 13 he wrote to ask, "Did Mrs. Garza say that Charlotte said anything about me to them? If she did, please tell me what. Did they say anything about me? [It was] good, I hope. I'm glad to hear that Charlotte doesn't care anything about a car. Maybe that leaves a chance for me. I sure hope so, but I doubt it." Because of Ralph's early mishap and Ida's never having learned to drive, the Wisners never owned a car, and they certainly didn't have the funds to buy one for Billy. So if Charlotte wanted to date Billy, she'd have to do it on foot.

In that letter, Billy also mentioned the 18-19 year-old draft law President Roosevelt had just asked Congress to pass. "I guess you and Dad listened to the president's speech last nite. If they do pass the law I may be Air Corps-bound. In fact, I'm sure of it." He signed off, saying he was heading for algebra class.

The new legislation would affect Billy's draft status if he didn't stay in school, and he wouldn't stand a chance of getting into the Air Corps if he dropped out. It seems he was facing important decisions every day.

He had met with some men from the different branches of the Army, Navy and Marine Corps. "I went in with a group of about twenty other boys to see about joining Naval aviation. The officer explained it all to us. I am going to join V-5. This is the group that is left in school for one year and then are called up for service. My call will come about next July, anyway, so I might as well join what I want to. If I do join this I will be given Civilian Pilot Training for about 5 weeks at Love Field this summer and then it will be about 2 months until I will go to Athens, Georgia, for pre-flight training. Now, don't go into hysterics, Mom, because I haven't signed anything yet."

It wouldn't be hard to imagine Ida's reaction to Billy's plans. She had never been in an airplane, and knowing her baby wanted to fly must have made her a little crazy. But Billy was on his own now, and there was little she could do but stand by and support his decisions.

On November 17 he wrote that he was taking his departmental tests. He thought he'd done well in algebra, but he was dreading chemistry on Friday. He would take his engineering exam that afternoon and expected to do well.

He still had girls on his mind. "So Arjorie came over last nite, huh? What all did she have to say? Why did she quit Sears? What pictures did she have? I don't remember them. Did Sis finally have some developed? Please send some of both of them to me, will you? How does Dad like his job by

now? Does he still get off early? What has happened around the house since
I left?"

He told them things were dull around school, because all he did was
study, "But I guess I'll have to get used to that if I am going into the Air
Corps."

He closed by asking about the outcome of Fannon's physical. Fannon's age, 26, made him eligible to enlist, but the results of his physical
didn't. He had double vision ever since he was hit in the eye on a Boy
Scout retreat and also had the world's flattest feet. Fannon was disappointed, but at least he knew his position with the phone company made him
essential to the war effort.*

Billy didn't save the letters Ida and Maxine wrote to him in college,
but he did keep one from Allen Rische, the son of Ida and Ralph's best
friends, Ruby and Kip. Allen was married and in the Army, assigned to the
Pentagon. Because Billy knew his mother was nervous about the prospect
of her "baby" going to war, he gave her Allen's letter as reassurance that he
was making the right choices.

November 19, 1942

Dear Bill: -

Just had a letter from home and your mother mentioned
that you were at N.T.A.C. taking engineering and I thought I
would write and congratulate you on your decision. Naturally, I
think you have made a very wise choice, since the time I spent there
has helped me tenfold.

Things here are just about the way they are pictured in the
papers. Washington is just about the most crowded place in
America, but even tho' there has been a lot of confusion because of
the immense job ahead of everyone, things are now taking shape
and we are beginning to see results now.

I have been enjoying my work very much and thank my
lucky stars that I took ROTC in school. I have had many a letter
from my friends who didn't take military training asking how
they can possibly get a commission, and I have to tell them they

---

*Fannon was re-classified in 1945 and all set to be called up when the war ended.

have to take their chances through the ranks, college degree or not.
Bill, be sure and keep on with your ROTC. Get that commission.
There is no comparison between the lot of an enlisted man and an
officer – and it is going to get harder and harder to get a
commission as time goes on.

Bill, if you have time drop me a short line and let me know
how you are making out there at Arlington. I suppose some of the
courses are still tough. I had some tough going myself, but a little
extra work in the tough ones will always pull you through.

How will this new drafting of 18 and 19 year olds affect
your status, Bill? I hope it will not keep you from finishing and
getting a commission.

I wish you could see the new Pentagon War Dept. building.
Since I have been moved into that building, I have gotten lost in it
several times but after you get yourself oriented it isn't as bad to
get around as you might have heard.

[…] If you ever get the feeling that you should be in there
with the fighting boys, just remember any farm boy that has no
education at all can do that job. The real shortage is in specialists
and officers, and you are doing more than your share training
yourself along the line you are.

Don't forget to drop us a line if you have time.

Your friends,
Allen and Kitty

The more Billy applied himself, the more his grades improved. On December 1 he wrote that he would try to get another furlough home if he could catch a ride back to Dallas. He'd gotten a 95 and a 99 in English for that half-year, and he was working on keeping all his grades that high.

But there was turmoil on campus. "This school sure is in an uproar," he wrote. "The war sure has played havoc on the students and faculty. So many boys are quitting to join the service that the classes are getting thinner and thinner every day. A boy who sits by me in some of my classes is going to quit and go to San Francisco to see his mother and dad in about a week.

"The dorm is also in an uproar. Some boy burned shoe polish, and smoke poured into every room. All of the boys in the dorm have been confined to quarters. They can't even go out to go to the library. They go out of the dorm to go eat and go to classes, but that is all. Boy, they are all so mad that they can't see straight."

Evidently, he wasn't getting as many letters from home as he'd like, because his February 7, 1943, letter begins, "Why in the heck don't you ever write? I was expecting a letter from you all week and when I didn't get one I sure was disappointed. Boy, if I ever get into the Army I hope I get letters quicker. So that is that."

He had been made house manager, but school was as "dead as it ever was." The new major had been keeping them "cooped up pretty close, here of late." He asked if Ida had received his classification yet, then added a P.S. posed by every college student since time began: "Mom, you couldn't by any chance send me a buck or two, could you? I am running pretty low."

By spring 1943 everyone had a family member in the service. Fannon's younger brother, Morris, was three years older than Billy and newly married to his high school sweetheart, Margie Nicholson. The two young men had become friends as well as family by the time Morris joined the Navy and was off in Hutchinson, Kansas, for training. Everyone teased Morris that Kansas was about as far from the ocean as he could get, so he must not have been too serious about going to sea. In his March 4 letter Billy asked how Morris liked Kansas and added that he would write to him right away.

Then he told his mother he'd been trying to catch up on his sleep, no doubt to make up for his active social life, which also had taken a toll on his finances. "Mom, do you think it would be alright if I wrote Fritz and asked him for some spending money? I don't think he would mind, do you?" He added he wouldn't come home that weekend, because, "I have a date with a girl next weekend but not with Elaine. She will probably try to give me heck if she finds out. Notice, I said just try. She won't mess with me but just once."

Billy rarely mentioned the same girl twice. Few boys were still at home, so with his good looks, easy-going nature, and skill on the dance floor, he could take his pick. He never went steady, and because he didn't have a car most of his dates were with groups of friends.

Billy's mind wasn't on going steady, anyway. He was ready to move on. According to the 1943 NTAC yearbook, the school had dedicated itself to getting its students onto the right track. Its foreword describes a campus preparing its graduates for war.

Conceived in a year when the very foundation of our nation was being shaken, this 1943 Junior Aggie has tried to show the part NTAC is playing in the war effort...Riveters were needed. We trained them. The Air Corps demanded men. Our Aggies volunteered. Boys and girls alike enrolled in defense courses. The entire corps became war-conscious.

Billy would soon put his own skills to use in the real thing.

5

THE NEW MYSTERY

Denver, Colorado
April 23, 1999

National Personnel Records Center
National Archives and Records Administration
9700 Page Blvd.
St. Louis, MO 63132 5100

Gentlemen:

I have been referred to you by the U.S. Total Army
Personnel Command in Alexandria, VA, for further information
on my uncle, William O. Wisner, 0-708778, killed in action in
Italy on October 20, 1944.

Under the Freedom of Information Act, I have received a
copy of his file from the above-mentioned agency. However, this file
has raised questions that need answers, and I hope you can help.

First of all, what has happened to the Army Effects Agency
that used to be at 601 Hardesty Avenue, Kansas City, Missouri?
Do the personal effects stored there after the war still exist?

According to the file, an I.D. bracelet with my uncle's
name on it was recovered some time after his death (the file
doesn't reveal when). The bracelet was first mentioned in a letter
dated December 15, 1952, from the Mortuary Service
Detachment to The Quartermaster General, Memorial Division,

Washington, DC. While the remains were never positively
identified, it seems an I.D. bracelet found with any remains,
however unidentifiable, should have been returned to his next of
kin, along with the circumstances of its find and final disposition
of the remains found with it. This was never done.

It appears the bracelet was forwarded from the Memorial
Division to the Army Effects Agency in Kansas City on August
20, 1954, to be kept "with the case file for Unknown CIL-5034
[…] until the case is resolved." There is no further mention of
the bracelet, and no further entries in the file except for a
Transfer of Records slip dated 1955.

I would appreciate copies of all records regarding my
uncle, as well as any information that would shed light on the
current location of the I.D. bracelet and of Lt. Wisner's remains
(or the address of the agency I may write for such information).
His sister, my mother, is 81, and I would like to help her learn of
his whereabouts before she dies.

Sincerely,
Diana T. Dale

* * *

I stared at the hard evidence that Billy had not vanished, but I still
couldn't believe it. In 1952 someone had found the I.D. bracelet he
was wearing when his plane went down. But who? And where did they
find it? I was afraid to hope we might find Billy, but at long last, there was a
possibility of learning where he crashed.

After I wrote the Army Personnel Records Center, I e-mailed Jim
Graham and Steve Duncan to tell them about the evidence in Billy's personnel file and asked them what they thought I should do next.

Jim replied he had "taken the liberty" of forwarding a portion of my
message to Bill Jordan, a former employee "(if not a director) of the Central Identification Laboratory (CIL), which deals with identification of the
remains of lost military personnel."

That explained the CIL number. Billy's case had been changed from an
unknown "Individual Deceased Personnel" entity to a "Central Identification
Laboratory" entity. The CIL would have the answers we were looking for.

Jim had said Bill Jordan could direct me to the bracelet's whereabouts, and the next day he forwarded me Jordan's response, which included names and phone numbers to call at the CIL in Hawaii.

I left a message for the deputy commander of the U.S.A. Central Identification Laboratory at Hickham AFB, Hawaii (CILHI), retired Col. Johnie Webb. When he called back the next day, he asked questions, took notes, and told me he would have his auditors pull Billy's file and let me know what they discovered. That's the only time the prospect of a government audit has ever sounded good to me. Webb said it would take some time, but I didn't mind. We had waited more than 50 years; another month or two wouldn't matter.

I followed up with a letter to Webb reiterating the questions buzzing in my head:

- Where and when was the I.D. bracelet found?
- Where are the remains associated with my uncle now?
- Is there the remotest possibility, given the advances of science and DNA testing, that these remains can be positively identified?
- If it is found, can we get the bracelet back?
- If the official story is that he went down over Italy, why were remains and the I.D. bracelet transferred from a mausoleum in Griesheim, Germany?

That tantalizing clue made me hungry for more. So instead of doing nothing while I waited for Webb's answer, I decided to see what else I could uncover.

The Internet had served me well so far, so I went back to it and found the address of a site on military air accidents. Billy's crash was technically an accident because he wasn't hit by enemy fire, so I thought they might have something on it. Mike Stowe answered my query right away, but all he had on Billy was "two minor P-39 accidents at Moses Lake AAF, WA, piloted by 2Lt William O. Wisner." No help there, but I was impressed by his research. I remembered seeing a newspaper clipping in Billy's scrapbook about one of those accidents and wondered why he'd never told his mother about the other one. Then I remembered how much she worried. Better she not know.

My excitement about the bracelet was hard to contain. I had to share the news with someone besides my husband and my sister, and I felt it was too soon to tell Mama. She became pretty emotional when Sister and I gave her the photos of Billy's name on the Wall of the Missing and the headstone rubbing, so I thought the next news I gave her had better be good news, or at least solid evidence we were onto something.

So I wrote John Chopelas, Billy's boyhood friend. John and I had never met, but we shared an interest in Billy and WWII, and had corresponded infrequently over for about 10 years. John had been a radioman with the 452nd Bomb Group, and one of his hobbies is collecting WWII aircraft nose art. I knew he'd be as intrigued by my find as I was.

I told him what I'd learned from the file and added a lot of speculation. "My imagination started to run wild when I saw Griesheim, so I went back and checked the accident report," I wrote. "One eyewitness said he saw Billy's plane in an uncontrolled spin, but no reports ever attest to seeing him crash. The witness doubted his chance of survival because he didn't see a parachute, but he also said the cockpit was intact, even though one engine was in flames. When I checked a map, I saw that Bolzano is very near western Austria where Austria is very narrow, and Germany is just on the other side. If Billy had continued past Bolzano in roughly the same direction he had been going from Foggia to Bolzano, he could easily have ended up in Germany near Griesheim. His squadron was headed for Regensburg, which would have required a right turn at Bolzano, but Billy could have gotten disoriented—especially if his plane had been hit."

I could envision a great story: Billy comes out of the spin and tries to get back on course. Then, either his other engine fails or he is shot down deep in German territory and captured, then perishes in a POW camp near Griesheim. I'd seen too many WWII movies, and I knew it was far-fetched, but without answers anything is possible. It was comforting to think he might have kept going after the attack. Being killed in a freak accident when Billy was doing everything right was just too sad to contemplate.

But until we knew for sure, all I could do was wait.

On May 6 the St. Louis records center replied to my request for information with a request form. I filled it out and mailed it back the next day.

Cruising the 'Net some more, I found a Web site for the American WWII Orphans Network (AWON), an association of children of WWII deceased (www.AWON.org) It looked interesting, so I asked for more information, and they sent me their newsletter and some background. It was an impressive network of people, many of whom, like me, were looking for a father, brother or uncle. I thought it might be a good back-up resource, so I sent in my membership dues.

In late June the St. Louis Personnel Records Center answered my request. Because a fire in 1973 had destroyed most of their files from WWII, all they had was a summary of Billy's records. There was nothing new in their recap, except for some reason they had put Bolzano in France. I wasn't too disappointed, because the burned files would have had Billy's active duty records, most of which I had. The bracelet and the clues to Billy's where-abouts were in the files being researched by Johnie Webb at CILHI.

Mike Stowe, the accident researcher, gave me another referral, this time a Ted Darcy of the WFI Research Group (www.cntn.net/wfirg/). Mike told me Ted performs detailed research on crashes, so I e-mailed Ted and told him what I had done so far. "I wish CILHI wasn't involved," Ted replied. "That could make it rough getting the file I need if I take the case. Anyway, do you have copies of the two applicable MACR's? Exactly what official paperwork do you have? I read through the Group History notes on the incident, but they were of no use." I faxed him the Missing Aircrew Report from the file I had, the one in the search report contained in Billy's personnel file.

Ted replied that the MACR I sent him was the short version, so he ordered the two full versions and asked if I had ordered Lowell Twedt's deceased personnel file. Twedt's plane had collided with Olson's above Billy's. Good suggestion.

On August 15 Ted e mailed me that the reports had arrived, and on August 19 he wrote again: "I went over both MACR's but there was noth-ing new. Suggest you order the other [file] as they won't let anyone play in the X-files but themselves." I made a mental note to order Twedt's file right away, but it got pushed aside by everything else going on in my life: work, being with family at our cabin, and my charity, Pack to School.

Nothing else happened for two months. Then, on October 20, the 55th anniversary of Billy's crash, Jim Graham popped back up. He said, "It has been some months since, as I recall it, you were tracking your uncle's I.D. bracelet in the government's archives of personal effects. Were you successful?" He gave me an update on the search for Carl Hoenshell, the pilot in Bulgaria. The team had just found his I.D. bracelet at his crash site. "The pilot's niece was there at the discovery and, of course, is elated. There are some successes." He signed his name and added "(former 71st pilot)" at the end, as a reminder.

As if I could forget who Jim was. His guidance had brought me this far, and it looked as if it might get me even farther. I wrote back and told him it must have been ESP, because just the day before I had written the CIL a follow-up letter. It had been six months since the CIL had promised the file audit. I congratulated Jim on his Hoenshell success and thanked him for his interest in my case.

I was intrigued by the search for Carl Hoenshell in Bulgaria. It was hard to believe they were able to find him after all these years. I wondered what his niece was like. Had she known her uncle, or was she like me, haunted by his presence and the mystery of his disappearance?

I asked Jim if he knew anything about Griesheim, and he replied on October 27th that he had asked a young German airwar historian about the place and had already heard back from him. "So I decided to take him up on his offer to write to the several Grieshams and see if they had burial sites," he said. "Maybe the specifics on the crashes might ring some bells somewhere." The historian, Roland Geiger, told Jim there were four Griesheims in Germany, one of which was in Bavaria, too far north to be considered. I knew the one we were looking for was near Frankfurt am Main, so I passed that information along to Jim.

Johnie Webb at the CIL responded on November 8. He said they had obtained a copy of the IDPF, the same file on Billy I had, but they, too, had come up empty. "In an attempt to locate additional information, we have requested that a search for the file Unknown X-70035, which subsequently became CIL-5034...be conducted by our headquarters... Once this file is received and reviewed by our analysts we should be able to provide you with the answers you seek."

That was disappointing. I could have told them the IDPF didn't have the answers, and it would have saved them a lot of time. But at least they were working on it. That CIL file was the key.

On December 7, 1999, the 58th anniversary of the bombing of Pearl Harbor, Jim forwarded an e-mail from Roland Geiger. Roland had checked with several archives, but no one knew anything about a mausoleum in Griesheim. He was under the mistaken impression that the bracelet was still with the remains at the mausoleum and wanted the exact source of my information. I had to tell him the bracelet had initially been with the remains at the mausoleum but that it had been placed in the CIL file, not the grave.

I finally remembered to order Lowell Twedt's file on December 10.

Four days later I got another letter from Webb at the CIL, and my heart sank. He wrote, "We did receive a reply to our request for the CIL

5034 file from the Washington National Records Center (WNRC) in Suitland, Maryland. Unfortunately the CIL 5034 file is 'missing'. Without this file to review, we are unable to answer the questions in your letter of April 27, 1999... Unless the CIL 5034 file can be reviewed, we are unable to provide you with factual data on the information you seek. If additional information is received concerning your questions, we will notify you..."

Webb enclosed a copy of the "Reclassification Sheet" that had changed Billy's records from "Unknown" to the "CIL" designation. It was a useless piece of paper.

I was more depressed than I thought possible. My hopes had been so high, and this looked like a dead end. I quoted Webb's letter to Jim Graham, and asked, "Jim, where do I go from here? Is there a next step I can take? Anyone who knows me knows I don't give up easily, and to have come this close to finding anything that might be associated with Billy makes me even more determined. It's so much more than his family ever knew existed."

I asked him if he knew what causes a file to be missing, and if there were any other avenues I could pursue. I told him I hoped the file on the other pilot, Lowell Twedt, might have some clues, but I wasn't optimistic.

"Of all the possible outcomes," I went on, "this is the last one I expected. I keep seeing the closing scene in *Raiders of the Lost Ark,* where the Ark of the Covenant is packed in a crate and wheeled into a U.S. Government warehouse containing thousands of crates exactly the same size and shape." I was sure Billy's "missing" file was in a warehouse somewhere, mis-filed. But where?

I couldn't give up, so I wrote Johnie Webb to thank him for the work he and his staff had done and asked him if that meant his office had completed its portion of the search. I persisted, "How does one go about finding a 'missing' file? And just what does 'missing' mean in such cases—mis-filed? destroyed? archived in the depths of some warehouse somewhere? Where do I go from here? Whom do I contact next?" It took five months for him to respond, and by that time our search had taken a different turn.

On December 14 Jim responded to my agonized e-mail with just what I needed—encouragement and an action plan. He agreed the CIL's response was disappointing, but "I think your pursuit of the IDPF on Lt. Twedt is a good effort. Another might be to see if we can find the Lt. Jack Anderson [who] wrote the report of sighting on the mid-air collision.

Another might be a visit to the records agency at Suitland, Maryland, to dither them for further search for the CIL file #5034." He said he would try to find the eyewitness, Jack Anderson, but said that Anderson didn't show up in his 71st squadron records.

I was grateful for reinforcements. I needed help. But I didn't need Jim to tell me not to give up. Now that I had a little information, I was more determined than ever.

Total Army Personnel Command advised me they were processing my request for Lowell Twedt's file so, given their time frame before, I figured I'd have it in about six weeks.

Michal Mucha, the Polish war researcher who was my first e-mail contact, sent me a cheery Christmas greeting on December 22. I couldn't believe it had been more than 18 months since we met over the Internet. I wrote back and told him what had happened, about the bracelet, the missing CIL file, and my hopes of finding Billy. I told him my wishes were that 2000 would be a good year for him and a lucky one for me.

On December 23 Jim wrote again. An e-mail from a friend of his, Dick Kahler, reminded him that it had been two weeks since he had last written. Kahler had been Internet-surfing, had just seen my old message on the wae.com bulletin board, and had written Jim, "Looks like someone could use help." Kahler was the man who had spearheaded the Carl Hoenshell search in Bulgaria, and his curiosity had been piqued by my Web message. He wasn't aware Jim was already way ahead of him.

Jim told me Kahler was a banker in San Leandro, California, who had sold his bank and was retiring in the spring, "so his energies are about to be unleashed." My story about Billy had ignited his itch to "get back into the hunt," so if I wanted Kahler's help, all I had to do was say the word, and Jim would get him caught up. He ended his message with "Tally ho!"

The 1900s were waning. I never could have guessed what 2000 would bring.

6

BILLY TAKES FLIGHT
1943-44

December 30, 1942

TO WHOM IT MAY CONCERN:

I have known the bearer, W. O. Wisner, since
his childhood, and know him to be a young man of
sterling character, thoroughly honest and
reliable, sober and industrious.

Mr. Wisner is a young man of excellent
family, has been well reared and trained, and in
the short time that he has been in the business
world since he left school, he has earned
commendation of his superiors in the line of
business in which he was engaged.

Any consideration shown his application will
be appreciated by the writer.

Yours very truly,
J.D. Sheppard
V. Pres. & Gen. Mgr.
Lingo Lumber Company

* * *

Cadet portrait 1943

B illy completed the necessary college prerequisites by March, 1943 and began his military career for real.

Ida started a scrapbook, not only to track his progress, but also to provide a repository for the memorabilia Billy sent home so he would have it all in one place when he got back. It was never finished, and its contents have few dates or explanations. Billy never got home to fill in the blanks.

The scrapbook's cover bears the symbol of a son in the service, a blue star on a white background in a red border. Inside is Billy's cadet portrait, but he looks like a little kid playing soldier. His face is boyish and soft, still rounded from baby fat. His uniform, however, is genuine and displays the Army Air Force insignia, a propeller crossing a pair of wings. His cap perches high on his head, round and flat, looking like a misplaced pie plate.

Ida put everything into the book—birthday, graduation, and Christmas cards, photos, souvenirs, and letters. Three letters of recommendation from friends of the family are the first entries. Each is written on company letterhead and dated December 30, 1942. All of them testify to Billy's character and sobriety; one says he doesn't use tobacco. Handsome, well-liked, devoted to his family, Billy was the quintessential all-American boy.

An envelope holds a souvenir napkin and the guest list from an open house Ida and Maxine hosted for him on March 21, 1943. Forty-five close friends and relatives had gathered to give Billy a proper send-off as he headed for boot camp at Camp Wolters, Texas, 77 miles west of Dallas.

Ida put an envelope marked "your first letter home" into the scrapbook, just as she would have done in his baby book. It looked as if Billy was doing well.

March 26, 1943

Dear Mom and Dad,

We got up this morning about six o'clock. We made up our bunks and went to chow. For breakfast we had cereal, pancakes, milk, bacon and toast. After chow we went over to the assembly hall and took our exams. The first exam had 150 questions and you were allowed 40 minutes to finish it. They told us that no one single person would finish, but I would have done so if I had not lost the place. Anyway, I got 130 of them. We then took a mechanical aptitude test. I finished these tests. They told us who

passed the first test and who didn't. I was one of the ones who
passed, although I don't know what I made. Afterwards, they kept
those of us who passed and gave us a radio code test first to see what
we could do on it. Boy, I think I made in the high nineties.

We will be interviewed tomorrow and then we will be told
what we made on the tests. I hope I made high on all of them.

All of us got our uniforms today. [...] They said the shoes
would be in in a few days. Oh, yes, I got my helmet. You know, the
good-looking one. I will probably have to turn all this stuff in when
I leave, but I will have some good out of it while I do have it.

Mom, you might drop me a line because I think we are
going to be here longer than I expected. Will stop now as I am
going to the show to see "Lucky Jordan."

Love,
Bill

While Billy was away Ida received a letter from Tommy Hamlin, one
of Billy's college chums who wanted to know how to get in touch with his
friend. That letter went into the scrapbook, too, no doubt because Tommy
had written, "Mrs. Wisner, you are very, very fortunate in having a son like
Bill, for he is one of the finest pals that I've ever known."

Other correspondence surviving from Billy's training at Camp
Wolters are a post card from Ida catching him up on the news and a short
reply from Billy, too busy to write much. He said he had received her letter
forwarding one to him from his buddy Jack Tarver and that he had tried to
call the night before, but no one was home. He announced he had been
officially transferred from the Army to the Army Air Corps.

In late May 1943 a letter to the Wisners from the office of the commanding general, Headquarters, Army Air Forces Gulf Coast Training
Center, Randolph Field, Texas, indicated Billy just might make it as a pilot,
although there were no guarantees.

But Billy was making headway. After boot camp, he was sent to the
San Antonio Aviation Cadet Center (now Lackland Air Force Base). Ida
kept the "Acres of Cadets" and "Your Life as an Aviation Cadet" booklets
describing S.A.A.C.C. and its training process.

After orientation, the cadets were issued clothing and given a close-
cropped "Kelly Klip" haircut, named for Kelly Field, part of which had

become the training center. Then came three days of testing and at least a week of re-checks on various aspects of the tests. Failure of any one phase would mean automatic elimination from the aviation cadet program, and it wasn't unusual for a new friend to disappear without warning.

The "medical 64" test was the most comprehensive of all medical examinations given by the Army, even tougher than West Point's, according to one booklet, because the slightest flaw in a cadet's physical soundness could put an entire crew of men at risk. Results were also used to determine which job a cadet would handle best. The psychological test was "designed to find out, not what you know, but what you are able to learn under proper instruction." Cadets were cautioned that doing their "level best" in all parts of it would give them the best chance of success. The psycho-motor tests were administered last. Cadets were advised to relax (nervousness would work against their abilities) while they played complicated games devised to test eye-hand-foot coordination and depth perception, followed by ones designed to reveal a cadet's level of patience, his reflexes, and responses under pressure.

Test results determined whether a cadet would go on to pre-flight navigation, pre-flight bombardment, or pre-flight pilot training, the six-week program for which Billy qualified. Equivalent to basic training for the infantry, pre-flight pilot training would identify and eliminate the dead wood early. Only the best made it. Billy's friend and fellow cadet John T. Zebrowski remembers, "Wash-out rate was about 40 percent, mostly because of their inability to handle the discipline, but our group of buddies passed 100 percent."

One hazing incident stands out in Zebrowski's mind. "A cadet failed to address an upperclassman properly, so he was taken to the barracks and ordered to do pull-ups from the rafters until further advised. The upperclassman left to go to the bathroom and forgot all about the cadet hanging from the ceiling. I don't know how long he had been hanging there, but he had passed out, and his color was grayish when I came into the barracks. I immediately grabbed him and took him down and had him rushed to the hospital, as his hands had cramped and he could not release himself from the rafter. We later found out that after another hour or so of hanging there the cadet would have died from the disruption of blood flow to the heart and brain."

Zebrowski also recalls mealtime discipline. "When we ate we could not move a muscle to start eating until we asked permission from the upperclassman at our table." Any infringement and a cadet would lose his chance to eat at that meal, so those not disciplined enough to follow procedures practically starved and washed out quickly. Because of the hazing, he adds, "Many of the cadets would come back to the barracks in tears. Our class, 44-B, was one of the last classes to experience this type of discipline, as there were many complaints that it was overkill. Because of the publicity it ended shortly after we graduated."

Up at 0600, cadets spent their days in class, at physical training, maintaining a perfect uniform, locker, and bunk (the blanket had to be taut enough that a quarter dropped on it would bounce), playing organized sports, and studying. Lights-out was at 2200, if they could stay awake that long. Cadets were allowed visitors two days a week and church on Sunday, but all other time was accounted for.

That explains why Billy wrote few letters home and his scrapbook contains so little from this period, only Billy's cadet club card stamped with his class number, 44-B, and a newspaper clipping from the San Antonio Sunday Light dated July 18, 1943–"Visiting Day for S.A.A.C.C. Cadet Wives." The front-page item shows wives and families of cadets lined up for passes to visit their loved ones. The caption reads, in part, "On Wednesdays and Sundays at the San Antonio Aviation Cadet Center wives and friends of cadets can visit the huge establishment. Many of the wives are newlyweds, others have followed their husbands from hometowns. During the cadet training course the women seldom see their husbands and the short visits are anxiously looked forward to." An X on the photo beneath one of the women standing in line is marked "Sis," but it's impossible to tell for sure if it's Maxine.

But she says she never will forget the trip down there. With money tight, gas rationed, and trains reserved for troops, Maxine and Ida agreed to share a car with strangers. They contributed their ration cards for gasoline; the 280-mile trip took all day but seemed even longer. Ida was distrustful of the Mexican-Americans in the back seat, so she kept a tight grip on Maxine's hand in the front seat, while the driver sang "Somebody Loves Me," off-key, over and over, all the way to San Antonio. Getting there must have been anticlimactic, because Maxine doesn't remember anything about their visit with Billy or the trip home.

Billy qualified as a fighter pilot, and his buddy John Zebrowski made bomber pilot, so their training eventually took separate paths.

By July 30, 1943, Billy was in primary training at Jones Field, Bonham,

Texas. A change-of-address notice and an account tally for $75.45 are the only scrapbook records of his stay there, but 13 birthday cards from friends and family pasted into the scrapbook show that he wasn't forgotten. A birthday letter from friends Maude and "Doc" Dial saluted "One of the grandest boys I have ever known." Maude went on, "Bill, it seems just yesterday your mother brought you home from the hospital a sweet little blue-eyed, black-haired baby and tho' nineteen years have made a man of you, you still seem like a little boy to us."

At Jones Field Billy logged 65 hours of flight training on the PT-19-A and PT-19-B. A scrapbook photo shows a group of 25 jubilant cadets raising large tin mugs. On the back of the picture Billy wrote: "The big beer party in the south hangar given in honor of class 44-B leaving primary for basic training, Oct. 1, 1943." Billy numbered and listed five of his class-mates, friends he wanted his family to meet if only in a photograph. Because the USAAF organized its units alphabetically, all of Billy's buddies had names at the end of the alphabet. The five Billy listed were Raymond Zurcher, E.J. Zitzman, Frank Zawadski, Richard A. Wood, and Louis W. Wust. In the picture Billy looks deliriously happy, as do the rest of the boys—so much for the sobriety attested to in his letters of recommendation.

The big beer party in the hangar at Jones Field after the completion of primary training. #1 – Raymond Zurcher, #2 – E.J. Zitzman, Billy, #3 – Frank Zawadski, #4 – Richard A. Wood, #5 – Louis W. Wust

Next was basic training at Perrin Field in Sherman, Texas, for single-engine flight training. Billy logged 74 hours on the Vultee BT-13-A. Sherman was close to Dallas, so he and some of his buddies spent weekends with the Wisners whenever they could. Ida kept one of the thank-you notes from Dan Wise and Louis Wust dated October 26, 1943. "We just wanted to thank you for a very nice weekend," it said. "Even if it was just one night and some delicious meals, you'll never know how it boosted our morale to stay with you all after nine continuous months of army life—almost as good as being home. We made the trip back in plenty of time and for the first time in many a day, we went to sleep without being homesick. Oh, yes, Mrs. Wisner, could you give us some solution to the problem of getting your son up in the morning—we've tried everything but cold water, and that will come tomorrow."

Photos from Perrin Field show planes, planes and more planes, plus groups of Billy with his buddies clowning around, waiting for ships, and posing proudly in their flight suits.

Billy, Frank Zdybel, John Zebrowski, and Frank Zawadski at Perrin Field

After a short leave Billy was assigned in December 1943 to Eagle Pass, Texas, near the Mexican border about 140 miles southwest of San Antonio. During those days he sent few letters home, but on a picture postcard of an AT-6 dated December 13 he described the plane and promised a longer letter later.

He must have been getting homesick, because in 1944 he began saving his mother's letters. From January 27 until February 2, Ida wrote him three letters and four postcards, all of them barely containing her excitement about seeing him graduate. Ralph, Ida, and Maxine would travel to the ceremony together, and Ruth Peck, Billy's friend and former Sears co-worker, would meet them there the next day.

In her January 27th letter, Ida said she and Maxine had started training at the Red Cross. Still worried about her "baby," she asked if he was getting nervous and counseled him not to get in a hurry and make mistakes, and adds, "Oh, me. I am so nutty thinking that we are going to see you tomorrow week. Isn't it a grand and g-l-o-r-i-o-u-s feeling."

Her postcard on February 1 detailed how they would make the trip. She was still keyed up. "Well, it's 5:20 a.m. I could not sleep, so I got up at 4:30. In fact, I had a headache and I just started thinking. We got our tickets yesterday and they are a yard long. When we transfer at San Antonio we take a Laredo bus and when we transfer at Dilly we take an Eagle Pass bus. So we will be seeing you soon. Dad told them at the plant and they said it was OK."

The next day she wrote "Well, AV/C W.O.W., this card will be the last 'til I see you…Sis is working till Sat. noon. I am taking the test at the Red Cross today. I sure hope I get a good grade. I dreamed I made 44—some grade! We will be seeing you soon."

At Eagle Pass Billy logged 99 hours in the AT-6. His Eagle Pass yearbook is peppered with signatures and notes from his friends; most have names at the end of the alphabet. According to their inscriptions, Billy had earned the nickname "Woo Woo," but how he got it is a mystery. It no doubt had something to do with his initials, W.O.W., but there must have been other reasons, too. John Chopelas and the gang had called Billy "Wiggle-Tail Willie" as a boy, and John Zebrowski remembers he was "Sonny" during cadet training. Billy's nicknames were growing up with him, and Woo Woo was the one that stuck.

A small envelope in the scrapbook holds eight 2"x2" snapshots of some lighter moments with his buddies at Eagle Pass. One was of a blonde pin-up poster stuck on the wall, but the rest were of Billy, Richard

"Woody" Woodruff, and Clarke Wiseley. Clarke had sent the photos to Billy after they left Eagle Pass, and Billy had sent them home, adding his comments to Clarke's on the back of each one. On the one of Clarke, shirtless and looking fit, Clarke had written, "Badly in need of a Drink!" Billy had added "My little buddy Clarke Wiseley, Eagle Pass AAF, March 1944." Billy called Woody his "Big Buddy" on the photo of the two of them smoking pipes (so much for being tobacco-free). On the one of Billy standing "at ease" in black shorts, a white T-shirt, and aviator sunglasses, Clarke had written, "Look at those cute legs."

Before final preliminary training at Eagle Pass, Billy went home on leave. A scrapbook photo shows him in uniform standing in front of the little house on Melbourne Street. Next to it is his graduation announcement for Eagle Pass Advanced Single Engine School, and under that a newspaper clipping reads, "Lt. William O. Wisner, Army Air Forces fighter pilot, will leave Sunday for Eagle Pass Advanced Flying School for a month's training on P-40 pursuit craft before overseas assignment, after spending a short leave with his parents, Mr. and Mrs. R. O. Wisner, 1619 Melbourne. Lieutenant Wisner, a Sunset High graduate, received his commission and wings at the Eagle Pass school, Feb. 8." His family was so proud.

He sat for a couple of formal portraits while on leave, one in his leather flight jacket, one in his uniform. In both photos his cap displays the eagle emblem of the U.S. Army and, unlike the one in his cadet portrait, this one sits comfortably on his head, tipped ever so slightly to one side. The stay has been removed, so the sides of the cap are relaxed and softened with tell-tale indentations made by the headset of a pilot who has logged many hours in the cockpit. His face is lean and sculpted; no trace of baby fat remains.

There are lots of snapshots, too, from this short time at home. In some, Ida, Ralph, Maxine, Fannon, and Ruth Peck pose with Billy on the front lawn. In others, the two young women pose together in Billy's caps, clowning and having a good time. In not one of them can you see a smile on Ida's face.

Billy must have made good use of his furlough. His high-school tennis buddy, Paul Tarver, remembers Billy borrowing his family's car for a date. Paul's big brother Jack was in the Marines, Dalton was in military training, and young Paul and Bobby were still in high school. Paul said Billy brought the car back so late he had to sneak into the Tarvers' screened-in porch to awaken him. Paul hadn't yet gotten his license, but he drove Billy home, anyway. "I don't think I ever told my dad about that," Paul recalled, chuckling.

Second Lieutenant William O. Wisner

Then he quietly added, "That was the last time I saw Bill."

During that leave Billy gathered with the family men one afternoon, no doubt to have a few beers, listen to some sports, and catch up on the news. One can almost hear the good-natured banter. At Uncle John's urging they each wrote a letter to Billy's cousin, Cecil Hill, Jr., who was fighting in the Pacific. Aunt Sadie's son Cecil was Maxine's age, four years younger than his sister Marshall and the same number of years older than twins Peggy Jean and Betty Jo. Because Cecil was the only boy, everyone called him Brother, and the rest of the family followed suit. That seems to be a Southern custom, and it's rampant in the McCue line.* In fact, because Billy called Maxine "Sister," Ida took to calling her that, too. Until the day she died, she still called her own daughter "Sister."

The letters to Brother mirror the camaraderie the men shared.

---

*I've never called my sister anything but "Sister," and cousin Marshall's daughter, Sue Ann, was always "Sister" to her younger daughter, Lynne. When I told my new sister-in-law about Cecil, I said he was a cousin, seemed more like an uncle, but we called him Brother. "That's rich," she hooted, "the man's name is Cousin Uncle Brother!"

March 26, 1944

Dear Cecil,

It's been a heck of a long time since I last wrote you, and John crawled all over me for neglecting it. I'm here at home for a couple of days before I leave for California.

I went back to Eagle Pass right after graduation to take some more P-40 training and gunnery. We received our orders yesterday to go to Salinas, Calif. to the 454th Fighter Squadron. I am going to fly a P-38 for I don't know how long and then from there we will probably go to the South Pacific. I'm really anxious to get out there and get started. I really wanted to fly a P-51, but I'll sure as the devil settle for a P-38. How about it?

[...] If you do get a furlough and even come near Salinas, please drop in and see me because I really want to see you. I'll close this Cecil and write a longer letter when I get to Calif.

Your cousin,
Bill

Dear Brother,

We are all over at Ida's this Sunday afternoon and Billy here is on his way to the West Coast. John is also here big as life and twice as gruesome. We have been talking about the war, etc., and John suggested we all drop you a note.

It's been a long time since you have had a furlough and from the reports we get here from the Pacific it seems like it might be even longer before you get back. I hope it's not too rough on you, but I know it's tough any way you look at it.

My deferment was up yesterday and I am waiting to see what will happen to me next—no one knows.

You fellows have sure been dealing out some bad news to Tojo and that is good news to us. We appreciate the job you are doing. There is nothing much going on here except the usual news—Red Cross drives, war bond drives, rationing, etc., but it's not bad at all—we're doing fine. [...]

Regards,
Fannon Thompson

Dear Bro.,

Well, we all decided to drop you a few lines so will add my two bits worth. Bill has just gotten in and we have had quite a chin fest for the past hour or so. I guess he has told you in his letter where he is headed for and all about everything. Sure wish you could drop in on us and guess you do, too. Can't seem to realize that you have been gone two years, but time slips away from you. Bill has been in a year now. It only seems like last week since we went to Mineral Wells to see him, and what a difference then and now, as he is six feet one inch tall and weighs 165, and you remember what a runt he used to be and always worried over getting tall.

There's not much in the news line, Bro., or everything is just running along same old line with plenty of work, leave before daylight and get in at dark. Am still at the Continental Motors and we have been working seven days a week up until last couple of weeks and working on Sundays.

John came out to have dinner with us to-day and we have been having a time. Wonder when we can all get to-gether again and hope it will not be long, so why don't you get the bunch to-gether and wind this thing up, for if you don't I am going to have to get John, and he and I will straighten it out, for you know he won the last one by himself and he and I to-gether, I know, can wind this up.

Know you have had it rough, boy, but keep your chin up and keep hitting them. Drop your heavy duties for a while and let us hear from you when you get a chance to write.

Best regards and best of luck.

> *Yours,*
> *Ralph*

As Ralph had said, Uncle John was in France during WWI, but he was so gentle, and unthreatening it would be hard to imagine him giving those "Huns" a hard time. It's a sure bet he didn't single-handedly win the war. However, he didn't get away uninjured. He was wounded when he fell out of his bunk onto his bayonet. Got a Purple Heart for it, too.

Even though Uncle John had instigated the letter-writing campaign, his hastily-added note was just four lines. He cited a paper shortage as his excuse.

While he was home, Billy made a recording at a do-it-yourself sound booth. His voice was soft and deep with a pleasant southern drawl, and in order to cheer up his mother, he sang her "Home on the Range" in a lovely baritone. The record's poor quality makes it difficult to understand, but one passage comes through loud and clear. "It's kinda hard to tell you what I mean to say right here before all these people, but I guess there are times when you have to carry out what's in your heart, no matter who's around. But I want you and Dad to know that you've always been so good to me, and I'll always try to uphold the things that you've taught me, to be the good man that you thought I'd make. And I don't think that any other boy in the world has gotten a better upbringing and had a better home than I've had. I want you and Dad to know that I'll always love you and you'll always be first in my heart." His voice broke at one point, and he had to stop to clear his throat and control his emotions.

Ralph, Billy and Ida (left); Maxine and Billy (right)

Billy was in Salinas, California, for 15 days of further instruction, and by May he had arrived at Moses Lake, Washington, having driven night and day with three of his buddies, William Karstetter, Eddy Steffani, and Paul Summer, in Eddy's Packard sedan.

A letter from Clarke Wiseley, Billy's closest Eagle Pass buddy, caught up with him there. Clarke's typing was as exuberant as the exploits he described.

Fort Worth, Texas
4-24-44
21:45

Dear Woo Woo,

Since I can't seem to get anywhere with the only Sec[retary] here at night, I decided to pass my spare time giving you the latest dope.

Just returned from a ferry trip from Stamford to Sheppard Field. Rode a damned ole train that turned out to be the milk "RUN" - stopping at every cow in the fields as we passed by, nothing but a two-car affair powered by a one-cylinder gas engine that was supposed to run an electric thingmabob, all we did was coast mostly uphill… Anyhow, we arrived at Stamford late at night. No beer, no women, you can imagine how we felt - we did.

To end, I had a dinner date with "Janio" for Sat. night. We were grounded because of rainy weather. Lost that date. Also had a date with my other woman for Sun. Had a dust storm the following day, so I had a date with one of the waitressss (enough S's??). She turned out to be typical of the ole home product and was as changeable as the weather. At least she didn't drink my beer, as I had none. You should have the proper slant by now, hmmmm?

After flying the railroad tracks back to Shep Field I hopped the ole train home to ask my women to forgive me, which they didn't, as usual. I now am dating the local talent in the workroom. Close to home.

I talked to your mother and got the low-down on your deal, and I fume every time I think of it. As Woody may have told you, or not knowing, Sgt. Langly, with the aid of another Sgt., went down the list and picked 12 guys for Salinas. He happens to be an ole friend of my family's but he

didn't notice my name on the list, which happened
to be at the tail end, as usual. T.S.

Listen, hardhead, let's be for writin' me all
the stuff you do and especially the type training
you take. I wish the Hell I was with you, but so
far I'm doing nothing but ferrying and once in a
while test-hoppin' in a couple single-engine jobs.
My P-40 is about repaired now, and I have
permission to give it the works or vice versa.
Outside of that, I'm unhappy naturally.

I will personally look up your "VIRGINia" and
see if she is treating you right. If not, I'll go
with her and treat her mean. OK?? OK!

Write now and let's have the ole stuff on how
the P-39 tumbles.

Keep your tail high and your nose clean.

                         Your buddy,
                         The ole man,
                         Clarke

Billy's cadet buddy, John Zebrowski, now an instructor back in Texas,
brought Billy up to date on their S.A.A.C.C. classmates. He, too, was
unhappy about being left behind. And it seemed being an instructor was
almost as perilous as flying combat.

                         5-15-44
                         Monday Night

Dear Bill–

*Boy, surprised wasn't the word when I received your letter. I
just thought you were never going to show up. You sure hooked
yourself up to a good deal–P-39's and then stepping into P-38's.
Wow! You know, Bill, I'm just about fed up with this instructing
deal. They have been shipping instructors out right and left, but
they always seem to miss me somehow. Maybe my luck will change
soon. Maybe a possibility that I'll meet up with you in P-38
school–by luck or something.*

*I'm on my second class now. Have eight boys this time
(44-F). Six of them are good boys, and two are rather slow. The two
aren't beyond repair but not up to par. Started formation
today—all of them were pretty good except one—he sure gave me grey
hair about four or five times, but he is improving slightly but
surely. And night flying is going to pop up again inside of a week.
I don't mind that much except for the four hours of formation
each cadet must have. This sure is wonderful experience. If I ever
do get into combat, I'll be as cool as a cucumber.*

*My kid sister got married last Saturday. I got one of their
AT-17's and Zawadski and I went up for Sat. & Sun. Even
Zawadski is leaving me now. He is going to Fresno, Calif., B-24
co-pilot, leaving Wednesday.*

*Now, I'll tell you where all the boys went. Danny [Wise]
and Jack [Wright] got their B-26's, as you know. Wrenn got B-24
co-pilot and is on his way over by now. LeRoy Woerner got
bombardier pilot. Yousling and Woodside are instructors here at
Lubbock. Old Zdybel, A.J. Wolfe, Hank Wollum, Zurcher, Zelasko
all went to Selman Field, Monroe, La., to ferry navigators around.
Withers and Wust went to Hurlingen for B 24's, Williamson and
Williams got B-24's at Kansas. W.G. Wright got bombardier pilot.
And old Joe Gremlin is flying B-25's in S.C., Greenville, to be
exact. C.R. Wood got bombardier pilot. I don't know what R.A.
Wood got. Youngie got instructor here at Lubbock, but was shipped
to Fresno, Calif., B-26 co-pilot. That about covers the bunch of our
boys, Bill. Some of our boys from here—44-B—have their own B-26's
and are leaving for combat. Fast work, eh?*

*Hey, Bill, how about sending me those twins' address in
Dallas. I might get down there soon to see your Mom and Pop and
Sis and may as well say hello to them—ahem!*

*I sure wish I could have made the rounds of Los Angeles,
Calif., and I sure do like eager women lately, but I have just been
looking lately.*

*Well, bub, I guess this about finishes this one up. And don't
forget, Jr., when you get those sights lined up from a P-38, get one
good blast in for me.*

Your old pal,
"Zeb"

The twins John referred to were Billy's pretty blonde cousins, Peggy and Betty Hill, both still single. Billy was playing matchmaker.

Another letter from Clarke Wiseley, this one in his expressive handwriting, reiterates his frustration at being left behind. Clarke's flying hadn't settled down, but his social life had—and fast. What a difference a month makes.

5-24-44

24:15

Dear Woo Woo,

Hell of a long wait, hm? Been so damn busy flying all over the state in PT-19s and L-2Ms, AT-7s, BT-13s, and every other piece of junk the Army has with a prop on. Had a ferry trip last week or two to Pittsburg, Kans. in L-2Ms. Nothing but a Goddamned ole Piper Cub. There were 30 of us, and from the direction of take-off we just weaved in and out. Couldn't go up or down, or right nor left. I'm still having bad dreams over it.

My P-40 is almost finished now and I'm growing more eager. How's the ole P-39? Remember Capt. Rawlson saying it was a 7% better ship all around than the P-40? How about that?? Oh, yes. No doubt you have had enough conversation with former P-39 pilots to debunk or prove the ole tumbling theory—what do they say??

How is the 37mm? Does it jam as much as Capt. Ral. said?? Damn it, I'd give my left ball if I could get in with you. Looks like you'll come home with lots of brass and braid before I ever get checked out in a jeep!!!

Well, lil chum, my women will have to hunt someone else to entertain them, as I am now an ole married rascal. Who would have thought it? Not I! Guess I stayed too close to Big "D." It wasn't Janie, wasn't Gerry, remember the girl who stood on the steps when we left for Perrin Field? Same one. We have a nice flat in Ft. Worth, close to the field and since I go to work when I get damned good and ready, I take life easy—naturally.

If I don't get my shipping orders soon I'm headin' for Mexico and will let them fight this war any damn way they please. I can't transfer to the Polish or Dutch air force, 'cause I asked the C.O. of the field. I told him what I though of his big boxcars. He had given a nice lecture before—called us buzz boys. We're quite P-O'ed.

We (15) were all turned in at Ballinger, Tex., for rat racing, buzzing, low altitude formation, and on our trip to San Antonio ran every car off the highway for 50 miles. I had a P4 with real small numbers—these ships are being stored—so I gets up about 1500' and peels off split-S right down the main street of some one-horse town. I was so low people were running all over the place!

I laughed so hard I almost ran into another guy who followed me down. He had a piece of telephone wire in his landing gear, but not a word was said. This is our sorry life. How does it feel to do some legal buzzin' and rat-racin'?? Have you started skip bombing and dive bombing? Christ, when I think back on our ole gunnery days and recall all the swell times we had, I get so blasted mad, I could join the infantry and peel spuds rather than sit on my ass.

Well, Woo Woo, take damned good care of yourself. I know you will—you've done a swell job, but you're not through. Guess you'll have to shoot the bastards for me, too. Please write, will you? I'm really sorry about not writing sooner, as I know what letters from ole buddies mean.

> *Your ole pal*
> *The ole man,*
> *Clarke*

Billy sent his mother a newspaper clipping about a close call he'd had on one of his training flights at Moses Lake. The article said, "A Fourth Air Force plane based at Moses Lake made a forced landing five miles southwest of Hartline at 2:00 yesterday afternoon, the Moses Lake public relations office announced, but the pilot escaped unscathed. Damage to the plane, a fighter craft, was not revealed, nor was the pilot's identity."

Knowing she would eventually find out about it, Billy reassured his mother: "I didn't want to tell anyone about it because I knew you would worry. It has been some time since this happened, so I guess it's alright. It was quite an experience. Will tell you all about it when I see you. Bill."

Clarke must have heard about the accident, too, and in a letter written on D-Day, June 6, 1944, Clarke wrote, "Damn it, Woo Woo, I'm too broke (married life) to send flowers, so dammit the Hell! Keep on the ball!!" Still frustrated by being stuck in Fort Worth, Clarke adds, "I'm listening to a blow-by-blow description of the invasion now. I'm really P-O'ed. When am I gonna get off of the can??" He asked Billy what dive-bombing was like and if he liked flying the P-39 with its shorter wingspan.

The same day Clarke was writing his letter, Ida and Ralph received a telegram.

> DEAREST FOLKS PLEASE EXCUSE DELAY AM HOSPITAL WITH
> MEASLES BE OUT IN FEW DAYS DON'T WORRY FEEL FINE
> WILL WRITE WHEN THEY'LL LET ME LOVE= BILL

Billy got no end of ribbing from his friends for catching a "kid's disease." What a way to celebrate the invasion of Europe.

But Billy didn't forget his dad on Father's Day, and on his June 8 card he added, "I just want you to know that if a fella looked the wide world over he could never find a Dad like you. I only wish I could live my whole life over so I could be with you just that much longer. Your devoted son, Bill." In spite of the measles and the accident, Billy logged 47 hours in the P-39, and he even got some time off to play. A letter from his high school tennis buddy, Dalton Tarver, expressed envy that Billy had gone salmon fishing. Dalton was following Billy's footsteps in the Air Corps and was proud to announce he'd just been classified a pilot.

In the scrapbook are photos of two squadrons at Moses Lake posed in front of a tarpaper building. Some of the men are circled and their names are marked, Steffani, Summer, Patton, Twedt, and Karstetter, among others, names that show up in other photos and in Billy's letters. Billy valued his friends and wanted his family to know them, too.

By July 1 he was at Ontario, California, where he began training on the P-38 Lightning. He was assigned to the 443rd Air Base Unit, Section 2, 4th Air Force, and he sent home a large photo of the class. Billy had written each man's name, noting "My Boys" above his friends Paul Summer and Eddy Steffani. At the bottom of the list he wrote, "NOT PICTURED: Wisner, W.O. – Patton, W[alter] H. (At link trainer when picture was taken, dammit!)" But Billy and "Pat" were photographed in a cafe on one of their double dates. That, too, is pasted in the scrapbook, but Billy neglected to identify the young women.

Three letters to Billy survive from this period. One from Uncle Fritz was as formal as he was, typewritten by his secretary on his firm's stationery with a carbon copy to Ida. It caught Billy up on some of the cousins' activities.

Moses Lake, Washington. Paul Summer (back row, 6th from left), Eddy Steffani (7th from left), Bill Ward (middle row, far left), Walter Patton (5th from left), Billy (6th from left), Bill Karstetter (front row, far left)

July 19, 1944

Dear Billy:

First of all, let me congratulate you on your birthday and wish you many a happy return of the same and that the next one will be celebrated in Texas with your own folks. [...]

Last night as I was coming from Jean's and stopped at a watermelon garden, I ran across Maxine and Fannon. Fannon was going to work about 11:30 and we rode to town in his car. All your folks are well and seem to be getting along all right.

Jean and [husband] Gordon came in late last Saturday night with [daughter] Sharon from Fort Benning, Georgia, where Gordon finished school at the Advanced Officers Training School. [...] Gordon will leave here this coming Tuesday to go back to Camp Cook, California, to join his division. He does not know, of course, where he is going but expects possibly that they will go to the Chinese sector.

Betty Jo wants to join the Waves but they have persuaded her to wait until Brother comes

home. For over a year it has been reported that
Brother would be home around the first of the
month each month, but he is still in Alaska and if
they continue to defer his furlough, it is
possible the war will be over before Betty Jo
enlists. I think she has taken all her
examinations and I am sure she is acceptable.

Peggy does not want to go. Betty Jo says she
is mooning about her boyfriend in the Marines, who
has been in the Southwest Pacific ever since the
beginning of the war. I am sure you know the boy.
His name is George. I recall him very well and he
is a nice boy and has been back one time, I think,
for a furlough.

Let us hear from you, Bill, and if there is
anything we can do, I am sure no one will object
to doing their part for you.

Again, a happy birthday to you and all the
love in the world.

                              Your uncle,
                              Fritz

The next was from Ida, disappointed that she wouldn't get to see her
son before he shipped out.

                              Dallas, Tex.
                              July 28, 1944

Hello darling—
     *Enjoyed your letter so much. Am looking forward to
getting the pictures. The enclosed card was sent from Eagle
Pass—guess you want to put it in your wallet.*
     *Guess what—Richard is going to be a paratooper. Isn't that
awful? Dad asked Mr. Hasty where Herbert was, and he said he is
somewhere in Calif., just like it was a military secret. Mrs. Tarver
said Dalton was going to Ontario (he thinks), the last of this week
or 1st of next week. Oh, yes, I do hope you both can get together.
Jack [Tarver] will be home around the 1st.*

We went to see "Lassie," and of course Sis and I cried. She is getting along fine, and F. is OK. He is working hard on his house. It looks good. He is on his vacation this week. Hope by this you have received the shoes and your box. Honey, I wanted to make you a big cake, but didn't know what condition it would arrive.

I sure am so disappointed I won't get to see you, darling. I would come, don't mind the hardships of the trip, but it costs so much. Dad is OK. His feet still swell, but he won't fight for another job.

Darling, now pay attention to this and answer it. Make two copies of a code you can make up. Example–If you are going to the Chinese/Burma [sector], you can say something like this–"Wouldn't it be grand if Sis would have twins." Now put your thinking cap on.[…]

I love you, honey, so much, and be so careful.

> *Gobs and gobs of love*
> *from Mom*

Maxine recalls that she and Ida had planned to visit Billy in California, but just before they were to leave Maxine's employer canceled her vacation. Her presence would have defrayed the cost of the trip, and without her Ida couldn't afford to go.

It was frowned upon, but Billy took Ida's suggestion and devised a code that would tell them where he would be sent. He also was getting his finances in order.

> *Ontario, Calif.*
> *July 31, 1944*

Dear Mom and Dad,

Received two letters today and was really glad to hear from home. I received your box a few days ago and Sis's box yesterday. Thanks a million. The fellows really enjoyed the box, but it sure made me mad when I found out they had taken those peaches out. I had my mouth all set for those peaches*[…]

---

*Shipping fruit to California has always been regulated, so those peaches never made it past the border.

You said Dalton was to be sent to Ontario. I don't think he will come here, but he will probably go to Cal. Aero Academy and that is only six miles from here. Maybe at last I will get to see him. I'm still mad and sick over the way that Snookie treated Jack. If a woman ever did me that way I swear I'd kill her.

Mom, I had an allotment made out yesterday in your name. Starting the 1st of Sept. you get $100.00 out of my pay each month. This will come in every month. Would you please open a bank account for me but fix it so you can draw out of it any time you want to. I will probably be sending more than that home but I want that much to be sent home for sure.

Now, Mom, any time you want anything, and I mean <u>anything</u>, Whether it's for you or Sis or Dad or Fannon or anyone you deem to give it to, don't hesitate an instant about drawing it out of the bank. If you can't fix the account so you can draw out of it, then just keep it at home in a sack or something. The reason I haven't been sending more money home than I have is that I had a personal debt that I had to pay off, but it is all cleaned up now, and I can really start putting it away.

Our section commander just told us that we were going out to the desert next week, so that messes up our last weekend in the States. By the weekend after this one, we will probably be on our way overseas. We leave there the 11th and only stay at Hamilton Field in Frisco for a couple of days.

Mom, about that code. Here's the way it will work. If I write a letter with any of the following sentences in it, you will know where I am going:

1. *"Won't it be swell if Sis has twins!"–South Pacific*
2. *"I have a feeling the road is going to be tough from here on in."–China/Burma*
3. *"I hope the yard looks as good this year as it did last year."–England*
4. *"How are the Hastys doing, these days?"–Aleutians*

If I do go anywhere else, I will be able to tell you about it. Mom, these, or rather one of these sentences will appear as the first sentence in the <u>second</u> paragraph in one of my next few letters, so be on the lookout for it.

Mom, I'll close this now and write more later.

Lots of love,
Bill

At Ontario he logged 62 hours in the P-38. A letter from Clarke, who had recently visited Billy's parents, expressed envy: "Bill, I'm sure glad to hear you talk about the P-38. I admit what I know about them comes from reading and talk, but I feel sure you couldn't ask for a better plane for speed, firepower and guts. As I look at it, the only way I can get even with you is to fly P-51s, but I doubt if I get the chance... Damn it, that P-38 looks slick!! What does she cruise at?? At what rpm and manifold pr? Can it out-dive a P-47, hm? Christ, I gotta have something on mine that's better than yours!"

On August 10, nine days after his 20th birthday, Billy's orders came through. He celebrated in Los Angeles, and in his scrapbook is a photo taken that night at the Earl Carroll Theatre Restaurant, Hollywood. Billy is seated at a table next to a lovely young woman, and they both look like they're having a good time. The date is hand-written at the bottom of the photo, but his companion's name is missing.

Billy's orders were to report to Hamilton Field, California, "not later than 1200, 13 August [1944] for further movement overseas." On August 16 he was directed to go "without delay" via rail from Hamilton Field to Camp Patrick Henry, Virginia, then to report to the Commanding General, Hampton Roads Port of Embarkation, "for further movement to the overseas destination of this shipment by water."

Among the 17 names on these orders were Lowell Twedt and Billy's buddies Ed Steffani and Paul Summer. After what must have seemed to him like an eternity, Billy was on his way.

And the war wasn't over yet.

7

SOMEBODY SOMEWHERE
KNOWS SOMETHING

From:	Dick Kahler
Sent:	Sunday, December 26, 1999
To:	Jim Graham; Diana Dale
Subject:	RE: Fw: Uncle Bill

Jim

Tis the day after Christmas and the thoughts of "Uncle Bill" started thru my mind. Let me get some facts in my head. Like Carl the crash site was never found? He went down over Bolzano, which I assume is in Northern Italy. Has this story been put in the 1st Fighter News? Who was his wingman? Has anyone in Bolzano been contacted? There are 5 listings in Bolzano for AOL, 4 in English 1 in German. We found Carl this way. Did anyone check Florence-American Cemetery? It seems that would have been the logical place to take him. Do you have the mission report as to who else was on the mission that may have reported something, other than the 71st? Has she been in contact with Ted Darcy at wreck1@cntn.net? He will cost a few bucks but this one looks tough and we will need all the help we can get.

OK, I am hooked, it looks like a project for the coming year. Mail me what you have or e-mail me whatever else you have. Happy New Year.

Dick

* * *

J im Graham's network of people who could help us find Billy included Dick Kahler. Kahler wasted no time in contacting Bill Mays, a researcher in Bulgaria who had helped them find Carl Hoenshell, the missing 71st Fighter Squadron pilot Jim and Steve Duncan had told me about. It was hard to believe, but somehow they had found local eyewitnesses who remembered where Hoenshell's plane had crashed more than 50 years before. I was afraid to get my hopes up, but I wondered who might have seen Billy's plane go down. Were they still living? Would they be friendly?

It was apparent we weren't going to get any more information from the U.S. Army, at least not any time soon, so I was grateful for Kahler's help.

I answered his questions, and Jim sent him copies of our earlier e-mails to get him caught up. Kahler responded by sending e-mails to every contact he could find in the Bolzano area—tourist bureaus, city halls, and hotels, as well as residents of Bolzano who were on line. Besides providing the particulars of Billy's crash, he said they could read about the search for Carl Hoenshell on the Web at www.behindbarbedwire.com/carlh.htm. I visited the site and was fascinated by the way the Hoenshell story unfolded. They had made it look easy, but I didn't dare hope Billy's story might turn out as well.

Kahler sent me the street address for the state archives in Bolzano and suggested I write them. He was an e-mail dynamo and copied Jim and me on every message he sent. Most days I would open my e-mail box and find at least 10 messages waiting for me.

Jim wrote Kahler on December 27, "You're as fast out of the starting blocks are you always were! Bolzano will know a lot more about history than they did before. There are a lot of odd strings to this ball of yarn. Keep winding...Good hunting."

The next day Kahler responded that he had found an American living in Bolzano who might be interested in helping and had sent him the Hoenshell story "to set the hook." He had already heard from two of the people in Bolzano who used AOL, and added that the terrain north of town "is the Italian Alps so my next step is to see if I can find ski runs there and find out if there are any P-38 parts in the middle of a run. In this day and age someone must have spotted something and if we can get the local paper to do a story perhaps it will jar someone's memory. All we need is one hit!"

While Kahler was working the overseas angle, Jim searched govern-ment records for more clues. The two men exchanged data relating to the crash and talked about potential eyewitnesses still living (Jack Anderson) and the relatives of Olson and Twedt. "[Jack Anderson] is not evident on any 1st FG Assoc. rosters as far back as 1977 when reunions began," Jim wrote Kahler. "I don't have any original home address for him. There are likely a zillion Jack or John Andersons, so a 'white pages' search might not be rational, but I'll try to find the gov't records source that would have the last recorded address for the Army. The only value of finding living relatives of Virgil Olson and Lowell Twedt might be to see if they have had any government tracking of their remains... When Diana gets the full file on Twedt, she will have more current addresses for his family."

Jim sent Kahler a scanned version of the Mission Report and the MACR; in the meantime one of the AOL members in Bolzano suggested we contact the provincial newspaper, the state archives, and the Italian Mil-itary. She also recommended a Bolzano researcher, Wolfgang Moroder.

Our network was growing.

Kahler found 49 Virgil Olsons listed in the U.S. and gave me the phone number for a Lowell J. Twedt living in Montana. I called and spoke to Mrs. Twedt, a nice woman who told me her husband was not related to our Lowell Twedt. She did offer to put me in touch with a cousin, howev-er, who had a book on the Twedt family, but that seemed like a reach, so I filed it for future reference. Everyone was being so helpful.

While scanning Billy's MACR, Jim noticed on line 7 "the A/C he was flying had 'no nose art nickname.' [Billy] either had not had it painted with his 'Golden Slipper' nickname, or he was flying another A/C." Jim's first assumption was probably correct. Even though I'd heard all my life that his plane was the *Golden Slipper*, Billy must not have been over there long enough to get his plane painted.

On December 29 I received more copies of e-mails Kahler had sent to the Bolzano addresses. He'd found a Web site on mountain climbing in the Dolomites (the part of the Alps nearest Bolzano) and told me, "This looks worthwhile. The region around there is really tough terrain. If these guys are climbing those mountains a crash site would be of great interest and would have been something everyone remembers."

That seemed like a good lead. I had always believed that if Billy had crashed near people, the U.S. had to have known about it and would have told the family. That meant Billy was probably in an area too remote to be

easily spotted, high up on a mountain, perhaps even in a glacier. I remembered reading about the "The Iceman," who had been uncovered in a glacier
only a few years before in the same region. It had been a monumental find
vis-à-vis prehistoric man, and because he was found so near the border, there
was a dispute over whether the 5,300-year-old specimen could be claimed by
Austria or Italy. Italy won by less than 100 meters. I searched for more information and found the museum's Web site (www.archaeologiemuseum.it).
I hoped it wouldn't be 5,000 years before anyone found Billy.

New Year's was upon us, and I told my e-mail pals that my husband
and I were escaping to our cabin in the mountains to celebrate Y2K and
would be out of touch. Jack had heard so many horror stories about power
outages, communications failures, and millennium crazies, he thought we
needed some peace and quiet. He was right. We slept late, played Scrabble©
and dominoes, ate great food, listened to jazz, read, partied with the neigh-
bors, and unwound. It was a wonderful way to usher in 2000, and we were
so far removed from e-mail and the real world I didn't even think about
finding Billy.

My absence brought good luck.

8

OVERSEAS
1944

Friday, September 8, 1944
Someplace in India

Dearest Woo Woo,

Well, bub, how's your end of the detail making out? Mine isn't worth a d- - -! India. Ug—Such a place. Shouldn't happen to a dog! But, at least we're outta the States. Maybe someday we'll get into combat. That's what we're working for!

Buddie, you never in your life have seen anything like this filthy country. The natives have no idea what soap is. They take their toilet on the sidewalk and just let it stay there. You can't even stand the smell, as you walk down the streets. But then, this is quite a mystic country. A number of very interesting sights. The natives are quaint, to say the least.

We left Hamilton Friday after you, by train, for Miami Beach. We had a 7-hour layover in L.A. Some fun. Then a 7-hour layover in New Orleans. What a trip. Really had a superb time. Then Miami. A very nice place. We didn't have enough time there to suit the Rabbit and me. Sweet action! We met two stars in a USO show and really painted the town. We're in hopes of seeing them out here some day.

We're all feeling fine now, but the third day after arrival, most of us came down with the GIs. What a mess that was (we have outside latrines). It afforded a number of laughs for all of us.

This set-up here is very nerve-wracking. We haven't so much as seen one of our "babies," much less fly one. I'm getting sick and tired of sitting on my dead ass from morning till nite. And, we've had no mail yet, none at all. Hope you're having better luck with your mail.

Well, Stud, it's time for me to sign off. Rabbit sends his love to each of you.

Good luck always,
Sarge
[Lt. Charles K. Sergeant]

* * *

Billy's friends were being shipped all over the world, and some of them got to choose where they would go. Bill Ward, a classmate of Billy's at Salinas, Moses Lake, and Ontario wrote in his memoirs, "We had all been asked our preference for transfer to the Pacific or Europe. I chose Europe because I didn't want to take the chance of being shot down over some large expanse of water and floating around in a rubber dinghy until I was, or was never, picked up by some passing ship." Billy must have felt the same way, because both of them ended up on a troop train headed for the East Coast, along with Lowell Twedt, Paul Summer and Eddy Steffani.

But before Billy left he cleaned out his footlocker and sent some things home. Fannon picked up his barracks bag August 24, and in one of her letters to Billy Maxine wrote, "Mom and I got a kick out of your many cards and your tooth! Some tusk! Why didn't you mount it on a chain or something? By the way, what the heck happened to your identification bracelet? Never saw anything in such a state!! Also, who is the girl pictured with you at Earl Carroll's? Some stuff. You never tell us nuttin'!"

Nothing in the file or in Billy's letters tells what day he left the States, so it's hard to know how long they were at sea. Bill Ward said they first landed at Gibraltar, then headed across the Mediterranean to Naples, Italy. "Thank goodness the trip was uneventful," Ward wrote, "with no German submarine scares. We docked at Naples in early September and debarked to a reassignment center in that city. Most [members] of the group were assigned to the 15th Air Force, located in the Foggia area. Five of us were

Billy and mystery girl at Earl Carroll's nightclub

assigned to the 1st Fighter Group and then to the 71st Fighter Squadron. We traveled to Salsola by truck and reported to Squadron Operations on September 10, 1944."

The first V-mails from Billy are undated, but he no doubt sent them as soon as he arrived. Billy knew how much his mother worried.

Somewhere in <u>Italy</u>

Dear Mom and Dad,

This is just a line to let you know where I am. This Italy is some country. I've never seen so many dirty people before in my life. The Germans sure left this place in a shambles. This outfit I'm in is really a good one. It is the oldest fighter outfit overseas. Summer, Steffani and I are still together and will be flying missions together.

The boat trip was very uneventful. We were pretty crowded, but it was not too bad. I've already seen the ruins of Pompeii and quite a few other things. This is about all for now, so will sign off and write a long letter tomorrow.

All my love,
Bill

Billy was not at liberty to reveal his exact location, but Foggia was in southeastern Italy, in the "spur" just above the boot heel. Ward recalled that once they arrived, "It was at this time that the five of us [Billy Wisner, Bill Ward, Eddy Steffani, Paul Summer, and Lowell Twedt] started to get to know each other. All of us had had a nodding, 'Hi, how are you today?' acquaintance, but now we were going to live and fight together."

Billy was making new friends, and it looked like he had hard work ahead of him.

Somewhere in Italy

Dearest Mom and Dad,

This is a letter to supplement the one I wrote last night. We got here three days ago and the set-up is pretty good. There are a bunch of swell fellows here, and the C.O. seems to be a regular fellow. We have not flown any missions as yet but hope to within the next few days. Our outfit is escorting heavy bombers on raids to Vienna, and other targets deeper in German-occupied territory. When this theater of operations folds up, our outfit will either move to China or to the S. Pacific. Whatever the case may be it looks as if I'll be over here for the duration. You have to have fifty missions or more in before you can come home.

I haven't received any mail for almost a month, but I'll probably get a big stack of it when it does finally catch up with me. I'm about out of space so will close for now.

All my love,
Bill

He wrote home often, and his airmail letters detailed more about his routine and surroundings than did the space-limited V-Mail. But those took longer to reach their destination, at least a month and sometimes more. Mail from home was just as slow, especially when it had to catch up with a serviceman on the move.

September 19, 1944
Somewhere in Italy

Dearest Mom and Dad,

Well, I've been here for two weeks now and still no mail. I know it will be some time before I hear from you but it is really hard to wait. We have been going through the same routine day in and day out since we got here. I went up with my flight leader today for some mock combat flying. They fly a bit different over here than we did in the States. We go buzzing just about any time we feel like it.

We are building a new officer's club for our squadron and while we are not flying we work like beavers on the club. The other day we went to the coast of Italy on the Adriatic Sea to get a load of sand for mixing with cement for the club. We stopped at a swell strip of beach, filled the truck with sand in about fifteen minutes and then went swimming for a couple of hours. The Adriatic Sea is very warm at this time of year and we had a swell time riding the waves into shore. I got a pretty good coat of tan out of the deal.

I'm really ashamed of myself. It was just the other day I remembered about Sis and Fannon's anniversary. Congratulations and may many happy others come year after year.

Here is what my squadron insignia looks like– [he included a sketch of the insignia, a skull and lightning bolts]*–71st Fighter Sqd. This is a crude drawing of it, but you can get the general idea of what it looks like. I'm having this insignia painted on the front of my jacket and a big beautiful P-38 painted on the back of the jacket. I'll let you know when I get my own plane. Right now I'm flying other fellows' planes.*

I take back what I said about not getting any mail. The mail came in a few minutes ago, and I got <u>fourteen</u> letters from you and Sis. I was glad to hear that Brother got home OK. He'll be gone to Corpus when this gets there. I was sure sorry to hear about Clarke's mother. Please send me his new address. I was really sorry to hear about Jack, too. His eye must be really giving him trouble, and if Snookie was my wife I'd turn her over my knee and give her a good spanking.

Well, folks, I'll close this now and write more later. Write as often as you can, as letters really boost my morale.

> *Lots of love,*
> *Bill*

P.S. I'm now 6'2" tall and weigh 175 lbs. Boy, I don't know when I'm going to stop growing.

Bill

The Jack Tarver/Snookie conflict must have been some soap opera. This wasn't the first time Billy had mentioned it.

Billy's flight log recorded four local missions on September 14, 15, 19 and 20. On September 21st he flew his first two combat missions, to Istandari (Budapest) and Munich.

It must have been difficult corresponding with such a long time between replies. Ida's first V-mail letter to Billy was dated September 23, but there's no way of knowing when it reached him. But she had received two from him, so far. She had written him every-other day since he left, and Maxine wrote on the "off" days, so he could expect a bunch once they did catch up with him. Ida said she was happy he was in with some "swell fellows," and predicted, "You will make friendships that will be good all your life and you will keep up with them after you come back."

She told Billy she had bought a gift for him to give to Maxine, a yellow silk nightgown and little blue jacket. "She was so thrilled. I am going to try and make everything pleasant and easy for her. She is so sweet, and Fannon is so thoughtful, and that goes a long way." As she closed, Ida reminded him to be careful.

On September 24th Billy flew another combat mission to Athens, then on the 26th and 27th a ferry trip and a local. He wrote home on the 28th saying he hoped his letters were getting through. He'd gotten five more that day from Ida and Maxine, "so my morale is very, very high tonight," but added, "by the way, Dad, why don't you let me have a few lines by your own hand? I know Mom puts everything in the letters you want to say, but you know old sentimental me, if I don't get letters from both you and Mom I feel that something is definitely lacking."

It was only the end of September, but because packages moved more slowly than air mail Ida asked him what he wanted for Christmas. In an earlier letter he had asked for a good lighter. In this one he added a few more: "1) another good pair of leather gloves, size $8\frac{1}{2}$ or 9 (you remember the other pair you gave me, well, I've flown so much in them and am going to fly so much more in them that I don't think they are going to last much longer); 2) a white scarf and a wool scarf (it really gets cold at 30,000 feet, even with the heater on); 3) a can of cocoa, some ground coffee, some cheese in those little bottles, a big jar of sweet pickles (oh, boy) and anything else good to eat you can think of. We can cook it right in our tent. Be sure and pack it well so it won't crush. Thanks a million."

He said he had flown two missions so far. "Both of them were the belly tank five- to six-hour kind. You've read in the papers where the heavy bombers of the 15th Air Force are pounding targets deep in enemy territory, well, we are the boys who do the escort work in P-38s and keep the German planes away from the bombers. Please don't worry about me, Mom and Dad, because we have the best fighter plane in the Air Force and have had the best training that could possibly be given us, so please don't worry. Just keep things going alright at home and little Bill will take care of himself."

Bill Ward confirmed how cold it got up there. "The P-38 was not a well-heated airplane, and was very cold at the 32,000-ft. to 34,000-ft. altitude we usually flew on bomber escort missions. I believe the temperature normally decreases three degrees per 1,000 feet, so you can see the temperature outside the plane was very low, and our heaters didn't do a very good job inside. I usually wore regular underwear, long johns, wool shirt and pants, maybe a wool sweater, ... coveralls, and a mohair-lined cloth jacket, which was warmer than a leather flight jacket." He cited another reason for so many clothes. "Since a good many of our missions required that we fly over the Alps or some other snow-covered mountain, it was a good idea to dress warmly, anyway, in case our plane was hit by flak and we had to parachute or crash-land in the snow."

So much clothing must have been an encumbrance in such a small cockpit. But there was even more to contend with. "We also wore our gun belt, or a shoulder holster, to carry our .45 caliber pistol. I believe most of us also carried some form of hunting knife, mainly to puncture the inflatable rubber dinghy packed in our parachute harness, in case it accidentally inflated while we were flying. One thing we didn't need was a cockpit full of dinghy." Ward says they also wore an inflatable vest, called a "Mae West," after the buxom movie star of the era. "The vest included a package of orange dye marker and maybe a flare. The vest and dinghy where with us just in case we had to parachute into or crash-land our damaged plane in the Adriatic. Over that was our parachute harness, which included either a 'seat pack' or 'back pack' parachute and our inflatable, one-man rubber dinghy. When we reported to the squadron, I was issued a harness with the parachute packed in the back and the dinghy in the seat. I remember how hard the CO_2 bottle (for inflating the dinghy) used to get on those longer 4 to 6 hour missions, and couldn't wait to inherit a 'seat pack' parachute from one of the pilots who was completing his 50 missions and going home soon.

"We wore three pairs of gloves–first a silk pair, then a woolen pair, then a leather pair… We always wore a leather helmet with built-in earphones, and a throat microphone for talking on the radio. This had two microphones placed a couple of inches apart, as part of an elastic strap, and was worn around the neck like a necklace. There was also a microphone in our oxygen mask, which we always wore starting at least at 10,000 to 12,000 feet on the way out on a mission. Some fellows didn't like the throat [mikes] and wore their oxygen mask[s] all the time. With the oxygen mask on and…goggles down, and with a scarf around the neck, we were completely covered and protected from flash burns from a damaged and leaking oxygen line ignited by an incendiary bullet. Flash burns could be very short in duration, but very devastating.

"So now we are completely dressed, except for one thing, a survival pack, which we strapped to our right or left leg. This was rectangular (approximately 6" by 9" by 3" thick), canvas-wrapped package. This pack contained some very durable cloth maps, a compass, a flare, and concentrated chocolate and other food. We used to attach the maps we used for the missions we were flying to the flat top of this package. The course and a line between our field and our destination [were] marked in pencil on the map. For the squadron or the group leader, who was responsible for the navigation of the mission, their gyro compass, clock, and landmarks along that line were all we had to reach our target during dive bombing and strafing missions. For bomber escort missions, all we had to do was find the bombers at a pre-determined time, altitude, and location."

If anything went wrong, bailing out was difficult. Because of the configuration of the P-38, the pilot couldn't just open the canopy and jump out. He had to climb out of the cockpit onto the wing, position himself to clear the tailpane connecting the twin fuselages, and jump. An easier way would be to flip the plane over, open the canopy, and "fall" out, but that would require having control of the plane.

Ward's memoirs include some interesting, if personal, trivia. "With all those clothes on, and flying reasonably close formations, it was best not to try to urinate on the way to the target area. Usually, when you are about halfway home, though, the formation loosens up, and you can 'make the effort.' The P-38 designer provided a relief tube, which is a removable funnel clipped under the seat and attached to a flexible plastic tube that leads out through the bottom of the fuselage and points aft. If you can reach what you need to with all those clothes on, and after unbuckling your parachute leg straps, you have it made. The suction from the outer tube would easily draw out any liquid and vaporize it very fast. It is very important for your plane crew chief to make sure the exit tube is clear and is pointed aft and not forward."

On September 29th and 30th Billy made two more local flights, and on October 4th he flew another combat mission to Munich. During this time the pilots were beginning to upgrade their living quarters. According to Ward, "At the time we reported to the squadron, most of the pilots and ground operations officers were living in tents on 'Officers' Row'…Quite a few officers, however, were living in 'shacks' constructed from sandstone (tufa), which was easily cut into building blocks and was readily available in the area. The five of us decided to build one of these shacks also, but while construction was in progress, we also lived in [a] tent. We used the plywood crates that our belly tanks were shipped in, for the sides of the tent, so that we could have windows. They were hinged at the top, so they could be pushed out at the bottom, and we could have air circulation…The tents were heated using homemade, oil-drum heaters."

Evidently, this took a lot of time and energy. In his October 4th letter, Billy apologized for not writing sooner. "Haven't written for the past few days. Please forgive me because we were working on our tent, building shelves, making a stove and the like, and I was pretty tired. We have to fix up our quarters just with the materials we have on hand."

But there was time for a few other activities, according to Ward. "When we were not flying on a mission, most of our time was spent working on our new home, except for some occasional recreation." Recreation included badminton, skeet shooting, reading, chess playing, he said, "and, I hope, writing letters to our parents, wives, and girlfriends at home."

Ward said the 71st Fighter Squadron flew four types of missions. "The first type…was [escorting] bombers to and from their targets to protect them from attack by German fighters. It was our job to intercept and attack the German fighters before they could get to the bombers. We usually flew 2,000 to 4,000 feet above them in a criss-cross pattern. We rendezvoused with the bombers before they reached enemy territory, stayed with them to their target and on their return, until they were out of enemy fighter reach.

"The second type of mission was where we did the bombing…Our targets were of the railroad or vehicular bridge type, rather than the factories and refineries the bombers went after.

"The third type of mission was what were called 'strafing missions,' where we flew at very low altitudes, with targets such as enemy convoys, troop trains, locomotives, and enemy airfields. These were especially dangerous for us, because when flying so close to the ground, everyone and his uncle would take a shot at you...On some missions we would first dive bomb a target, and then stay down low and go on a strafing run along some railroad line, or go across country on a fighter sweep."

The fourth type of mission escorted photographic reconnaissance planes on intelligence-gathering trips. Only five planes went on these, and Ward said it got pretty lonely up there.

Billy's log documents only escort and strafing missions. His October 4th letter described how his missions went, and it also spoke of tragedy. "So far, I've flown three missions and am going on another one soon. The missions are all five to six hours long and all of them are escorting the big boys on their bombing raids. Boy, you don't know what a good feeling it is to see German industrial centers blown to bits. It gives you a funny feeling, though, when you see one of the bombers explode in mid-air. This happens seldom, but it still gives you a funny feeling."

He told his mom she'd be getting a $200 government check and a $50 bond, half of his $100 allotment. He would save half of what he'd keep with him and expected to have a "goodly amount of cash on hand" when he came home.

He'd finally gotten his own airplane and was "pretty happy" about it. "I still haven't decided what to name it. Enclosed is a caricature that an Italian drew of me when I was in Naples. I thought it was pretty good. Save it for me, will you please? This is a short letter, but it brings me all up to date." He sent all his love and ended with a P.S. that they would get to hear the first game of the World Series that night, then added a P.P.S. saying the Browns had won the game, and he'd won ten bucks.

Ida pasted Billy's caricature into his scrapbook. While the resemblance is faint, his dimples are unmistakable.

Between the October 4th letter and the next one, Billy flew four more local flights and one combat mission to Vienna. According to Bill Ward, when flying combat, "We usually carried two or three 500-pound bombs, or a 1,000-pound bomb under the left wing, in place of the belly tank, on bombing missions. It was extremely rare for us to carry bombs

under both wings, since our range without an extra fuel tank under the right wing was not long enough to reach our targets in Austria and northern Italy. I remember most of our bombing targets were railroad or vehicular bridges over streams, rivers, culverts, etc.

"For each mission, in preparing for take-off at the end of the field, we lined up four abreast by flight: Red flight first, then White, then Blue, and the last was Green. Each color designation consisted of four planes, for a total of sixteen planes per squadron. When ready to start take-off, the first flight locked their brakes, revved their engines to take-off RPM, checked each magneto separately, and when the flight leader was ready, released their brakes and took off down the field, side-by-side. Each flight used the same procedure and followed each other closely, so the squadron completed take-off in a relatively short period of time…All three squadrons in the 1st Fighter Group (27th, 71st, and 94th) used the same field, but our living quarters and operations areas were entirely separated from each other."

By October 12 Billy said he was flying missions "pretty regularly." He had received a V-mail letter from his dad, which boosted his morale "100%." By this time, the family was getting excited about Maxine's baby, due in January, and Billy was trying to decide what to do for the child. "Mom, I started to buy a certain thing for Sis's forthcoming baby, but I decided not to buy it. What I did decide to do was this–take $100.00 out of my allotment and start a bank account in the baby's name. Sis and Fannon can add to it through the years and he or she can have it for a college education. What do you think of the idea? Now, if you don't like it, well, don't hesitate to say so. How is Sis getting along? I hope everything goes alright. Be sure and take good care of her, Mom." It's a wonder he had any money to spare, because he said he had just lost his pants betting on the World Series.

"Be on the lookout in either the Dallas Morning News or Times Herald for my picture. Another Texas boy, Nash by name, and I had our picture taken today for our hometown newspapers. I'll send you the original in my next letter."

Public relations support for the men overseas was strong, but no less so than the support the men had for each other, as Ward recalled. "For each mission many of the pilots who were not flying that day would all go down near the end of the field and wave to the fellows as they taxied by on their way to the take-off end of the field. It always gave you a good feeling to see your friends giving you support as you started on a mission. You knew as you started out that the chance of being shot at during some part of the mission was about 95%." He added that a crash truck and ambulance were there all the time for take-off and landings, "in case their services were needed immediately."

On the 13th Billy flew another combat mission to Vienna, and on the 14th he recorded a mission to Blackheimer. Under Remarks, he added "Strafing Score: 3 locomotives." He flew a cross-country to Torrento on October 15, a combat mission with an early return from Brussels and a test hop on the 16th, then another combat mission to Vienna on the 17th. His score on the Blackheimer mission was a thrill, and he told his family about it in great detail.

Somewhere in Italy
Oct. 17, 1944

Dearest Mom and Dad,

　　Well, how are the swellest parents in the world feeling tonight? I say night, because that's what it is here now. Back home now it's 2:30 in the afternoon.

　　I feel swell and things here have been moving right along. I now have six missions and am going on another one tomorrow. We found out that we now have to complete seventy missions before we can come home. We went on a mission escorting big bombers to Czechoslovakia the other day and on the way back we dropped down to find something to strafe. We located a railroad yard that had quite a few engines steamed up and ready to move. Boy, what a field day we had shooting up those engines. I blew up three of them with gunfire from my ship. That 20 mm cannon sure plays hell on locomotives. I now have three small locomotives painted on the side of my ship. I hope to add some German crosses to the score soon. All in all our flight destroyed quite a few engines. I also strafed a train full of German soldiers. Boy, you should have seen those birds run for the ditches. I think there are quite a few German soldiers that will never fight for Hitler again.

　　Mom and Dad, I'm having the painter in our squadron paint the name and picture on the side of my ship. I'm calling it "Golden Slipper" and am having a big slipper put on the side of the ship all done up in gold. I wanted to put yours and Dad's name on the ship but couldn't do it, so I decided to put something on it that symbolized some of the happiest days of yours and Dad's lives. I knew how much you liked the song, so that's what I named her. How do you like it?

　　These pictures I am enclosing will appear in either the News or Herald along with a write-up. Be on the lookout for it. There is a photographer here on the field who is from Texas. He takes pictures of all the Texas boys and sends them to their hometown newspapers. The other boy is James Nash from Beaumont.

　　How is Sis doing? Tell her to take good care of herself, and Sis, you'll get a good long letter from me in a few days. I sure do miss everybody and am only waiting for the big day when all this is over. That's about :30 for now, folks. God bless everyone and take good care of yourselves.

Your loving son,
Bill

P.S. I'm in line for the Air Medal, as of my fifth mission.

Ward said there was much more to strafing than the movies would have you believe. "Strafing was a very, very dangerous mission, because everybody was shooting at you from all over the place, with everything from pistols to heavy automatic cannon..." Billy neglected to mention that in his letter. His mother was worried enough.

He enclosed the two well-staged pictures of him with James Nash, the flyer from Beaumont, all decked out in their flight suits and walking toward the camera. Both boys were so handsome the photos could be mistaken for movie stills.

The Texas Boys, James C. Nash and Billy

Billy's logbook shows no mission on the 18th, as he had said there would be. The last entry in the book is in a different handwriting. It's dated October 20, "From: Foggia #3 / To: Bolzano / Remarks: MIA." It's signed by Paul Summer.

November 3 was the Wisners' 28th wedding anniversary, and that morning Ida answered a telephone call from Western Union. They told her she had received a telegram and asked her to come get it. They gave no explanation for not delivering it, nor would they read it to her over the phone. Ralph was at work and Maxine was six months pregnant, so Ida caught a streetcar and went downtown by herself.

She signed for the telegram and took it outside. Holding on to a telephone pole for support, she opened the envelope. There, alone on a busy street in downtown Dallas, she read the terrible news.

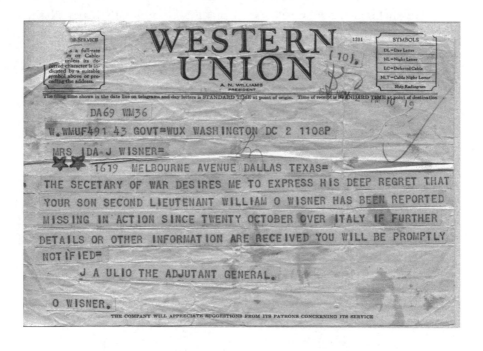

9

ON THE SCENT

From: Hotel Poder [info@hotel-poeder.com]
Sent: Friday, December 31, 1999
To: Dick Kahler
Subject: Aircrash P-38 in the year 1944

Dear Mr. Kahler,
I am writing to you regarding your request to get some
information about a P-38 crashed in the end of the year 1944
northwest of Bolzano. I am a student and interested in South
Tyrolian history during and after the Second World War. I
received your e-mail from an organisation named "Staff Sudtirol".
However, my investigation about an aircraft (probably a P-38)
crashed approximately 15-25 KM in the north west of Bolzano, a
village called SIRMIAN/SIRMIANO (In Southtyrol all villages,
towns cities, streets, etc., have both an Italian or-and a German
name, because they are bi-lingual). This aircrash happened in
the end of the year 1944 (in autumn). I know this, because a
man, which I know, once told me this story.
It is quite interesting because in this area not many aircrafts
crashed or were shoot down. There were defensive weapons on
the other side on the top of the mountain (a village called
MOLTEN/MOLTINA).
In autumn 1944, then, an aircraft with 5 people in there was
shoot down from the sky; after that the aircraft burned for
another 2-3 days. 4 people survived and 1 person died.

The old men from the village in Sirmian tell, that one soldier cut
in two the cable from his parachute while he was flying down
from the sky to the earth and died immediately.
The other 4 persons were put into prison in a village called
NALS/NALLES; from there they were moved to another prison.
This is all I know about an aircraft crashed in this area in the end
of the year 1944. I hope this information will be helpful, if you are
interested in more information do not hesitate to contact me; I
will see if I can get more information.
Yours sincerely,
P.G.

* * *

It was certain the crash P.G. referred to was a bad lead, because Billy
would have been alone in his plane. But it meant people there still
remembered, and best of all, we had found a contact willing to send
out feelers. Now all we needed was luck.

Leads were coming in steadily. The staff of www.sudtirol.com, the
Web site for the province of South Tyrol (*Südtirol* in German, *Alto Adige*
in Italian) had forwarded Dick Kahler's e-mail to the Hotel Lichtenstern.
The Hohenegger family, who owns the hotel, wrote they have a good
friend who collects everything about WWII, "and he also knows about the
crash. We will contact you when we know more." Kahler sent us the hotel's
Web site, and I looked it up. Very charming, near a place called
Ritten/Renon, which I had never heard of before. I didn't know then just
how important that location would become.

Jim tried to find the two hotels on a map in an effort to pinpoint the
crash site. The Poder was about five miles beyond Billy's last sighting and
well within our estimate of where he might have crashed, but Jim couldn't
find the Lichtenstern. I looked at my maps, but they weren't very detailed.
I could see, however, that north of where Bolzano was clearly marked there
was nothing but mountains, and just as P.G. had said, each city had both a
German and an Italian name. It was all very confusing.

Kahler copied me on the e-mail he'd sent to the Bolzano newspaper
on January 2, and he and Jim put together a recap of information on Billy
and a list of military contacts we had made so far. We compared notes to be
sure we all had matching, complete, and accurate data. We couldn't afford

to miss a single clue.

On January 3 Dick Kahler e-mailed Jim that he had heard from someone at the newspaper in Bolzano, and Jim sent me a copy of Jim's response to Dick: "Looks good! What data does he have? It would be good to have him know that three P-38's crashed in the same area on 10-20-44. The debris from two of them was likely scattered due to their explosion in mid-air at about 20,000 feet. The third dove in, in a spin—that was Wisner. He might also benefit from the scanned mission report and the Anderson eye witness report. If not really readable, the mission report might stimulate his interest. Likely the anti-aircraft battery that downed them was German, so it might even be of value to find out the actual German outfits stationed in the area. Then I might get my friend Roland Geiger to see what he could find in the German records for the outfit..."

Jim was full of suggestions, and I told Kahler I felt useless. In response, he reminded me to write to the hiking and mountaineering schools in the Dolomites. Happy to have something to do, I composed letters to 10 different locations and asked each to post it at the school. Maybe someone had seen something and would contact me.

On January 4 the Office of Information for the City of Bolzano acknowledged Jim's request for "e-mail addresses of individuals or organizations who might know of crashes within a 25 KM radius of Bolzano during October 1944." They had forwarded his message to the tourist information bureau for the whole region and suggested he also write the office of the Italian military for South Tyrol. They didn't have an e-mail address for them but gave Jim the street address, and he wrote them the same day.

The pace of our search was picking up, so Jim thought it would be a good time to fill Bill Jordan in on what we'd been doing. Jordan had left the Central Identification Laboratory in 1996, but Jim hoped he might still have some strings to pull if we got stuck. Jim told Jordan about the CIL's letter to me saying Billy's file was missing, and Jordan replied that he was "more than glad to help," but that he'd have to do some research. I was glad someone in an official capacity would be making inquiries, too. Maybe he could nudge the CIL toward finding that missing file.

The Bolzano newspaper replied on January 9. Kahler had meant to attach a fact sheet to his e-mail, but it didn't go through and he got the unsigned, curt reply, "There is no fact sheet, 'cause there is no attachment. I'm waiting. Bye." So Kahler re-sent the request, this time with the attachment. I was glad to see I wasn't the only one who could screw up an e-mail.

Those few inquiries to civilian organizations were making progress, and with each response I wished my grandmother had known about these resources. Every letter she had written 50-some years ago hit a dead end. But if it had ever occurred to her to write to civilians, she wouldn't have known which ones to write or even how to identify them.

Kahler summed up our status on January 10th. "The hooks are in the water now and it is a matter of time till we get a bite. With your letters out, Jim's letters out and about six or eight people that responded by e-mail it is a matter of time until someone takes the time to look for information. Waiting is the most difficult thing we have to do. You are probably like me, patience is not a virtue of mine. We will wait a couple of days and if we don't get a bite we will look around to put more hooks out."

I confirmed for Kahler what he assumed about me. "My husband knows me well: if he says, 'It can't be done,' that's just a challenge for me to prove him wrong. I'm glad you're impatient. After 55 years, time is running out. I wish we'd had the Internet 20 years ago. Memories would be clearer, more people would be alive to tell the stories, and maybe Billy's CIL file wouldn't be 'missing' (I love the quotation marks they used), and we'd know how, when, and where they found what they found." I was grateful for his encouragement.

Kahler mentioned the Web site for the Florence American Cemetery, and I told him about our visit to the real thing. Kahler said he had found out that his friend, Jesse Ray Dorris, is buried there, and he wanted to visit the site, so I gave him suggestions of what to see while he was in Florence.

While Dick and I were trading travel tips, Jim got a message from the Bolzano Tourist Bureau asking for a more precise location of the crash. Jim sent them the text of Jack Anderson's report, but still the best we could do was "five miles northwest of Bolzano," and that was anything but a pinpoint.

I composed a letter to the Archivio di Stato, Provincia di Bolzano (State Archives, Bolzano Province) citing the details of the crash and asked them for suggestions on who else we should approach. I forwarded Jim the text of my letter to see if I should send it. He replied, "Good letter. It's hard to keep track of 'who's on first' in this e-mail merry-go-round, but I, for one, have not written them…"

Then he asked a question that surprised me a little. "Where did you get the info that Lt. Virgil Olson parachuted and survived? John Mullins' history of the 1st Ftr. Group states that Olson was KIA. We need to straighten that anomaly out.

"Also, as you may have detected in my other e-mail, I have made a mistake of reporting the crashes occurred northwest of Bolzano. As I was transcribing Anderson's account and rechecked the mission report, I found that it SHOULD BE NORTHEAST! In my correspondence with the Hotel Lichtenstern, I have found that their location is about where I would imagine it all happened..."

Uh-oh. Could we have been looking in the wrong place? And where did I get the idea Olson had survived? I wrote Jim that I'd have to check my files and said, "I seem to remember running across a letter from [Olson] to my grandmother stating he had no knowledge of the accident until later, when he was released from POW camp and questioned about it. But I may have confused him with another flier in the squadron. If I'm right, I'll scan [the letter] and send it to you. But I'm beginning to doubt my memory, because that isn't the kind of thing John Mullins would have missed."

Jim told Kahler about the change in location after studying the maps again, noting that in Billy's MACR the crash is indicated slightly northwest of Bolzano, but on Twedt's it's slightly northeast. However, the "X" marking the spot was typed in, so it wasn't a precise indicator. Jim said, "I would certainly rely more on the mission report which said '5 miles northeast.' It was typed from the IO's notes. Where the three planes hit is another question. I would think that they would have hit within a four to five-mile diameter circle as they started falling from about 20-22,000 feet. You'd think that three at once would have gotten someone's attention."

You'd think so. I dug into the cedar chest and discovered I wasn't mistaken. There were two letters from Olson to my grandmother. He told her he had survived the accident and spent the remainder of the war in a POW camp but hadn't known Billy had been hit, too. I thought it was odd that John Mullins didn't have that information, but then I realized he had compiled the text of his book from the 1944 Mission Reports, which listed Olson as missing. He may not have had access to later reports correcting that information. I scanned Olson's letters and e-mailed them to Jim on January 11.

Jim's response was interesting. He said Olson's account puts a "bit of a hole" in Anderson's account. "As you may recall, Anderson said that upon Twedt's collision with him, the two planes blew up and debris fell onto your uncle's plane. If they blew up, I doubt that Olson would have escaped. I would be willing to bet that Anderson had the identity of the planes mixed up and that the plane that dove and spun in was Olson's. Maybe after Twedt hit Olson, he swerved back and hit your uncle's plane, and they were the ones that blew up. In any case, it sure would be of interest if Olson could be queried. If he returned, I wonder if he is still living. I'll have to check on government files."

Then he went on, "Another astounding discovery! In reading the War Dept. letter, they referred to Paul Summer, who was on the mission, too. As it turns out, Paul was my favorite flight leader, and we kept in contact for many years. He died about 15 years ago from a diabetic heart condition. I have kept in contact with his widow, Edna. Recently I was looking for pictures of the squadron when it was in Foggia. Edna sent me out Paul's scrapbook to look through. I just checked it and found the copy of the orders that assigned Paul AND your uncle to the squadron at the same time in September 1944. Paul had three names underlined. One was Twedt's, and [an]other was your uncle's. Both were annotated 'KIA.' I got on the phone to Edna to see if she knew your uncle. She said Paul had talked about that mission and said he had followed your uncle's plane down 'til it crashed. (That statement DOES support Anderson's story that it was your uncle's plane that spun in.) I asked Edna about Virgil Olson, but she doesn't recall Paul ever mentioning him."

Jim closed, saying, "Small world, isn't it?"

"That brought tears to my eyes," I wrote back. "It's the first personal memory of my uncle I've been able to get out of Foggia... Thank you, even if it is third-hand. And thank you for the interpretation of the crash. It makes a lot of sense, but it still saddens me that the 'official' record contains no mention of Paul's account that he followed Billy's plane all the way down." I recognized Paul's name from some of Idy's letters and promised Jim copies.

An e-mail from Dick Kahler on January 12 had a promising lead-in: "We may have 'our man in Bolzano.' This is the guy from the local newspaper." He attached the e-mail from Paolo Cagnan, a reporter for the *Alto Adige*, Bolzano's daily newspaper, the same anonymous person who had responded to Kahler's first e-mail to the newspaper. Cagnan complimented him on the Hoenshell search and promised to check with the historical society about Billy, but before he could get started he had a lot of questions. "Are you absolutely sure about the date of the air crash? Don't you know exactly where the crash happened (the name of the nearest village or something else)? Could you send me a picture of a P-38? Is Jack Anderson still alive? You wrote that the aircraft and the pilot were never found, but then you mention the cemetery of Mirandola, possible remains at

Griesheim and a bracelet (found where?); could you explain it to me, please?"

I answered Mr. Cagnan's e-mail directly and gave as much information as I could, clarifying where necessary. I could now recite the story of Billy's disappearance in my sleep.

Bill Mays, who had helped Dick Kahler in Bulgaria and was included in the correspondence, had been passively observing the blizzard of e-mails. He piped up, "Hi All, I have the same questions about the bracelet. Where was the bracelet found and how does the Quartermaster Corps have it? Was it in his footlocker, or did by chance someone find it onsite? From my experiences here in Bulgaria, the Allied Commission did some checking in 1947 after the war, but they were short-handed and pressed for time so details were not really recorded very well."

I explained the mystery of the bracelet. I knew that once Bill Mays realized it had been found years after Billy's crash, he'd recognize its importance. In fact, that had been the clue that had gotten everyone involved in the first place, but Mays hadn't been in the loop when all that was happening. Dick Kahler had brought him on board when he realized we might be able to use his help when and if there was an actual search.

I was discouraged by Mays's comment that the Allied Commission's investigations after the war were "pressed for time." I knew that might also mean "careless," and I tried not to let it get me down. I thought about my grandmother and her dogged refusal to accept the government's official line. But maybe that's all we would ever have.

I had a sinking feeling we would never get the answers we needed.

10

MISSING
1944-45

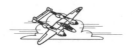

Dallas, Texas
November 9, 1944

Dear Mrs. Nash,
    We have received a telegram saying that our son Lt.
William O. Wisner is missing in action over Italy. He sent us
pictures of himself and your son, and I wonder if you have received
any word from James in regard to Billy. We would certainly
appreciate any news you can send us. We are so upset and worried.
You have a lovely son, and that big boy of ours is our baby.

Very sincerely,
Mrs. R. O. Wisner

* * *

After Billy's MIA announcement appeared in the Dallas papers, letters poured in from Ida and Ralph's friends. Some of them shared stories of pilots they knew who had returned months after having crashed; all of them conveyed messages of hope and love.

Now, instead of a scrapbook, Ida started documenting her efforts to find out what happened to her son. She enlisted the help of her brother-in-law, Fritz, hoping letters he would write on his law firm stationery might carry more weight.

On November 4, the day after Ida had received the telegram, Fritz wrote both Eddy Steffani and Paul Summer at their home addresses. On November 8 Eddy's mother, Mrs. Peter Steffani, replied. "I was just writing my son when I got your letter this morning. We haven't heard from our boy for nearly fourteen days and in his last letter he hasn't mentioned anything about your son Bill. I only know that they were good pals and buddies, as I heard Edward and his wife talk so much of Bill while they were in Washington and California. And when they were sent overseas my boy wrote that Bill and Paul and another pal got to be in his squadron."

She said she had asked Eddy to write the Wisners directly if he learned anything new, then told of his narrow escape from death about a month before. "His plane blew up and caught fire. He was trapped in it and only with God's grace it blew up the second time and blew Ed out of the cockpit. He was put in the hospital for a few days and X-rayed, found he had strained muscles in his back, a slight concussion of the head, with cuts all over it. And his body was black and blue from his knees up. But is feeling fine now, is out of the hospital and flying again."

Ida had written to the Prisoner of War Division, but their November 9 response was that no report had come in from either the International Red Cross or the Protecting Power indicating that he was a prisoner of war. They would be notified immediately if any information did come in.

On the same day she received a letter from the Adjutant General at the War Department confirming the telegram. He, too, said he would send more information as soon as it came in or, at the very latest, would write again in three months.

Three months with no official word would have been hard to bear, so Ida kept busy. She wrote to the parents of James Nash in Beaumont, the boy in the photo with Billy, but it came back undeliverable due to an insufficient address.

As more time went by with no word, the family grew more anxious. Now seven months pregnant, Maxine's emotions were difficult to control. Fannon was working the night shift and was home sleeping during the day, so when the waves of grief overwhelmed Maxine, she would go into the alley to cry so as not to disturb him. One day a neighbor heard the weeping from inside her house and came out to see if she could help.

Everyone tried to hold up the family's morale. Billy's high school chum, Dalton Tarver, wrote Ida that he was sad but optimistic. "I feel the same way, almost, because I have always thought of Bill as another brother. Before I say any more, please don't worry too much. That sounds a bit crazy, I know, but if you haven't heard anything else, try to think of him as just being forced down or something like that. Even if he is a prisoner he is not so bad off. I am taking the same training that he took, and we have seen hundreds of films and actual facts about pilots missing in action. He has got a hundred to one chance of even being injured. He knows how to take care of any situation; believe me he has been trained for it. Think this over and try to picture him in the best conditions possible... He wouldn't want either of you to worry too much about him. I am sure that he is safe and sound right now."

Paul Summer's mother replied to Fritz's letter a few days later. "Dear Friends," it began. "I just can't tell you how badly Mr. Summer and I felt this noon when we received your heart-broken letter, Mrs. Wisner. You know we were out to Moses Lake, Washington, last June to visit Paul and met your son Bill and liked him so very much. And he, Ed Steffani, and Paul have been so close to each other for many, many months. I only wish I could give you the news you are hoping for, but we did not know of this misfortune until you wrote us. In fact, our last letter from Paul (dated Oct. 25th) was so late coming that we began to feel something was wrong— now we realize that Paul probably just felt so terribly bad about Bill that he couldn't write anyone. And when he did write he didn't tell us about it, as I suppose he thought it would worry us, too, and that he would wait until perhaps he had better news to report."

She, too, would let the Wisners know if her son heard any thing new, but there wasn't much more she could say that could comfort them, "except that you can be very proud of your fine young son. And we'll all be hoping and praying that God is taking care of him wherever he is and that he will eventually get back home to you again." She would be happy to hear from the Wisners again.

Family-friend Allen Rische was still at the Pentagon, and Ida asked for his help. His response was encouraging. "I don't want to be unduly optimistic, but in many cases of Air Corps personnel reported missing in action they eventually turn up either in our own lines or as prisoners of war. In the cases of prisoners of war the international Red Cross makes the notifications to the next of kin and usually several months are required before the records are cleared." Allen said he had checked on Billy's status, but there was no additional information.

An official letter from the 15th Air Force dated November 14 confirmed the telegram and provided details of the incident. It said, "On the flight to the target, in the vicinity of Bolzano, Italy, flak was encountered and as a result your son's ship received a direct hit which caused it to fall from formation and lost altitude. His chute was not seen before the craft entered the undercast." In closing it said that Billy had made a valuable contribution "to the struggle that engages us all at this time. He proved that he was well qualified as a pilot and leader of men. He discharged his duties in a manner reflecting much credit upon himself and the air force of which he was so proud to be a part."

Ida wrote again to the Red Cross. She told of the circumstances of his disappearance and where he was stationed, and she enclosed a letter to Billy and asked them to forward it to him if they found him.

> *Dallas, Tex.*
> *Nov. 15, 1944*

> *My darling boy –*
> *Hope and pray that you receive this note. We have received news from one of the boys that they saw a parachute open and was sure it was you. I just want you to know we are taking it on the chin and we are taking the best care of Sister. The baby won't be here until January, so she has time to get over the shock. I have stacks and stacks of letters about you. Clarke phoned from Baton Rouge and Edith from Chicago. You are well liked, honey, and we all hope you are OK.*
> *Am sending this thru the Red Cross in hopes they have news of you. I am writing you every day so when we see you again you will sure have a stack to read. Don't forget to pray, darling. Mom loves you very dearly and always will think of you as a little boy.*

> *Be sweet, as ever*
> *Mom*

> <u>*Kisses xxxxX*</u>

But the letter was intercepted by the Office of Censorship in New York, because Ida had mentioned Billy's unit and location, which was not allowed with the war still going on. They returned it and its enclosure with a note saying, "...We suggest that inquiry be directed to the Office of the Provost Marshal General, Washington, D.C., from whom may be obtained the only official information concerning Lt. Wisner."

A reply from the Adjutant of the 71st Fighter Squadron on November 20 said they couldn't help at this time, because "Regulations will not let us give information of this type until a period of six months has passed. We are all hoping that he will turn up before too long."

Six months—an eternity.

Then a letter from the headquarters of the Army Air Forces in Washington corrected the November 14 letter from the 15th Air Force and provided a little more information about the crash. "...Full details are not available, but the report indicates that during this mission at about 11:20 a.m., while in the vicinity of Bolzano, Italy two of our aircraft collided in mid-air and your son's fighter sustained damage from some of the debris coming from the wrecked planes. The report further indicates that Lieutenant Wisner's aircraft was last seen in a spin falling toward the earth. Inasmuch as the crew members of accompanying planes returning from this mission were unable to furnish any further details, these facts constitute all the information presently obtainable."

He wasn't shot down, so maybe there was hope. It was an accident, so maybe he got out. No one saw the plane hit the ground, so maybe it didn't crash. These thoughts must have run through Ida's head over and over again.

A bright spot in the correspondence came from Billy's Eagle Pass buddy, Clarke Wiseley. Clarke's mother had passed away not long before, and Clarke, along with his buddy and the Wisners' family-friend Walter Patton, had adopted Ida as his new mom. He wrote from Harding Field, Baton Rouge, Louisiana, and it looked like he was on the move, at last. Now Ida had another boy to worry about.

11-22-44
10:30

Dearest "Mom"
    Looks like you have acquired some more members to your family. You would really be decked out in gray hair if your three boys were all in your kitchen!!

I agree with Patty [Walter Patton]—*if anyone gets to call you "Mom," I'm going to be one of them.*

I wrote Paul [Summer] *a letter – as yet no reply. I'm going to write Patty and see how he's doing and what to do in case I get hijacked his way. They tell us here that one of the largest pilot pools we have is in India, so I'm sure glad Pat didn't get stuck in one of them.*

Say, while I think of it, did you notify the Red Cross? Sometimes they have obtained information about prisoners of war. I think the whole thing is operated through their channels. I have heard where the Red Cross in Switzerland receives notification of P.W.'s and they in turn notify their branch in the Italian theater, who in turn notifies his group. I don't know whether this is always the case, but I have heard of some cases that went along similar channels. Talking to one of our instructors who returned from there who was held a P.W. but got away, I asked him about the treatment the pilots and Army men got from the Germans. He said he expected the worst, but as far as treatment, physical and medical, not bad. Nothing like we have, but better than what we hear from the Japs. The food wasn't anything to brag about, but you had sufficient. He said they try to trick you into talking, as is expected, but he didn't recall anyone being beaten while he was there. The Germans were notified that any attempt of brutality to U.S. P.W.'s would result in similar action to our German P.W.'s, so it's all in sweatin' it out. [...]

Write when you find time, and you'd better get the Red flannels out if it's as cold there as in "La" Baton Rouge, exclusive residence of innumerable species of insects.

> *Love to all*
> *Always,*
> *The ole man*
> *Clarke*

That letter was followed by a Thanksgiving card from Clarke and his wife, Avis. Their baby was due in January, the same time as Maxine's. Avis was in poor health, so Clarke's sister, Evelyn Croft, was staying with them in Baton Rouge to help. Evelyn's husband John had been the chief radio control tower inspector in Seattle when Billy was at Moses Lake, and Clarke had told Billy to look them up. They'd all become good friends.

Avis thanked Ida for a baby present and told her Clarke had been set up a month early to ship out. "He is so anxious to be on his way across. Thank goodness he will at least have to stay here until the baby comes…Have you heard any more about Woo Woo?"

On November 28, Paul Summer was finally able to answer Fritz's first letter to him. He said he'd been expecting a letter from Billy's folks "and your letter and one from Mrs. Thompson came as no surprise to me." He told Fritz he had been intending to write, but there was a 90-day censorship period and until then he couldn't give any details.

"Bill and I were close buddies and had been together for a long time. Needless to say, we all miss him and are anxious for word of his safety. Although I can't give you the particulars, you may find some comfort in that I was a witness, and I believe his chances are good. I will leave it up to your discretion as to what you tell his parents. I would hate to rain false hopes. The nature of our operations carr[ies] us far into enemy territory, and when a man goes down we have little way of knowing the outcome. The Army lists them MIA, and that is all you would hear until the party either made good an escape or listed as prisoner. Such news may take months. In case he is taken POW, you may hear before I do, so I wish you would notify me.

"Tell his parents I will be only too glad to do anything I can over here. Also, when 90 days are up I will gladly answer all their questions. Bill was very well-liked in the squadron and was doing a fine job. The rest of the boys never give up hope for lost members, and many have returned or been POW." Paul hoped to remain in touch.

Another relative of one of Billy's friends, this time Eddy Steffani's wife, Rosemary, wrote on December 3rd with bad news of her own. "Last Thursday we received a telegram from the War Department telling us Ed has been missing in action since the 16th of November over Yugoslavia. We are very hopeful that he will come out of it all right. It seems that all one can do is to pray, keep hoping, and wait for further news. Don't give up— just keep thinking Bill is all right. I know it is hard to do, but that's what we are all doing, or at least trying to do, about Ed.

"I felt very bad when Ed wrote about Bill. You see, we both think so much of him and consider him as one of our best friends. We first met him in Eagle Pass. Bill may have mentioned in some of his letters about Carol, our little girl, and I being at Moses Lake and Ontario with Ed. We all went around together quite a bit, and had a lot of fun. Just before they left for overseas, Bill wrote me a very nice letter telling me not to worry about Ed, etc. He also sent me his picture, as I had asked for one before. Not many boys are so thoughtful."

She wondered if they'd heard from Paul Summer and assured them she would let them know if she heard anything more and if Ida would do the same for her. She closed with, "I hope and pray that both Bill and Ed will come through all right," and signed it "Mrs. Edward Steffani."

Ida was hoping and praying, too. And poor Paul—in one month he had lost two of his best friends. Paul's mother provided what support she could, and in her December 11 letter she said she'd heard another of Paul's friends was missing and was sad to learn it was Eddy, "altho I sort of felt he was the one. I surely feel sorry for his wife and folks."

Eva went on to say Paul had told her that he hadn't flown since his last letter. "Knowing now about Bill and Ed," she added, "I sort of read between the lines that perhaps they may have kept Paul on the ground for a while, knowing how badly he feels about the two boys being missing."

Paul had written that there wasn't any news about them yet, she said, "but that sort of news is slow in reaching us. Some have escaped and shown up in person. I wrote to Bill's uncle, but couldn't tell him much; censorship security is 90 days on such matters." Paul said he had been made first lieutenant, "and that they are living in a stone house that he and some of the other boys built out of materials salvaged from bombed buildings," just as Bill Ward had described in his memoirs.

Eva closed with some personal information, noting that she and her husband were about the same age as the Wisners (57 and 55) and adding that they have another son still at home. Her husband "is a conductor on the great Northern RR and works here on the Iron Range."

Clarke's sister Evelyn passed through Dallas on her way to Baton Rouge, met the Wisners, and wrote a sweet thank-you note for the lovely evening she had spent with them. Clarke added a note to Evelyn's to thank them for the baby gift, saying, "If it was a wee bit bigger, I'd sure have to crawl in it myself." Good old Clarke, always trying to stay cheerful for Ida's sake.

At last, Paul Summer wrote the Wisners directly on December 12. "I can realize your great anxiety and I sincerely wish I could give you assurance of your son's safety. Bill and I were close buddies and I miss him very much," he said. Paul knew the Wisners had the official report, but now he was able to add his perspective.

"I was flying at approximately 1,000 ft. above and observed the whole thing. Bill's ship was intact, but damaged as evidenced by smoke trailing out of it. It was apparently under control for a minute or so before going into a spin which would indicate that Bill was O.K. and able to bail out. Because of our difference in altitude it would be impossible for us to observe the tiny speck he would present in bailing out against a patchy background of clouds and earth. We have good hope for his safety and many have recovered from worse circumstances. Word of his capture may be many months in coming in if that is the case. You would undoubtedly be notified before we were."

Some good news came announcing the birth of "Clarke Milton Wiseley, III, on December 13 (red-headed, too), 7 lbs. 10-1/2 oz." The baby was a month early. It's a good thing Evelyn was already there to help.

The Christmas season brought with it cards and letters from old friends and new, from the Summer family and the Steffanis. Ida and Ralph also got a sweet note from Maxine, who was trying to keep morale high in the Wisner house.

12-20-44

Merry Xmas to My Dearest Mom & Dad,

> *I just want to tell you that I think I have two of the most wonderful parents on earth and to thank you, for Billy, too, for being what you are. I want you both to remember that wherever our precious boy is that God is watching over him.*

> *Now, Mom, quit that crying, 'cause I'm rooting for you and Dad to keep those chins up as I'm trying so very hard to do.*

> *This is very inadequate, but I'm not very good at saying what is in my heart. I love you both very much, and I want to see more broad grins on your adorable faces.*

All my love,
Sister

Clarke added to his Christmas card, "The reports from Wash. are typical in their info. They just don't jibe. They have the area down where he bailed out, but I'm inclined to take their reports with a grain of salt—a large one, at that. When Paul writes and if there is any news, don't worry, I'll have that phone ringing its headset off."

And he sent a chatty letter just after the holiday. He indicated he was up for the last feeding till 0200, getting used to taking care of a new baby and a sick wife. "Boy what a life I've led this past week!!! With the 'Sad Sack' (nickname for Lil Clarke, because he sleeps at the wrong times) squallin' and my clumsy actions knocking over an ink bottle and a few other incidents for today's program, I've yet to finish the night so I'll say no more...I'm an apt pupil at changing, feeding and gettin' the bedpan. I realize this is quite a different letter than usual, at least in topic, but I'm sure you would get a kick out of it since you no doubt have a good 'recollection' of those days. Guess you should have taken me aside and explained—hm!" The baby's early arrival had caught everyone off guard. "The Doc must have had his glasses on backwards, because he said not to worry—the baby would arrive around the latter part of January."

He had enclosed a letter from Paul, but there was no news in it about Billy or Eddy. He said, "I know you haven't given up hope, because that would be lettin' him down, too. I was so in hopes that somehow I could have gotten a letter from Paul saying Bill was OK, and I could cheer you up so on Xmas, but such was my luck." He signed his letter from Evelyn, Avis, Clarke and "Lil" Clarke.

In addition to asking Paul about Billy, no doubt Clarke had complained about being stuck Stateside flying the P-47. The letter from Paul that Clarke had shared with the Wisners was dated December 15. It opened, "Glad to hear from you, old man. Don't fret about being held in the States, this damn job isn't everything it's cracked up to be." Paul mentioned he had gotten several letters from Dallas, and he was optimistic. "My idea is that Bill had a good chance, but I can't be sure under the circumstances. If he did make it, the Jerries have probably got him by now and there's no telling how long it'll take them to pass the word out."

He had flown 24 missions and hoped to finish up by spring, "if my luck holds out. The Luftwaffe has perked up a bit lately and will probably have some good scraps yet." In closing, he gave Clarke a bit of advice: "Well, don't sell the 47 short, old boy; it's doing a good job over here."

Christmas must have been dreary at the Wisner house and New Year's even worse with still no word about Billy. But on January 2, 1945, Eva Summer had heard again from Paul and shared what was in his November 23rd letter to them. She quoted Paul: "I will say that we have good hopes for Bill, but I hesitate to write [the Wisners], as I would not want to be guilty of giving his folks false hope. You may as well know that this is a pretty rough game, and if you ever should receive word that I am 'missing in action,' don't get all excited about it as the chances are as good one way as the other."

Eva added that she was enclosing two color photos taken in Washington that Paul had asked her to have made for Eddy and Billy before either had been reported missing, "altho' I know they will make you feel bad all over again. The one of Bill and Ed is such a grand picture of both boys—it is taken in a boat on one of their fishing trips, or perhaps when they went to Wenatchee—I'm not just sure. The other one, which Paul says is of the three of them is not quite so good. If the middle boy is Paul, it surely doesn't look one bit like him to us."

Billy and Eddy Steffani at the oars on Moses Lake

Paul's letter to his mother had given the Wisners some reason to hope, and it looked like Rosemary Steffani had something to cling to for Eddy's prospects, as well. "I received a letter from Ed's commanding officer over in Italy, and he gave us some additional information about Ed which to me sounded quite hopeful. He said, 'Ed's ship was seriously damaged by anti-aircraft fire while he was on a strafing mission. En route from the target he informed his flight leader that an emergency landing would be necessary. When last sighted Ed was seen to make a crash landing in a field near the target area.' "

Reassured, Rosemary added, "At least I know he was not wounded while in the air, unless he got hurt in landing. I'm not going to think of that part of it, though. He no doubt is a prisoner of war. We'll just have to keep on praying and waiting until we know for sure."

Her life was upside-down, but she was trying to keep it normal for the sake of her young daughter. "In spite of everything we had a nice Christmas and New Years. Carol was so happy and excited over the tree, Santa Claus and her presents that we just couldn't help but be happy with her. My folks bought her a black cocker pup about two months old, so between the two of them they have quite a time."

She closed, saying Eddy had been awarded the Air Medal. "We are very proud of him, but I'd rather have Ed alive and well than all the medals in the world."

On January 13 Maxine gave birth to a daughter. She and Fannon named her Billie Gene, after their only siblings, Billy Wisner and Morris Eugene Thompson. There was little debate about the choice; the names would work for either a girl or a boy, and with both brothers in the service the parents wanted to honor them. By this time Morris was serving in the Pacific on the *U.S.S. Cowpens*, and if he and Billy both made it back, they could share pride in their new niece and namesake.

The excitement of the birth must have diverted Ida from her correspondence, and her silence worried Eva Summer, who wrote on January 25, "I have felt so uneasy about you folks the past week I just have to write you a few lines today. I sent you a letter Jan. 2 with a couple of colored prints of Bill, Ed, and Paul, but I haven't had any word from you since. I knew the pictures would probably make you feel bad all over again, and yet I felt you would like to have them, too. Please forgive me if I did the wrong thing."

She asked if the baby had arrived yet and whether they'd had any word about Billy. She hadn't heard from Paul in quite a while, either, and was getting nervous, but the war news was looking good and she was hopeful it would be over soon. She had received a nice letter from Rosemary Steffani and remarked, "She is so brave."

Eva's worried letter worked, and Ida responded to catch her up on the news. But now Eva had worries of her own.

Kelly Lake, Minnesota
Feb. 3, 1945

Dear Friend:

I was so relieved to receive your letter—also glad to hear all about your new baby. Please congratulate your daughter and husband for us. I just know little Billie Gene is so sweet and will be a lot of comfort to you at this time.

Well, dear friend, I have more sad news for you—we also have received one of those much dreaded telegrams from the War Dept. about our oldest boy, Charles. Our own dear Charles has been reported missing in action in the Pacific Ocean Area since the 27th of January. We received the word Thursday noon, and you folks can truly appreciate how we are all feeling now. Charles' birthday was Sunday, the 28th—God only knows how the poor boy spent it. He was 24 years old Sunday, and I had him on my mind all day—couldn't keep from wondering about the five B-29 Superfortresses that failed to return the day before from a big air-raid over Tokyo. We had heard about them on the radio. Of course, I hoped and prayed that one of them was not his plane, but it must have been, as that is the day he was reported missing. I just can't think of anything else but the boys—but we just have to have faith that our boys are safe somewhere and will get back into friendly hands as soon as possible. That old Pacific Ocean is so big—if he came down on the water it might be days and days before the crew would be found. The more I think the more confused I get. We haven't heard from Paul directly since a letter dated Jan. 12th, but he and a high school friend had spent two hours together on Jan. 21st, so he was O.K. then.

Will try to really write a letter when I feel more like it.

Sincerely,
Eva Summer

Eva's letters to Ida must have been mirror images of the ones Ida had been writing to Eva and Rosemary. The agony of not knowing was terrible to bear. On February 11th Eva wrote that there had been no further word about Charles. "[I]t is so hard to take—we can really sympathize with you folks now." She didn't feel equal to writing much but knew the Wisners had worried, because she hadn't heard from Paul in a long time. "We final-ly received a letter from him a few days ago—it had taken almost <u>three</u> <u>weeks</u> to come. He was O.K.—said he had completed 32 missions, that there wasn't much news to write. He made no mention of Bill or Ed, so I feel sure he knows nothing new to tell us.

'We have been hoping every day that you might receive good news— the days of waiting are so long, and ours are just beginning. I did hate to write and tell Paul about his own brother but we decided it was the best thing to do. May God bless <u>all</u> the boys and take care of them, wherever they are, and bring them safely back to us."

She added a P.S. "We received a letter Charles had written us on Jan. 26th, the day before his bad luck. I just can't realize yet that this awful thing has happened to us, too."

With the long delay in overseas mail delivery, Ida must have contin-ued to get letters from Billy after she knew he was missing, too. His hand-writing on the envelope would have made her heart leap, even if she could see that the postmark was old.

Now that the 90-day censorship period had gone by, Paul was able to give the Wisners some encouragement, but the news was still the same. "We lost three men in that accident and although none of our outfit observed any chutes, another group in the area reported later that they had been a witness and had seen two chutes open. If such were the case, I feel confident that one was Bill, as I believe his chances were the best of the three. I hesitated in telling you this for fear of raising false hopes. If he did make it OK, he was probably captured and it may be quite some time before you hear of him."

He said there had been no word of Eddy Steffani yet. "I correspond with Clarke W. and Walt Patton. Pat, as you probably know, is in the CBI theatre and doing alright." He closed, telling the Wisners not to hesitate to write him any time. He would do whatever he could for them

Clarke's letters were a poor substitute for good news about Billy, but he did the best he could to keep spirits high. He had managed a short visit with the Wisners while on leave, and wrote, "I was awfully sorry I couldn't spend more time with you folks. I really enjoy being with you all. Some-thing seems to remind me of my home—guess it's just [that] you are my kinda people." He added that he was proud of his wife and son. "I guess ole mother luck really patted me on the back that time."

The news about Maxine's baby finally caught up with Rosemary Steffani, and she wrote to congratulate Ida on her first grandchild. "Billie is surely a cute name, and I know just how proud her Uncle Bill will be when he hears the good news."

Rosemary was looking forward to the birth of her next child in about two weeks, but she still hadn't received any good news about Eddy. And now that she'd heard about Eva Summer's son, Charles, the three women were pulled together by a bond of fear and grief. "If only this awful war would end," she wrote.

In reply to Ida's sympathy letter Eva wrote, "It seems that sympathy from one who has also had an experience like mine means an extra lot. We can really understand how each other feels. I have been so in hope you would have had good news by this time, but it seems not yet..." She said the government had changed Charles's status from "missing in action in the Pacific Ocean Area" to "missing in action over Tokyo," but they still had no further information.

Rosemary sent an announcement that Mary Jean Steffani arrived March 2, 1945, weighing 6 lb. 9-1/4 oz., "parents Lt. & Mrs. Edward Steffani."

Then Ida received a different kind of announcement. This one said Billy had won the Air Medal, "for meritorious achievement in aerial flight while participating in sustained operational activities against the enemy from 21 September to 14 October 1944." Because it couldn't be presented to Billy, it would be forwarded to the Commanding General in Dallas, who would select an officer to make the presentation.

Ida made arrangements to receive the medal at home. A photo taken as the officer presented it to Ida shows them facing each other, in front of a wall on which hangs a formal photo of Billy in uniform. The officer holds the medal as if to pin it on Ida's blouse. Ida has turned to the camera and stares at it through tired, vacant eyes.

Clarke had been shipped overseas to the 371st Fighter Group, so it took some time for the letters he wrote in transit to make it home. In the meantime his sister Evelyn had "adopted" Ida and Ralph, too, and she caught them up on the news in a March 19 note. "Dearest Family," she wrote. "Avis finally heard from Bud [Clarke]—a cable and a V-letter dated Mar. 1st, so it took him a little over a week to get to England or France. He says he was doing his laundry, so I offered him a job right quick. Have you heard from him? I'm sending him Terry and the Pirates and Sunday funnies, so he can keep up with the times. Ha!"

With no more news about Billy, it must have been hard for Ida to keep corresponding with her new friends. To take her mind off her worries she spent as much time as she could with the new baby.

As a result, Eva Summer hadn't heard from Ida since Febuary 28, so she wrote again with a little more information on Charles. "We finally received a letter from the commanding officer of Charles' squadron, but the news was not good. He wrote that while on a mission over Tokyo, Charles' plane was seen to pull out of formation just after leaving the target, and was last seen dropping down into the clouds over Tokyo Bay, as tho' damaged by enemy aircraft. Just how bad this damage was the rest of the squadron was not able to determine, as they received no report of any kind from the plane. He also said that every facility at their disposal had been exhausted in an attempted rescue of the crew, but to date nothing had been seen or heard of either the plane or any member of the crew." She added, "Like you, there are days when I feel quite hopeful, but every so often I have a bad day when I am nearly crazy with worry and grief. Easter, the season of hope, is near—may it give us all the renewed hope and faith we need during this trial."

Clarke's first V-mail letter to Ida and Ralph came from England. He squeezed a lot into a small page that had been rendered even smaller after it was reduced and folded into a 3-by-4-inch envelope.

Dearest Mom & Folks,
Kinda slow in writing but I've been traveling, so to speak. As you know, I came by boat and the trip wasn't at all bad. We had very good food, only 2 meals a day. Most of the gang either "rattled the bones" or chased the USO and WACs all over the deck. But this ole man won $15 and settled down to a nice, long novel. Shows I'm taking my married life seriously, hm? Ha ha. Say, how's the "Lil One"? Avis wrote and said Lil Clarke is gettin' more "Red on the head" every day. [...] England's countryside is lovely—everything is nice and green, but I can't say much for their cities—too crowded together and all houses look too much alike. The city is filled with coal dust and gives you a grimy feeling. Food is sorry here. We generally eat a snack after each meal, because we are still hungry. We are running out of snacks—then what? Ha ha. I know this letter will find you all in good health. Take good care of yourself, Mom, and remember, I'm right in there pitching with you. Love to all. Always the ole man, Clarke.

Once he got settled, he wrote more, but mail from home wasn't catching up with him, and now he'd been moved to France. He described a foray into Paris: "Drank a wee bit too much champagne and cognac and had quite a time gettin' my boys home (six of us). The subways are nice and some of the fellows enjoy them more than the American [ones], but I can't see what enjoyment one could find in any subway except push and shove to get past the narrow door. Also, these confounded things stop running whenever they get ready. One nite they quit at 22:30, next at 23:30. The nite we were stranded ended at 22:30, and besides, it was quite difficult for me to keep all my boys together near departing time. Surprising how keen their sight was, being intoxicated, at that. They'd swear up and down they saw an ole friend clear across the club—not an American dame in the place—hm!"

But at last Clarke was seeing action. "Mom, I'm really having the time of my life! We really have a big show 'shootin' up' Jerry trucks and 'locos.' I haven't run into any tanks, but there is so much to shoot at, and it really burns nicely–hm! Everybody in our outfit is either plane-happy or motorcycle-crazy. Every time someone calls in a Jerry screamin' down a dirt road on a motorcycle, everyone takes after him. Me, I'm 'loco' happy. I think the steam shootin' out of a train is quite a sight. Enough of my bull. Don't worry, Mom, I'm not giving them much time to shoot at me— not this ole rascal. Ha ha!" He added that he was homesick and worried about Billy and Eddy.

Ida attended the March 14th "Meeting of Relatives and Friends of Prisoners of War, Civilian Internees, and Missing Personnel" and the regular meeting on April 2nd of relatives of men in the Air Corps either missing or prisoners of war. The first meeting featured three speakers who were repatriated prisoners and escaped POWs; twelve more would be on hand to speak to the families personally after the program. The March War Prisoners Aid Bulletin was distributed at the second meeting. Ida was leaving no stone unturned.

And she had gotten more bad news. Dalton Tarver was dead. Dalton, who was like a little brother to Billy, had crashed March 15, 1945, on an instrument training flight outside Phoenix, according to a clipping and obituary in Billy's scrapbook. Dalton had followed in Billy's Air Corps footsteps, but he never made it to the war.

The stress made Ida ill, and both Eva and Rosemary worried about her. Eva tried to make it better in her April 12th letter. "I'm afraid you folks feel that perhaps Paul has not been as cooperative with you as he might have been. But I do hope you understand his position. His heart is heavy, too, over his experiences concerning Bill, Ed, and Charles, all three. And I know there is nothing that would make him any happier than to be able to send both you folks and the Steffanis some hopeful news. But when he just doesn't know anything to write, he hesitates to even attempt a letter to you."

She said Paul had been made a flight commander and was trying to finish his missions so he could leave Italy. But Eva was afraid he would be sent to the South Pacific as soon as the war in Europe was over and hoped they'd let him come home first. Plus, they'd had no more news about Charles. "One day just seems like another," she wrote, "and I keep thinking around in circles and get nowhere. But when I think about how brave all our boys have been it makes me ashamed of my weak faith and courage."

Rosemary thanked Ida and Maxine for the baby gift. She said she still hadn't heard any news about Eddy, but had heard from Paul about Eddy's crash. "He wrote and told me he was flying with him that day and saw the whole thing. Ed's plane was hit by anti-aircraft fire and he radioed in telling the flight leader about the damage done. He tried to get back into formation, but the plane lost altitude and hit the ground. I asked Paul for the truth, so he told me in his opinion it was a fairly bad crash, but he had seen fellows come out of worse ones O.K." That's the same thing he had said about Billy's crash.

Ida was sick with worry, and Rosemary recognized the symptoms. "I know you are terribly worried about Bill, but do try to take care of yourself. I am a graduate nurse, so I know that worry can cause lots of sickness. Ed's father hasn't been feeling well, either, for about a month now, and it is due to the fact that he is worrying terribly about Ed and his younger brother who is in the Navy..."

She added a bittersweet note: "I forgot to mention the baby looks just like Ed, even to the dimple in her cheek. I surely am glad, as Carol looks more like me. She has dark hair and eyes, while Mary Jean is blonde and has blue eyes."

By now the war in Europe was all but won. Clarke had gotten over there just in time, and he was taking every opportunity to give the Germans a run for their money. He had been in Metz, and on April 29 he was in Germany, where his mail had finally caught up with him. Things were pretty exciting. "'Bout two weeks ago we had two boys do a stunt like McCord.* They were strafing a train and blew up some dynamite, and the blast was felt at 10,000 ft. The planes went through about 100 feet, and one was flipped on his back, but both recovered, and despite the planes being badly scorched and suffering some damage, they made it home OK! The bubble part on the canopy was turned a milky color due to the extreme heat. Buddy in our tent was shot down and cracked his head a little when he bellied in. The Jerries put him in a hospital, and Patton liberated it! He's going home in a few days!! Lots of pilots coming walkin' in. The tank corps goes so fast, they liberate the prisoners, and they come walkin' home. I'm keepin' my eye out for our Boy, since we have hit Czechoslovakia pretty good!!"

---

*Warren G. McCord graduated from Eagle Pass with Billy and Clarke and was assigned to the 455th Bomb Group; MIA January 1945.

Clarke's reports were encouraging, but a letter dated May arrived from the Army Effects Bureau in Kansas City, Mo., brought the Wisners back to reality. It was addressed to Ralph. All other correspondence up until now had been addressed to Ida, since Billy had named her as next of kin and beneficiary in the will he had executed April 7, 1944, while he was at Salinas. The form letter, with the blanks filled in with Billy's name, stated the bureau was forwarding some personal effects belonging to Billy in a separate carton. The letter asserted that transmission of the property did not vest title in the recipient; Ralph was to be the custodian. "The items are forwarded in order that you may act as gratuitous bailee in caring for them pending the return of the owner, who has been reported missing in action. In the event he later is reported a casualty, and I sincerely hope he never is, it will be necessary that the property be turned over to the person or persons legally entitled to receive it."

Ralph signed and returned the receipt on May 7th, adding below his signature, "box received intact and appreciate your letter." The box contained Billy's sunglasses, a hunting knife, insignia, a New Testament, a pipe and fingernail set, toothbrush holder, belt buckle, leather name plates, playing cards, wings, second lieutenant bar, good-conduct ribbon, souvenir coins, aircraft insignias, U.S. insignias, marksman medals, personal papers, and a billfold. It also included his shoes and clothing.

It's hard to know what Ida and Ralph must have felt when they opened the box. If the clothes still carried his scent, having them home may have been comforting. But because they were no longer with their owner, it was apparent he might never return to claim them.

Evelyn Croft visited the Wisners on her way back to Seattle after Avis's recovery. When she got home, she dropped them a postcard May 7 saying Clarke was single-handedly trying to end the war in Europe to make up for the time he had been stuck in the States. "Avis heard [from Clarke] Friday, and he'd completed 29 missions. She doesn't know he got three ships shortly after transfer to France. She might worry. His ship was shot full of holes but he said it was worth it. He wants to get one for every one of his buddies that are missing. Soon as we get full control of the Italian situation, you'll hear good news, I betcha!"

Clarke's enthusiastic, last-minute contribution to the war effort must have helped, because May 8th was V-E Day. Surely, now that the war was over in Europe, information would flow more easily. Maybe they would find Billy, at last.

And Clarke kept hopes high. In a May 15 letter, this time written from Germany, he said, "Every day, now that the war here has ended, we have P.W.s who are traveling back, looking for their outfit, having been shot down or forced down due to weather or engine failure. We had two lieutenants from Italy who were captured and sent to Frankfurt on the Main. They had been down for eight months and no report of capture. Had been turned in by the Jerries. They had been shoved from one camp to the other till no one seemed to know who or how they got in. I have been assigned by our Sqd. C.O. to make a thorough search for one of our personnel missing in action. Since no one knows whether he was captured or escaped, how his plane looked after bellying in, so I'll first find the plane and then work on back till I find out the final score. Each Sqd. is making an attempt to discover what happened to their pilots missing in action in order to close the files and records they have…"

The Summers couldn't expect to hear any more about their son Charles until the war in the Pacific was over, but they, too, hoped the victory in Europe would bring good news for the Wisners. And Paul had completed 46 missions in Italy, so there was a good chance he wouldn't be sent to the Pacific. Eva wrote Ida June 12, "Imagine our surprise and joy when Paul walked in at 3:30 Monday morning. He arrived at New York June 6th by transport plane but didn't send us any kind of word—just surprised us by coming all the way home.

"He is quite a bit thinner—has lost twenty pounds—but he surely looks good to us. It is so nice to have him home—and how we wish that Charles, Bill, Ed and many others could be home now, too. Paul had enough points to get out of service now, but he has chosen to remain in for a while longer. He will have a thirty-day leave at home and will then report to Santa Ana, California, for further orders."

She added that Paul was going to write Ida a few lines, "but what a hard task it is for him, dear friend. He would so love to be able to give you good news about Bill, but he just doesn't have it to give. We surely hope you have had something definite from some source by this time. I can truly sympathize with you in this terrible suspense of waiting."

Eva was no doubt relieved Paul wouldn't continue in combat. Being assigned Stateside was no guarantee of safety, but it was a damn sight better than being shot at. Paul's letter to the Wisners had nothing more to tell, but he did give them a current address for James Nash, the Texan photographed with Billy just before his last mission. Paul said Nash should be back in Texas by now, too.

First Billy's belongings, and now his friends were coming home without him. But his mother wouldn't give up that he would soon follow.

11

IDA'S WAR
1945

Mon. A.M.

Dear Fritz –

    Enclosed find letters I received Sat. They don't give us any further information but seems like they are still working on it. A Mrs. Chas Collins living on Clarendon Drive phoned me last night and she said the gov. is not reporting all the amnesia cases in the hospitals in Tex. She is trying to locate her boy, too. She has visited three gov. hospitals in Tex. and this week she is going to Waco and invited me to go too, then maybe we can contact the others thru correspondence. What do you think of this? Ralph and I do appreciate your letter. It was to the point and maybe they will work harder. I do know this, Fritz—if Billy is alive, he just doesn't know who he is. I will let you know what I learn. Keep the letters and I will pick them up soon. Appreciating everything you have done,

                As ever,
                Love,
                Ida

* * *

T he war in Europe was over, but a personal struggle continued on the home front. Fritz Wencker worked hard at finding Billy, and Ida helped with the letter writing, but they both kept getting the same disappointing results.

Newpapers all over America covered solemn memorial services, jubilant celebrations, and stories of heroism and tragedy. But history downplays the other casualties of war, agonized families whose sons and husbands were missing. Fearing the worst, they continued to hope for the best. For her part, Ida clung to every shred of information that filtered back to her, but until there was certain truth, no one wanted to give her bad news.

Ida now had a home address for Lowell Twedt, one of the pilots in Billy's accident, so she wrote to him. His mother, Gertrude Twedt, replied in his place, in a stream-of-consciousness onrush of information, speculation, grief, and agony.

San Diego, Calif.
July 3, 1945

Dear Mrs. Wisner:

Rec'd letter yesterday you wrote to my son, and am very sorry we have not heard a word from our boy since the word from the War Dept. that he was missing in action, but you have it different from our message. I will quote you as we got it he was reported by "the Adjutant Genl as missing in action over Italy since Oct. 20. Further information dated Oct. 21 has just been rec'd which indicates that Lt. Twedt was the pilot of a P-38 Lightning fighter plane which departed from a base in Italy on a bomber escort mission to Regensburg, Germany on Oct. 20. Full details are not available, but the report indicates that during this mission at about 11:30 A.M. while in the target area your son's plane collided in mid-air with another of our aircraft and both planes were last seen falling toward the earth. The crew members of accompanying planes returning from this mission were unable to furnish any further details." End of quote. We have had one more letter from the war dept but could not give us any more information which we rec'd March 26. So you know just what we have rec'd. I can sure tell you I can know how you feel. I have had a nervous breakdown and had to quit work. I have been working for an aircraft factory for 2-1/2 yrs and it was really the only thing that kept me up so

long and the Dr. said I should work as long as I could but when the
news came over the radio about how those poor prisoners were treated I
just got down. I feel they are still alive and I am afraid they were hurt
so badly they might be mentally off and don't know who or where they
are. You may not be like I am but I just lay awake nights and can't
sleep and only pray there will be something I can do. I have gone to the
Red Cross and they don't seem to be able to do anything. I sure
sympathize with you and was very glad to hear from you and if I get
any more word I will let you know right away and if you do I would
sure be very grateful to you for any information. I wrote to a man in
Ohio I read in the paper that had a short wave radio set and he spent
his time getting messages from boys over in the war zone and a
neighbor of ours had a boy missing and he was hurt so bad he is still in
hospital in England not been able to be moved. And they hadn't heard
from him for a long time and this man found out about him over his
short wave radio and let his folks here know. I wrote this man where I
seen it in the paper in Nov. and asked him to keep Lowell in mind and
I had an answer back right away that he had rec'd my letter and it
might be 30 days or longer before Berlin Station would put his name
on the air if he was P.O.W. I will give you his address if you would like
to write him. I wrote right away to the Crew Chief. I didn't know his
name but Lowell had written about him and as his Crew Chief that
took care of his plane and liked him very much. I asked him if he could
tell me anything and he answered back and said he couldn't give any
more than I had rec'd and wrote a beautiful letter and how he prayed
for the boys to return when they went out on a mission. His name was
S/Sgt Robert E. Rahe. Now this is all I can tell you. I didn't know the
names of any of the boys in his Sqd and this boy Paul Summer was he
in the same Sqd as Lowell? I only wish I could tell you something that
would be a little comfort to you. [...]

I have another boy in the Navy is a Seabee in Tinian and
we only hope he can come home. He has been in 2 yrs and is very
anxious to get home. He has had the fever but is well again, he says.

Will write you if I hear anything and you do the same.
Never give up keep on praying for their return.

Sincerely,
Mrs. R. M. Twedt

This boy Olson we write about was he in the same Sqd and
do you know his address or his folks address?

Ida wrote to the man with the radio, but he replied July 9th that he had discontinued the service in May, "after relaying over 12,000 short-wave pickups from foreign stations about missing men during three years working night and day without [compensation]...I relayed first news to many Dallas families that their sons were alive in the hands of the Italians, Japs, or Nazis and practically every town, city, and village in the U.S. knew of my work for the boys and their loved ones. I know just how you feel because I've read thousands of similar letters, later helping lots of mothers."

He may have helped a lot of mothers, but he couldn't help Ida or Mrs. Twedt.

James Nash answered Ida's letter about a month after she had written him at the address Paul had given her. But he was no help, either, "because I wasn't on the mission that day; in fact I flew my first mission in November, although I got into the Squadron Oct. 2. Bill and I had our picture made together because we were both from Texas and we were the only two Texans in our Squadron at the time. I had talked to him several times and liked him very much." He offered to visit Ida if he was ever in Dallas.

Now that Ida and Gertrude Twedt had found each other, they joined forces. Perhaps together they could get to the truth of their sons' crashes. Gertrude had spoken to a man with the Red Cross, just back from Germany. In a non-stop thought train, Gertrude related what he'd told her. "He was sorry he could not give me any information only said if they were hurt and in a hospital and their identification was gone it took a long time to get them identified again if they were unconscious and could not explain and they would have to write here to the war dept to get things straight and that was a slow process because he said they were very particular." Ripley's *Believe It or Not!* lists the longest sentence on record as one in Victor Hugo's *Les Misérables*. Evidently Ripley never met Gertrude Twedt.

Ida had sent Gertrude a photo of Billy, and she promised one of Lowell in return. "Your nice letter just kind of does something for me to know someone has sympathy for me. And I am trying to believe we will have our dear boys home with us again soon," she wrote.

Ida continued to poll Billy's friends and their families. A reply came from Dan Wise, the boy who had written Ida for advice on how to get Billy up in the morning. This time Dan was writing from Burma. "I've often thought about [Billy] and the rest of the ole boys who were with us at that time, but of course, the Army seems to have different ideas for us all, and as a result we're spread to the four corners of the world. I know how you and your family must feel, but let me beg you not to give up hope. So many boys have gone down, been given up and returned. I've seen it here and the chances of you all hearing from him might have been cut off by some idiotic German reason and there are so many possibilities that a long time would have to pass before I would even think of him not coming back.

"This war has brought many a tragic and terrible thing," Dan went on to say, "but I don't believe it can go and take Billy with it. He's too much a part of what makes the American people great. I'm proud to know your son, Mrs. Wisner, and you, too, must be proud of him." Dan sent his love to the whole family and asked to be told the minute Ida heard anything.

A July 17th letter to Ralph from the Army Effects Bureau enclosed some of Billy's personal papers and his flight log, and on July 26, 1945, the bureau forwarded a check for $10.82. Ralph signed for it on August 6 and added a note at the bottom: "Would appreciate if you could tell me what this was. Thanks kindly." The bureau didn't get around to answering that question until October 30. It was the cash Billy had in his locker when his plane went down. The check was dated 26 October 1944. It had taken the government just six days to make an accounting of Billy's personal belongings, but it took more than six months for them to forward his money.

John Zebrowski, Billy's cadet-school classmate, replied to a letter from Ida as soon as it caught up with him. He said he hoped Billy would turn up soon and, given his own experience, thought that might be possible. "I went down over Vienna, Austria, myself, last Dec. 11, and my folks didn't hear a thing about me until just this May—so maybe you'll be getting word from him one of these days—I sure hope he turns up as one of the two that were in Paris." He asked Ida to pass his congratulations on to Maxine for the new baby and closed by saying, "Gosh, Mrs. Wisner—I hope by the time you get this letter that you've heard from Bill and know that he's safe and on his way home. Goodbye and may God Bless you."

Ida must have asked what John had meant about Paris, and Clarke's reply revealed his embarrassment. He clearly had some explaining to do. His July 26th reply began, "Lordy I must be slipping!

"I would have sworn that I had written you about running into two fellows that were in a concentration camp located in the northern part of Germany, near the Baltic Sea. Both boys were quite positive that they had two

Wisners, one was called 'John' and the other one they didn't know for sure, as he was in the opposite end of the barracks and since each barracks contains 80-120 persons, they hadn't been there long enough to get acquainted with all the first names and etc. They did believe that the boy came from Texas and also was not a member of the 8th or 9th AAF, but he was a pilot and that put him in the 12th or 15th, which at that time was located in Italy.

"The description fits well, said he was tall and slender and had dark hair, young as most pilots are, the only description that made the whole thing off key was the description that the lad from Texas was quite gullible and the fellows were always telling him that the Jerries would turn them loose the next day or something to that effect. That's all I have on that, Mom. Wish I could say more. One thing when the Russians were a couple days from the area the Jerries pulled out and some of the boys started to hitchhike to meet the American troops and rejoin their outfit. Some of these boys who left camp ran into pockets of Jerry troops that were still holding out and some were wiped out, also the German home guard is being tried in some places for killing X-PWs after their town had surrendered and the PWs were passing thru on the way home or to their outfit."

Ida must have hoped the rumor about the Texan in the POW camp was true, even though his personality didn't fit Billy's at all.

Another story had come out of Paris, one that Clarke didn't want to tell Ida but shared with his sister, instead. He had written Evelyn on June 16 from Nuremberg, saying of Ida, "She's really gettin' worried, now that most all of the P.W.'s have been released and still no news from Woo Woo. I get so I can hardly write her the news as it comes in, for there is so little to work on. They are such swell folks, and Bill was my 'flying buddy' and that's tops for my money. I sorta looked after him and saw he didn't get out of hand. Typical of the Wiseleys—always run someone else's business better than our own."

He continued, "While I was in Paris I ran across one of our classmates who was in Bill's squadron. He wasn't on the mission, but he said the fellows were flying through flak, and the man in front of Bill was hit and also Bill. But Bill flew through the explosion of the man ahead and he exploded, too. This seems to be a bit different from the account given before. Even this is rather hazy, as the buddy who told it to me was an ex-P.W., having been shot down a lil after—or before—don't recall. Anyhow, don't pass it on, just keep it under your hat. Don't want her to ever find out, unless someone who was there tells the real story."

In spite of Clarke's request to keep it from her, Ida had that letter in her files.

While many of the boys in Clarke's 9th Air Force were on their way home, some were being shipped to the China/Burma/India Theater. He wrote, "As for us we are moving into Austria before long and looks like we are heading the wrong way to get home, Hmmm? Something about transportation being too crowded. Still doesn't explain Austria. Guess I'll see more of the Ole Country. I really like the scenery and have one big time scroungin' and hunting for cameras, etc."

He'd read about a food shortage back home, but he'd been hunting and had shot ten deer, "so you know they are plentiful and also delicious." That way, he, said, he could save his C rations, "so I won't go hungry if and when I come home."

The news that they weren't going home yet had hit some of his boys hard. "Boy you could hardly walk down the hallway for the poor kids that hit the bottle too hard…, ha ha! What the hell I'm laughing for, I don't know!! But I'm making the most of it as usual and I have some good perfume from the Riviera, Cannes, France, so my women are going to smell pretty and all that there stuff!! Ha ha. You'll have to tell me which is the best, I'm not too familiar with the feminine stuff—says here in small print…"

Poor Clarke, so eager to get into the war and now that it was over he couldn't wait to get home.

Ida related the latest version of the crash to Eva Summer and received a chatty letter in reply. No news yet of Eva's son Charles, only the same old government rhetoric, but she said Paul had been home for 30 days before being shipped to Santa Ana for reprocessing. "[Paul] said about half his old squadron were there with him and many of them were taking their discharges…I do know, too, that he finds it hard to write to either you folks or Rosemary Steffani, as he feels so badly about not having any definite or very good news to tell either of you. But as for me, I have never heard him say that Billy's plane exploded—in fact I think all this while he really had big hopes for Billy's return, but of course that has lessened considerably since V-E Day when no more word has been received."

Fritz's July 2 letter to the War Department was answered July 30. They said only that all information would be reviewed twelve months after the date of Billy's disappearance, at which point they would decide whether to continue listing him as missing or make a finding of death, "as the facts appear to justify."

Fritz's reply gushed with gratitude, uncharacteristic of this no-non-sense, stern man. He told them it was the most information they had ever received in response to any of their inquiries and took the opportunity to add a personal note. "I am sure you are not interested in the intimate sur-roundings of each one of our brave boys who was a casualty or missing, but Lt. Wisner was his parents' only son and, if alive, was twenty-one years of age on August 1 of this year...Wealth or money can be replaced and, if not, the lack of it will equalize itself among our citizens, but, as contended by the founding fathers of our Government, Life, Liberty and the Pursuit of Happiness are inalienable to the citizens of our country, and if any of these are taken away from you, you have lost something substantial and that which makes life worth living...I am sure you have no time to read this, so disregard everything that is said except the appreciation because of the receipt of your letter."

He forwarded a copy of both letters to Ida with a cover letter telling her to keep them with the others, then added, "Although my hopes are dimming, I am still praying we may have Billy with us in time for the Christmas celebration."

Ida hoped for the same and did the only thing she knew how, to make that possible. She wrote the American Red Cross in U.S. Occupied Territory, the International Red Cross in Geneva, the U.S. House of Representatives, the Foreign Service, the Allied Military Government in Bolzano Province, and the American Legion in Washington. The replies trickled in during the following month, but each was the same: "no further information," "deepest sympathy," "will keep you informed," etc., etc., *ad nauseam*.

And now that Nagasaki had been bombed on August 9, 1945, the war in the Pacific was over. America celebrated, but nothing changed for the Wisners. And Ida wasn't the only one desperate for information. Gertrude Twedt still clung to the hope that their boys were victims of amnesia somewhere. In one of her letters she said someone had told her husband that "...boys that were missing like ours they had taken them and were put to F.B.I. work and he told of a boy in some circumstance was one and his wife had been hunting for him. She was like we are trying every-thing to find him had traveled different places and then some way she found out something and went where he was and he was one but when she came to him he said I don't know you and wouldn't have anything to do with her but he said they just could not let anyone know where they are and this fellow was in the States and they seem to be looking for any sabotage. He had been overseas. Now I don't know if I can believe if I met my boy that he would not want to know me. They have a good many he says and it is boys that they think would be capable to serve."

Then, another letter from the Adjutant General's office of the War Department on August 30th informed the family that "no report of any change in status has been received" since their last letter. It reiterated their policy of waiting 12 months then reviewing all information pertinent to the disappearance and making a decision about a finding of death at that time. Then it added a request: "Occasionally relatives and friends of missing persons receive communications containing pertinent and reliable information which has not been reported officially to the War Department. If you have received any such communications, it will be greatly appreciated if you will forward them or photostatic copies thereof to this office. After examination they will be returned to you if you so desire."

Ironic. Not only did they have nothing to tell Ida, they were asking her what she knew, when all she knew was what they told her.

Desperate to forestall the change in Billy's official status from "missing" to "presumed dead," Ida made another plea on September 13th. "Before I get that dreaded letter when the year is up, can't you try to get the War Dept. to make a more thorough search for my boy? One of his buddies has been searching in a plane, but what can anyone see from a plane? Why can't there be a search by guides on foot from Bolzano, Italy, who know the country? Believe me, I don't want you to do more for me, as I am not any better than other mothers, but we all feel just the same. There have been 14 fliers from Billy's graduation all from Dallas class in Eagle Pass. Six have been reported missing and nothing else. I am awake half the night, and the rest of the night I am trying to find a little boy lost in the mountains of Italy. Try something. I know, or think I do, what you are [up] against, but I just can't do anything but write letters, and I have written hundreds."

Her request didn't seem unreasonable. After all, if Clarke's situation was typical, there were a lot of young men overseas waiting for orders to get home. Why couldn't they be put to use finding the missing?

Gertrude Twedt wrote September 26th to tell Ida about a letter the government had sent her, but it was exactly the same one they'd sent Ida. However, Gertrude had believed the War Department when they said they might not have all the facts, and she told Ida in great detail how she had set them straight. It was a waste of her ink and paper.

Eva Summer, still worrying about Ida's health, wrote in October, "I think you owe me a letter, but I have you on my mind so much that I am going to write you a few lines anyway. I have been wondering whether perhaps you may be ill and it surely would not be surprising after your experience of the past year."

Eva was going through the same agony, having had no word of Charles. But the good news was that Paul was home for good, she said, released from active duty. "He is now on a 43-day 'terminal leave,' at the end of which he will be on the 'inactive status' list, retaining his captain commission in the Air Corps Reserves. That means he will again be a civilian until such time as they may need to recall him into the Air Corps. God forbid that there will ever be another war, and that will not be necessary." She apologized for Paul's not having written Ida, and said he just didn't have any more information.

Ida was grasping at straws. She sounded delirious when whe wrote Lt. Col. Ida Danielson, director of nursing service at Theater Service Forces Headquarters in Paris. "Is there any way you can check lists in hospitals—or I know most of the boys have lost their memory and have lost their identification tags—I guess you think I am very incoherent—Is there any way there to take fingerprints or do that when they are brought to the States or if their fingers are mutilated—what then? William has a bad scar on his index finger on his right hand.* I write this and after reading it think I am silly but I am just about crazy—and I have written hundreds of letters and nobody pays any attention. Would you try and help me? You and I have one thing in common—our names."

Despite Ida's efforts to keep it at bay, the "dreaded letter" arrived right on schedule. It was dated 21 October 1945, the day after a full year had passed since the crash. It was signed by Maj. Gen. Edward F. Witsell, acting adjutant general of the Army, who had written so many of the official letters. He recounted the circumstances of the accident, saying Billy's plane had been damaged by debris from the two that had collided above him.

They had reviewed all records, reports, and circumstances on Billy's absence, Witsell wrote, "without the receipt of evidence to support a continued presumption of survival [and] must terminate such absence by a presumptive finding of death." But because they couldn't establish an actual date of death, they set the presumptive date as 21 October 1945. Witsell

---

*From that time in the mumbly-peg game when he saved the caterpillar.

regretted the necessity of the message, but trusted "that the ending of a long period of uncertainty may give at least some small measure of consolation. I hope you may find sustaining comfort in the thought that the uncertainty with which war has surrounded the absence of your son has enhanced the honor of his service to his country and of his sacrifice."

How could that possibly be of any consolation?

Ida drafted an announcement for the Dallas newspapers in pencil on the back of Witsell's letter. She slipped the published clipping from the November 4, 1945, *Dallas Morning News* into the front of Billy's Eagle Pass yearbook. Over the years it yellowed and stained the pages of the book, leaving an indelible shadow of an inevitable conclusion.

The headline read, "Missing Pilot Presumed To Be Dead." In the margin above Billy's photo, Ida had written "Blessed darling."

12

DESPERATION
1945-46

Midland, Texas
October 27, 1945

Dear Mrs. Wisner:

I was in Stalag Luft I, south compound, located on the
Baltic near Barth, Germany. I never knew anyone in my camp
with a name similar to yours. However, there were around ten
thousand prisoners in the camp so it was impossible for me to know
them all.

I am sorry that I am not able to help you with this
information. I hope that you will have had some good news by the
time you receive this.

Yours very truly,
Henry A. Wieser
1st Lt., Air Corps

* * *

The announcement of Billy's presumed death generated another
onslaught of cards and letters from friends and relatives, merchants
and bankers. This time they sent condolences, and the constant
reminders compounded the sadness.

Ida's oldest and dearest friend, Ruby Rische, came for a visit to help ease Ida's grief. Ruby's love and support had always sustained Ida, and this time it must have allowed her to let go, just a little, because Ida gave Ruby some of Billy's things to take back to her niece.

Ida received a sweet thank-you note in return: "[Aunt Ruby] gave me the wings of Billy's that you sent me. I will treasure them all my life and thank you for giving it to me. I played the records and they are swell. I played the Hut Sut Song on the second hole* and it tickled me. Aunt Ruby said it tickled me as much as it did Billy."

Perhaps Ida was beginning to believe Billy wasn't coming back alive; the official word made it seem more certain. And more replies from Headquarters of the U.S. Air Forces in Europe and the Veterans of Foreign Wars carried the same, tired old message: no further information on the whereabouts of Billy Wisner.

Adding finality was a letter from the Secretary of War, written one year to the day after the Wisners had received the telegram about Billy's MIA status. Billy had been awarded the Purple Heart posthumously.

Clarke, unaware of Billy's new, "official" status, was still trying to cheer Ida up. He said in his October 26th letter he was still having a hard time getting home and enclosed a photo he'd had taken in Brussels. Smiling broadly, he wears his flight jacket with his fox mascot emblazoned on the left front. The emblem shows a cartoon fox wearing a top hat and holding a bomb. On the back Clarke had written: "Brussels, Belgium, 15 Oct. 45. Started out in B-25 13 Oct 45. Lintz—Munich—Stuttgart—Nurnberg—Amsterdam—Brussels—U-78 forced down—Bad Gottingen—jeep. Wiesbaden—Munich—C-47—Salzburg—L-5—Lintz in a jeep. 9 days. Gad!!"

Clarke was worn out, but he was alive and well. And he would get home eventually.

Gertrude Twedt still clung to the hope that Lowell and Billy were hospitalized somewhere. She wrote, "I just don't want to give up that they are gone and what I am afraid of if they are still alive, they are brain cases, and there is a hospital in New York that has those cases. I don't know how they spell the name but the name is pronounced like Pauline. I heard it over the Army Hour last Sunday. A.C. (Pauline) Hospital New York...One

---

*Some 78-rpm records were manufactured with a second, off-center hole, so that when the record was played with the spindle through the second hole, the music was distorted. *The Hut Sut Song* had nonsensical lyrics, and that would have added to its humor.

Clarke M. Wiseley

of Lowell's best friends has just been found in India been missing a long time, a pilot. Well I only trust in God to bring back our boys and hope this finds you well and lots of love." Her older son had finally made it back from Saipan, thin and nervous, but alive.

A letter from Eva Summer darkened the mood. It was written on what was then called Armistice Day, November 11, and it no doubt described what Ida was feeling, too. "I have two unanswered letters from you now so will try to write a few lines this afternoon. It is such a gloomy day—dark outside, and full of memories—my mother passed away eleven years ago this morning. That and thinking about other Armistice Days when we had Charles at home with us has given me a very bad case of blues."

She continued, "We knew no doubt you folks had received that inevitable notice from the War Dept. which comes about all missing boys at the end of a year. I'm afraid we are going to get the same kind of message not many weeks off. We have had no more word of any kind about Charles.

And coupled with the misgivings about his not coming back are the thoughts we can't help having about what he may have had to suffer. There are constantly new tales of the tortures our B-29 boys had to suffer over there. Of course we do know that Charles was in a terrible air battle that particular mission over Tokyo (350 enemy planes in opposition to our small group of 62 B-29s), so if he had to die, God grant that he went quickly and didn't have to suffer abuse like many did."

Perhaps in an attempt to be less depressing, she reiterated what Paul had told her, that he thought Billy had a good chance of bailing out but couldn't tell for sure. "However," she went on, "Bill's plane seemed to be intact the last he could see of it. Paul says to his best knowledge only one of the three planes exploded, and sifting everything down it must have been Twedt's. Of course that is only Paul's guess, and he just doesn't like to say anything that he isn't sure about."

But she knew she wasn't helping Ida. "This is a poor letter to cheer you up, but I too am so heartbroken I just can't seem to lift myself out of this terrible depression. Maybe I can do better next time."

With their official letter-writing campaign winding down, the Wisners began settling Billy's affairs. Ida wrote Fritz to thank him for all he had done and offer reimbursement for Billy's college tuition. Fritz wouldn't allow it. "I do not want any of it back, as it was a pleasure to help him along, and the only regret now is that we could not help him some more as he was willing to take advantage of opportunities, applied himself, made good grades, and would have had a very bright future."

On December 5th the adjutant general sent Ida the home addresses of the airmen who had participated in the mission "from which your son failed to return." Besides Paul Summer's and Virgil Olson's, he furnished addresses for Lt. Claude A. Babb and Cpt. Albert G. Martin.

Ida wrote to Lieutenants Olson, Babb, and Martin right away, but her letter to Babb was returned, marked "unclaimed" and "undeliverable." No reply came from Martin, but Virgil Olson's neatly typed letter arrived a week later.

```
                              Portland Oregon
                              December 12, 1945


     Dear Mrs. Wisner,
             Please understand that I am writing you with
```

deepest sympathy, what little information I can
give you concerning that most unfortunate
incident. I was totally unaware that your son was
involved until a very short time ago when I
received a questionnaire from the government. Up
till that time I did not know that a third ship
was involved and I can't say from my own
standpoint who was in the ship that ran into me or
the outcome of the collision. I was fortunate
enough to bail out and was taken prisoner but I
have heard nothing concerning your son, Lt.
Wisner, or Lt. Twedt, either, in P.W. camp or
since having been returned to this country.

                         Sincerely,
                         Virgil O. Olson

That had been one of Ida's last hopes for news of Billy, and it, too,
was fruitless. And now she had a letter from the claims department of the
American National Life Insurance Company saying that before they could
process Billy's claim they needed a copy of his death certificate. Fortunate-
ly, they had already sent for it, sparing Ida and Ralph that grim task.

In her Christmas card Gertrude Twedt wrote, "I just had to write
you a few lines and hope you are well, and tell you I had a letter from a boy
that is over in Italy that went to school with Lowell and he went and
phoned up 'graves registration' and he was not listed or registered there
and he said he had heard that the American Military Gov. has a provision
whereby the Italian families that have harbored stricken U.S. aviators or
soldiers get a certain remuneration and he said under this plan the A.M.G.
might be able to gather further information which the Italians otherwise
would not have bothered to disclose. He has a brother also working in
northern Italy and they were going to do all they could to get some information and they are also asking about Olson and your boy."

Following Gertrude's lead, Ida queried the Memorial Division of the
Office of the Quartermaster General for burial records on Billy, but the
response was "no information on the burial of Lt. Wisner."

Ida wrote Gertrude about Virgil Olson's letter, who took it as a sign
of hope. "I have prayed the boys would come home, and seems to me if

Olson could bail out, our boys could have bailed out also." Gertrude still wanted to believe they were in a hospital somewhere and added, "I don't believe the Gov. knows about all of them." She told Ida she, too, had been getting her son's papers in order.

Virgil Olson answered some of Ida's follow-up questions in a letter dated two days after Christmas. "No two ships break up the same places or to the same extent," he wrote, "so frankly nobody but the Almighty knows how badly Lt. Wisner's ship was broken up or how severely he himself was injured. My captors (three) informed me later in the day that my friend was dead—in their own words 'amico caput.' Not knowing at that time that a third party was involved, I presumed that they spoke of the pilot who ran into me [Twedt]."

Olson disagreed with one of Ida's theories. "As to the possibility of the Russians or Partisans holding your son, Mrs. Wisner, I don't like to say this but I myself don't believe there is any possibility of that." But he asked her not to give up after reading his letter, "because a person never knows how many wonderful things can happen out of a clear sky."

Her hope now exhausted for the return of her living son, Ida turned her search toward finding Billy's body. She wrote Texas Senator Tom Connally, chairman of the Committee on Foreign Relations. He had no information for her and closed his response with, "As I depart tomorrow for my duties as a delegate to the United Nations meeting in London, I shall carry ever with me the memory of those, like your son, who gave their lives to bring us victory. I shall not forget the terrible price we have paid for peace, in the loss of such fine young men as Lieutenant Wisner ..." Everyone Ida wrote replied with all the politic words, none of which she wanted to hear.

Connelly enclosed a press release describing how the government searched for remains of the missing and killed in battle. At least that was something.

Maybe if Billy's body could be found, Ida could have some peace.

13

CLOSING IN

From: Jim Graham
Sent: Wednesday, January 12, 2000
To: Dale, Diana
Subject: Re: Virgil O. Olson

Hi Diana –

I'm at my daughter's house up in Blaine, WA. I brought my new toy (the laptop) & have managed to get online & read the current flurry of messages. I feel like I'm just checking out in a new plane before taking it up, so I'm operating on a wing & a prayer! I don't want to lose anything & I'll probably send my outgoing into 'outer space.'

I was amazed at the coincidence w/r to Paul Summer, too. Since Paul was relatively new in the squadron at the time, the Intelligence Officer likely took Anderson's statement as being more 'senior' or maybe he had better overall recall. In any case, the IO listened to all members of the mission before he wrote up reports & if there were not conflicting stories he would usually try to gather the 'facts' into a single report.

You don't need to send me your uncle's flight log as I have all of the squadron mission reports back to about March 1943. I have been cross-correlating all of the mission reports vs. all of the 71st pilots & the three squadrons of the 1st FG, but have only gotten back to Nov. 44 so far. It's fairly tedious & I'm assembling the summaries on the computer files, so it takes a while. I hope to

complete a tabulation before our next reunion in May. In any
case, I will send you copies when I get there – but tweak me
later in case I slip – I'm trying to provide the data to other guys in
the outfit, too.

I sure will be interested in copies of stuff you find with Paul
Summer involved.

I see Dick has uncovered a live contact in Bolzano. I think we've
got to get him data in as clear a sequence as possible. I see Dick
told Paolo, the contact, to communicate directly with you, so let
me know how I can assist in feeding him. I have maintained
copies of all of our 'Wisner' search messages on disk, so I can
pull up anything you need from that. I'll be able to respond more
reliably when I get home tomorrow night.

I haven't been able to check out Anderson, to see if he is still
alive. Do you have any 'current' data on him? Edna Summer
gave me a phone # for a guy who was there with Paul & your
uncle & was a close buddy of Paul's, so I will check him out
when I get home.

The hunt is getting lively! Keep charging!

Jim

* * *

Bless Jim Graham's heart. I wanted to help him as much as I could,
so I sent him excerpts my grandmother had taken from every letter
that contained references to Billy's crash or mentioned the sighting
of one or two parachutes. She had transcribed them in pencil on a piece of
tablet paper; certainly they kept her hope alive. Jim wrote back, "Fascinating reading. I can better understand the thrust and energy of your search."

Because Jim had known Paul Summer, I sent him scanned copies of
Paul's letters, and Jim asked if he could share the letters with Paul's wife
Edna. Of course he could. I told him, "I keep hanging on to the accounts
that say it was Billy's plane that didn't explode (I don't know why that
makes a difference—it doesn't change the outcome). I guess it makes it
seem more possible that we'll find him if he crashed. Besides, it's the story
I heard all my life." I was getting more like my grandmother every day,
clinging to any shred of hope.

On January 13th Bill Mays said that in our case, as in the Hoenshell case, "Someone who was alive and living in the vicinity of the crash will remember an event like that and should be much more willing to tell the story now vs. back in 1947 when things were still in turmoil. Most people were afraid to talk about things back then." I hoped he was right.

Paolo Cagnan, the Italian newspaper reporter who had agreed to help, wanted to know what a P-38 looked like, but I didn't have a scan of one handy so Jim gave him some P-38 Web sites to look at. I felt silly for not having thought of such a simple solution, but then Paolo hadn't thought of it, either, and he was a reporter. Paolo said he would try to look for some witnesses once he knew the exact location of the crash. Good luck, I thought. If we knew the exact location we wouldn't need Paolo, or anyone else, for that matter.

Jim sent Paolo copies of Anderson's eyewitness report and letters he had written to the various military and tourist entities in Bolzano. He closed his e-mail with "Ciao!" and added that that was all he knew of the Italian language. Paolo's reply was gracious. "Don't worry about your Italian. If you can survive to my written English, that will be the best you can do…" Paolo added he would spend the weekend organizing what he had received and then begin his investigation.

He said he had already checked the German newspaper archives, the only source of contemporary information, and had found nothing about the crash. "What most surprised me," he added, "was that I couldn't find any little article about what happened and that's a little bit strange because, you know, for the Nazis' propaganda it could have been important to let the local population know that the German flak worked so well. In fact, it was a success for them, wasn't it?!?" Next he would consult an Italian book on the Allied missions over Bolzano. He said the city had been bombed many times because its railway and main road were strategic passageways north to Austria and Germany. U.S. squadrons would often bomb Bolzano on their way to or from Germany, but there isn't a lot of information on those. "The reason why is that here are still living a lot of people involved with the Nazis and they don't want to remember it."

He described the area. "You know, Bolzano is the capital of South Tyrol/Alto Adige, the northernmost part of Italy, in the heart of the Dolomites, a very beautiful place where to live. South Tyrol was part of Austria since WWI, when we Italians 'arrived.' Now, three quarters of the local population is composed by German-speaking people. We Italians are only one quarter. All of us are bilingual, but the local Government is run by the

Germans. It's quite an interesting story, isn't it?" I appreciated the insight.

The archives were also run by the Germans, he said, and he was hoping to get their cooperation. His e-mail didn't help our case, but it did give us a glimpse into the local culture. By "Germans," he no doubt meant the German-speaking Italians, not German citizens. I worried if the cultural division might make our search more difficult.

Bill Mays wrote his next e-mail in Italian to Paolo and in English to our group, and it provided another helpful tidbit. "Another thing to keep in mind when chatting with locals and/or writing letters,...over here (Europe) most foreign aircraft were not called by their technical names, i.e., P-38, B-24, but were known by their nicknames, 'Lightning' or 'Fortress.' Here in Bulgaria a P-38 could have been a garage door opener, so nobody understood what I was talking about until I said, 'Lightning'— then they all remembered."

For Paolo's benefit Mays added that when he first started researching the Hoenshell case he had a location about the size of Switzerland to work with. "What we knew for sure was the date of the crash and where and what time the plane was last sighted. Since [your] crash and crashes (three planes) should have been a big event that day, 20 October 1944, anyone 10 years old or older at the time might have a good memory of the details of the crashes and be able to provide more exact locations."

That was exactly what we were looking for. Somebody somewhere had to know something, and that's what my grandmother kept trying to find.

But she was looking in the wrong places.

14

LAST-DITCH EFFORTS
1946

January 5, 1946

Dear Sir:

    The writer is the mother of Lt. William O.
Wisner, who graduated with you at Eagle Pass,
Texas. William went across in August 1944 and was
assigned to the 15th Air Force based at Foggia,
Italy. He was pilot of 38's. His ship was named
the Golden Slipper and had a gold slipper painted
on it.

    On October 20, 1944, [on] a mission to
Regensburg, Germany, two ships piloted by Lt.
Lowell Twedt and Lt. V. O. Olson collided. The
debris of their ships hit Lt. Wisner's, and he was
last seen going into a steep dive, followed by a
spin, over Bolzano, Italy. This was his 10th
mission. He has been presumed dead by the
Government.

    I am sending each of the boys in his class
this letter in the hope that they might have heard
something about him or the circumstances
surrounding the accident. The above is all the
information we have from the Government.

> If you have any information concerning him or
> anything from the other boys you have talked to, I
> would certainly appreciate hearing from you. I
> would also like to bring William's book up to date
> concerning his classmates.
>
> Sincerely,
> Mrs. R. O. Wisner

* * *

Another year had begun with no further news about Billy. Ida had to keep trying, so she wrote to Billy's Eagle Pass classmates in hopes of squeezing something else out of the grapevine. She sent a mimeographed form letter to each graduate, but not one of the replies had any new information on Billy.

They did, however, help her bring his Eagle Pass yearbook up to date. As the letters came in, Ida and Ralph added to the entries Clarke would make in the book every time he visited them. Next to Billy's photo Ralph transcribed a quote from one of the letters: "All of us have to die sometime, but only a few can die for something." Ida added, "God bless you darling."

Answers to her 232 letters poured in during January and February, and a few more trickled in the rest of the year. Of the 85 responses in the file, 20 were from mothers or wives of boys who were killed or lost. Some of the classmates had never met Billy, but they took time to answer, anyway. Others volunteered names of boys they had known from other classes who had been stationed in Italy. Ida followed every lead, acknowledged every letter, and to those who had lost touch with their friends she passed along news and current addresses. It kept her busy and made her feel useful. But it must have been hard. So many of those boys weren't coming back.

Each letter was heartfelt in its condolences, and each had its own poignant story to tell. Taken together, they tell the story of WWII from the viewpoints of the home-front casualties, those who waited helplessly for word of their sons and husbands.

The letters from mothers were heartbreaking.

Arkoma, Okla.
Jan 5, 1946

Dear Mrs. Wisner,

As I am the mother of Lt. Richard C. Davis received your letter today and am so sorry to know of another one of his buddies going down. You see I lost him Aug. 26, 1944. The War Department notified me he was seen to fall in the North Sea just off the coast of Holland, but I had another son in England that was based 40 miles from Richard and he told me since he come home how Richard was lost, and all of Richard's buddies that I have wrote to have been lost.

It seems hard sometimes that they had to go when they were so young but God in Heaven only knows the cause and why they were taken and I am hoping God will take care of us all and some day we can all be together again and Richard will meet all his buddies in a better place, for he loved them so much. So may God bless you.

A friend
Mrs. Davis

Some shared Ida's agony of not knowing where their sons were.

Cleveland, Tenn.
April 10, 1946

Dear Mrs. Wisner:

I received your letter that you wrote to my son, Harold E. Spicer, telling of the loss of your son.

I am writing you to let you know that on Sept. 21st, 1944, Harold was reported missing near the vicinity of Arnhem, Holland. The only information we had was that he was last seen going down in a dive to meet 15 enemy planes about 15 miles northeast of Arnhem, and that was the last seen of his plane.

He was also presumed dead by the Government this last September 1945. He was pilot of a P-47 and had been across since July '44 and was based in England with the 56th Fighter Group, 8th Air Force.

I, too, have tried to find out something in every way I know how but have never been able to find out anything. [...] I, too, would like to know about any of the boys that you have heard about. [...]

If I get any information concerning anything about your son or any of the boys of their class, I'll be glad to send it to you and would appreciate if you would do the same.

Sincerely,

Mrs. T. J. Spicer

Mrs. Spicer wrote again later that year to say that the government had located her son's grave in a military plot in Barchem Civil Cemetery in Holland. "The letter stated," she wrote Ida, "that Harold was killed in action on Sept. 21, 1944, the day he went down. I am trying now to realize I must become reconciled to his death."

But many mothers would never know where their sons were buried. This one, like Eva Summer, knew her boy had died, but there was no hope of recovering his body.

January 7, 1945

Dear Mrs. Wisner,

Your letter came today telling us of the loss of your son, Lt. Wisner. I am so sorry for you. You are the third mother to write to us telling of the loss of a son from the Group our son trained with.

I am Lt. [Peter H.] Montgomery's mother and he, too, is gone. He left the States the latter part of March 1945 for some destination in the Pacific. He was a fighter pilot. On April 23 about two hours out from Oahu, something went wrong with his ship. He called his captain and said he was going down. His ship plunged into the ocean and altho' they hunted for two days no trace of him was found. The weather was bad and they were only flying at about 600 ft. and that is all we know of his accident.

I hope you are able to get more information about your son, as it helps some to know. But it seems there is so little they really know to tell.

Sincerely,
Mrs. P. H. Montgomery
Wellington, Kansas

Not all of Billy's classmates were killed in combat. This one, like Billy's friend Dalton Tarver, never even made it overseas.

Chappell, Neb.
January 4, 1946

Dear friend
   We received your letter today concerning your son, Lt. William O. Wisner and we are very sorrie not to be able to give you any information concerning him.
   You see our son, Lt. Carroll L. Becker was fatally injured at Waycross, Georgia, when they were out on their last mission, practice before they were to go over seas. His engine refused to work and he had to make a forced landing on June 15, 1944, and he died June 17. We brought him home and layed him to rest in his home town cemetery.
   Our grief was beyond words, as he was our first lost in our immediate family, but as time has gone by and there has been several of our home boys that have been missing overseas, and we have know their parents anxious hours of waiting, we are grateful to know where he rests, and our sincere sympathy goes to so many whoes homes have been saden by this terrable war. May God be with you and give you strength to endure your grief.

Sincerely yours,
Mrs. L. H. Becker

Some survived the war and arrived home safely, only to die needlessly.

Querdado, Texas
Jan. 4, 1946

Dear sister in trouble,
   I just received your letter, and I guess you already know

what this is about. I am the mother of Lt. Percy Bingham. My son Percy was killed April 15, 1945. He went across July 1944, was shot down over Germany Sept. 5, '44. Made his way back to our lines and was sent home Oct. 5, '44. He was a fighter pilot. Wasn't hurt, but came down with his plane.

At the time of his death, he was stationed at Pyote, Texas. Col. Bundy wanted him to fly in this last graduation, also memorial services for the President. His plane came apart in the air. He was killed instantly. I never got to see him after. My son was killed in sight of his home. I live about three miles from the Eagle Pass flying field. I am sure I met William. I think I met all the boys in Percy's class. I cooked many meals for the boys. It was a treat for them. Percy enjoyed it so much and said he was so lucky to be near home. Every time he was free he would gather all the boys he could and bring them home with him. I tried to mother them all. I never saw a finer group of boys. I am sorry I can't give you any information concerning William. But according to dates Percy couldn't of known anything of him, either. I hope when you have news it won't be bad.

I had word from the War Department Percy was missing and the next word I had was a telegram from him. He was in the States. I know something of what you are going through. Only mine is certain. May God give you courage to face whatever is in store for you. Try to be as brave as that fine boy of yours. God has gathered many, many of his choicest flowers in this war. I get awful low sometimes. But I know I am just one of many mothers going through this. I had one wounded in New Guinea. He is home now but a cripple always will be. But some mothers have lost all their boys. I hope this will learn us to fight wars and rumors of wars. Oh God we have had a hard lesson.

Please excuse my poor efforts and just know my heart goes out to you, little mother. May God bless and comfort you. And when you pray, ask Him to remember me.

Percy's Mother,
Mrs. T. H. Bingham

A couple of letters came from mothers whose sons were heroes, even though they didn't die in combat.

Beaumont, Tex.
Jan. 10, 1946

My dear Mrs. Wisner,
How truly we can sympathize with you! Our son [Joseph P. Litherland] was killed in an airplane crash on September 25th, 1944. He left the U.S. to go across about the 29th or 30th of June 1944 and was in the 9th Air Force stationed in France flying the P51 Mustangs. Then in September he was sent to England to escort some bombers from the 8th Air Force on some long missions over Germany and it seems the gas they were using in France was different from that used in England and they had a lot of difficulty with their planes and some wouldn't take off so they had to be worked on and then tested, so our son was sent on a test hop in one of the planes and as he was flying over Colchester, England, the tail came off of his plane and of course he didn't have much control but instead of bailing out he stayed with his plane and managed to get it out to the edge of town and barely missed some houses and was attempting to make a crash landing in a vacant field but a large elm tree was in his way and he hit it and crashed, killing him instantly. Some of the ladies who saw him crash go over and put flowers on his grave as often as they can for they know that he gave his life to save theirs. They also correspond with me and sent me some pictures of his grave. I've often wondered just how many of the boys from their class lost their lives and when you hear from all of them I would be so glad if you would send me a list of those who won't be coming back. [...]

Sincerely,
Mrs. Litherland

And one was from the mother of one of Billy's best friends at Eagle Pass, Richard "Woody" Woodruff. Ida should have recognized the name from the photos Billy sent home. She already knew Woody was dead, but in doing such a large mailing, she must not have realized Richard Woodruff was the same boy.

Elizabeth, N.J.
July 26, 1946

Dear Mrs. Wisner:

Your letter to my son, Richard, has been re-addressed to me here at Ocean Grove, N.J., where I am spending my vacation. Needless to say how I felt when I received it, since Richard was killed over Nadzab, New Guinea, last January 9th. He had trained as a dive bomber pilot and only left the States the day after Christmas 1944. He flew to New Guinea and was only there ten days or so when he was killed. It seems he was sent to a replacement and training center, which has a young commanding officer in charge who makes a practice of bringing back aces who have had actual fighting experience to give the new arrivals tips and instructions on all the latest flying tactics.

Evidently, Richard was up with one of these aces, as he was reported as being a passenger on a training flight when I first had word that he was missing. Whatever he was being instructed in, it was concluded when the wreck was finally located on February 27th that he and his instructor had been killed outright, because Richard's body was found with his trap and parachute intact. He had been missing since January 9th, and I think I know some of the agony you are undergoing, with no definite word of you son's whereabouts.

I am sure I know who your son was, as Richard had spoken of a very particular buddy, and particularly of graduation day, when his pal's sister had pinned his wings on for him. Am I correct in assuming this was your son and his sister? It certainly does grieve me to learn about the accident. [...]

I have been told Richard had a funeral with full military honors, and was flown to Finchafen, New Guinea, for burial. I am assured his grave will be carefully kept and identified.

Please accept my heartfelt sympathy, and should you have any news of your son at any future time, I shall be happy to learn of it.

Most sincerely,
Ethel M. Woodruff

Like Rosemary Steffani, the young wives had it especially hard.

Whitewater, Wis.
January 4, 1946

Dear Mrs. Wisner:

   I am very sorry I am unable to help you by giving any information at all about your son.

   My husband, Lt. Ivan Bogie, was reported MIA Sept. 20th, 1944, one month before your son. He was missing for a year before I had official word of this death.

   Ivan flew a 47 and was doing strafing when he was hit by flak. His plane hit the ground and blew up. I didn't know any of this until the year was up. I don't imagine the two boys were together over there, as Ivan was in the 9th Air Force.

   I have a baby girl that will be a year old the 26th of this month, that he will never see.

   I certainly hope with all my heart that some of the boys can tell you something that will bring you some comfort, as I have some idea what a mother has gone through in losing a son.

   Wishing you the best of everything, I remain

Sincerely,
Mrs. Ivan Bogie

The responses from Billy's classmates, many of whom were already back in college, were of little help, because most had served in other units. But the letter from David Bastel must have made Ida proud.

23 Jan 46

Dear Mrs. Wisner,

   Received your letter and am very sorry to hear about William, and also sorry that I can give you no information concerning him. Your son went to the 15th Air Force at the same time I was assigned to the 9th Air Force, and being stationed in Belgium. As for Wiz, I can say that regardless of what news the future holds you can be justly proud of your son. Being closely

*associated with Wiz during our training, and also as a close
friend and pal during our free time, I can honestly say that he was
a fine pilot, officer and gentleman. If God decreed that Wiz
should go, I am sure it was as he lived, an outstanding example of
America and American manhood as it should be.*

*As for me, I was also flying P-38s and was shot down
during the breakthrough of the Belgian Bulge on 17 Dec. 44. Was
injured but fortunate enough to get back after being a prisoner of
war until liberated 29 April 45 at Moosburg, Germany.*

*Please call on me if I can be of any service to you, and
would appreciate it ever so much if you would advise me of any
further news of Wiz.*

*Sincerely,
David H. Bastel*

One letter gave the Wisners an accounting of Billy's whereabouts during his last months in training on the West Coast, a lot more than they had
known at the time.

14 Jan. 46

Dear Mrs. Wisner

*This is in reply to your letter of Jan. 5th, requesting some
information, if I happened to know any, in regards to your son.*

*I will start at the beginning and try to tell you of some of
our experiences from our graduation at Eagle Pass. William
attended a different basic school than I as I went through Perrin
Field, Sherman, Tex. I was not in his same squadron at advanced
either so did not become too well acquainted with him there. Here
the story may start becoming interesting to you. A small group of
us were re-assigned to Salinas AAB California. Oh, Boy, thought
everyone, P-38s. We all knew that the West Coast was the center of
that type of training. This is the place that we came to know one
another a bit better. We were sadly disappointed at Salinas,
however, as we didn't even see the inside of a cockpit there. Our
orders were finally made up and we were again transferred, this
time to Moses Lake AAB Washington. At Salinas four of us got*

together and decided to drive to our next station. Lt. Steffani owned a Packard sedan so he, your son, Lt. (now Captain) Paul S. Summer and myself drove night and day in getting to Seattle. Capt. Summer was in your son's squadron in advanced flying school and also Lt. Steffani. They were all in the same group overseas, also. Capt. Summer came home at approximately the same time as I but Lt. Steffani is also among the missing. I am a bit ahead of myself, I guess.

Our time at Moses Lake was spent in Bell Aire Cobras, P-39s, and we were in the same group there. Upon completion of our course at MLAAB we were assigned again to Ontario AAB California. There our training in 38s began, but your son and I were assigned to different sections and more or less lost track of one another again. When we were finished at Ontario we were shipped to Hamilton Field at San Francisco for further movement overseas. At this point your son and his group were shipped ahead of me. You will hear more of that if you contact Capt. Summer. His picture and address is in the EPAAF class book.

The reason that they got ahead is the fact that there were two flight officers, one of them myself, and two boys whose names began with the letter Z, so the four of us were at the last of the list, of course. We shipped from Hamilton about a week after your son. As near as I know he went to Newport News, Virginia, and from there to Naples via water transport. It took my boat, a liberty ship, 27 days to get to Naples. We were assigned, the four I mean, to the 14th fighter group, also near Foggia. When in the Officers Club in town one day shortly after we were assigned to our squadrons, I again ran across Lt. Summer. We sat down and had a long talk, and he told us that all the friends of the four that were left behind at Hamilton were located with the first fighter group. Their field was only about five miles from ours and we figured that we would go over at the first opportunity, but the opportunity didn't come up until quite a few of our friends were no longer there.

The only information I can give you about the accident is through what Capt. Summer told me at the Officers Club in Foggia one afternoon, this line of communication, known popularly as the old "grapevine." You have asked me for information that is hard to give, but I imagine that you, as a mother, would appreciate the truth as I heard it. Summer told me that the first group was on its way out on a mission and that very heavy anti-aircraft fire was encountered over the Brenner Pass, he did not exactly name the place. One hard thing to get a P-38 pilot to admit is the fact that their type of ship will more or less explode in mid-air, but that fact is true. It seems as though the leader received a direct hit and wreckage from his plane caused similar accidents to several others in the formation, one of them your son. The first fighter group was always famous for very tight formations of planes, but when flak is coming up and explosions occur, the tight formation proved to be their undoing. In similar circumstances returning pilots hold no hope for buddies who have been in such type of spots.

Doubtless you will hear from quite a few people—parents— that will like to get information also. If you should have time I'd like to hear a bit about some of the boys in my own squadron at EPAAF, sqdn 3, to be exact.

Did your son ever send you from Moses Lake AAB a group picture taken in front of a tarpaper barracks? I have that group picture here now and you might have one also, so will not send one along. If you do not have a copy, I'll try to have a print made to be sent to you. In case you do have it, Lt. Twedt is sitting in the first row, no. 2 man from the right side of the picture. I didn't know Lt. Olson but believe he was in the group somewhere.

I got 37 missions before V-E Day. I would probably have finished my 50 and come home but had a bit of hard luck on my 4th mission. Had to bail out over enemy-occupied northern Yugoslavia, but partisans picked me up and got me safely back to base where I continued my missions.

I'm now a civilian and a farmer. We have 230 acres here in central Illinois, and it is the life for me.

I am in hopes that this small bit of information will prove to be of help to you. Feel free to contact me any time if anything comes up that I could be of assistance to you. In case you should ever travel through Illinois and come near Peoria I'd certainly appreciate seeing you.

Yours sincerely,
W. B. Karstetter

The Wisners were thrilled to get Karstetter's letter. They'd had little knowledge of Billy's last months in the States, because he was kept so busy training and moving from base to base.

Ida wrote Karstetter as soon as she got his letter, on January 18. She was so excited her typing was full of mistakes, but her emotions came through loud and clear. "Dear William," it began. "I like to call you William, 'cause I love that name. I just want to tell you right now I never received a nicer letter. You certainly did give us some data we have never received, that is, we never knew just where William was, he would telephone and failed to let us know where he was or maybe he was not allowed to tell. We knew he was in Salinas, Calif. Bless his heart, he was so full of his flying and could not talk about anything else."

She recapped the details of Billy's last mission and told him she would send him a list of the boys as soon as she had heard from all of them. She asked if he could send two copies of the group photo, because, "I have a little grand-daughter one year old, blonde curly hair, she is a darling, Billy was so tickled to know that he was going to be 'Uncle Bill,' he was so crazy about kids. He, Ed, wife and little girl ran around together in Washington. Poor Ed never saw the last little girl, his wife wrote me that Ed's plane exploded and burned. [James G.] Newman, [Warren G.] McCord and [Warner H.] Marsh, all Dallas boys and in the class, the gov. presumed them dead.

"Mr. Wisner cries nearly all the time, Billy was our baby and our pride and joy. He was such a good kid, I miss him so much. He and I worked in the yard, washed the clothes and he liked to cook, and dared any of the kids to call him sissy. Do you know anything of his dates, he was so crazy about a girl in Calif. and Mrs. Patton (Pat's mother, who died while Pat was in India) talked to him like a Dutch uncle, she said Billy was going to marry this girl, I never heard anything else, thought you might know. Billy wrote us that she was keen and she knew the ropes, his Dad said maybe she was quite a bit older.

"You can see by my typewriting I am kinda rusty. After reading your letter my husband said, 'Yes, sir, I would like to meet that boy, he has given us more data than anybody.' If we are ever in Illinois will certainly look you up. My Dad and Mama were farmers and I think it is the most wonderful profession in the world. If you can think of anything else or hear anything I certainly appreciate your writing. Thanking you very, very much for your wonderful letter, I am, Sincerely, Ida Wisner."

Ida's curiosity about Billy's girlfriend in California reveals he must have mentioned her on the phone, but there's nothing about her in his letters. Was she the one in the photo taken at Earl Carroll's in August?

Ida wasn't the only one curious about her. In one of Maxine's letters that never caught up with Billy overseas, she wrote, "By the way, why didn't you mention your Los Angeles flame. Kid, you can't put anything over on us! Ha Ha." Billy may not have mentioned her, but Walter Patton's mother, a friend of Ida's, had been spreading the rumor, thanks to Pat's letters home. Like the photo taken at Earl Carroll's, the photo of Billy, Pat, and two young women in a restaurant has no caption. Those photos and the Do Not Disturb tag came home in Billy's barracks bag unescorted by explanations, and it's difficult to tell if they are the same girl.

Billy, W.H. "Pat" Patton, and unknown dates

Then again, if Billy had been serious about a girl, he would have had her photo with him for luck.

One classmate's letter gave a glimpse into the camaraderie of the boys in Italy.

Las Vegas, Nevada
January 28, 1946

Dear Mrs. Wisner:

I received your letter inquiring about the
accident that Bill had in Italy. I was flying that
day, but was not on the same mission that Bill was
on. However, the 17 of us who went overseas
together stuck together pretty closely, and when
anything happened to any one of the boys, the rest
of us usually knew about it. I was in a different
Fighter Group, the 82nd, and heard about the
accident the next day. According to what the other
boys told me, Lt. Twedt's P-38 was hit by flak,
and the result was a collision with the debris of
Lt. Olson's P-38 and Bill's. According to all
information that I gathered, the three went down,
and it is very unlikely that any of the boys
escaped.

Bill, Lt. Twedt and I were very good friends.
We had trained together in the States and went
overseas together, as you know. Upon our arrival
in Italy, however, we were assigned to different
groups, but managed to see each other quite
frequently.

I was shot down in Yugoslavia on my first
mission, but managed to return to complete my tour
of duty. I know that when I went down, all of the
boys heard about it immediately, and were very
happy to see me return. We all felt that way about
one another, and have always hoped that those of
us who did go down in enemy country would someday
return. Bill was a very good friend and very
popular with all the boys, and of course, it hit
us pretty hard to hear of this loss. Lowell was
also one of my best friends, so you can see that I
felt doubly bad about this unfortunate accident.

The last any of us heard about it was that

all three P-38s were last seen heading toward the
ground at a very rapid rate. It is unknown to me
whether any of the boys managed to escape and
parachute from the wreckage. Many miraculous
escapes have been made during the war, however, as
I know from my own personal experience, and I
would like to believe that Bill will come back
some day, too. According to the eyewitnesses, it
was a very bad situation, and it looked hopeless
to them, as was related to me the next day.

    If I can be of any further assistance, or
give you any more possible information, Mrs.
Wisner, I would be very glad to do so.

                         Yours very truly,
                         Lt. Donald H. Swan

Although Swan got the crash details mixed up, his letter was more
realistic, and Ida hated to hear the truth about Billy's prospects for survival.

One response, from a serviceman who never met Billy but had been
referred by another Eagle Pass classmate, must have hit Ida hard. It was
important enough, however, for her to file it with the official letters, separate from the bundle of Eagle Pass responses. Its envelope was missing, and
the letter was undated.

Austin, Texas

My Dear Mrs. Wisner,
    *I am so sorry that I cannot help you in your time of need.
There is really nothing I can do except give advice.*
    *After having served in a prison camp, I have heard many
men explain how they were shot down. I should be a fair judge. It is
my firm belief that your son is dead. Many of the Air Force men
were buried in unnamed graves, so you may never know where.
Try to see it my way, and spend your spare time praying for him.*

                  My deepest sympathy,
                  Philo Howard

Billy was not coming back alive.

But a letter from the chief of staff at Headquarters, Army Air Forces Flying Training Command gave hope that they might at least learn where his body was. "I know that in all theaters there are men working on the missing-in-action list, and all of these countries are being scoured for information relative to missing or killed-in-action people. Whenever anything new is brought to light, the Adjutant General is immediately notified, and he in turn notifies the next of kin."

Gertrude Twedt was still hoping for miracles, and her January 31, 1946, letter enclosed a newspaper clipping about Tech. Sgt. Ralph Lindley, who had been shot down at the same time as Sgt. Alston Gergerheis over India on Jan. 11, 1945. Gergerheis had been reported dead, and Lindley returned home to Iowa after spending the duration of the war in a Singapore prison camp. Lindley's commanding officer had suggested he go to Minnesota to extend the sympathy of his fellow fliers to the Gergerheis family. When Lindley knocked on the door, Gergerheis himself answered. Each thought the other was dead, and they were both wrong. It was the kind of serendipity Gertrude Twedt and Ida Wisner still hoped for.

Clarke Wiseley, stuck in Lintz, Austria, wrote Ida on February 17 that he was dealing with the Russians, shopping for crystal in Czechoslovakia and silver in Vienna and expecting to go home in three months. Still no news about Billy, though.

The Italian ambassador replied to Ida that he couldn't help families of U.S. servicemen, only Italians.

Billy's insurance policy would pay the Wisners $10,000 in equal installments, and the U.S. Army Air Forces sent Billy's back pay of $1,000 for the period between his being reported missing and being declared "presumed killed." That was a lot of money in those days, but Ida would have given it all back, sold her soul and everything she owned, just to know where her son was.

In March Gertrude Twedt said she had been writing to a schoolmate of Lowell's, Henry Mukai, who was still stationed in Italy and was doing what he could to find out about Lowell while he was still overseas. So far no luck, but Gertrude had given Ida Henry's address, so she could write to him, too.

Eva Summer dropped Ida a note. They had received their own "dreaded letter" that submitted a finding of death for Charles as of January 28, 1946, and said, "We had a nice Memorial Service for Charles in our home church here on March 3." Paul was still home, "hoping to get start-ed in a resort business on one of the border lakes this spring."

Unlike Eva, Ida couldn't face having a memorial service for Billy. That would have been too final, and it wasn't in her nature to give up.

Clarke telegrammed Easter greetings to the Wisners, and Henry Mukai dropped them a note at about the same time, saying he had checked with the Central Postal Directory and would check the Central Graves Registration when he could. Those were the only two leads he was able to obtain from the Red Cross, he said. "I'm sorry you must bear all this sus-pense—it becomes agonizing, I know, for myself." He wrote often and sent deepest sympathies in every letter, but he never learned anything new. It was ironic Ida would accept help from a Japanese-American. She blamed the Japanese for her son's death, because it was their attack on Pearl Har-bor that had brought the U.S. into the war, and for the rest of her life she refused to buy anything made in Japan.

Word came that everyone still hospitalized by the war had been checked and identified. Yet Ida continued to hope Billy might be a victim of amnesia somewhere. As long as she could imagine him alive, under whatever circumstances, he still was.

In October she sent an agonized letter to Major Brown of the Casual-ty Section. It appears she knew she had to start letting go, but it was killing her. Still she persisted: "Just another mother trying to get some informa-tion concerning her boy…I have since heard from one of the boys who col-lided above. He was taken prisoner and they told him the other boy was dead. Of course, we can't know that was Billy or the other boy. Billy's ship had a gold slipper painted on it. This is the 350th letter I have written and can't hear anything. Of course, Major Brown, I know that time is against us, but maybe he is in a hospital somewhere and doesn't know who he is and if he is now I know that bone structure can only tell one of his little fingers was broken and just before he left the dentist extracted his upper left 6th or 7th molar. He sent it to me and that's all I have left. I know what a job is before you and I certainly appreciate the efforts you all are putting forth, but we are so heartsick just waiting and learning nothing. We have given our all. I hope all graves marked unknown will have attention."

In December she tried Virgil Olson again, saying, "Have to do some-thing and I write and write, on and on." Olson was prompt with an answer, but it didn't help. He told her once again that he had been unaware that a third ship was involved until after he got home.

Ida's helper, Fritz Wencker, suffered a heart attack and died on December 29, 1946. He had been a steadying influence during Ida's grief and her search, so his sudden loss must have been a blow. A month after his death, Ida received a letter from one of the attorneys in his office. Referring to Fritz's efforts to find Billy, the lawyer asked if "I may discover what is to be done in the future with [Billy's] file and the matter now pending." Since there was nothing else a lawyer could do and Ida couldn't afford to pay one, anyway, the file was closed.

One by one, Ida's resources dwindled, and so did her correspondence.

Two-and-a-half months after Ida's letter to Major Brown, the Memorial Division of the Quartermaster General answered. It was the last day of 1946, and they apologized for the delay. They told her American Graves Registration Service units were now basing their searching operations on captured enemy records, combat unit reports, and POW reports. But still nothing on Billy.

On March 4, 1947, as he promised he would, Bill Karstetter sent Ida reprints of the photo taken of their group at Moses Lake. He included copies of their orders and a list of as many pilots' names as he could remember. "There are a great many I can't even place by the process of eliminating names, as you can well see," he wrote. Memories dimmed as the war faded into the past and the boys got on with their lives.

But Ida couldn't and wouldn't forget her mission. In May 1948 she wrote again to the quartermaster, asking if there was additional information and if the government would at least furnish a headstone for a burial plot in Dallas.

At last she was considering a memorial to Billy, but even that wasn't to be: "[T]here is no authority to furnish a stone to be erected as a memorial in a family plot when the remains of the decedent are not interred therein," they replied. Ida couldn't even bury her son symbolically.

The last letters she received came in 1949. On April 18th the adjutant general amended Billy's death from the "presumptive" date of death on 21 October 1945, to killed in action on 20 October 1944. He added, "The issuance of this official Report of Death will not affect any payment or settlement of accounts which has been made on the basis of the Finding of Death." At least they wouldn't take away Billy's back pay.

A follow-up letter enclosed a corrected Presidential Accolade and Purple Heart Certificate to reflect the official date of death.

The last letter in Ida's file punctuated the case with finality.

29 August 1949

Dear Mr. and Mrs. Wisner:

Almost four years have elapsed since the
cessation of hostilities of World War II, which
cost the life of your son, the late Second
Lieutenant William O. Wisner.

The unfortunate circumstances surrounding the
death of your son have been thoroughly reviewed
and, based upon information presently available,
the Department of the Army has been forced to
determine that his remains are not recoverable. I
wish to assure you that, should any additional
evidence come to our attention indicating that his
remains are in our possession, you will be
informed immediately.

Realizing the extent of your grief and
anxiety, it is not easy to express condolence to
you who gave your loved one under circumstances so
difficult that there is no grave at which to pay
homage. May the knowledge of your son's honorable
service to his country be a source of sustaining
comfort to you.

Sincerely yours,
W. E. CAMPBELL
Lt. Colonel, QMC
Memorial Division

"Not recoverable" obviously meant "we can't find him." That was
the last official word Ida received. But they had neglected to mention that
their conclusions were drawn from a search made of the crash area the previous year, and the family wouldn't know that for a long, long time. Just
over three years later his identification bracelet was found, another fact Ida
would never know.

The last items Ida put in Billy's file were two copies of the program
from a 1951 memorial service honoring the Sunset High School graduates

who had given their lives for their country. William O. Wisner was next to last on the list of 114 names. Unlike the correspondence, which Ida had kept in scrupulous order, neatly affixed to the folder, she had slipped the programs in loose, as if even opening the file would be too difficult for her to think about.

After seven years of grief and denial, Ida and Ralph had begun to get on with their lives. Nearly half a century would pass before a clue to finding Billy would come to light.

15

WITNESSES

From: Jim Graham
Sent: Saturday, January 15, 2000
To: Dale, Diana; Dick Kahler, Stephen W Duncan;
               Bill Mays
Subject: MAJOR BREAKTHROUGH!!!!

Hi All & especially Diana! –
I have just received a message from one of the tourist offices
in the Bolzano region and it identifies two individuals who
witnessed the crash of one of the P-38's on Oct. 20.
I AM TAKING THIS MODE OF LETTING YOU KNOW SO
THAT WE DON'T GO OFF HALF-COCKED & MESS UP ON
APPROACHING THESE PEOPLE. AS YOU RECALL IN
PAOLO'S LAST MESSAGE, HE DESCRIBED THE
POSSIBLE RETICENCE OF THE GERMAN SECTOR OF
THAT REGION TO SPEAK OUT ON WWII SUBJECTS. THE
NAMES OF THE TWO INDIVIDUALS MENTIONED APPEAR
TO BE GERMAN.
First, I think that Diana should think it over & express her
wishes. Then I think we should do a bit of strategizing as to
how to approach the two individuals and probably have Diana
make the contact. In the meantime, I will reply to the individual
at the Tourist Office and have him ask the two if & how they
would like to receive questions about the event.
Let's hear from Diana before we make any moves.

I'll include an excerpt here to show you the source of my
excitement.
Jim

The name of this persons are: Dr. Bruno Hosp—today the
regional culture dept. and he lives just in front of the incident
place. He was 6 years old and he remembers a dead man with a
parachute other victims were scattered around the aircraft.
Another person—he was a little bit older is Mr. Hans Frotscher—
living in Riggermoos and he knows exactly the place where the
bomber crashed down.
This boys were one of the first persons they saw the crashed
aircraft.

* * *

I answered Jim as soon as I saw there were potential crash witnesses,
excited but fearful this would be another dead end. I was shaking when
I typed my e-mail and agreed with Jim that we should move cautiously.
I didn't want to offend anyone or push too hard. But I was puzzled by the
memory of other victims in the crash. If the pilot with the parachute was
Olson, he would have been alive; the other victims would have been Twedt
and Wisner. But I doubted a parachutist would have come down at the
same spot as the crash. I was also concerned about the word "bomber."

I agreed with Jim that his strategy of approaching the witnesses
through the tourist office and "testing the waters" was the way to go. I
asked for suggestions and affirmed that, as a relative of the deceased and
not a military entity, I should approach the witnesses directly. "I'm sure
their families lost a lot of loved ones in the war, too," I said, "and they will
empathize with my desire to get closure." I had a million questions and
knew if I ever got any answers, I would be indebted to my helpers for the
rest of my life.

Bill Mays responded, "One problem I had when searching here in
Bulgaria was that the Lightnings were often mistaken for bombers, or classified as bombers due to the twin tail booms, and also the drop tanks
looked like bombs from a distance. Does anyone know if any bombers were
downed in that area on or approx. to 20 October 1944? There could have
also been civilian victims from the crash."

Oh, dear. I hadn't even considered the possibility that Billy's crash might have taken the lives of innocent residents of the area. But that would explain more than one body at this site, and I feared it might be so. But, then, if Billy's plane had killed civilians, the U.S. government should have known where he hit, and so we would have, too. On the other hand, if several bodies had come from one plane, we had the wrong plane. I didn't know what to think.

Jim checked his MACR (Missing Aircrew Report) index and found four bombers downed in Italy then, one B-17G, one B-25, and two B-24s. "I guess we should not get our hopes up too high 'til the designated witnesses relate a bit from memory," he said. "As Bill [Mays] says, too, we need to make it known to them just what a P-38 looks like."

Jim forwarded me the complete message from Peter Righi of the Bolzano Tourist Bureau, which included a phone number for Bruno Hosp, one of the witnesses. I didn't have the courage to call Hosp directly and didn't even know if he spoke English. I speak a little Italian, just enough to get by when traveling, but my vocabulary isn't adequate to explain what I was looking for. And the extent of my German was *gesundheit* and *danke schön*.

According to Mr. Righi the exact location of the crash was Gebrack (just a few hundred yards from his home), at a place called Riggermoos near the Hotel Kematen in Ritten. All of those places were in a part of Italy I had only vaguely imagined, and I wasn't prepared for such Teutonic names.

Jim thanked Mr. Righi for his e-mail and asked him if he would approach Dr. Hosp and Mr. Frotscher on our behalf to see if they would be willing to correspond with me. He also inquired about written records or photos of the crash and its victims or any items recovered from the crash.

I told Jim I would wait for Mr. Righi's answer before doing anything. "My heart tells me to jump in and get involved," I wrote, "but my head tells me to proceed with caution. Your comments about media attention and the four bomber crashes in Italy keep me from getting my hopes up just yet." I knew I had to wait, but my heart was pounding. I was afraid to let myself hope we might find Billy's crash site, or perhaps even Billy himself.

While we waited for Righi's response, Bill Mays offered to translate any Italian I might need help with and told me about a translation Web site that would get me about 75% accuracy. Jim wrote: "Waiting is agonizing. Dick [Kahler] and I recall waiting for Bill [Mays] to reply after he made the trip to the Hoenshell site near Dragoman, Bulgaria. Time drags and imagination wanders." How right he was. My imagination was running wild, and my hopes were skyrocketing.

On January 18, after a long silence, we heard again from our newspaper friend, Paolo Cagnan. I had assumed he was off on other stories, but he had been investigating ours. In fact, he had gotten deeply involved. "I'm almost obsessed with this story," he wrote "I begin to dream about planes, flak and so on."

He took the opportunity to tell us a little about himself. "No one of you knows exactly who am I. I am an investigative journalist, age 32. I work for a local newspaper called 'Alto Adige' in Bolzano. I work with State Television RAI, too. I wrote some books about crimes and mysteries. Not a very big success, in fact." He added a personal message to Bill Mays thanking him for his message in Italian, then asked Jim for some technical information: "If an airplane crashes like the Wisner's P-38 did, from an altitude of 22.000 feet, how big will the area on the ground where is possible, in theory, to find some pieces of the broken plane?"

He asked me for every piece of information regarding the accident, including scans of the official reports and letters. He also wanted to know "what exactly is the CIL, where is located and which is its specialisation?"

Jim and I coordinated sending him what he needed, and I told Jim despite Paolo's association with the media, which would make most people suspicious, I felt he would be a good resource for communicating with the witnesses. At least he would be getting paid for his time; others might not be so forthcoming if they weren't compensated for theirs.

On January 21 Peter Righi at the tourist bureau wrote Jim that the two gentlemen, Mr. Frotscher and Dr. Hosp, didn't speak English, but the wife of Dr. Hosp did. Her name was Dr. Inga Hosp, and he included her phone and fax number. He also asked for our addresses so he could send us some tourist information about the Ritten area.

I was terrified at the prospect of speaking to Inga Hosp over the phone, because I wasn't comfortable with the potential language barrier, especially if her English was anything like my Italian. There was also the time difference and, most of all, the intrusion. I told Jim I would write instead of call. I had her fax number and could get the letter to her right away.

I composed it carefully. It was far too long, but I wanted to be sure I made the most of this opportunity. I might not get another chance to ask some very important questions.

21 January 2000

Dr. Inga Hosp
Ritten, Italy

Dear Dr. Hosp:

I must apologize for writing you in English, but I speak
no German, and my Italian is inadequate for this request. I have a
very big favor to ask of your husband, and I understand he speaks
no English. This is where your help is needed.

Mr. Peter Righi of the tourist bureau referred me to you.
He tells me your husband witnessed the crash of an airplane during World War II, when he was a boy. If that crash occurred on
the morning of 20 October 1944, there is a very good chance the
pilot of that plane was my uncle, William O. Wisner.

I realize it was a long time ago, but it is very important to
my family to find out what happened to him. [...]He was my
grandmother's only son, just 20 years old, and for years she never
gave up hope that he may have survived or that more would be
known of his fate. I grew up hearing about him, and I seem to
have inherited my grandmother's stubborn will to know more.
My mother, who is almost 82, is William's older sister. I have not
told her of my search, but I am doing it on her behalf.

William's official file leaves many questions unanswered,
and now that the records are available to us we see that a vital
part is missing. We are searching for more information through
the U.S. government, but that may prove fruitless, so I am hoping your husband's memories of the crash will add some pieces to
the puzzle.

May I impose on you to ask your husband to recall the
incident and translate his response for me? I don't expect a childhood memory to be perfect after 55 years, but I will be grateful
for anything he can contribute. I would specifically like to know
the following, if possible:

• Exactly where was the crash?
• Were civilians hurt? (I pray they were not)
• Was the pilot inside the plane when it crashed?

- Did anyone keep any records of the crash, any photographs or souvenirs?
- Did the plane burn; how intact was the wreckage?
- Were there any identifiable markings or pictures on the plane?
- What became of the wreckage?
- What became of the body of the pilot?
- Was it possible to describe what the pilot looked like, or did he wear any identification tags or bracelet?
- After the war, did the U.S. government ever search the area and/or recover the pilot's remains?

I don't expect your husband to remember explicit details, but I feel I must ask these questions to be sure nothing is overlooked. Words cannot express my gratitude for anything he might add to our story.

If you know of any other witnesses that could help, I would appreciate learning how to reach them. Mr. Righi of the tourist office said that a Mr. Hans Frotscher also knows about the crash, but he doesn't speak English. I have not yet approached him, and with the language barrier, I am not quite sure how I should. I thank you in advance for your efforts on our behalf. My very best wishes to you and Dr. Hosp.

> Yours most sincerely,
> Diana T. Dale

I took the letter to a shipping/faxing/mail-box store and asked them to fax it, but I didn't notice that the fax number was also the home phone number until it was too late. After the clerk dialed, I heard her announce she was sending a fax. I looked at the clock and realized it was the middle of the night in Italy and I had awakened someone. How rude of me—I feared I may have made an enemy before we even got started.

Again we had to wait. In the meantime, I heard from the Italian State Archives, but they had no information for me and didn't know where such records could be found. That might have been a disappointment had it come earlier in our search, but now I had a feeling we getting along fine without their help.

That same day we all heard from Paolo. He had been working hard, and he shared his strategy with us. First, he had sent a fax to a general in Rome asking for a complete list of all American soldiers buried in Italian cemeteries. That was a waste of time, he said, because the U.S. government had come in after the war and moved everyone to U.S. battlefield cemeteries.

He drew a map indicating the area he was searching. It was far more detailed than the map in Billy's MACR with only a vague indication of the crash site. Paolo's map indicated the possible location five miles northeast of Bolzano, in the Isarco Valley, between Bolzano and Bressanone. "I'm quite sure this is the exact location: it made no sense for the 'lightning' and the 'fortresses' to fly NW of Bolzano. But it's only my opinion."

He told us the German flak was positioned on the mountain of Schlerngebiet about 1200-1500 meters in elevation, from which they could check the "air traffic" going north through the Brenner Pass, to Austria and Germany. "In the next days I will begin to ask old locals for information: I'll try to 'force' all the friends and parents to help me. This is the 'oral history.' "

Next, he would look for the official flak reports which, he said, may exist only in theory because many documents were destroyed by the Germans before their retreat in April/May 1945. He confirmed what the state archives had told me, that they had no information. But he did say it was possible some reports may survive at the "Bundesarchiv" at Koblenz, Germany. "I'll try to give them a call, fax or e-mail an SOS."

He finished with a list of questions and requests of Jim and me. From me he wanted the memos from 1952 that mentioned the bracelet and remains. From Jim he wanted to know what happened to the mission after the crash, and how many P-38s and bombers were ultimately involved.

Jim had received copies of captured German records from the National Archives. The researcher there had found Olson's capture record, as well as a chronological listing of downed aircraft on 20 October 44. Jim forwarded them to me and to Roland Geiger for translation.

The capture record was fascinating, even though I couldn't understand it. As I looked it over, I tried to imagine what must have happened after Olson was caught. He would have been taken at gunpoint by German soldiers and transported to some sort of headquarters, where he would have been processed and questioned. I wondered how he was treated.

As I pored over the report, I looked for anything I could understand. I recognized the date, October 23, 1944, and the place, Bozen (the German equivalent of Bolzano). The report was dated three days after the crash.

Why? Did Olson manage to hide out for a while before he was captured? Or was the report made after he had been moved to another location?

I could read Olson's name and birthdate (August 27, 1915), and his rank. The word "Lightning" appears near the bottom of the form, no doubt in the space marked "type of aircraft." Nothing else meant anything to me. Geiger's translation would certainly help.

On January 26 a fax was waiting for me when I got to my office. It was from Dr. Inga Hosp, and I held my breath as I read it.

Dear Mrs. Dale,

Thank you for your Fax letter. Certainly I am ready for helping you, but it will take some time for the research.
After talking again with my husband who was only 6 years old when an American airplane crashed into the forest near Riggermoos/Ritten (which is called Renon by the Italians, but we are German speaking by mother language, like most of the native people in South Tyrol, which belonged to Austria until 1918, as you may know) I will first talk to my husband's elder brother Josef (born 1934) who took along his younger brother to the wrecked plane. Then I will talk to Mr. Froetscher who grew up near that place and may know more than even my husband's brother. (My husband's family lived then two miles away from the place in the village Klobenstein.) Occasionally our house, where we live since 1974, is only 200 metres away from the place. But most of all I want to talk to Mr. Ramoser (over 80 years old), who stayed at Ritten all the years throughout the war (which is not normal because most of the German speaking native people in south Tyrol had been expelled by the Italian Fascists). And after the war he had some official competencies as a kind of mayor or so—so that he could know perhaps something about the remainings, burial place, etc.
So please be so kind to wait just one or two weeks. Then I'll come over with more news.

Best wishes and yours sincerely
Inga Hosp

I could barely contain my excitement. She sounded so nice! Not one word about having been awakened in the middle of the night to answer the phone. And not only had she done her homework, she had expanded her research beyond the people we mentioned.

My Southern upbringing mandated a written, personal thank-you for her efforts, so I hand-wrote a note on stationery with a Colorado broadtail hummingbird on it and enclosed my favorite photo of Billy, the one of him kneeling down with the dog. I hoped putting a face with Billy's name would help her take my mission to heart. Photographs don't fax well, so snail-mail had to do.

I e-mailed everyone the news that Dr. Hosp was willing to help and included excerpts from her letter. Dick Kahler replied, "Looks like a good one." Jim said, "Wonderful to get such a gracious and cooperative response...As you say—how do we wait patiently for two weeks?" Jim suggested I inform Dr. Hosp of Paolo's involvement and tell Paolo we had found some potential witnesses through the tourist bureau. He didn't want anyone working at cross-purposes, and I was grateful for his foresight. Because we had found our two resources independent of each other, it was probably a good idea to keep them that way. But each should know of the other's efforts, so if they wanted to work together it would be their choice. I didn't care either way, as long as we got results.

It looked as if we were on our way.

16

TWO PATHS,
ONE DESTINATION

From: Paolo Cagnan
Sent: Friday, January 28, 2000
To: Jim Graham
Subject: Re: Pictures & letters

Hi Jim & Diana
Thank you for the pictures and the letters. I will stay abroad for about a week. When I'm back, I'll speak to a former Luftwaffe pilot who seems to know everything about the flak's activity during WWII in Alto Adige, its position and its "successes." It will be quite difficult for you to build up contacts with locals via e-mail because of the distance and the language. No one studied English here since some years ago.
I suggest the following: if you find out someone who knows (or seems to know) something, tell it immediately to me and I will talk to him personally. I think my intermediation will be the best for practical use.
Ciao

* * *

Even though Paolo's salutation was to Jim and me, his e-mail went to Jim only, so Jim forwarded it to me. It seemed to both of us Paolo was trying to keep all the contacts for himself, as a good reporter would, but we didn't feel comfortable putting him in touch with people we hadn't even had a chance to hear from, especially without their permission.

My next fax to Dr. Hosp told her about Paolo but that I had not given him her name or anyone else's, because the intrusion of one stranger in her life, me, was enough. But I did ask her permission to share with him any information she gave me "because he has worked very hard on our behalf and deserves to know the outcome." I warned her that he had offered to print a story asking for possible witnesses if other sources proved unproductive and that he may want to write a feature story about the search.

This time I sent the fax in the middle of the day so she would receive it at a "civilized" hour. I wasn't taking any chances.

Roland Geiger had translated Olson's capture report, and Jim forwarded it to me on February 1.

> formular 1a
> Data about capture of a member of an enemy air force
> Office: Flieger Horst Kommandantur (Air Base Command)
> location: Bosen
> date: Oct 23, 1944
> distribution:
> Kgf = Kriegsgefangenen = POW
> Weiterleitstelle = office responsible for leading POW from
> collection point
> to Stalag
> FLGK = (I don't know)
> Auswertestelle West = Interrogation Center, Oberursel
> Entwurf = sketch = where to be filed
> name and first name: Virgil O. Olson, born Aug 27, 1915
> rank: 1st Lt
> residence before the war: unknown
> serial number O-762394 T43 44 A (blood number and faith)
> Location and exact time of downing (downing by whom, fighter
> plane, flak?)
> on Oct 20, 1944 about 12 o'clock in the Sarn Valley
> Alpenvorland = the area in front of the Alps (no English

expression = no Alps outside Europe)
not known who shot him down
Location and exact time of capture: in the Sarn Valley
(Alpenvorland see above) on Oct 20, 1944 about 12 o'clock
Details about capture (crashed, bailed out, parachuted?): the
pilot was salvaged from the wreck of his airplane (slightly
wounded)
type of plane (exact sign of the fuselage): Lightning
Crew members (alive, dead, wounded, where do they stay): The
pilot was salvaged slightly wounded.

signature
Lt and taking-over officer

The translation didn't tell us much more than we already knew, except that Olson was captured as soon as he crashed. It took time either to process him or to get him to a central location before the report could be made. I didn't take note of the capture location, Sarn Valley, assuming it was just another name for the region surrounding the Hosp home. Thank goodness Jim was paying attention.

That same day I received my packet of regional tourist information from Peter Righi. It had a very good road map in it showing a detailed perspective view of the region, much like a Colorado ski area map, showing 3-D renderings of mountains, roads, and other landmarks. It was so detailed, in fact, I could even see the street Inga Hosp lived on. If we knew exactly where her house was on the Gebrack Road, we could pinpoint the location of the crash that they said was in front of their home.

Jim put out a request through the 71st Fighter Squadron to track down Virgil Olson. We hoped Virgil's memory of where he landed would help us narrow down the crash site. But John Mullins's response came back that he hadn't even known that Olson had been captured. He had been on the same mission, with the 94th Fighter Squadron and said that he didn't see how anyone could have survived the collision. Olson had been his classmate, and he wanted to know where Jim had found him listed as POW.

I wrote Jim, "I'm absolutely astounded John didn't know Virgil was captured and eventually returned, but we have his letters to prove it. You did mention that Olson was listed as KIA in John's book; I thought that was just an oversight. I'm glad we were able to enlighten him." I went on to say it was beginning to sound like it may have been Olson's plane that went down near Ritten, and Wisner and Twedt were the ones who blew up, but that wouldn't account for the I.D. bracelet and whatever remains were found.

Jim wrote back he, too, was astounded about Olson, saying, "If Olson had ever made contact with the 1st Ftr. Assoc. I am sure John would have heard about it. Olson apparently has made no contacts with fellow squadron members." He then theorized that perhaps it wasn't Olson who crashed at Ritten. "The translated capture report states he was found in the Sarn Valley. I also just received my tourism packet from Ritten this afternoon and have studied the maps. I assumed that the 'Sarn' was a river and the valley named for it, but I could find no Sarn River on the map. However, off to the NW of the map there are arrows pointing West to 'Sarntal/Val Sarentina.' If this nomenclature is Italian for the 'Sarn' area, it would seem that Olson may have landed over there somewhere—not near Riggermoos or Kematen/Caminata where our witnesses live." He closed with, "Come on, Frau Dr. … Tell us a story!"

Jim was a true friend. By this time I was sure his meticulous attention to detail would keep the search on track. He was also sympathetic, so I could unload my wild imaginings and erratic emotions on him, and he would understand. I wrote back that I hadn't thought to look for the Sarn Valley on a map, assuming it was in the same area as Klobenstein. I went on, "Jim, I believe things have been unfolding backwards for a reason. If there hadn't been gaps in the [Individual Deceased Personnel File], I wouldn't have gotten so tenacious about solving the mystery of the bracelet. And I never would have met you and Dick and all the other wonderful people who have been involved in the search. (And John Mullins would never have found out Olson's true story.)

"I also think the CIL file is missing for a reason—to allow us time to find the witnesses who can add a personal aspect to the story. The CIL file will eventually resurface (thanks to Bill Jordan, I hope) to complete the picture from the official military viewpoint. I'm being philosophical while we wait. Frau Dr. Hosp can take all the time she needs (within reason), to make sure the information she gets is complete. No more unanswered questions. But the time is just creeping along."

John Mullins had another thought, which he shared with Jim. "I'm surprised that neither of the other two bodies was located." Either John hadn't been paying attention or we hadn't filled him in, because one of them, Billy, had been found somewhere—that was the whole point—because we had the bracelet to prove it, or at least evidence of a bracelet. Now, if we could just figure out where it was found.

I checked a genealogy Web site to try to see if Virgil Olson was listed, alive or dead. I found a deceased one born in 1915, but it was the wrong birthday. Maybe Virgil was still alive somewhere and just wanted to put the war behind him. He'd spent six months in a German POW camp, and that's not something one would want to remember. We knew finding him wouldn't help us, because he had written Idy that he didn't even know a third plane was involved in the accident, but it would be interesting to hear his version of the crash and find out what happened during his capture and imprisonment.

It was interesting that Idy never thought to ask Olson where he was captured and take her search there. Our search relied on finding the location of the crash; hers depended solely on what the Army knew.

Jim found an e-mail address for the tourist office in the Sarn Valley, where Olson was captured. Assuming the valley was named for a river, Jim had asked about the Sarn River. The answer came back there was no such river, that the river flowing through the Sarn Valley is the Talfer/Talvera River. They included some tourist information on the valley, but it was all in German and Italian and not much help.

But Jim had also inquired about plane crashes in their valley, and it turns out that was the right question to ask.

Paolo checked in on February 7. I noticed he was calling me Diane, not Diana, a pet peeve of mine, and I thought of my grandfather's reaction whenever anyone would mispronounce his name "Wise-ner," with a long "i." Papa would say, "It's pronounced 'Wizzner.' The 'e' is silent like the 'p' in Mary."

"There's no 'p' in Mary," would come the usual reply.

And Papa would say, "That's right. And there's no 'e' in Wisner."

I wondered how long Paolo would insist on getting my name wrong. He took no note of how I spelled it in my e-mails, and it was beginning to bug me a little.

But he was making progress, thanks to information from a former Luftwaffe pilot. "It seems to be that Lt. Olson finished with his parachute on the 'Cima Santner,' in the middle of the Sciliar planos. In fact it is in the area of the crash, I mean 5 KM NE of Bolzano, at the altitude of about

2500 meter...I'll verify as soon as possible, maybe already tomorrow. It could really be the key-information!!! ciao!!!!!!!!!!!!!!"

Jim asked Paolo for more information about the Luftwaffe pilot but told me he was taking the information with a grain of salt. He couldn't find the area in his Ritten brochure, and the altitude of 2500 meters didn't jibe with the Sarn Valley in the capture report, because the whole mountain area above Ritten and the Sarn Valley is about 2300 meters. "My guess is that we should encourage him to get the former Luftwaffe pilot to give some detail of Olson's condition, capture & disposition." He cautioned against getting Paolo's information mixed up with the witnesses near Riggermoos.

That evening Jim went back to organizing his 71st Fighter Squadron records and came across another version of the crash. He was logging and correlating the group and squadron reports and had come across a supplemental one dated October 31 that had been filed with the later missions. "Group intelligence had received a tie-in from a B-17 group that was in the Bolzano area at the time of the incident your uncle was involved in. It is too ragged and fuzzy to scan for the computer, so I'll transcribe it.

> "On 20 October 1944, five miles northeast of Bolzano (4633N-1122E) at 1115 hours, 3 P-38s, 2nd Lt. Lowell S. Twedt, William O. Wisner and 1st Lt. Virgil O. Olson, were lost due to mid-air collision. Lt. Knapp, pilot of a B-17, (772nd Squadron, 463rd Bomb Group) reports two chutes were seen to open below the wreckage, from a distance. The incident was originally reported as a B-24 blowing up but further interrogation reveals that Lt. Knapp did not identify the explosion as any type of aircraft but the observation of the falling wreckage and the two chutes was the approximate time of the collision of 3 P-38s. [...]"

Idy must have heard that version, too, because she had it in her notes, but there was no indication where she had gotten it. Her sources had been a lot more thorough than I realized, and the sighting of two parachutes were what had fueled her hope.

The next morning I received Inga Hosp's fax. She had been thorough.

2000-02-08, 21.30

Dear Mrs. Dale,

Today I received your lovely wildlife letter and your uncle's
image. Thank you very much! My own son Matthias has his age
right now: 20 years! Studying veterinary medicine at Vienna
University. And just thinking that he could be involved in war
activities makes me upset. Even more: as a little girl (born 1943 in
Munich) I grew up with first childish memories of kindly
laughing American soldiers and their gifts of chewing gums, Baby
Ruth-bars and baby dolls (which could drink "milk" and even
piss). One of the old friendships from that time lasted for 50
years! But this, I guess is not what you want to hear from me.
During the last seven days I did the following:

1.- talking to all the eye-witnesses, you know already: all of
them reported that there was a lot of snow when the plane
crashed. This is unusual for the altitude (1350m) and for
October but could have occurred nevertheless. All of them
reported two soldiers who saved themselves by parachutes, and
one dead between the wreckage; the parachute jumpers being
arrested by German security SOD (South Tyrol by this time,
after Mussolini's end, was occupied by German troops), the
corpse and other remainings transported away;

2.- calling the local priest; no registration of a grave;

3.- contacting Black Cross organisation; they look after soldiers'
graves. The research is still going on.

I'll now try to get contact to a former American Airforce officer
living at Innsbruck who is said to own lists of crashed American
aircrafts in this part of the Alps. Let me, please, check if this is a
mere rumour or more. I also want to know which other aircrafts
crashed in our region round Oct. 20, 1944. The only
newspaper, I've been told, did not report such events, but I
want to check personally in a library and in an archive. All this
will need some time, but I won't give up, and I think you
would do the same for me: question of humanitarianism.

While I write this, your fax letter arrived. Strange thing: I am a
journalist myself, free lancer and working more in the fields of
culture, and have no primal interest to write about the case.

And perhaps the results could increase if the reporter goes his
way and I go mine. So let's leave it like it is now.
To me it seems important not to rely too much upon the
conviction that the Ritten aircraft was your uncle's. By the way: Do
you have any personal file, numbers like those, every soldier had?
That's all for today, more soon, I hope.
Yours sincerely
Inga
P.S. Last weekend my new I-Mac has been delivered, so we now
can correspond by e-mail, too: [...]
PPS. I wonder what's the job you are doing, Diana.

I was so excited I nearly fell over myself responding by e-mail. I had
made a new friend, and I wanted to nurture the relationship. I gave her the
details of the crash and what we'd found out so far, filled her in on some
information about me, and then congratulated her on going on-line. I
signed the e-mail, "Fondly," because I was fond of her already.

I told Jim what she had said, and he got excited, too, saying we now
had another member of the team. But he cautioned us to "tread softly." He
suggested feeding her some of the mission documentation to "give her a
better feel for the incident and to get her 'hooked' on the mystery of the
search." I should feel her out on her willingness to be included as part of
the team and warn her that the result would be "multilateral e-mail messages." We don't want to overload her, he added.

He suggested getting Dr. Hosp's Innsbruck contact to tie in with
Roland Geiger, who had helped Jim earlier in our search. "They might
have a lot of mutual interest. I hope she can identify him. It would be good
to get some of these parallel efforts going. One danger might be that they
might walk all over each other."

I was grateful for Jim's discretion. He had just the right touch when
it came to working with people for maximum cooperation. I, on the other
hand, was buzzing when I wrote back. "Of course, all kinds of wild scenar-
ios are going through my head—if his was one of the parachutes and he
survived, was captured, then died in a POW camp, that would explain the
bracelet. But, then, so would the scenario of his being killed in the crash
and being 'disposed of' by the Germans. (And if his plane was hit by falling
debris, there's a good chance his canopy was damaged and he couldn't
parachute out.) But why would they take a body (or what's left of one) all

the way to Griesheim? I forgot to check the location of the POW camp Olson was taken to. Was it near Griesheim? I've got to stop thinking about it and just focus on what we know to be true." I sent Jim a copy of my e-mail to Inga.

On February 9 Jim's query about crashes in the Sarn Valley came in an answer, with some creative spelling, from the Sarn Valley Tourist Bureau. "After a few day of researches I have Information of 3-4 airplanes that went down in the Sarnvalley during the Second Worldwar. In one or two days I can send you a detailed map of the areas. Today a friend of mine will send you a detailed information of one airplane that was shut down by a German Flack. I need informations about the P-38 Lightning of Mr. Olson, I need to know how many pilots or soldiers have place in the P-38 Lightning. I hope you can understand my english." It was signed Mair Christoph.*

Jim wrote back immediately and introduced himself. "I am a 76-year-old former P-38 pilot in World War II and am doing some historical research on my squadron's lost pilots. Your assistance is very much appreciated. I would be pleased to know just a bit about you to assist in our e-mail conversation." He said he hoped he was writing in a manner that could be understood and thanked him for his research. He promised the eyewitness report and attached a photo of a P-38, adding, "There is only one person that flies in the P-38. He is the pilot, and he sits over the wing in the cockpit between the two engine fuselages. The color of the planes that crashed were probably silver as in the photo, but the back part of each of the two fuselages would have been painted black."

Jim also wrote Roland Geiger to ask about Griesheim's location and whether it was near the POW camp where Olson was taken. Once again, I was way off base. It's a good thing I wasn't controlling the search. The POW camp was Stalag Luft VIIA near Moosburg, which was 200 miles from Griesheim. But since we were making such good progress, I wasn't too disappointed that my theory was wrong.

Meanwhile, Paolo told Jim that the Luftwaffe pilot had given him second-hand information. But he was "quite sure that the 'parachute story' is the Olson's story, but I need more informations; if it is the right story, I'll

---

*Names in Europe are commonly written with the surname first, then given name. This gave us some confusion at first, and we would address this young man as "Mair," thinking that was his first name.

have made half of my job: locate the area of the crash. My intention is to know where Lt. Olson was captured, where the Wisner's P-38 crashed and so on. I know it could only be an illusion, but the area is correct, there was a flak in Castelrotto on the Altopiano dello Sciliar, controlling the air-floor in the middle Val d'Isarco, which is 5 KM NE of Bolzano. I hope so…"

At the same time Jim received a response from someone else at the Sarn Valley Tourist Office. We were creating quite a stir in the neighborhood. "Hello Mr. Jim Graham," the e-mail began. "My name is Göller Andreas and I am a friend of Mair Christoph, that is the teenager that make the practise job on the tourist office in the Sarnvalley, where you have asked Herr Perkmann about some information during the second world war. We two go to the same school and at the moment we have only two weeks something like a practise job at some offices in our valley. We are very interested in your research and so we both the last days worked very hard on your questions, but now to our results about this historical event."

He and Christoph had checked the archives in the valley with no success, then went to the Bolzano library to look for news items dated October 21. Still no luck. But Andreas said he had even better information. "My grandfather was witnessed of this crash of the airplane, at this time he was 14 years old and his father at this time was a 'Sodmann' (that means he had to work at something like a soldier for Hitler) here in the Sarnvalley. So the american airplane with the pilot Virgil O. Olson was shot by a german Flak (that was a big cannon or gun). This Flak was situated on the mountain (the exact place is called Kirchkorn in german), it is a place in the mountains between Pens and Durnholz (this are two short valleys of the big Sarnvalley). So when the american airplane was took by the shot of the Flak so the airplane began to smoke and my grandfather saw also that [about]. 3 or 4 persons made a parachute jump out of the airplane. The airplane afterward crashed to a mountain it's called in dialect german Garmesegg and there the pilot was capture, he has not big hurts. The other three american soldiers were founded in the mountains of Durnholz and also captured by german soldiers, also the other american soldier was captured."

He wished Jim luck and said he hoped he could understand everything, "because my English is not so good."

Sadly, Jim had to inform Andreas that his grandfather had seen the wrong plane. "Your description of the airplane knocked down by flak is probably not the one we are looking for, because the P-38 had only one man in it. There were two other P-38's in the air crash, so there were 3 pilots that came down, and at least one parachuted (maybe two), but we think the third one crashed in his plane."

It looked as if the Sarn Valley might be the wrong place to look if the only plane that had crashed there was the bomber at Garmesegg.

Two more places not to look came in the only letter I received from one of the climbing schools I had written months before. A Mr. Karl Lanthaler had taken the time to research his area, but all he could find was information on a crash in late March/early April 1944, 40 km north-north-west of Bolzano and another on January 5, 1945, 25 km west of Bolzano. At least, that's what I think the letter said, because it was in German. Since the dates didn't coincide with our crash, I didn't pass the information along or try to get the letter translated.

I received Inga's first e-mail. She told me she had grown up in upper Bavaria. "I am glad not to be a Nazi's daughter," she said. "My father was an architect and oppositional as can be to the regime. So after the war Americans were his 'natural' friends." She had studied literature and theater at Vienna University, and she and husband Bruno, a politician and member of the autonomous provincial government for cultural affairs, would celebrate their 30th anniversary that summer. She went on, "As you perhaps know, the province of South Tyrol or, Italian, Alto Adige, is inhabited by three ethnic groups: the German speaking (which we belong to) as the largest (about 300,000 people), the Ladins (oldest, but smallest group, about 20,000, speaking an old Alpine language similar to Provençal) and the Italians (about 170,000 people, most of their ancestors immigrated between World War I and II). To protect the "German" (which is, historically, an Austrian minority, because our region belonged to Austria until 1918) and Ladin minority we enjoy a far ranging political autonomy including school education from Kindergarten up to the High School level. My activities are formed by organizing cultural events, writing and broadcasting (for the Bavarians, too), but I try to reduce this more and more—so I can say I just work now for my own pleasure. I have written several books, but unfortunately no one is in English. My family is formed by my husband Bruno, son Matthias, daughter Julia (22, studying microbiology at Vienna) and 15-year-old Siamese cat named Thai.

"Concerning the main object of our correspondence I am glad to tell you that I found another person to deal with your inquiry, Mr. Keith Bullock, American, married to a Tyrolean lady in the northern part of Tyrol (i.e. in the Austrian part) who was involved in other, similar inquiries and has special knowledge about American bombers operating in Northern Italy during World War II."

It was so nice to know more about her. I had worried that I might run into some loyalty to the Third Reich, but I certainly didn't have the courage (or insensitivity) to ask. Besides, I wasn't stupid; I needed her help. But I was relieved her family had opposed Hitler.

Inga gave me Keith Bullock's address and told me she had sent him parts of my letters concerning my uncle and hoped it had been all right to do so. She, too, closed her e-mail with "Fondly." What a lovely lady.

I wrote to tell her about Jim and his role in our project and asked her to share Jim's name and e-mail address with Keith Bullock so they might collaborate on other research. I also told her about the Carl Hoenshell case, pointed her toward the Web site story on him, and told her Jim had been in Billy's squadron and how valuable Jim was to me. It was nice to be able to forward Inga's messages to Jim in their entirety instead of having to transcribe her faxes.

But I couldn't do that for Paolo; I had to respect Inga's wishes for Paolo to "go his way" and keep her identity from him. We had to see to it that he got Inga's research second-hand.

On February 10 Christoph Mair answered Jim's message. He would soon complete his internship at the Sarn Valley Tourist Bureau and wanted to give Jim his home e-mail address and some information about himself. "I am an 18 year old boy, and I attend a commercial school in Bolzano. At the moment I am here in the Tourist Office to make two weeks of practice, to learn more about business. ...My interests are history, the armed forces and technology. I hope you have received the e-mail from my friend, about a aircraft, that came from north and was shut down by a german Fluck. As soon as possible I will send you a map of our area with the crashpoints. At least I want say you that I can understand your language, my mother language is German, my second language is Italian and the third is English."

Andreas Göller wrote Jim the same day. "Yes the computer was able to show us the picture (photo) of the P-38. It's also true that the story that I have told you in the last e-mail is not correct, because my grandfather said also that in this airplane were eight people, because it was a Bomber."

Andreas went on to answer some of the questions Jim had asked him. "Yes our first language here is German, the second one is Italian and the third one is English. So we studied English only for three years at school and our written English is not so good. I think my speak much better in

English, because I was four months ago in America (New York, Washington and Amherst).

"So I hope you will find more information about the event, and it would be perfect if you let us know all of the research that you make, because it is a very interesting historical adventure."

The next day Christoph reported in again: "A friend told to me that during the summer, when he must going in the mountain, he can see pieces of aircrafts and a big railgun. I must now ask him better." Then, later that day, came the message, "With luck we have found the aircraft you are searching...One of the pilots was arrested by the german army, his right foot was in a bad situation but he could walk. I have another information about a pilot, I think but I am not secure, he died in the crash, men found his body without live. I hope to can give you further information next week, when I have spoken with the persons who saw the pilots and aircrafts in 1944. The first information can underline the date and the time when the aircrafts crashed. Can you tell me how was the [weather] 20.10.1944 with sun or rain."

Jim answered Christoph that night and said, "The weather was clear and visibility unlimited, so the sun was likely shining at 11:20 AM ..." He asked Christoph if he would question the witnesses to find out if there were any pieces of the aircraft still around. "Sometimes the people liked to save a small remembrance of the event. We would also like to know the details and people who were the first to find the pilot who parachuted to the ground."

This looked promising.

17

THE PATHS CONVERGE

From:	Dr. Inga Hosp
Sent:	Saturday, February 12, 2000
To:	Diana Dale
Subject:	Lost Uncle

Dear Diana,

More news, fresh as can be, and: the puzzle is complete!

Half an hour ago I got a phone call from Mr. Hans Grimminger from Augsburg/Germany who studied, for another research some years ago, the Washington Archives. He found the missing link in his computer. William O Wisner was one of four members of 1st. Fighter Group-Lightnings, downed Oct. 20, 1944 after being hit over Bozen/Bolzano some miles north of Sarnthein, near the village of Weißenbach. The pilots' names are Olsen [sic] (71st. Fighter Squadron, Nr. 9314), Tweed [sic] (9313), Elliot (he brought down his plane near Ancona in an emergency landing) and Wisner (9312). In the Missing Aircrew Report he is mentioned as "lost". Also the German reports (Abschußberichte) which are in Washington, too, mention the loss under [their number] KSUJ 2323.

After several interviews I did during the last days I was already almost sure that the plane crashed near our house at Ritten was not your uncle's; this must have been a bomber and it must have been during winter 44.

Before starting this letter I phoned a friend in the neighboured

community of Sarntal/Val Sarentino who will do the local inquiry
for me. About next Wednesday I will be ready to give you the rest
of the details. The research concerning the grave will go on.
Please be so kind to contact Mr. Grimminger. He was a member
of the 15 Luftflotte and did much research for both Americans
and Germans. Perhaps he would be pleased by a thankful word.
His address [...]
Best regards until soon
Inga

* * *

At last we had confirmation from the "other side," the Germans, and it matched everything we knew so far. Inga's message had arrived February 14th, and it was the best Valentine's Day greeting I could have imagined.

I thanked Inga and told her about the two students we had found in the Sarn Valley. I didn't want them to cross paths unexpectedly, and I thought she might be more willing to work with them than with a reporter.

I then wrote Hans Grimminger to thank him for his research. My letter was two pages long, but I thought he needed to know why this search was so important to me.

Jim agreed that a loop had been closed on Sarn Valley and said he'd send Keith Bullock, the pilot in Austria, a summary of the mission and ask for his research on that area.

Jim also told me he would be going on a trip in a few days and wouldn't be back until after the first of March but would try to stay in touch. I panicked at the thought of being without my guidance system for two weeks.

Inga wrote the next day saying she had already tried to get in touch with Christoph Mair. He had left the tourist office, so she left a message at his home to call her.

"In the meantime," she went on, "a friend in the Sarn valley did a research for me which proved the three crashes and the localizations. Christoph will look after the local details so that we do no double work. Is that o.k.? Until now we are rather sure only about Olson's way down from the crash point high up in the mountains down to the street where he seems to be taken as POW. It is a pity that we couldn't research some years earlier, because most of the eyewitnesses now are dead. My friend has been said that one of the two victims was buried at the crash point, and that the other one died during the transport to the next village, Weißenbach. But who was who? Anyway: we won't give up."

Thank goodness she was as tenacious as we were. I was so grateful and thrilled she had made contact with Christoph already, I wrote her back immediately. I asked if her friend could identify the three crash sites on a detailed map. Jim already knew where Virgil Olson's plane had hit, but I wasn't sure he knew the other two sites had been identified. I also asked for more details on which pilots died in the crash and which died during transport.

"Who was who, indeed?" I echoed. "It will be good to find out what happened to the bodies of both of them. Is there some official record of what was done in those days? I'm sure the Germans have records somewhere, but did the local government keep any files?" I told her about the search in 1948, that no crash sites were found, but that 14 bodies had been removed from a cemetery in Mirandola. I asked her if Mirandola was near the Sarn Valley and would it have been a logical place to bury unknown foreigners.

"You're right;" I went on, "It is a shame we didn't do this years ago. My grandmother never gave up hope, but by 1950 she stopped writing the government and the embassies, having gained no more information. But I really don't think this would have been possible without today's Internet. It would have taken so long to get correspondence back and forth, the immediacy would be lost and enthusiasm would diminish. Every incorrect lead would have used too much time. With the Internet, a dead end is just a fork in the road that is easily corrected with little time wasted."

I hoped my mother would stay healthy long enough for us to have some answers. It was getting close to the time when she and Daddy would be in Colorado at their mountain cabin for the summer. I was looking forward to telling them the whole story, face to face.

Keith Bullock wrote me, prompted by Inga's inquiries. She had told him some of my personal information, too, no doubt to open the channels of communication and encourage his cooperation. But while he would have been a great resource for bomber crashes, he had no information on P-38s. He told me he was British, not with the U.S. Army Air Force but the Royal Air Force. He had adopted Austria as his home, having married a woman from North Tyrol, and he spent his time researching Flying Fortresses (B-17Gs) and Liberators (B-24s). I liked his sense of humor and hoped I could meet him some day. His last paragraph included a bit of a dig at Jack. "I close by wishing you, your husband and your seven animals, would love to have written and *seven other animals*, but as I am not sure how big Jack is and if he is of the aggressive nature I didn't, but I did, sorry, Jack, British (80% English 20% Scottish) humour will out at times..."

I answered his questions in a too-long e-mail, but I sensed he was a good audience. I added that when Jack had read his last paragraph, he replied, "Tell [Keith] I'm deeply offended, and if I could slip my leash and get out of my collar I'd bite him on the ankle."

Inga received more information from Christoph on the 16th. He had been busy, and she and he were now working together. A snowfall postponed their visit. Her home was at 1350 meters (4,455 feet), half an hour's drive up from Bolzano, at 350 meters. Christoph's home was at an elevation somewhere in between, around 1,000 meters, so the terrain was interesting, to say the least.

Christoph had asked for a photo of Billy and wanted to know how tall he was and the color of his hair, as a result of some interviews he had conducted. Inga wrote, "One of the downed dead Sarn valley Pilots is remembered as with red hair. Your uncle could have been the other one. Without being too optimistic: perhaps these informations could help. But I don't want to speculate. After he would have received the image and done more interviews I'll go down to his place and talk to him personally. And I'll gather picture postcards, a map and so on and send it to you."

I told Inga I would e-mail Billy's photo to Christoph. It was a good opportunity to thank him personally for his work. I said I didn't know what color hair Lowell Twedt had, but I told Inga I would scan my photo of him and send it to Christoph, too.

Keith Bullock e-mailed a reply, re-emphasizing how sorry he was that he couldn't help. But something else was coming out of his contact with Inga. "I have already sent her six possibilities of crashes in and around Bolzano (Bozen) with the hope that one of them may have been the one that her husband witnessed," he said. I thought it would be great if Inga could find out about the crash in her front yard, too.

Meanwhile, in the excitement of the discoveries in the Sarn Valley, I had forgotten about Paolo. We hadn't heard from him in quite a while, and I assumed it was because he was covering other stories. But his February 18th e-mail said he had been busy traveling the region, only researching ours. He said he would have liked to tell us that he'd found the exact location of the crash, but was still investigating. "You know, working with this kind of oral and written sources is quite difficult: believe me, it's almost impossible to find documents regarding this case. I couldn't even find the exact location of every Flak group in this Land, because of the absolute lack of informations: every piece of paper was destroyed.

"Working with the oral history is hard, too, because everyone remembers different things in a different way and different times. In addition, most of the male locals which are now 70-80 years old were abroad—mostly in Russia—during WWII. So, almost no direct witnesses of the events. As I've already told you, I establish that the crash location, I mean 5 km NE of Bolzano, should be between the middle Isarco valley and two planos [plateaus]: Renon and Sciliar. Speaking with a former Luftwaffe pilot, he told me that he has heard many times the story/legend of an American pilot, who [landed] with his parachute on some rocks in the middle of the Sciliar, at about 2500 metres, during 1944. He was 'saved' by local climbers and then captured by the Germans."

He thought that could have been Olson but needed more information. "Specially, I needed the remains of the Wisner's P-38. I spoke to many locals, then I simply decided to go there, arranging some meetings. I did it Thursday, with the former Luftwaffe pilot—Anton Weissteiner—and a journalist—Giancarlo Ansaloni—who has been lived there, between the villages of Siusi and Castelrotto, for many years.

"After a very hard day, interviewing about ten people, I still don't know if I've found the solution or not. I have to distinguish between real facts, legends and mental confusion after so many years. So, I'm trying to give you the most objective picture of what I got. It's absolutely sure that an American airplane crashed in the area in 1944. It crashed in the middle of some trees in San Costantino, few houses between the villages of Fiè and Siusi. It crashed during the daytime: it could have been around 11.30, that means 'our' time. Apparently, no one can distinguish between a fighter and a bomber, but many locals think it was a fighter. Two or three persons remember that the airplane, which was partially in flames, circled around the villages of Fiè and Siusi at about 300 meters, before crashing between the trees with a very noisy ground impact. I would say, it couldn't have been a B-17 or a B-24."

It seems Paolo's research had led him to the same expert Inga had found. "I spoke to Keith Bullock, a former RAF pilot which lives in Tyrol. He made a list of the allied bombers-crashes in the area (only bombers, unfortunately) and he has no informations regarding this case. After the crash, many locals went there, as you can imagine. And many took several pieces of the airplane. I found one piece, which was used by a local farmer to create a monument made by this piece and other bomb-pieces. It's what we call a 'longherone,' which I can't translate into English. It's a tube with this characteristics: it's about 120 cm long, it has a square shape and a diametre of 5-6 cm. Weissteiner believes that an expert of the USAAF could determine if it was part of a P-38."

He said he had taken some photos and would send us scans of them in a few days. "The farmer— [who] is 73—thinks that some remains could still be there, but we should wait for the good season (now it's snowing) and try to locate them, maybe with a metal detector which I don't have. Speaking about the period, many locals believe that it could be October, but a local historian—not a professional one, a retired teacher—wrote a book in which he set the event in July, 1944. If he's right, we're wrong and the case is closed."

But Paolo thought he had the right location. "Many locals remember that a corpse was found inside the plane. Only one corpse. So again, it couldn't have been a bomber. Was it Wisner's body? I tried to find an indication in the official documentation of the local cemetery, 'cause someone told me that the body was buried there, before it was given to the Americans, probably in 1946. I have to check the reports of the local Town council. It could be the best way to find out the truth. I'll do it in the next week, 'cause it was closed."

One thing didn't fit our story, though, and it bothered him. "Now the biggest problem: no one seems to have noticed an explosion in the air (Olson's plane against Twedt's plane) but many—almost all—remember that two pilots went down on parachute. The first, as I told you, finished between the rocks at about 2500 m. The second it's another stuff, because everyone has different memories. Someone it's not sure that the two episodes (the crash in San Costantino and the two parachutes) happened the same day. And all this is very confusing. One survivor it's enough: it could have been Olson and it were 'perfect': Wisner died, Olson survived and was captured. But what about the second prisoner?"

Of course, by now we had information Paolo didn't: the location of Olson's capture. And that was his next question. He also wanted to know if we were absolutely sure Twedt had died in the crash. He wondered if his remains were never recovered, how could we be sure he wasn't also captured. And one of the locals had told Paolo he thought one of the prisoners was "a coloured: what about Twedt and Olson?"

He was excited. "If that's 'our' case," he added, "I would feel like a Pulitzer-winner. If not, I'll have to start again. But don't worry, in every case I'll survive!!!"

I was relieved Paolo would survive, because we now had evidence proving he was wrong. While he had been investigating his leads we had focused quite a distance west of where he was looking. I was guessing, though, and without a good map I couldn't be sure.

Nevertheless, I didn't want him chasing a wild goose if he didn't have to, so I told him about the capture report that put Olson in the Sarn Valley and answered the rest of his questions to the best of my ability. Working at a full-time job, I was not as organized as Jim or able to pull records the way he could. But I knew for sure that Twedt had died, and I told Paolo that. I also told him I was waiting for Twedt's file, which might give us some more information about his disappearance and what happened to his remains. At the very least I could tell him there was no doubt both Twedt and Olson were white. The U.S. military wasn't desegregated until the Korean Conflict, and the only African-American pilots at that time were the Tuskeegee Airmen.

I also tried to correct Paolo's spelling of my name by signing off, "Diana, like the princess *(come la principessa)*." Perhaps the association would help.

With everything I sent him, Paolo was now armed with the same information as the rest of us. I e-mailed Jim to let him know Paolo had re-surfaced, and I attached Paolo's e-mail. But there was no response. Wherever Jim was, he didn't have his computer hooked up.

I forwarded Paolo's message to Inga, who had already checked the area he had been investigating. She wrote to tell me about it.

"Our 'newspaper reporter,' as you call him, is really on the wrong side: If you check the Ritten map you got by the local tourism office, you will see that Ritten is in between the two localities: the Schlern (what Cagnan calls Sciliar) side, and the Sarn valley. 'Our' crash has nothing to do with the one near Völs in July 1944 (what he calls 'Fiè,' as the Italian version; but this is the moment for you to know that after WW I, when the South Tyrol became part of Italy, and during the Italian Fascist period, the old names were moved to Italian versions; Völs got moved to Fiè, Ritten to Renon, Sarntal to Sarentino, and so on). But the ex-teacher he mentions is the one I called (because I knew he once was researching about the Völs crash) and he led me to Mr. Grimminger at Augsburg who was the one who solved the puzzle. But the Völs-event is fully researched, reported and solved; the ex-teacher has sent me his report."

She went on, "No doubt: We have to look after your uncle's further fate in the Sarn valley. And therefore I have given a short article (which will be published without my name but in personal contact to the editor) to a Sunday paper in German language (you should know: the Italian-speaking population is mainly at Bozen/Bolzano town, the German-speaking spread over the whole region) to help Christoph Mair with his interviews. But there are no names of the 'investigators'! As I told you, I am not interested in this case as a journalist, there's only human interest! And no 'Pulitzer ambitions' at all!!"

She closed saying it had turned into a wonderful evening, so her husband and some friends were heading out for a toboggan ride under the full moon.

An evening toboggan ride in the Alps. What a lovely scenario! I felt we had formed a friendship and thought I could vent some frustration on her, as I would any close girlfriend. I told Inga my weekend had been just the opposite of hers. "I spent the weekend baby-sitting the electricians who were upgrading our wiring, baby-sitting some friends' neurotic dog who is staying the week while they're out of town, baby-sitting a very needy parrot who gets more so when Jack is out of town, and baby-sitting an elderly cat who is now being fed through a tube that goes into his neck and down into his stomach. Come to think of it, it wasn't a nice weekend, at all. After wading through four dogs and having to stop every hour or two to 'feed' the cat, I felt like I didn't accomplish a thing. It was as if I was being nibbled to death by ducks."

The article Inga mentioned worried me. I thought her idea of using a neighborhood newspaper to help Christoph was a good, because it might flush out more witnesses, but I feared it would alienate Paolo. After all, he had come into the investigation before Inga, and now she was beating him to the story. I hoped her local paper was one Paolo didn't read.

In the meantime, Paolo e-mailed everyone a photo of what he found in the Isarco Valley, but once again he left me out of the distribution of the message. I found out about it when Dick Kahler sent me a copy of his response to Paolo. Bill Mays wrote Dick he thought the part Paolo had found looked like a strut, which should have a serial number, and if Paolo could get the number, Dick could determine if the part came from a P-38.

But it was beginning to look like a moot point. We all were zeroing in on the Sarn Valley, and I told Paolo so. He wrote back, undaunted, and opened his e-mail with an exuberant, "Ciaooooooo!

"Sorry Diane but I was so excited that I deleted your message for mistake. The news are very important, because I know very well where the Sarntal is: not far away from Bolzano, in the area which I determined exactly in the 'map' I sent to you. But it has nothing to do with the area I was investigating some days ago: that means that my story should be wrong for the two parachutes, not for the air-crash in San Costantino.

"It's possible in theory that the P-38 with your uncle crashed where I told you, that the 'parachute story' it's another war-episode and that Olson landed in Sarentino. All of this is not incompatible, because of the small air-distance. Our group seems to be very efficient, don't you think so? The capture report says that it was impossible to determine from whom the plane was hit. Olson was lightly injured. I will immediately go to Sarntal to look for further documents in the archive of the village: it's possible that they could find a connection between the Olson's capture and the crash, which could have happened in the same area. If you have some news, tell me as soon as possible." He closed with, "Ciao principessa."

At least Paolo was open-minded about the crash location, but he had missed the point entirely about my name and was now calling me "princess." He must have thought I had some grand illusion about myself. Instead of belaboring the point, I thanked him for his hard work and told him I hoped it would pay off in a very good story for him, whether it was the right place to look, or not.

He wrote back the next day, having read Olson's capture report. "No parachute at all", he said. "It's written that the pilot was 'rescued' from the remains of its Lightning. That means only one thing: Anderson was wrong when he spoke about a collision between Olson's and Twedt's planes. No explosion in the air. No deflagration. Olson landed in the Sarntal Valley, and landed so softly that he could survive the crash. The valley is mountainous with lots of trees. I can't imagine how could the P-38 land in this territory, but we have to believe that the German report is correct."

I had to agree with him there. The Germans were nothing if not precise in their recordkeeping.

My hope that Paolo wouldn't find out about Inga's story didn't last long. He went on, "Today I had a very bad surprise: a local German-speaking newspaper wrote the story, for the first time. The article says that three

P-38 were hit by the FLAK in the Sarntal Valley. It doesn't mention any remains of both the other two airplanes and pilots. I was very disappointed: this was 'my' story. I think, it was <u>Inga Hosp</u> who gave the information to the newspaper. Have you ever heard from her? She is the wife of a local German politician. Someone told me two weeks ago that she was investigating the case, too. I tried to reach her, but I couldn't. Maybe, she doesn't want to speak to me. Actually, I don't know what she knows. Do you?"

I felt my color rise as I read between the lines. Paolo felt betrayed. But he didn't stay down long, and as a good reporter would, took it in stride. "Tomorrow morning I'll go to Sarntal and look for any document. Please, if you are in touch with several other locals, tell it to me. I don't want to be the only one, but I worked very hard at this case and my editor will fire me if he knows that another newspaper publish the story at first, after all of my work."

I don't know why I hadn't warned Paolo about the article. Perhaps it all happened too fast. If Jim had been in the loop, maybe it wouldn't have happened. I felt awful about Paolo's getting "scooped" by Inga. I was positive I told him there were others working on the research and that my other contact didn't want to be approached by him. But even though all's fair in love and newsgathering, I still felt guilty.

I sent Paolo's e-mail to Inga and said, "It seems I've hurt him, and I didn't mean to. He has worked hard on this, and he deserves to publish his story…I hope the newspaper that published it doesn't compete directly with Paolo's. I would never forgive myself if he loses his job."

By this time, everything was happening so fast, I could barely keep track. I needed Jim's steadying hand, and he was still out of reach. I sent Jim every e-mail, anyway, and I tried to imitate his diplomacy when I smoothed Paolo's ruffled feathers.

I admitted to Paolo I knew Inga and told him how we had gotten her name. I said I hadn't mentioned her to him because the information on the crash her husband had seen turned out to be a dead end.

Then I came clean. "She did tell me she was a free-lance writer, but I had no idea she was going to write a story until today, when I got an email from her telling me she had already done it. I'm very, very sorry. I had told her at the beginning you were working on research for us and asked if you might contact her. She declined, as she said, 'for now,' but I assumed that was to protect her privacy. She has been very helpful to us even though 'her' crash was the wrong one. With the scope and complicated nature of the search, we didn't want to turn down anyone willing to help."

I added, "Please continue your work. I know your story will be very thorough and accurate…If your editor is angry with you, blame me. Of course, our purpose is not to get a good story, but to get the answers we need, so we will take all the help we can get."

I told him when Jim got back in town he'd have more for him and told him about Christoph, adding I would ask permission for Paolo to contact him directly.

I wanted to ease Paolo's bruised ego, so I said, "Your analysis of Olson's capture report is very interesting. No one else caught the fact that he was rescued from his plane. We always assumed the parachute was his. That makes the question of my uncle's fate even more puzzling. More than one eyewitness said they saw either one or two chutes, depending on who's telling the story. But there was a lot going on when the incident happened, so everyone could have been mistaken."

I thanked Paolo for staying in there despite the setback we had caused and told him I had sent a copy of his e-mail to Inga. "Perhaps she will get in touch with you now," I added.

This had turned into a diplomatic soap opera. Understanding there is no love lost between the Germanic people and the Italians, I knew I was treading a fine line, but I needed both Inga's and Paolo's help. If two people were investigating the same story from different angles we could get twice the information, possibly reaching our goal from two different starting-points, and each would corroborate the other's.

But as the tension mounted between the two, I found myself wailing, "Jim, where are you?" and even sent him e-mails with that heading. But still no response.

Inga faxed me her article, and I was relieved to see how short it was. But it was in German, so I ran it through my translation software to get the gist of it, then later got the translation refined with the help of one of my sister's students.

In the article Inga told the story of the crash and my search for Billy, and asked a lot of questions in a dramatic writing style (or at least that's what the translation seems to reveal). Her closing paragraph summed up my feelings: "If help can come for a former enemy, perhaps it is a small work of kindness."

Thank goodness it wasn't in-depth, less than 400 words. It was just enough information to get local people interested, but it wouldn't detract from Paolo's lengthy investigative story. And maybe it would flush out some more answers.

By February 22 Paolo had rebounded and was back on the case, this time in the right location. The paths were coming together. He said, "I think we are really next to the truth.

"Yesterday I went to Sarntal, where Olson was captured. A fighter hit by the flak crashed between some trees at about 1200 meters, after having flew over the village of Sarentino at about 2-300 meters of altitude. Old locals are remembering of one dead pilot and two parachutes. These two pilots were both captured and immediately transfer to Bolzano, where—as you know—I live.

"One is certainly Olson, the other could have been either Twedt or Wisner. There are still two or three direct witnesses. I will speak to them next Friday. I will go to the place of the crash, too. This place called 'Garmesegg Wiesen' is quite isolated, about half an hour of hike or trek, I don't know. There is still a piece of the airplane, next to a hut. I'll find it and take some pictures for documentation."

He added that he had no idea who the dead pilot was, but he did ascertain that he was not buried at the local cemetery. The people of Sarentino had been very cooperative. "I suggest, if everything goes right it will be possible to organise a ceremony in the next summer. Maybe, to put there a small monument or something else for all the people who died making their duty during WWII and against every war."

How sweet. He was taking our story to heart. And he added a bit of trivia to the capture report. "I can tell you that the document you sent to me is coming from Wetzlar, a small town north of Frankfurt. It used to be a 'transit camp' for the air officer[s] captured during WWII. Olson arrived there at the 23rd of October 1944: quite a long journey from South Tyrol. The document doesn't come directly from the FLAK: that means that it could be not so precise, speaking about Olson being extracted from the remains of the Lightning. It could be decisive to obtain informations regarding Twedt."

His e-mail had attached five photos of a monument near San Costantino, one of the villages he had investigated. He thought one of the pieces incorporated into the sculpture might be from a P-38, even if it wasn't one from our crash.

The monument was an abstract sculpture assembled from wreckage and bomb scraps, but it was unmistakable as a G.I. wearing a helmet and holding his weapon at present arms. A plaque, which I couldn't read, probably dedicated it to the people who had lost their lives either in that crash or in the area during the war. It was touching someone would take the time and trouble to erect such a monument in a place where so few Americans would see it. But, then, war touches everyone's lives, no matter their loyalty.

I sent Paolo the transcript of Inga's article to let him see that it was a different kind of story than he was going for. Thankfully, my anxiety over his reaction had been unfounded. Paolo had thick skin and a strong ego.

"Don't worry: everything is OK," he said. "The 'diplomatic incident' is closed. I could imagine what happened with Mrs. Hosp and you gave me yesterday a confirmation. So, the article was written directly by Mrs. Hosp, who won't be able to make what I did. I want to tell you that not only am I looking for a good story, but also I feel to be part of a great group. I mean, I feel as [if] I have always known you. This cooperation it's a very nice experience, in the sense of human contacts. I'll remember it, hoping I could be proud to have helped.

"Now back to the research. The name of the student is Christoph, but I wasn't able to reach him because I don't know his address nor his e-mail at school. As I told you, Friday I'll spend my day-off going to the Sarntal, taking pictures and interviewing the former direct witnesses. If we are lucky, Friday night we could have THE FINALE SOLUTION. If not, we'll investigate further."

So Paolo figured out who the student was. That was good. I had written Christoph about Paolo, but he hadn't answered any of my e-mails so I didn't know if they had connected or not. Now neither Paolo nor Christoph would be blind-sided, and since Christoph was working with Inga, too, I hoped the awkward situation would ease a bit.

I told Paolo I was grateful for his reassurance. I had lost sleep worrying that I had handled the conflict poorly, but all I was trying to do was respect everyone's wishes.

On February 25 he reported in again, saying it would be brief, because he was very tired. "In two different places in Sarntal I founded one oxygen-cylinder(?), another unidentified small piece of a fighter, two wheels Goodyear and some cartridges. Everything has a numeration. I measured all the pieces and took many pictures which shows very good the objects." He promised a complete report on Sunday and photos and I.D. numbers on Monday. He went on, "No one seems to have died in the accident. No witness reports of dead pilots, many report of two or more parachute[s]. But the story is more complicated: I'll tell you. I believe 75% this is 'our' story." He closed by saying Monday would be my D-Day.

But this was curious. Two or more parachutes didn't seem right. The Garmesegg name didn't register as the site Andreas Göller's grandfather had seen the bomber crash. I needed Jim's critical thinking again, but he was still incommunicado.

The next day I got Inga's report of her journey to the Sarn Valley. In all her previous e-mails she had put "Lost Uncle" in the subject line. On this February 26th e-mail she had written "Found Uncle." My heart was in my throat as I read it.

Dear Diana,

The following is only for you because Christoph and I made this research for you and for your mother—not for a newspaper reporter!

Today I picked up Christoph after school - a beautiful "first spring day" in late February - and we went to his home valley, the inner Sarntal behind the village of Aberstückl. We visited Jakob Weger, an old but vivid man and very friendly and cooperative, at his farm named Pluner (a site named "Plunerbach", which means brook near Pluner farm, was mentioned in the German report, Mr. Grimminger had sent me). He told us to have seen one plane crash in front of him (the site is called Aberstückler Nock, and the pilot must have been), and one behind him but much closer in northerly direction. The plane was going down in a stoop dive, he saw smoke and he heard it crash down between the trees. When reaching the place (about half an hour's walk above his farmhouse) he saw the wrecked plane and a totally burned body on the floor. And he saw, also on the floor near the corpse, a bracelet, black of smoke, but a name on it with two W, one of which he thought to be Werner. A neighbour has buried the corpse at this place, and he formed a wooden cross and put it into the earth.

Later on, after the end of the war, some merchant came to get away the metal parts of the wreckage, and with him a Carabiniere to look after the body. And Jakob is sure the human remains buried there have never been taken away because the exact place of the grave could not be found. Maybe the cross had been lost in the meantime - or they did not look at the burial place itself.

Then Jakob told us where to find one part of the wreckage. We went there (near to the farmhouse) and found a strangely shaped (but which ever part of a wreckage is not strangely shaped) rather complex, heavy piece formed by several metals with numbers on it. Christoph digged it out from the snow and carried it to the farmhouse. It is undoubtedly a part of the engine. (As I never thought to be able really to find something I did not bring along a camera.) But on Monday or so I'll go again (it's about 45 minutes by car, up and down and down and up from my home) and take some photographs.

In the meantime I give you the numbers:

W 8438920 FD C 8621   H H (or K) 8

There were other numbers on another place on the same piece, a kind of scale 1 2 3 4 5 6 7 with other numbers in between these numbers, each three lined off with an elliptic shape.

Then Jakob brought an iron saw which he has made himself out of another piece of the wreckage (i.e. he fastened the blade on this piece). On a screw I found a gravure "Rockford S.P. Co". Jakob told us, all the pieces of the wreckage must consist by very good materials because there was never any rust on them. Out of another piece he has made an ashtray which he estimates very much.

Well, Diana, that was it, and we were rather content, as you can imagine. Christoph and I (and as well Jakob and his wife) are sure that we found the place where your uncle's life had really come to an end, and where his remains had been buried. The scenery is most beautiful. If Christoph had been alive in 1944 he could have watched the crash like a movie scene from the opposite side of the valley where his home is. (I will take a photograph from there, too.)

If we are able to find the crash site (after the snow would have melted away totally, and Jakob will certainly join us and do his best), we could try to search with a metal detector (my husband's idea; he can get one)... at least we could form a new wooden cross, a better one this time, and leave it there as a sign of pity and remembrance.

Next week I will send you a map and the photographs.
Best regards
Inga

That had to be it! I hoped Mr. Weger's memory of the two W's on the bracelet was a good one and not prejudiced by any mention of Billy's name. Nevertheless, the memory of a bracelet—any bracelet—was a good indication Inga had found the place where Billy crashed.

But knowing that beautiful young man had been badly burned broke my heart. Either his canopy had been jammed by the falling debris and he couldn't bail out, or he was unconscious as a result of the impact or smoke from the flaming engine. I pushed the former scenario out of my mind and settled on the latter, but I knew we'd never know the truth. I was just grateful someone had shown enough respect to bury him. It would have meant a lot to my grandparents.

But what about the bracelet? How did it come to light in 1952? Was it buried with Billy, then later found and taken by the Carabinieri after the war? Or did someone take it when they buried him and turn it over to the authorities later?

So much new information, so many new questions, and still no Jim to keep my speculations under control.

Paolo was off doing his homework, but after seeing Inga's account I was sure he was still, at least partially, on the wrong track. But he was adamant. In his next e-mail, he said. "The truth is very near, and not only a grain of it."

He had been to the Garmesegg crash site "with some helpful locals. It was a challenging trek. Between the trees, ice, mud and snow we could find 20-30 different remains. Some quite big, some smaller. Even bolts and spiral springs. You will receive this pictures on Tuesday or Wednesday."

He said it was time to review all the evidence, but he felt sure that with his descriptions, photos, and serial numbers we should be able to tell if the parts he had found had come from our P-38. "In theory," he said, "it could be only Wisner's plane. In theory."

He had found one piece of iron with writing on it. One of the words ended in "…tning." He immediately thought "Lightning."

He went on to re-state and then add his opinions (in parentheses) to the information he had gathered from the official sources.

- "20 October, 1944 at 11.20 AM (right, undirectly confirm by the Olson capture report)
- 5 km NE of Bolzano (partially wrong, Sarntal is north of Bolzano)
- the Olson letter of 1952 statues that: he parachuted himself, he survived, he was slightly injured, he was captured, he didn't realise that Wisner was involved in the accident, too. In his letter he didn't mention Twedt, too. So, he didn't see nor Wisner or Twedt after the crash, nor in prison or in the Dulag-Luft of Wetzlar. In my opinion, it's realistic to think that if Wisner or Twedt survived the crash, too, they should have been captured and put together with Olson. I think it didn't happen. But many eyewitnesses remember of more than one parachute: this is still one of the most difficult points in our research.
- Anderson report: no parachutes (wrong), two planes exploded in the air (possible, but still with no evidence), another one crashed (true)
- Anderson report: the third plane (Wisner) went into a deep spin and crashed (true, according to my eyewitnesses)
- Olson capture report: he was extracted from the plane (wrong, he said he parachuted himself)
- Twedt and Wisner died by the explosions/crashes (could be or not, no corpse was apparently discovered or buried in the valley, at the crash A no one saw a body or his remains)"

Paolo then analyzed the wreckage he found at the three sites he was investigating: Garmesegg, Aberstückl/Sonvigo, and Pens/Pennes. Most came from Garmesegg, including the oxygen cylinder, but two wheels and submachine gun bullets came from Pens.

"This is what I collected last Friday. All this objects were taken by locals from the places of the crashes. Yesterday I went for the first time at Garmesegg with some locals; we could find 20-30 different remains. We have found a bone, too. Animal or human? I will let it analyse by a pathologist. I found many other pieces with perfect inscription... You will receive the pictures of this second part of remains in the next days. If I can do it without paying some billions, I'll give some pieces to a metal-restorer who could find out all the inscriptions, again."

He said he had spoken with Christoph Mair, who told him he had found something at the Pens crash, which he knew I had been told about.

Then he analyzed the eyewitness reports but said he would hold off telling most of what he'd learned until we had identified the items in the photos. I tried to imagine the faces of the people he talked to. "For now, I can tell you that I've found 4-5 eyewitnesses between 60 and 95(!) years. As always, there are some 'perfect' informations and some new problems. No one saw an explosion in the air, for instance. Everyone believes that the P-38 [at Garmesegg] crashed without a pilot; no one saw his remains and the fighter went down complete out of control. It was a very impressive crash, with an explosion and a fire which destroyed about 400 square metre of wooded hills at about 1300 metres, cutting into two pieces many trees. Now it's snowy and icy.

"One eyewitness told me that there were 13-14 planes in group of 4 or 5: almost perfect, in fact there were 15! They were hit by the FLAK at Penserjoch/Passo Pennes, north of Sarentino. Someone believes to have seen 4-5-6 parachutes, in different places. Two old men said to me, there were WHITE parachutes.

"According to the Olson letter of 1952, it's impossible that Olson and Wisner were captured together. What else? I think, that's enough. I concentrated my research in [Garmesegg], while Christoph Mair believes the 'right' place was [Pens]. Both possibilities could be right. Waiting for your answer (Jim, please, come back home!!!) I'll send you the other pictures between Tuesday and Wednesday. According to your investigations, I'll go further."

He added a P.S. to his four-page e-mail: "Is the Pulitzer-prize only for Americano?!?"

Paolo had given us a lot of information to wade through, and now he was wishing for Jim, too. We both knew we needed someone with a clear head to sort through all the discoveries. The scent of a story was pulling Paolo along, so he wasn't a good judge, and I was too emotional and confused by the place names to make sense of any of it.

I studied Paolo's photographs. The only items I recognized were wheels, so I consulted my book on P-38s,* which Jack had given me when we started the search. His dad had flown a P-38 in the Pacific at the beginning of the war, so we both had a connection to the unusual plane. I could

---

*O'Leary, Michael, *Lockheed P-38 Lightning,* Osprey Publishing Limited, Oxford: 1999.

tell the wheel design in Paolo's photos matched the ones in my book, but the number of spokes was wrong. The P-38 had six; Paolo's wheels had eight. I tried to keep an open mind about the Garmesegg site, but the eye-witness reports of four, five, or six parachutes were worrisome. That didn't dampen my hopes, though, because I hadn't remembered that we had already decided Garmesegg was the site of a bomber crash. I was still overwhelmed by the multiple names of the sites, but I know Jim would have caught it. He cross-referenced everything. I needed his sharp eye to get me back on track.

Dick Kahler and Bill Mays, who had been quietly monitoring the flurry of e-mails, congratulated Paolo on his hard work. Dick said the serial numbers would help Steve Duncan identify the aircraft. Bill Mays said he would soon be on his way to Stuttgart, Germany, and might be able to extend his trip for a visit with Paolo.

I wrote to both of them and Jim, with a ton of questions. I was so excited about the progress we'd made, I was certain both Inga and Paolo were getting us the answers we needed. I wanted to know what would happen if (or when) we matched the serial numbers on the wreckage to the planes. I wanted to know if the CIL would get involved, as they did with the Hoenshell search, and if so, when would we contact them. I didn't even know who would foot the bill to bring him home if we did find the grave. I wondered if I should be arranging time off for a trip to Italy.

I asked Inga to find out if Mr. Weger knew what had happened to the bracelet.

It was now the end of February. We'd been at this two months, and already we had more information than we could process, especially with Jim out of the picture.

Inga mentioned in one of her e-mails that she and her family were coming to the States in the fall and would be in San Francisco over Labor Day weekend. If they could get to the States, I could get to San Francisco. These were people I wanted to meet.

So Jack and I started making travel plans.

18

ZEROING IN

From: Dr. Inga Hosp
Sent: Monday, February 28, 2000
To: Diana Dale
Subject: Uncle

Dear Diana,
Thanks for your message. And thank you, too, for offering to
come to San Francisco next summer. But please don't feel
disturbed (perhaps our travelling period during holiday time does
not match very well with your husband's working period), and
you don't owe me nothing at all. San Francisco is scheduled
between Aug. 31 and Sept. 4. From there we will return to
Europe. But I would certainly like very much to meet you.
Yes, Jakob mentioned that the Carabiniere who came to look
after the remains, accompanied by that Italian merchant of used
metals, took away the bracelet. So it could very well had been
sent to American officials – and gathered at the U.S. mausoleum
in Germany. But I don't want to speculate too much. I cling to the
facts, and I only give to you what I was told. By now you should
also have my second message (by Fax) about what I did today.
And this is at least a confirmation for the Lightning crash above
Jakob's farm. As I told you, we could try to find the gravesite after
the snow will have melted away.
I would really propose not to give my last results to Cagnan at
once. He should do his research by his own—this should enforce

our chance to find the truth; I mean results, which are confirmed
by independent research!
I know that he was at Garmesegg (it is the home of Christoph's
grandmother), but Garmesegg (also called Urstettberg) is
mentioned as crash site of a bomber! At Aberstückl I was today,
as I wrote you. (Aberstückl is the native name, Sonvigo is the
same village, only the Italian translation, invented – like
thousands – during the Twenties, to make a historic marginalia.)
As soon as we have confirmation by the numbers or something
else, I will give you Jakob's address.
Good night, Diana, and best regards!
Inga

* * *

Things began moving even faster. Lowell Twedt's personnel file arrived on February 28th, but there was nothing in it about Billy's disappearance and no more specific location of Lowell's crash than of Billy's. However, there had been a wife, Ruth, and a son listed as Lowell's beneficiaries. The son's name was William Lowell Twedt—another Bill.

I looked for Ruth Twedt in Qwestdex.com, an online directory, with no luck, then found two William Twedts and left messages with both. Within a couple of hours one of them called back.

"This is Bill Twedt. You left me a message," he said. I noticed he pronounced his name "Tweed"; I'd always wondered about that. He was curt and highly suspicious, especially when I started asking a lot of questions about his father. I was aggressively trying to qualify him as the right Bill Twedt, and he was probably thinking I was some scam artist aiming to bilk him. But as I got farther into my story and told him we may have located his father's crash site, he opened up. In fact, he was almost speechless. His family had never learned any more than mine had. They, too, thought Lowell had vanished without a trace.

Twedt told me he was six when Lowell died, and because his father was in the service and away from home before that time, his memories of him are faint. He said his grandmother, Gertrude Twedt, had never given up hope she would someday know something about her son's fate. That much I already knew. His mother, Lowell's widow, was still living and had remarried. He had Lowell's flight log and a few of his belongings and documents. If I needed copies he'd be happy to send them to me.

I told him we didn't have an exact crash location yet, but we were getting close. When I related Jakob Weger's story of the crash and how he had seen an I.D. bracelet with my uncle's initials on it, Twedt said, "You know, 'Lowell Twedt' has two W's in it, too." I hadn't thought of that. I started to worry, then shoved the doubt into the back of my mind.

I told him we were trying to get enough information for a full investigation and I'd keep him informed. I copied Lowell's file for myself and sent him the original. In my cover letter I told him about the players in the search and how they had gotten us to that point. I hoped one day both of us would be able to thank them for finding our loved ones.

About that same time I received a two-page letter from Hans Grimminger, the German researcher Inga knew. In responding to my thank-you letter he cited chapter and verse on his research, which Inga had only paraphrased. His compassion was evident in his opening paragraph, and his English was charming. "Thank you for your letter, written with much [feeling] for your Uncle Willy, you never met, but standing very near to you. I understand your feelings because of two reasons, first I still have an uncle Willy, which will be 85 years in summer and second I had a uncle Ludwig (my second Christian name), which was killed as a German soldier in 1942 in Russia, years before I was born."

He apologized for his English and for not being able to do more for me. His hobby was the airwar history of South Bavaria, but he did have documents on South Tyrol that had narrowed down the locations of our three crashed aircraft. His information had been pivotal; without it, we might still have been floundering around in the wrong places.

> I don't have many documents about the "shooting down" of the four P-38s at 20.10.44 in the Bozen (Bolzano) area:
> A very short version of the report of the German flak (anti-aircraft-artillery) units of the Flakgruppe (Group) Bozen (Bolzano), on microfilm of the German Bundesarchiv. This reports are saying that between 11.30 and 11.35 hours four "lightnings" were shot down and crashed at the following places:
> 1. North slope of the Kirchberg (Churchmountain) at Aberstückl (Sonvigo), north of Sarnthein (Sarentino) in the Sarntal (Valle di Sarentino), by 1. +3. +4. Batterie (battery)/schwere (heavy) Flakabteilung 490; 4./schw. Flakabtl. 547; 1.+3./schw.Flakabtl. 548

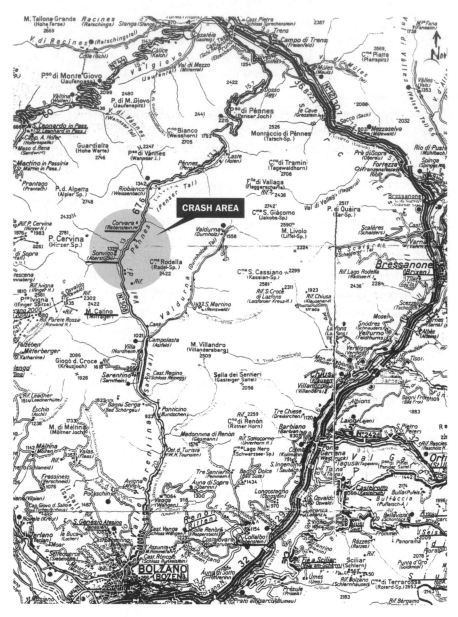

2. Messner Basai, 9-10 Km North of Sarnthein (Sarentino), by 3.
    Batterie/schw. Flakabtl. 490; 1. + 3./schw. Flakabtl. 548.
3. East of Rabenstein (Corvara), Blunabachtal (Bluna-brook-
    valley), 10 Km North of Sarnthein (Sarentino), by 1. + 3.
    Batterie/schw. Flakabtl. 548; 3./schw. Flakabtl. 490.

4. Kesselberg (Monte Catino), East of Meran (Merano), by 3.
    Batterie/schw. Flakabtl. 490; 1. +3./schw. Flakabt. 548.
The four crashplaces of the German reports are not wrong. I do
not know how far each aircraft from the other came down,
maybe very near. The aircrafts broke into parts in the air, when
this fell down, they were often away from the other parts of the
same aircraft, especially in a mountain area.

This was great data. And Grimminger had included a copy of the U.S.
Intops Summary of the 15th USAAF of October 20 showing the targets. One
was for 71 B-17s from the 99th and 463rd Bomber Groups to hit the Regensburg oil storage depot. The escorts were 92 P-38s from the 1st and 82nd
Fighter Groups; four from the 1st FG were lost by intense, accurate, heavy flak
at Bozen (the ones in Billy's accident). He also recapped the information from
the MACR he had on file and suggested I get a copy of it from the National
Archives. He provided me the address and went on to describe the area.

> In your search and the disappointment, you had to
> recognize, you must know something about this area Südtirol
> (Alto Adige), the Sarntal (Valle Sarentina), higher up Penser Tal
> (Valle di Pennes). Look at the enclosed copy of a map
> (1:200.000). This valley is surrounded by high mountains, at
> the west and north side up to 2,800 meters, at the east side to
> 2,500 meters. At the end of October, you can have a beautiful
> fall in the valley, but also in the mountains deep snow. I don't
> know how it was in 1944, maybe Dr. Hosp knows it. The
> crashplaces were (minimum) at a sealevel of 1,000 meters,
> maybe in the snow.
> The Luftwaffe (German Air Force) was responsible for
> the crashes of [m]any aircraft. In this area were Luftwaffe-
> soldiers of the airfield Bozen (Bolzano) and soldiers of the
> Luftwaffe-flak-batteries. Normally they searched for the
> crashplace, captured enemy aircrews, gave orders to bury the
> remains of killed crewmen and salvaged the wreck and parts of
> the crashed airplanes. A German order said that the remains had
> to be buried at the cemetery of that village or town, where they
> were found (normally), but in many events, the remains were
> buried at the crashsite or taken to a larger town, but not far

away. In U.S. reports I saw that the Germans buried U.S. aircrews from different crashes at Bozen (Bolzano), aircrews from a B-24 of 29.03.44, B-17 of 18.07.44 and B-24 of 12.11.44.

If the crashplaces of 20.10.44 were high up in the mountains, maybe in the snow, the German soldiers did not much searching when they couldn't reach this. At this time, the situation was very strain[ed] for the German Armed Forces. Since five years war, very high losses at all battlefronts – Sowjet Union – in France at two (north and south) – Italy – at sea – in the air. Millions of German soldiers were killed, wounded or in war prisons. Many air raids over the Alps gave much to do for the flak-soldiers there. The XV USAAF bombed targets in South Germany and also in North Italy, especially the railroad-tracks. The Brenner (Brennero) line through Südtirol (Alto Adige) was bombed many times. It was the No. 1 transport line for the Germans to Italy.

During the winter 1944/45, there was also much snow, and in spring the war was over. So I guess that there was not much research from the Germans.

But if the German soldiers found remains of your uncle, they gave orders to bury this there. It was absolutely unusual to bring remains of Allied soldiers over longer distances. If the German soldiers found [personal] effects, documents and other informations about aircraft, target, unit or crew, they sended this to an office of the German Luftwaffe at Oberursel near Frankfurt, named Dulag Luft. There was the interrogation camp of the Luftwaffe, all captured Allied aircrew came into this camp. I think that was the reason that the Mortuary Division wrote you that a bracelet of your uncle was found at Griesheim. This town is near Darmstadt and this is just south of Frankfurt.

This Luftwaffe-office at Oberursel kept all documents and informations about enemy aircraft that crashed, crashlanded or landed in Germany or in the occupied states in Europe. The office had a numbered portfolio for every aircraft. This included documents and reports (of the flak-units and fighters) which claimed the "shot down" of officers of the police, military units, villages, towns about the crashplace, the aircraft, the crew

(captured, injured, killed) with details like, who was where
captured, taken to which hospital or where and when buried.
Also reports of the salvage of the rests of the airplane. Also
included were the [personal] effects of the crew, effects like
identification tags and all what was in the pockets.

This portfolios were captured by U.S. soldiers at the end
of the war, maybe at Griesheim. Many of the portfolios are
today at the National Archives, but you can find only rest of the
documents and effects in it. I don't know where all the others
went. The Americans came into this area in April/Mai 1945,
U.S. Quartermaster units searched later for the missing U.S.
soldiers, and if they found graves of this, they exhumed the
remains, tried to identificate this and sended this to larger U.S.
military cemeteries. I don't know how good the QM unit at
Südtirol (Alto Adige) worked. From the unit which worked at
my home-area, sorry, I must say, that this soldiers worked very
lazy. I know incidents that remains of fighter pilots were
declared "unknown" by this QM-unit. This remains were
buried by Germany with the full name of the pilot, or with
some research the QM unit could find out the name, if this
soldiers had done more.

That last paragraph confirmed the comment Bill Mays made earlier
that the search units were "pressed for time." So many dead spread over
such a large area, and so few people assigned to find them, it's no wonder
there were so many still missing. But I had to hand it to the Germans; they
did keep scrupulous records, and the papers that did survive carried a lot of
answers. Mr. Grimminger's research had given us everything we needed.

About this time, Paolo piped up with a reasonable request. "This is
like an open-letter that you can send to both Dr. Inga Hosp and Christoph.
It seems to me that it would be absurd that in this friendly and 'worldwide'
research-group we could have two different 'local groups' splitting the
investigations, the results and maybe also the remains of the airplane[s]. It
would be a great defeat of everyone here. It's absurd that we can communicate all around the world, but we have many difficulties here in South
Tyrol. Which is my interest in the search? Both professional and human. As
you can imagine, I'd like to write a reportage in my newspaper, as soon as
we are absolutely sure about what happened and where."

Writing a book was on his mind, but "Where's the problem?" he asked. "You can publish in English, me in Italian, Mrs. Hosp in German. If someone is interested...

"Here is my proposal, he continued. "I'm ready to share all the information I gathered. We three could both work together or organize different tasks, so that we won't make the same things at the same time, maybe interviewing the same people and so on. Christoph knows many locals there in Sarntal, Mrs. Inga Hosp is a trained researcher, and she's looking for a metal-detector. I have got professional photographer and all technical equipment. So again, where's the problem? The best will be to organise a meeting between the three of us. I think this is the best proposal: to cooperate and share the results. Diane, you know very well that I can go further without any help, but I want to show my attitude towards the cooperation. If it is not possible, it's not my fault."

In my heart I agreed with Paolo, and I forwarded his message to Inga with no recommendation one way or the other. I hated being caught in the middle, and I couldn't speak for Inga. I hoped events would solve the issue for me, and I started counting the days until Jim would get back, perhaps with a solution. Inga let the matter drop.

Inga sent two faxes on the 28th. The message of the first one was the same as her e-mail of February 26, but it included a drawing of the item she and Christoph had dug out of the snow on Jakob's farm. It was nothing I recognized, and I hoped her photographs would be more helpful to the experts. The second fax was short, but it gave a little more information on her findings. "I was in Sarntal again this morning, taking photographs, talking to people. Another 70-year-old man at Aberstückl confirmed to me the three Lightning crashes at the places mentioned in the German reports from Mr. Grimminger. He also has seen the captured pilot pass by his home on his accompanied way down to the street. He also knows that one plane crashed near Pluner farm.

"Then I went again to talk to Jakob Weger (Pluner). He confirmed everything he mentioned on Saturday. I took photographs of him holding the metal saw, and I took photographs of the large piece, too. On the opposite side of the valley I met another eyewitness, also a 70 year old man who saw the crash as well as the burnt corpse which he confirmed being buried at the crash site..."

With all the information pointing at the Sarn Valley, Bill Mays thought it was time for us to get the government involved, and he sent them a copy of his message to me. He had forwarded Inga's last e-mail and photos, along with a brief description of our search, to the mortuary affairs office at the European Command headquarters in Frankfurt and to the office in charge of any potential excavation. "The person who came to Bulgaria from EU Command name is David Roath, and he was instrumental in the excavation of Lt. Hoenshell. EU Command is who actually orders an excavation and sometimes they use a CILHI (Central Investigations Laboratory Hawaii) team to do them, but not always. It's the EU Command's decision, so we should begin there. It will also help to be prepared to write your favorite congressperson(s), and find out who is the US Ambassador to Italy. They also enjoy feel-good PR missions like these."

He would compile the information we had so far and emphasized that the crash (and burial) sites should not be disturbed in the meantime. "My advice is that once we determine ... that this is your uncle's crash site from evidence and witness testimony, David Roath and/or a team will go to the site themselves to do an 'official' military investigation as to the likelihood of recovering the bodily remains of a US military vet, hopefully your uncle."

After Roath visits the site and concludes that the probability is high, Mays predicted, he will "most likely order an excavation. I should tell you that the time from when we determine this is your uncle's site to the time an excavation crew would be there...assuming all that I previously mentioned...is probably 2 years or so."

Mays had high praise for David Roath, "a great guy, very fair and super to work with." He counseled that we should get Roath good evidence from the witness as to time and exact location, "as well as the locations in the MACR's Jim has that are the official US military guide to this crash. This will reduce Mr. Roath's investigative time needed and shorten the overall time. I'll also ask Liz Wilson [niece of Carl Hoenshell] to provide some additional insight as to the steps she took, phone calls she made, and letters she wrote to get the ball rolling. Liz and EU Command also have the entire parts manual for a P-38, so what we need are pictures with the corresponding serial numbers. A serial number off a machine gun or an engine block part are very good identifiers. I called the EU Command office, and they could not positively I.D. any of the parts, so we need more pictures and more serial numbers. Liz e-mailed me back and said the wheel was from a P-38 or P-51 by sight, but will have Colin look it up in the book to be sure."

He added a personal message to David Roath, saying there was some irony and coincidence with the Hoenshell case and with ours—both were started by the niece of the pilot. He attached a file with all the particulars, adding that he was leaving for Stuttgart the next day, March 1, and would be back in five days but would be available by mobile phone.

I sent Paolo Bill Mays's e-mail to let him know the U.S. government would be involved soon. Paolo replied, giving me the name of the U.S. ambassador in Italy, Thomas Foglietta, and agreed with Bill Mays that I should write him. Paolo added, Foglietta "knows very well our region; some weeks ago he went to Cavalese, where an American jet caused the fall of a cable-way which determined the death of 20 people; he's used to coming in South Tyrol for vacation; I think he could be personally very interested in our search." That story of the U.S. flier severing the ski-lift cable had been big news in America, and I feared the reckless actions of that U.S. pilot might create hostility toward ours. I didn't dwell on it, but it niggled at the back of my mind. I composed my letter to Foglietta telling him there might soon be a U.S. investigation in his back yard and sent it off that day.

Paolo attached some more photos of the wheels he had found, asked for more information about Mr. Grimminger, and added an interesting note. "I'm quite sure that the owner of the barn where I found the two wheels has still a machine gun. He told me he has sold it, but I'm quite sure he still has it, but he's quite suspicious: it's forbidden—for the Italian law—to detain war guns. I think, with some money he could 'find' the machine gun again, but we'd better wait to know if the wheels are part of 'our' P-38." He added that he had not heard from either Inga or Christoph.

But in spite of getting no help from the others, Paolo was doing just fine. He now had the same information they did; how he used it was up to him.

Only three more days before Jim would be back.

19

EVIDENCE

From: Jim Graham
Sent: Thursday, March 2, 2000
To: Diana Dale
Subject: WOW!

Hi Diana –

Got home tonight & collected 20 [pounds of] mail, 18 recorded telecons, & 93 e-mail messages! You've been on a real merry-go-round, almost started a war, made peace & set up a Wisner NATO! I feel like I've just walked into the final chapter of an epic movie!

Tomorrow I'll have to sort through your messages & see what my homework is. I just hope the hoards of investigators swarming over the Sarn Valley & hills don't meddle so much with the evidence that the Euro-CIL can't put the puzzle back together. You've been through the wringer – tell me your first order of business.

Jim

* * *

Words could not express my relief when I saw Jim's e-mail. At last, my drifting ship had re-connected with its rudder.

All the photos Paolo had sent came from Garmesegg. He had had some parts cleaned so he could read the serial numbers, but I was pretty sure he was wasting time and money at the wrong place. I wrote Inga to get a better grasp of the exact locations of the sites in Mr. Grimminger's letter and the one she investigated. There were so many different names for the same places I couldn't keep them straight.

Her reply was that Paolo's Garmesegg site was where a bomber had crashed, and she was emphatic about it. "I have another confirmation that he is wrong. I knew already from several sources and eyewitnesses that it was a BOMBER which crashed near Garmesegg above Astfeld. Now Keith Bullock, whom I asked as a bomber crash expert, was helpful again: He has sent to me a letter by another eye witness of the Garmesegg crash which was a BOMBER, was in April 1945 and from which 9 men could escape with parachutes. I called this man and got exactly the same information. As I wrote you recently I had the same story by an eyewitness at Aberstückl, also the 9 parachutes."

She was also a little triumphant. "Now I am looking forward to have revealed the numbers found by Christoph and me—and I am glad that I am, for the second time, able to help our reporter while he [Paolo] is jubilating on a wrong track. I would call this cooperation. Again: It was a BOMBER WHICH CRASHED AT Garmesegg… It was a bomber which crashed at Weissenbach near Pens. And there were three Lightnings to crash near Aberstückl (…which is Christoph's and my only site, confirmed by German Flak-Reports and by the diary of my German Flak-member)."

She said she couldn't access the photos in my last e-mail to her. "Have to upgrade my RAM. Damned computers! They never can get enough."

I believed Inga, but I wanted a second opinion. I was afraid Paolo might think we were leading him on. Before I set him straight I wanted to be sure we were right, so I e-mailed Keith Bullock and asked him to confirm what Inga had told me. I included some of the text of Inga's e-mail, and Keith wrote back March 4, "If you hear (or see) any swearing that's me. Had almost finished a long e-mail in answer to your just received message titled Garmesegg and Penserjoch when I did something that I am told by computer experts is impossible to do. I wiped the whole messsge out, and now I do not have the time to do it all again, visitors have just arrived from England and Germany.

"But briefly, I knew that I was back on the hook when I sent that letter to Inga, she reacted exactly as I thought and hoped she would, my interest being with a bomber that the witness, Hr. Ignaz Premsteller, had told me about. I hoped that Inga would telephone him on my behalf as it were, which of course she did." He said he would study the names on some accurate maps of the area. He thought he might have the Garmesegg bomber and would try to get the documents from the U.S. Archives. "I am not a person to offend ANYONE," he added, "and I certainly would not want to do this to Inga, or the young reporter, who, I am now going to suggest comes to see me.

"From what I have read and sense, I feel that Inga is on the right track, but I would very much like written proof: My wife is getting impatient and has just called out to remind me that it is impolite to be sitting in front of the computer when we have guests waiting for me to join them for breakfast. It will most likely be a few days before you hear from me again." He sent his best regards to me and to "haveyoulethimofftheleadtobiteanyone."

I was pleased Keith would be willing to work with Paolo. They were both reliable sources and could help each other on future projects. I told Paolo what Inga and Keith had said about the site at Garmesegg, but he steadfastly believed he was on the right three tracks.

He said he had spoken with Keith Bullock, who told him he didn't list any bombers that had crashed in the area during the war. Paolo, too, was comparing photos of the wheels he had found, but to bomber wheels. "There is a big difference," he said. "And the wheels I founded (Pens) are perfectly similar to the P-38's. The diameter is the same, too. It's true that for Garmesegg many people remember many parachutes, which let me think of a bomber, not a fighter. But everyone speaks about fighters, no bombers. I'll bet I'm right. Who knows? The only thing is to check the pictures of the remains. In fact, how many planes are we looking for? Only Wisner's or three different?" He punctuated his theory with, "That's the point."

I had to concede we were looking for three different crash sites, so I let it drop. With absolutely no feel for the scope of the region we were talking about, I couldn't make a judgment one way or another, but I felt sure that the site Inga and Christoph had investigated at Weger's farm was Billy's.

Jim had hit the ground running. He copied me on an e-mail he had sent to his contacts at the 1st Fighter Group updating them on the status of our search and asking for their help in confirming the parts. A P-38 expert named Bob Cardin had spoken at one of the 1st Fighter Group reunions and had helped Jim and Dick Kahler identify the parts from Carl Hoenshell's plane in Bulgaria. Cardin had restored *Glacier Girl*, one of a group of P-38s that had force-landed in Greenland in 1942. *Glacier Girl* was found in 1992, 250 feet down in an ice field, and its recovery, told in detail in John Mullins's book, was quite a feat. Cardin had restored the plane, and if he couldn't identify the parts we'd found, no one could.

Jim said that if our searchers could just recover a gun or an engine— parts that have serial numbers identified with specific P-38s—we could positively connect each site to its pilot. It would take direct and incontrovertible evidence to get the U.S. government to mount an investigation, so Jim asked his friends from the Hoenshell search if they had any detailed P-38 drawings and forwarded them some of Paolo's pictures.

I noticed Jim was having as much difficulty as I was pinning down the size of the terrain we were dealing with. His e-mail to Inga and Christoph summarized what we had thus far, and it helped me get things straight, too. "It is somewhat unlikely that all three of the P-38s involved in the October 20, 1944 incident would fall and crash very close to each other, even if they all fell from the same point in the sky, as the aerodynamics involved would probably scatter them.

"This is where [a] detailed map of the region would help to conjecture about the separation between the three crashes. What amount of area in the Aberstückl region would you estimate is likely to hold parts of the fallen airplanes? Mr. Grimminger's flak reports list four sites: 1) north slope of Kirchberg, 2) Messner Basai, 3) east of Rabenstein (Corvara), Blunabachtal and 4) Kesselberg (Monte Catino). Are all of these sites within what you call the Aberstückl area—or do some of them correspond to the a, b &c sites that Paolo Cagnan defines? Is it your belief that all three of the P-38s (Olson, Wisner & Twedt) crashed near Aberstückl (Mr. Grimminger's site of Kirchberg)? If so, does that mean that the 3 other Grimminger sites are not likely to be sites of our P-38 crashes?

"In our mission reports it is stated that two of the P-38s in a flight of four were hit simultaneously by two flak bursts. It is likely that the two bursts came from one flak battery as the three guns in one battery were controlled by the same ground radar. One of those two P-38s was Olson. The other was Capt. Elliott, who survived and was able to guide his plane to Ancona. The P-38s of Wisner and Twedt were damaged by collisions resulting from the violent maneuvers of the flight as the two P-38s hit by flak lost power and moved radically. Twedt's plane hit Olson's plane, and one of those two fell onto Wisner's plane. One of my friends I flew with wrote that he followed one of the planes down as it burned and spiraled to crash and he did not see the pilot bail out. He thought he was following Wisner down. My friend is dead now, so he can't expand on the story. Another report from a bomber pilot flying somewhat east of the P-38 flight stated in a report that he saw what he believed was the P-38 collisions and he believed he saw two parachutes come from the planes. We know Olson parachuted, but we don't know which one of the other two may have parachuted—maybe Twedt, maybe Wisner, maybe the bomber pilot was mistaken?"

He hypothesized, "It is my vague and unfounded guess that the three P-38 crashes would probably be separated from each other by at least 1 to 2 kilometers. My guessing isn't going to help determine the facts, so we need all of the witness data you can find and hopefully some parts that will be identifiable as coming from a specific P-38."

He confirmed that for the three P-38s we have serial numbers for each airplane, its two engines, all four of its 50-caliber machine guns, and its 20 mm cannons. "Of course, if we could find any of those," he said, "we would be absolutely sure of the plane's identity. Part numbers on other parts will determine if they came from a P-38, but not which one."

Like me, Jim was hoping Bill Mays would get down to the area on his way back from Stuttgart. "He knows the importance of preserving the location data for the plane parts and any human remains that might be found so that the quality of the evidence is not contaminated or confused. If I remember my reading of two weeks of e mail correctly, one of your witnesses says that remains were put into a gravesite which is believed to be undisturbed. It would be very valuable to know the precise location of that gravesite and to leave it undisturbed until experts might get permission to investigate it."

Jim had also said that he was hoping to correlate the information he had found at the National Archives with more information from the Bundesarchiv that Hans Grimminger had. "I think with Mr. Grimminger's coaching I can possibly correlate his flak battery reports with our search objectives. I also may be of help to Mr. Grimminger in getting at some data in our Archives for his historical work."

Jim asked that Inga convey our appreciation to all of the witnesses and helpers they had spoken with. He and I both knew that it had taken a lot of their time, and we hoped it hadn't interfered with Christoph's schoolwork. "I hope we can meet in the future to say thanks to you both personally."

Which brought him to Inga's trip. "In fact, Inga, maybe we can meet each other on your trip to the U.S. in August. I live in Seattle, Washington,

which is only about 130 miles south of Vancouver, Canada, and I understand you intend to travel south to San Francisco on highway 101. Is it
possible that you will be coming through Seattle? If so, I certainly would
look forward to meeting you. Please inform me of your plans."

I told Jim how grateful I was that he got us back on track. I added
that if Inga's trip down 101 did include a stop in Seattle, then Jack and I
could go there instead of San Francisco and meet Jim at the same time.
The date would be preferable, too, because we wouldn't be traveling over a
busy holiday weekend.

Then I added some news that disturbed me. "My niece spilled the
beans to my mother yesterday. Evidently, my sister thought she had told
Katie I was holding off on telling Mother until I knew more, but the message either didn't get through or my sister had told someone else twice. No
harm done. Mother was very emotional about it and very grateful for all
the work everyone has done. My husband was relieved—he said he wasn't
looking forward to the 'Maxine-Diana sob-fest' that would have taken
place when they came out here in June. She offered to pay my way to Italy
if/when it comes to that, and she wants to reimburse anyone and everyone
for their time and expenses. I guess she feels a little helpless, not being
instrumental in the search, so she wants to do something to help. I'm glad
she found out when we're so close, instead of earlier when everything was
so speculative. The ups and downs of the past few months would have
made her nuttier (and weepier) than she already is…"

It was a relief at last to tell Mother and Daddy about the search. I'd
felt guilty about not letting them in on the project, and now I could keep
them informed as things happened. And we were making good progress.

Bill Mays got back in touch March 7. Unfortunately, he had lost his
planner with all his contact numbers, so he couldn't call anyone from the
road. And once he found out a trip to northern Italy would have been cost-
ly and added seven hours each way, he realized it wasn't feasible to go. I
was touched he'd even considered making the extra effort.

In spite of the aborted side trip, he came back with some good news.
"EU Command does have a new open file (Lt. Wisner), and they are gathering info that I forward [in] their direction. I've sent them info and pictures that we've received from our friends on the ground in Italy and I
spoke with them on the telephone before I left for Germany. They are also
searching for what could have happened to the missing file. I hope to hear
from them soon, but part of their investigation team is currently working in

Turkey. They couldn't find the part numbers from the wheels in the P-38 parts manual. I don't want to swamp them with a bunch of e-mails because I know they don't have time to go through all of them, so I'm only forwarding data that we have already confirmed to be fairly accurate. Pictures and part numbers with locations and confirming testimony are great."

That same day, Jim told me Bob Cardin had agreed to review Paolo's pictures. "Since he has restored the recovered 1942 P-38 from inside and out, we can have no better expert opinion," Jim said. He expected a judgment within a day or so.

Then he added, "I think it would be SUPER if we could rendezvous with Inga in Seattle! I would be delighted if you could come up this way. We could have quite a chin-fest! Let's watch for Inga's response and nudge it to happen." Jim was empathetic about Mother's tip-off, and he understood my reaction. "But it is probably for the best. Some of her emotion may be vented and she may want to follow the chase to the finale—whatever. She should get over any feeling of obligation [to repay us] because we're all in it for the joy of discovery."

What a lovely man.

Jim forwarded me Inga's answer to his lengthy e-mail of March 5. Hers was equally lengthy but very helpful and addressed each of Jim's questions.

- Correlation between flak battery reports and your search objectives: In his response Mr. Grimminger resembled both the MACRs of the 3 P 38 (9312,9313,9314) with pilots Wisner, Olson and Twedt (plus, without MACR, the Elliot—P 38 which landed near Ancona), who were hit on Oct. 20, 1944 and crashed "near Bozen", and the German flak reports, speaking of 4 crash-sites ("Kirchberg", "Messner Basai" = Patzei, "Blunabachtal" = creek near Pluner farm, "Kesselberg"). These sites mark a rather wide range of many square miles, as you will see from the map you hopefully will receive very soon (sorry I have no scanner and a Telefax transmission of the map will undoubtedly be too bad). It may also be that parts of the colliding planes dropped in an even wider range! Three of the sites are situated in an area of which you can call Aberstückl the center, only Kesselberg is more distant, but it could also be that "Kesselberg" was the

site where the observers had guessed Elliot's plane to be hit
- but he escaped.

- Is it my belief that all three of the P 38's crashed near
  Aberstückl? Yes it is, but as I said, it was a wide range round
  Aberstückl. All the eyewitnesses I interviewed do say so.

- Your guess that the three P-38 crashes are separated from
  each other by 1-2 kilometers. My guess, too, even more than
  1-2 kilometers, as you will see from the map.

Inga said that if Jim really had all the numbers he listed, it would be possible to identify the pieces she and Christoph had found. But, "To find the gravesite of 'Plunerbach' may be difficult, but not impossible. Perhaps the Italian metal merchandiser left some small pieces there which could be found with a metal detector. Should we achieve that Jakob is more lucky now to find the grave site than some 50 years ago when he tried to localize it for the Carabiniere? I would not be too optimistic. Anyway—the investigators should await the melting of the snow and start an investigation not before late April/May (it is rather high up in the mountains)."

She said that their plans for their trip to Canada and the U.S. had been completed. They would be in Seattle August 23-25, arriving from Victoria. Then they would drive to Portland, then south on Highway 101. "It would be great to have a cup of coffee or a glass of the famous local wine with you in Seattle."

How civilized of her to include Jim's home town in the trip. That settled it. Jack and I would go to Seattle. We'd been promising to visit some friends there, anyway, so I e-mailed Dick and Julie Hamann to reserve a room at their house.

Bob Cardin's response to Jim's e-mail about Paolo's photographs from Garmesegg was encouraging but not definitive. He could identify a P-38 main landing gear wheel, a possible carburetor, maybe an oxygen tank, and 50-caliber bullets–same as on a P-38. All the wheels were from the P-38 main, and the gear with teeth on both sides could be from the propeller system, but he wasn't sure.

Inga's packet with her photographs, postcards, and map of the area finally arrived by mail on March 10th. She had marked the detailed map with the exact locations of the three crash sites and highlighted the farms of the eyewitnesses. At last I could get a feel for the terrain.

The postcards were of children in traditional costumes and aerial views of Astfeld, Aberstückl and the beautiful Sarn Valley. Inga marked an arrow on the Sarn Valley card showing the hill where Billy's plane had hit. There was still a visible notch in the trees.

The photos she had taken included a man named Josef Thaler, an eyewitness to the crash, holding his granddaughter's hand as they stood by the side of the road; the hillsides where Billy and possibly Twedt had crashed; the Garmesegg farm, home of the bomber crash site; the home of an eyewitness in Aberstückl who had seen Olson as he was marched through town after his capture; two views of the large piece of wreckage Inga and Christoph had dug out of the snow on Jakob Weger's farm; and Jakob holding the hacksaw he had fashioned out of another piece of the wreckage from his property.

Inga also included a photo of the view from her home, a breathtaking scene of a birdhouse, birdbath, and trees, all covered in fluffy, deep snow, with the pale lavender Dolomites in the background across the valley, back-lit in the late afternoon sun.

Thanks to those pictures, I had a new perspective on the crash. All my life I had visualized it as if I were riding in a plane above and behind the squadron as it flew over the mountains, much as Jack Anderson would have seen it, and I had played that mental film clip over and over. Anti-aircraft flak bursts among the planes and hits one, which goes out of formation. In the confusion another plane collides with the first, and pieces of wreckage fall onto Billy's plane. Billy's right engine catches fire and his plane goes into a dive, then spins toward earth and disappears into the clouds and out of sight. That's where it always ended.

But now I could see what happened next, as if I were standing in the valley that day. I hear a noise from above and look up. A plane appears out of the clouds with a trail of smoke tracing its trajectory as it hurtles toward earth. It spins around and around, then disappears into the crest of a hill. It takes a couple of seconds for the sound of the impact to reach my ears, then flames and smoke fill the sky above the ridge.

My previous vision had been dreamlike; this one was very real.

20

CONFIRMATION

From: Robert L. Cardin
Sent: Thursday, March 09, 2000
To: Jim Graham
Subject: Photos

Jim, I have received the 3 photos and I do confirm that the first 2
are of a P-38 turbo charger. The 3rd I think is a man, but I cannot
identify what he is holding.
Bob Cardin

* * *

Bob Cardin was a comic, and his last comment made me chuckle. The
third photo he was talking about was the one Inga had taken of
Jakob holding the hacksaw he made from a piece of Billy's wreckage.

Cardin's follow-up e-mail to Jim said he was 99.9% sure the part Inga
and Christoph had found on Jakob Weger's farm was a turbocharger from a
P-38. That news, combined with the two W's on the bracelet, confirmed that
this was the site we were looking for, the one where Billy may still be buried.

Jim added a succinct "Yee-Haw!" to Cardin's message.

Yee-haw, indeed. I was dancing on the ceiling. I asked Bill Mays if he
had received the information, too. He said he had but hadn't yet forwarded it to the investigators in Germany. He did know, however, they were
busy ordering files and taking note of the sites we'd identified.

On March 12 Inga sent me a message about our proposed ren-dezvous Seattle. "That's a splendid idea: meeting in Seattle, Jim included! I look forward to summer with great pleasure, even more because of this meeting with you and your husband. The research has also established—except the informational level—a kind of emotionally defined network, if you can understand what I mean, at least with some of you—and with you a very special one."

And on the subject of the search, she added, "Late this night, before sleeping, I checked my e-mails and found Robert Cardin's message to Jim Graham. As I understand, the Plunerbach-piece belongs in fact to a Light-ning. I will await now Jim's and your decisions for the further procedure. I had the impression Jim was overcrowded by results and should first get solid soil under his feet. I hope the map I sent him this night by Telefax can be helpful in this sense, too. But perhaps he got it already from you."

I seconded Inga's feelings about our visit in Seattle and warned her Paolo's article would be published the next day. Paolo had just faxed me a copy of it and told me how to access the whole thing on line.

It started on the front page, then jumped inside with several associat-ed articles about the P-38, the missing file, the people who helped with the research, an appeal for more witnesses, and the Internet search. The photo of Billy with the little dog was front and center, and it was strange to see such a familiar photo in a foreign newspaper. But it was also comforting, because I felt we were coming to his rescue.

From what I could translate using my two semesters of college Italian, Paolo had done a thorough job. Not everything in the story was pertinent to Billy's crash, but at least it was out. We could go forward from there.

I e-mailed the Web pages to Bill Twedt's son Chad, who was on line, so he could share them with his dad, who wasn't. I also sent Chad a scan of my only photo of his grandfather, Lowell, which I found in Billy's scrap-book. I was sure Chad knew that photo, because Idy had gotten it from Gertrude Twedt, Chad's great-grandmother.

When I told Jim about the articles, he said he had printed them off and was going to have to find someone at a good pizza parlor to read him the text.

I congratulated Paolo on his article and told him I wanted him to be there if we ever got around to an excavation. Unfortunately, he had spelled my name wrong throughout the article, so I told him outright he had got-ten it wrong. I quoted him the saying, "I don't care what they say about me, as long as they get my name right."

His plane collided above Billy's 10·20·44

Lowell Twedt — San Diego Calif

Lowell Twedt exiting a P-39

He got my point, and fired back an enthusiastic response with more information. "If you have thought that I would have stopped my researches after the reportage, you were completely wrong. In fact, I already have got ***NEW EVIDENCE!!!***" But first he apologized for his mistake and promised he would never do it again.

"I'm glad to tell everybody that now I'm cooperating with Christoph, a very tough guy, which means that 'almost' the whole group is now working together… Now something about the article: It was read by almost 80% of the local Italian-speaking population and by many South-Tyrolean. Everyone was very interested in the story, the feedback was really great and it was quite a satisfaction for me, after all this hard job. In fact, I published an SOS in both Italian and German, looking for new eyewitnesses and remains. Between Sunday and today I was called [at] home by 7 people: eyewitnesses of many different crashes, happened in South Tyrol during WWII."

He said he would document all their stories, even if they don't have anything to do with our case. There was one that was very interesting. "One old man living in Bolzano gave me an engine part of the P-38 hit near Aberstückl/Sonvigo. Now I'm referring to the ***crash-site 1) Aberstückl,*** which in fact is the same as the crash-site Messner Basai, which is called also Pazzei (how many different names in our story) ...This is the place from which the turbo-charger comes from. The object I received...is I'm pretty sure a DISTRIBUTOR—with 12 plugs. It's MADE IN U.S.A. by the famous SCINTILLA."

He described the piece and provided a drawing and the serial number, promising photos of it the next day. "This object was found in the early Sixties by this man in the wood next to Messner Basai/Pazzei. He saw two air-crashes, not very far away: less than one Km. He said, at one crash-site there were only thousands of pieces, at the other the fuselage was only partially destroyed. He heard that there were four hit planes in this area... He heard also that a pilot was shoot. After reading my article, he believes he could have been the same pilot who was later buried by the locals. I heard this rumours, too. No evidence, only 'voices.' In fact, he personally saw 'only' two crash-points."

Paolo agonized over the number of crashes, still not certain which was which. "Oh God, how many planes were hit by the Flak in that area?!? The only thing, you know, will be to compare this distributor and its number. Could be 'the' solution, don't you think so? Maybe I'll receive new evidence. Tomorrow and Wednesday I'll be there, 'in the middle of the action,' with or without the snow. The man is too old to come with me, but I'm sure many farmers know the exact location. I hope the sun will come soon...

"Speaking about the 'famous' machine-gun. The farmer told me, he spoke to the man who buyed it, but he says he sell it to another one... I believe it could be true. The farmer still promised me to try to find out where the gun is now..."

He closed with, "Ok, for today it's enough"

I was sure Jim would agree. He was tying all of Paolo's research to members of the 71st Fighter Squadron so that every scrap of evidence would be linked with the right crash and all go into the squadron historical record. Jim ran across a bit of information he thought the Twedt family might find interesting and asked Chad to "tell your dad that the P-38 that Lowell was flying, *Mon Ami*, was the airplane that belonged previously to Stub Hatch of the 71st FS. Stub became an ace (5 enemy A/C shot down) in one day on a mission to Ploesti on June 10, 1944. Stub returned to the US in August 1944, as I recall."

Too bad *Mon Ami* wasn't as lucky for Lowell as she had been for Stub.

21

CLEAN-UP

From:	Jim Graham
Sent:	Tuesday, March 14, 2000
To:	Dale, Diana
Subject:	Jordan-Baldwin

Hi Diana –

Now that we have more or less descended upon Mark Baldwin at the Euro-command, and he is aware of the missing CIL file, I think it might be time to tweak Bill Jordan as to what he has done to investigate it. Having the two of them in contact might avoid some confusion and concentrate energy in the caverns of Suitland, MD. OK with you?

Jim

* * *

I told Jim *of course* he could get Bill Jordan involved. The Washington National Records Center at Suitland had told Johnie Webb in Hawaii that they couldn't find the file that held Billy's bracelet and the answer to where his remains had been found in 1952. In fact, it was the absence of that file that had started our international search in the first place, and it was time to link the two.

Jim composed a draft of his letter to the investigators for Bill Mays's and my approval on March 14.

On that same day Paolo sent us yet another location confirmation, calling the subject of his message The Final Solution, an unfortunate choice of words, but I knew what he meant. "What would you say or think if I tell you that today I've found an eyewitness who remembers those particulars without any suggestion?

- it was October 1944
- there were 3-4 fighters together
- there was an explosion in the air
- three planes were hit
- I saw one parachuted pilot who was lightly enjured and captured
- I know where the other two planes crashed
- one pilot was buried next to the crash"

He had been collecting testimony since January 4, and this was the best yet. His conclusion: "The solution is between Plunerbach, Aberstückl, Kirchnock and Leiterspitz. Forget Penserjoch and Garmesegg... Inga was right, I have a full confirmation of the testimony of Mr. Weger. Tomorrow I'll write for you my final report. Now I'm too tired."

He closed with an exuberant "CIAOOOOOOOOOOOOOOOOOO."

He must really love his job. I forwarded his message to Inga and gave her a pat on the back for having been right all along. I know she wasn't surprised, but Paolo's concession was a relief. At last we could all read from the same page.

Paolo had photographed the distributor found at Aberstückl and it was confirmed by Bob Cardin to be "identical to one I have on an engine here in the shop."

Bill Jordan answered Jim's query, but he said he was moving on to a new assignment and wouldn't be able to help. He told us we were on the right track with Baldwin's group at the 21st TAACOM and probably didn't need him, anyway. I was sad to lose one of our first helpers, but Jordan hadn't been an active participant for quite a while, and he was right—we were getting answers without him.

Paolo came back the next day with the eyewitness's report.

Yesterday I went to Aberstückl/Sonvigo and interviewed Alois Messner, 70 years old. Someone told me that he is the last eyewitness of the P-38 crashes. He has quite a good memory, but he can't walk without any help. I don't think he would be able to personally show us the crash-locations, but some of his sons could do it for him.

Here is his report.

I remember the crashes here in the area. It was 1944. It was October, I'm sure. I saw the fighters, three or four. They were flying North, coming from South. I was 14 years old. I didn't hear the FLAK, but the day later a woman told me that the planes were hit by the FLAK of Renon/Ritten. There was an explosion in the air. I didn't notice it, but many did. I can't remember who told me about the explosion: it was 56 years ago, you know. But I'm sure there was.

I saw a fighter going down over the Hüberhof, which is the last hut over the village of Muls/Mules. I didn't see the crash, but the day after I went there with a neighbour and my brother. There [was wreckage] everywhere. We collected some of those. This area is near the Plunerbach, the wood east of Muls/Mules. Another plane, the second, went down at Kirchnock (p.s. Hosp's location: Aberstückler Nock). There was a pilot. I don't know if he died from the crash in itself or if, as someone says, he was shooted by some locals. In every case, he was buried next to the crash-site, I mean 20 to 30 meters away. The burial site had a wooden cross, about 1,5 meter high. The cross is not there yet, I won't be able to determine the exact location but I will be able to distinguish a perimeter of about 20 meter: in that area you could look for remains.

After WWII the Italians came here and remove all the wreckage. They destroyed the biggest remains and took all of that stuff away. I think, there is nothing left, if not hidden under the ground. In the 80's, next to the burial site a small road (Forststrasse) was constructed, but during the excavations they didn't find anything. I never heard of some discover.

The third hit plane went down in the area of Pazzei Alm (p.s. Grimminger location Messner Basai). My sons used to carry the cattle over there. There is still the upper part of a machine-gun. I mean, it has been there since last year. Maybe, you could find out a serial number on it. I think no one removed it. Me and my sons know where it is. The pilot of this third plane parachuted himself and was catched. I saw him between German officials,

coming across the hut where I've been living. He was a very tall
man, I think more than 180 cm. He didn't seem to be injured, but
someone told me, he had some internal injuries. He walked
normally. Someone asked later me if he was blond or black hair:
I can't remember the particular. He was brought to
Sarentino/Sarnthein.

Paolo went on, "This transcription is the result of a very difficult
interview: The man, who is now 70, speaks German with an awful accent,
related to a local dialect. Don't forget that I'm Italian... But I recorded the
interview. I let it be checked by a German woman and she confirmed the
main allegations." Paolo said that before any investigation could be made,
we would have to wait for the snow to melt, at least until mid-May.

Then he suggested we re-read the testimony of Jakob Weger, "which
is perfectly coincident with Messner's report. Then you have to read accu-
rately Grimminger's list of crash-sites, according to the FLAK documents,
and you will find out that everything fits.

"Let's do it together:

- Northslope of the Kirchberg: this is the Kirchnock or Aberstückler
  Nock: crash-site and burial site, bracelet with double W. The
  corpse should be still there.
- Messner Basai: same as Pazzei Alm, no human remains (it was
  Olson's plane), we could check the machine-gun.
- East of Rabenstein/Blunabachtal: this is the area we called
  Blunerbach, possibly Twedt's crash-sites, no human remains are
  remembered, Weger could indicate the exact location;
- Kesselberg/Monte Catino: nothing to do with our case.
- I didn't understand if the P-38 turbo-charger came from
  Kirchnock or Blunerbachtal. Please, ask Mrs. Hosp for detailed
  informations. The distributor could come from both Kirchnock or
  Pazzei Alm, for sure not from Blunerbachtal."

And once more, Paolo faced the possibility that he had been on the
wrong track at Garmesegg. "Messner thinks that Garmesegg's crash-site is
connected to a bomber, not a fighter. He speaks about 9 parachutes. I
don't know. I don't know either what to think about the P-38 wheels at
the barn next to Penserjoch (Pens)." Paolo suggested we forget those two

crashes and concentrate on the others, then enumerated all the documentation we had for the official investigation, saying, "I think the first part of
June will be the right time to come here and checked all this sites. I won't
go there, I will just wait for further instructions.

"My work is not finished, but I've got the feeling that I reached my
main goal. So, this is the right occasion to thank everyone for cooperation.
It has been a very hard investigation, but it has been also such an unforget-
table experience. I hope to meet every one of you and warmly shake your
hands. My reward will be the final success in the operation. I will also took
part in a literary competition with the diary of this adventure. I remain at
your complete disposition. I still have got the original pictures, the inscriptions, some of the remains, addresses and phone number of every witness. I
can provide logistical support. In one word, just tell what do you need and
I'll try to satisfy you. If you think I'm wrong with my conclusions, just tell
it to me and I will be ready to restart."

Paolo wouldn't have to "restart," I was sure. We had what we needed. I looked forward to shaking Paolo's hand, too, but what I really wanted
to do was give him a big hug.

But once again, something in his report confused me. I wrote to Jim,
"[Paolo] insists the turbocharger could not have come from Plunerbach, and
I'm sure Inga said it did." I wasn't sure about Aberstückler Nock and Plunerbach (a/k/a Blunerbachtal), because the names confused me. I wrote Inga
for yet another confirmation. Frustrated by my muddle, she put "Big Sigh"
in the subject line of her response, but at least she set me straight.

"You are very right if you are confused by our reporter's conclusions.
Because he is wrong again! Please be so kind to re-read my messages from
February 26. And if you don't want to (or don't have them any more)
please notice the following which I think I made clear weeks ago:

- crash site Plunerbach (Weger's farm, where I found the large P-
  38 part and the smaller ones, and where the bracelet was mentioned by Jakob Weger): this should be Bill Wisner's crash site,
  and there he should have been buried - and never excavated. And
  there the investigation should be situated for your uncle.
- crash site Pazzei-Alm: should be Olson's site from where he
  could get down to Aberstückl and to the valley. My eye-witness
  Alois Gramm (Messner farm) 70 years old - and I can understand
  his dialect (which is not awful at all; I would call it strong and

characteristic) and that of the others very well! without translator - saw the captured man walking down lightly injured, accompanied into prisonship (as I reported to you).

- crash site Kirchnock or Aberstückler Nock: should be Twedt's site and burial-site. No bracelet! And the corpse could be there. Was not burnt, as my eyewitnesses said. Was a tall, strong man (as I reported to you)."

She reconfirmed that the Garmesegg crash site was a bomber with nine parachutes. "Maybe you have the impression that I am a little bit angry, resulting also from the lecture of the *Alto Adige* article which deals with a lot of details (two large pages!) with dead ends, and reporting the successful parts of the investigation for your uncle as made by the author. And mentioning the successful investigators (Christoph and me) only as 'also involved.' But anyway: let him be. He is young and perhaps ambitious in a way which does not fit for my old fashioned conviction of how a journalist should act. During the last two days I cleared up all my material and wrote the story in my way. It will be published partially in a newspaper, and later on otherwhere. And certainly I will send it immediately to you! But it is of course in German. I remember you have a person to translate it, like my first article."

She said that she and Christoph would go visit Jakob Weger again and ask him to protect the burial site.

Paolo had transposed the Aberstückl site with the Plunerbach site. The turbo charger came from Plunerbach—that was Billy's site—and the distributor came from Aberstückl, which was Twedt's site. I was finally clear on which was which.

But Inga had written another article. I hoped it wouldn't mean more trouble for Paolo.

Bill Mays called the investigators to get a read on what, if anything, they needed from us. Jim had expressed concern that the conflict between our on-site researchers might interfere with their investigation, so Bill's response was informative and reassuring. He said they had already requested the files and documents on Wisner and Twedt, but it would take a while for them to arrive by snail-mail, maybe as long as two months. "They welcome and document all related info and are keeping it in a file in Germany as they wait for the official files to come in. The better our work, the more efficient they can be. Liz Wilson and Bill Jordan are the best sources for what to do on Washington's/DOD's side. Case priorities do get changed based on this factor as I understand.

"The 21TSC-EUC people will be completely bias-less," he added. "They were with me, anyway. Very cordial and professional, but they have their own rules to follow and once they get the approval to investigate, they will with our friends' help or not. From my experiences here in Bulgaria, the best thing to keep for them is the logistical information. Names, addresses, contact info, etc. They will go and record their own testimonies for their own file, take their own pictures, complete accounting of the site(s), and determine on their own the likelihood of recovering bodily remains from the site(s). The EUC team will do their best to include our friends in their search, but on a limited basis. Most of the time I wasn't even with them, since they didn't want me to influence any responses from the witnesses. I wouldn't have, anyway, but that's not the case in all of their investigations. They won't take any side except the U.S. Army's."

Mays went on, "The best thing we can help accomplish is to narrow the search with supporting evidence ideally to one crash site, package it up, give it to them, and wait for their response. This is where Diana's 'family' influence will help and also that of her congressperson. Politicians like nice, 'feelgood' stories, as do we all. It would be especially nice to be able to tell a story of cooperation between some American people, the U.S. government, and some ethnic Italian and German 'locals' in NE Italy, where the only negative news is from the cablecar disaster. The U.S. Ambassador to Italy should also like this story for political reasons too."

He said things were kept very low-key during the investigation in Bulgaria. There were no local news stories and only two short radio interviews when they were gathering evidence. "We didn't seek any local publicity because I didn't want it (or any treasure hunters) to get in our way. They tried to, anyway, but that's another story."

Then he added his own insight into the Inga/Paolo conflict. "From the info I've received, Inga's reluctance to acknowledge Paolo is her problem...and ours, but since she's old enough to form her own opinions that we aren't going to change and she does live there, we'll have to accept it and keep moving forward. She sounds like a wonderful person and a definite asset and I don't think this is as big as a problem as we think. Just my opinion. The same is true of Paolo. He's young (around my age - 29), energetic, and lucky that this story will fit in with his profession. Kudos to him and in my opinion, I hope he writes one heck of a story and it helps launch his international reporting career. That would make me feel pretty good, and you can't have enough reporters on your side."

In Mays's own experience and hindsight, he felt it was important to keep everyone involved in all correspondence. "Psychologically, everyone wants to be part of something good and time will help put everyone in their desired place. Heck, I've lived in the heart of the Balkans (through one big conflict) for over two years. The antipathy between Italians/Germans is nothing (I haven't heard that they want to kill each other, but let me know if they do). Personally, I don't care for Italian guys that much either (sorry, nothing personal, Paolo). Some [of them] kind of pissed me off by the way they stared and hooted at my girlfriend every time we walked by...on the street. I'm flattered they felt she was attractive, but it gets a little disgusting after a while. Generally speaking of course; they're not all like that! Cultural differences. There's my 2 1/2 cents' worth. Keep everyone in the loop all the time when evidence is involved and it concerns the mission and let's find Lt. Wisner!"

Bill's 2 1/2 cents' worth was priceless. In just one e-mail he had put everything into perspective vis-à-vis Inga and Paolo, and he had told us what to expect from the investigators. But he was wrong about the ambassador's interest; I never heard back from him.

Something else was confusing me, and this time it wasn't northern Italy's multiple names for the same place. By this point we had referred to the European investigation team no less than six ways: EU Command, Euro-CIL, Euro Command, 21st TAACOM, 21st TSC at EUC, Baldwin's group, Roath's group, and probably some others, too. I didn't know which was their official name; I just knew they were the ones we would ultimately depend on, whatever they were called. I did know David Roath was the director of the USAMAA-E, which I assumed stood for United States Army Mortuary Affairs Activity in Europe. He was the man Carl Hoenshell's successful case had gone through, and Jim was making sure we followed the same protocol. As long as they got the information they needed and followed up, I was happy.

Bill Mays clarified who did what: David Roath's office was at European Command Headquarters, 21st Theater Army Area Command (TAACOM), in the Mortuary Affairs Department, located just outside Frankfurt; he was director. Mays wrote, "It is David's Mortuary Affairs Dept. [that] writes the report to be sent on to the DOD (Dept. of Defense) to request an excavation. This will depend on what David finds in his preliminary visit to the crash site(s) and interviews, etc. It is David's dept. [that] is responsible for doing any excavation and sometimes they use CILHI [Central Identification Laboratory, Hawaii] to do the work." Mays didn't have Mark Baldwin's exact title, but Baldwin worked in Roath's office. At last we knew who the U.S. players were.

While reviewing the crash-site information I realized I was missing one of the Sarn Valley players. I must have overlooked a message, because in one of her e-mails Inga had mentioned Alois Gramm as a name I should recognize. But it didn't ring a bell, so I asked her about it. It turns out in an attempt not to confuse me she had deliberately left out his name. She quoted the e-mail, which I had received after all, but she added, "I didn't want to confuse you with too many exotic names, but here they are: the first. 70-year-old was Luis (=Alois) Gramm, Messner farm, Aberstückl...Luis Gramm is also the owner of Messner Pazzei, where Olson must have landed. Our reporter calls him Alois Messner, but Messner is the farm's name. I phoned him today for not being confused by those names. And he [Gramm] is convinced that the pilot died in a 'normal' way, not 'shooted by some locals.' "

Then Inga quoted Gramm, who had told her, "I saw a fighter going down over the Hueberhof..." and explained that the Huber farm is next to the Pluner farm. "So it's always the Plunerbach crash: Plunerbach in the Flak report. And it was a Huber-farm cowboy who buried the burnt remains of the pilot."

She went on: "The second 70-year-old man's name was Josef Thaler, Hamann-farm, Muls near Aberstückl (photo with girl, you remember). Opposite side of Plunerbach crash site." She thought that the Kesselberg site, Paolo's fourth site, might have something to do with our case, "But not as a crash site, more as a site where observers perhaps saw a Lightning which was hit but finally did not go down. Maybe it was the plane that made it back to Ancona."

She closed, saying she had mailed me a copy of her story and wishing me "an unspoilt weekend."

Thank goodness I wasn't losing my mind. Now all the players fit. Paolo's Alois Messner was actually Alois Gramm from Messner farm. Paolo had more difficulty understanding Mr. Gramm's accent than he thought.

On March 19 Paolo published three more articles following up his first ones. These were shorter, and only one of them dealt with Billy's crash site, but they tied up the loose ends in his first story and set some facts straight. Best of all, he spelled my name right.

I scanned Inga's map and e-mailed it to Jim. He superimposed a grid over it, so now we could use coordinates to be sure we were talking about the same location; the names would be secondary. He did a similar thing with Mr. Grimminger's map, which was less detailed but covered the over-all search area. We spent the next few days making sure each of us under-stood and agreed which crash site was whose: Plunerbach (Blunabachtal) was Wisner's (Jakob Weger's farm), Kirchberg (Aberstückl) was Twedt's, and Pazzei-Alm (Messner Basai or Pazzei) was Olson's.

Inga's article arrived March 23rd. She enclosed a lovely photo taken last spring of the view out her window, a lush, green meadow dotted with wildflowers and accented by an imposing abstract sculpture. The flower petals glowed in the sunlight, and I could almost smell the fragrance of the grass. A case of spring fever caused by a season a year old and half a world away nearly carried me away.

Inga's story was long, translating it was harder than it should have been, and my results were disappointing. I had to scan the printed copy into a text program before I could run it through my computer's transla-tion software, but even though I set everything for German text, either the scanning software or the text-converter didn't recognize the special Ger-man characters. As a result, any letter with an umlaut came out wrong: the ä turned into an "e," the ö was a "6," the ü was an "O," and the German character for a double "S" was interpreted as either "f" or a "B."

As a result, the scanned text would have been garbage to a computer, so before I could run it through the translation software I had to fix each mis-scanned character individually. By midnight I was going cross-eyed, so I quit and went to bed. I dreamed in German all night long and woke up the next morning wondering what I had said.

In spite of the problems I did get the general sense of her article. It was a charming diary of her search and recounted most of what she had told me in her e-mails. But there was one passage about the recollections of a German soldier who had manned an anti-aircraft gun on October 20, 1944, that I could only guess at. Inga had mentioned the diary of an anti-aircraft gunner in one of her early e-mails, but its significance hadn't struck me at the time. Here it looked important, and I needed a better transla-tion, so I set the article aside for the time being.

About this time Jim told me about a friend of his, Bill Ward, who had shipped over to Italy with Billy and shared a tent at Foggia with him, Paul Sum-mer, and Eddy Steffani. They had become acquainted through Paul Summer in

1945, and through the years had stayed in touch through the 71st Fighter Squadron alumni association. When Jim told Bill Ward about our project, he said he wanted to help, so he sent Jim copies of relevant parts of his files. Jim forwarded them to me, and I was touched by the thoughtfulness.

In the package was a photo of Billy Wisner and Bill Ward leaning against the side of a building. Billy looked relaxed and happy, his legs crossed and his cap set back on his head, revealing his handsome face and the widow's peak he inherited from Idy. It was eerie to see a "new" photo of Billy, and for a split second he came to life.

The documents he enclosed were his transfer orders from Salinas, Moses Lake, Ontario, and Hamilton Field, the same ones I'd seen in Billy's file. But he included two I hadn't seen. One was dated 10 September 1944 assigning five pilots out of the Hamilton Field group—Steffani, Twedt, Wisner, Summer, and Ward—to the 71st Fighter Squadron. The other, dated 13 September, confirmed their assignment to the 1st Fighter Group. Those documents filled two gaps in Billy's file.

Other gaps were filling in, too. Inga's research on the bomber crash her husband had seen as a boy, the one that had brought Inga into the search in the first place, had been left an open-ended issue when our search for Billy turned to the Sarn Valley. But now that Inga was bitten by the WWII bug, she wanted to know if Jim had any more information on that crash. The date, February 16, 1945, and the facts that two crew members were KIA and two were taken prisoner were all the information she had. Keith Bullock's records were incomplete, so she wrote Hans Grimminger for his help, too.

Jim told her it was a B-17G bomber of the 97th Bomb Group of the 5th Wing of the 15th Air Force flying out of Foggia. He had the serial number and knew there had been 10 crewmen aboard. But that's all he could tell her, because in February 1945 he was part of a group escorting Roosevelt and Churchill through the Mediterranean to the Yalta Conference with Stalin and didn't have the mission reports from that period.

However, he said he could look it up when he got to the National Archives in April. He was pretty sure he would find something on the crash and recovery of the bomber's crew in their captured German documents section.

It was almost the end of March, and we were pretty sure we had as much information as we were going to get through the means available to us. It was time for a physical search of the area.

And, as if on cue, Christoph e-mailed Jim to say he would visit Mr. Gramm and Mr. Weger on March 26. He added, "another thing is to say, in a few days the snow will melt, the [Plunerbach] crash site will be free by snow in a week, but at the other crashsites the snow doesn't melt until May."

Come on, sunshine...

Bill Ward and Billy at Foggia, October 1944

22

THE PACKAGE

March 30, 2000

Dear Jim,

Per your outline, here are the following documents, in the order you asked for them:

- Family tree
- Picture of Bill
- E-mail from Bill Jordan (with my notes of who I called)
- My first letter to Johnie Webb
- Webb's response saying the CIL file is missing
- My follow-up letter to Webb asking what to do next (never got a response)
- 71st website bulletin board notice and responses posted

The rest is coming. As I understand your outline, I still need to furnish:

- A letter from me stating my family objective and desire for an expedited resolution of the search
- My summary of the gov't files on Wisner to 1946 (or should I go further?)
- Copy of the letter(s) indicating the bracelet and remains

What else? I have copies of all the e-mails we sent back and forth, so I can give you any of them that you deem important, but I'm not sure where to start.

Diana

* * *

Now that our research was complete, we tied up loose ends for the investigators. I desperately hoped our evidence would convince Roath's group to pursue a site excavation.

Inga pursued her research on the Ritten bomber crash. It was becoming a worthwhile project, and I was glad more good would come out of her hard work. And something had moved in her investigation. "Immediately after the Ritten crash," she wrote, "a 56 year old man hurried up to the crash site—so fast that he got heart problems and died suddenly on his way! Knowing his name I called up the priest and asked him for looking into the list of the died people. And there he was at Feb. 16! And now I have the MACR (from Mr. Grimminger and Keith Bullock, too). I have even the 1945 addresses of the two widows. So the Wisner investigation was able to solve two other cases. Nice or not this coincidence?"

Jim put our search chronology together, assembled the materials, and prepared the formal request for David Roath's office to make a complete investigation. His trip to Maryland was set for April 17-20 and would include a stop in Pennsylvania to visit his friend and fellow squadron member, Bill Ward. This would be their first face-to-face meeting since 1945, and I was glad the search for Billy was instrumental in getting them together.

Jim's primary objective was to visit the National Archives in College Park for more research on the 71st Fighter Squadron, but he was considering a visit to Suitland to see if he could shake Billy's "missing" CIL file out of the Washington National Records Center there. Bill Jordan had told him it wouldn't hurt to ask, so Jim e-mailed three people at the WNRC to request an appointment specifically "for consultation concerning the acquisition, location, content and disposition of the Central Identification Laboratory (CIL) file 5034." I wrote a letter for Jim to take along that granted him permission to "act on my behalf in reviewing CIL file 5034, to receive copies of it and of any other files or information relating to same, as well as to receive any personal effects attached thereto." I felt like a lawyer when I composed the letter, but I didn't want him to get there and not have access to the files we needed.

We agreed that it was "nail-biting and finger-crossing time."

When Bill Ward got my letter thanking him for the photo of him with Billy and the copies of their orders, he called me. He reminisced about the old days, describing in great detail their living arrangements at Foggia and how they had built their quarters out of tufa, the native sandstone. It was interesting, but I was pretty sure Billy hadn't been there long enough to help with the construction, or he would have mentioned it in his letters. Bill told me Billy was a great guy, and they had started to become good friends in the short five weeks Billy was there.

I promised him a copy of my photo of Lowell Twedt and told him how close we were to making an official request for excavation. I loved meeting him; thanks to Billy I had made another new friend. And it came to me that, at long last, I had done what I had originally set out to do— find someone in Billy's squadron who remembered him.

But now we might even find Billy.

It took Jim the first two weeks of April to put together the package for the 21st TAACOM. The investigators needed letters from Billy Wisner's next of kin (my mother and me) specifically requesting an investigation. We asked for the same from Lowell Twedt's family in the hope that the investigators might be more willing to visit the area if they could find two MIAs on one trip.

As I reviewed the records to be sure we had covered everything, it struck me that Billy's IDP file had arrived almost exactly one year before, kicking off this whole incredible journey. "What a difference a year makes," I wrote Jim. It didn't seem that long, because once the search had started it had taken us just four months to do what the U.S. Army hadn't done in 56 years.

But after so much excitement and discovery, once we were ready for the government to get involved, things stalled. On April 10 Jim wrote that he had heard no response from either 21st TAACOM or Suitland. "I feel like a telemarketer who has just been hung up on at dinner hour. Do I have bad breath?...Do you have a shovel? Maybe we'll have to do our own thing in Sarntal!"

I told him I had three shovels and was willing to use them all, and "no, you don't have bad breath—at least not at this range!"

But on April 11 we hit pay dirt, a response from Mark Baldwin. He and David Roath had been out of the office for a couple of weeks. In my obsession with our search it never occurred to me they might be working on other investigations. But Baldwin said he would "very much like to receive the information you have regarding the site in northern Italy...As soon as I receive the information, I will most likely plan a trip to the site, especially if the location of the graves of the pilots are believed to be known."

When Jim forwarded the e-mail to me, he added, "Hooray!!!"

We'd done our part, and as a result the daily e-mails dwindled. I missed them. Inga sent me a package containing a travel book, a pamphlet, and a recent photo of the scene outside her office window. The snow was still deep, so I knew it would be a while before they could get up to the site. I took time out with the book, *Walks and Tours in South Tyrol,* for a virtual visit to her region. I even allowed myself to hope that someday I might be able to see it in person.

The pamphlet, written in three languages, was from a war memorial near Brixen/Bressanone, not far from our search area. A local resident had erected a monument to the crews of two U.S. bombers that crashed there December 29, 1944, and February 28, 1945. The introductory letter from the mayor said the memorial symbolized peace for those who once were enemies, but the last paragraph of the pamphlet related the more realistic local sentiment at the time of the crashes—anything but friendly toward the Allied invaders.

> The last few years of the war proved also for Brixen to be rather dramatic, especially since the Italian armistice of September 8, 1943, when the Germans occupied Italy. In the Province of Bozen (the South Tirol) the [G]ermans were more than welcome as there was hope now that the South Tirol would (again) be separated from Italy. The whole administration and all public services were [G]ermanised without delay. Prefect Froggio gave way to Peter Hofer: in the municipalities the Italian Podestà (a sort of mayor) gave way to German-speaking mayors. But soon fresh conflicts arose between those who had opted for Germany in 1939 (the vast majority) and those who had not. Contrary to expectations, the war went on and on in spite of D-Day (June 6, 1944) and the catastrophes on the eastern front. In Italy the Allied Forces made slow progress, and the long agony of the Third Reich badly affected the civilian population. As the railway over the Brenner [Pass] was the main supply

route for the Germans in Italy the line and especially the numerous bridges were the principal target for the Allied bombers. October 4, 1944 was the beginning of massive air raids on the railway bridge in Albeins: 14 civilians and 6 soldiers died on that day. The frequent air raids gave rise to considerable hatred for the Allied personnel. Some crew members who survived the crash of their aircraft, regretfully, met with mal-treatment, or worse, with a sad end. When the guns fell silent on May 2, 1945, the people of the Tirol awaited the new era with mixed feelings. They were happy they could live in peace once again, but they had to do so without many of their ablest young men. Moreover, the prospect of having to remain part of Italy was depressing. The uncertainty lasted more than a year.

Thank goodness relations are friendly now. I checked Billy's flight log and was relieved he flew a combat mission to Munich on October 4 and was nowhere near the bridge at Albeins that day. I was falling in love with the people of Südtirol, and I didn't want to think my uncle might have been responsible for the deaths of our new friends' loved ones.

Serendipity solved my problem of translating Inga's article when Jim got an e-mail from Janet Hagen, the wife of Carl Hagen, a retired USAF colonel and Jim's tentmate and fellow pilot at Foggia. She offered the translation services of her son-in-law and his father, both fluent in German. The father, Martin I. Selling, was a German native and had been a translator for the U.S. Army in Europe during WWII.* Jim asked me if I could use their help, and I readily accepted. I was feeling guilty for not yet having shared Inga's article with Jim.

In the meantime, Inga's research on the Ritten crash inched forward.

---

*Martin I. Selling's story would make a good book. He grew up in Germany and was imprisoned in Nuremburg on Kristallnacht in 1938 and later at Dachau because he was Jewish. Before Hitler's Final Solution was put in place, the Nazis tried to rid itself of its Jews by allowing them to emigrate. Selling's aunt secured his release on the condition he leave Germany within six months. He joined a refugee camp in England, then emigrated to the U.S. in 1940. He tried to join the Army Air Corps after Pearl Harbor ("to drop bombs on my oppressors") but was rejected as an enemy alien. But in 1942 he was drafted into the U.S. Army, trained as an interrogator, and arrived in France 30 days after the D-Day invasion. He gained satisfaction and some measure of revenge in helping the winning side as American troops recaptured enemy territory and took Nazi prisoners.

She would soon meet Keith Bullock in person. He and the mayor of a village on the other side of the Eisack Valley would be in her area to attend a ceremony honoring the crew of another crashed American bomber.

"I think, nowadays, friendships are absolutely the best result from yesterday wars, aren't they?" she asked. I started counting up the new friends I'd made over the past year and ran out of fingers. I couldn't have agreed more.

Baldwin was eager to receive Jim's packet of information, and on April 13 he asked Jim to fax it to him so they could get started. But Jim told him it was over 100 pages long, too long to fax, so he e-mailed Baldwin the names of our on-site researchers to get them started. He followed up with messages to Inga, Christoph, and Paolo alerting them that the investigators would soon be involved, and he asked everyone to let us know when Baldwin contacted them.

Jim express-mailed the package on Friday, April 14. The Post Office told him it would arrive in Germany the following Monday or Tuesday.

It was out of our hands now.

23

THE BRACELET

From: Jim Graham
Sent: Monday, April 17, 2000
To: Dale, Diana
Subject: SUITLAND

Hi Diana—

Brought my laptop with me, so I can keep in touch with what's going on. I saw Janet Hagen's message re the translation, so jump in if you feel like it. I think the whole Hagen crew will enjoy the result as will we. I wish we could compare the two stories— Inga & Paolo.

Today I called Suitland to see if they had acknowledged my e-mail. Leanne T. said she had been out of town & barely remembered there had been an e-mail for her. Anyway, she said that we have to get CILHI to send accession permission. I told her that Johnie Webb had been behind it, but she said there is only one person in CILHI that she responds to. She says that RACHEL PHILLIPS must send her (1) an accession #, (2) the box #, (3) Records Central Locator #, and (4) the file # (CIL 5034).

I told Leanne that we would try to contact Rachel via e-mail & get her to send Leanne the right stuff. Leanne said that they would run another search & if I can get an appointment thereafter, she says that their accession records would show history of the original receipt and any subsequent accession or movement. She said they get many such requests as ours, but all records

are owned by the agency that committed them, so they only
retrieve them at the order of the responsible agency.
Do you think you could contact Johnie Webb or even Bill Jordan
& ask what Rachel's e-mail address is? If you can, maybe you
could get Rachel to do the necessary tricks for Leanne. I'll be
here through Friday, so maybe we can swing it.
Any news from Mark Baldwin yet? He should have the package
by tomorrow. Today I was digging up some MACR's for Inga &
Grimminger. I printed out the one dealing with the B-17 that fell in
the Hosp back yard. One of the surviving crew members was
from Seattle.
Let me know what's going on once Mark gets the bundle.
Jim

* * *

Now in Maryland and without the proper permission protocols, Jim was being stonewalled by the National Records Center, and I felt responsible. As soon as I got his request I called Johnie Webb in Hawaii, who returned my call within minutes. After I hung up with Webb, I wrote Jim that Webb remembered the case and was calling Rachel Phillips to tell her to call me back within the half-hour. Webb had said he seemed to remember that more information about the bracelet had come to light since we talked nearly five months before, but he didn't remember enough details to be able to elaborate. He would check his files to see if there was anything they hadn't told me yet. I wrote all this in my e-mail to Jim while I waited for Rachel's call and said, "[Webb] may end up obviating the whole point of this thing, if they've actually found the file." I told Jim that Webb was very interested to learn we had found the crash sites, but I didn't give Webb any details, telling him all the information was now in the hands of the team in Europe.

No sooner had I sent that message to Jim than the phone rang. This time it was Rachel Phillips from Hawaii. I wrote Jim again to tell him about the call. "Rachel called me back in just the time it took me to write the last e-mail to you. She had the [CIL] file in her hands, and a package marked, 'Identification bracelet for William O. Wisner, 0-708778.' I asked her if the package felt like it had the bracelet in it, and she said it was thickly padded, and she couldn't tell. I told her to open it."

The tone of my e-mail to Jim was light and breezy, but my emotions had been off the chart while Rachel Phillips opened the envelope. I held my breath and gripped the phone until my hand ached while I waited. The packet was wrapped in several layers of paper and tape, and Rachel had had a hard time getting into it. I was a blindfolded witness at the opening of a time capsule, but I couldn't—and wouldn't—wait for them to send me the file so I could open it myself. I had to know if the bracelet was there.

I continued in my e-mail to Jim, "After what seemed like hours, she finally got it open. It's there—Lt. William O. Wisner. The chain is broken, but it's there. I asked her if it looked like it had been burned, and she said it wasn't shiny at all. So I guess you're off the hook to find the file and can do your other research without bureaucratic snafus, I hope. Rachel is going to make a copy of the file and send me the bracelet and the papers 'within a week.' I'll shoot you a copy as soon as I get it."

I closed with, "Whew! I'm going to go have a stiff drink. Have one with me."

Jim answered that night. "Amazing!" he said. "Now how did Rachel get it? I thought it was on file in Suitland! Whatever!!! If nothing else, all of our flapping around trying to find the crash site has kept you occupied while the bureaucrats stumbled through their filing system. What reaction does your Mom have? I guess you probably are going to wait for it to show up before you tell her. I can't believe that the Hoenshell and Wisner searches both ended up with bracelets! You may get a trip to the Sarntal yet! Go Mark Baldwin!! I'm pleased for you and your family. I just got back from dinner or I would have hoisted one." He asked me to keep him posted.

I had the same question Jim had—how did they get the bracelet? But I could only tell him what I knew: "Johnie and Rachel said they had just kept after Suitland to find the file. I wish he had told me before, that they were still looking; I would have kept in better touch. If you remember, I had fired back a letter after the one he wrote saying it was 'missing' and asked what do we do now; he never responded to that one, so I just assumed the thing was dead in the water."

I wouldn't tell my mother just yet. I wanted to wait until they came to Colorado in early June and just give it to her. I have a flair for drama, and I wanted to see her reaction for myself. I knew there would be lots of tears and blubbering from both of us.

Thank goodness Jim had other research to do while he was in D.C.; otherwise, the trip would have been a complete waste of his time and money.

After he had dug out as much information from the National Archives as he could, Jim headed for Pennsylvania to visit Bill Ward. I wished I could have been a mouse in the corner listening to the two of them reminisce about their days at Foggia. Jim had said Bill was working hard on his memoirs and would send me the parts relating to Billy.

Jim also wrote about what he found at the National Archives. "Today I was looking through the captured German 'Dead Lists' trying to find a possible entry about Wisner or Twedt, but found nothing specific. There are a couple entries of 'unknowns' in the Bolzano area for October 20, 1944, but no information other than an entry against a P-38, so who knows—maybe they were the subjects. It is amazing to handle those original hand-written pages that the Germans so meticulously kept. In roughly counting the number of their recorded U.S. air crashes listed, I get nearly 10,000. That's a lot of guys, considering that the heavy bombers had crews of 8-10! Just the 'dead lists' containing about 30-40 names per sheet occupied two boxes about four inches thick each. I kept wondering how many families have never known where their guys were buried. I think graves registration people did an earnest job, but take your Uncle Bill's case."

Exactly what I was thinking. In Billy's case, there were two unsolved deaths from just one incident. Add Carl Hoenshell and possibly Eddy Steffani, and that's four that were unaccounted for out of just one squadron. How many other unsolved cases are still out there? Thousands? Tens of thousands? What about Korea and Vietnam? The numbers must be staggering.* I began to gain new respect for the efforts of the people at Mortuary Affairs and the CIL.

On April 19 Jim started getting impatient for the package to arrive at Baldwin's. He was still on the road, so he asked me for the tracking number, which he'd forgotten to take with him. I passed it along, then looked it up myself on the U.S. Postal Service Web site, www.usps.gov, to see if it had arrived. It had made it as far as the jumping-off point for Europe, but beyond that there was no information.

After he got back to Seattle, Jim collected his thoughts about his trip. He had accomplished a lot. The 71st Fighter Squadron was lucky to have such a dedicated researcher. He reconfirmed that the captured German records didn't reveal anything on the Wisner or Twedt crashes. "I think

---

*According to the Department of Defense Web site, there are approximately 78,000 still missing from WWII; 8,000 from Korea, and 3,600 from Vietnam.

that Mr. Grimminger's look in the German Bundesarchiv for the flak outfit's records was the only contact we've had on that score except Olson's
ME capture record. I sorted through every [German report] they had at
the Archives and found lots of cases where the pilots were buried next to
the crash site or in a local cemetery. It makes me wonder if the families in
those cases are aware of the burial location."

He asked if the package from CILHI had shown up yet. "I'll be interested in the detail contents and any records of the routing of the file. I still
wonder what circumstances led to routing of 'remains' including the
bracelet through the Griesheim mausoleum and wonder if that was just a
temporary Army processing point for remains recovered in the years immediately after the end of the war." He said he never checked back with Suitland once the bracelet was found. "Someone in Suitland had to have
routed it to Hawaii, and as you were wondering—how come they hadn't
kept you apprised of the progress in locating it? Best not meddle with the
bureaucracy once they've scratched your itch!"

He had brought back the MACRs that Inga and Keith Bullock had
asked for, but he was unable to find the mission reports for the groups
involved. "It seems that the bomber groups only kept statistical tables on
their operations, such as bomb tonnage, hit estimates, fuel data, A/C and
crew losses etc. The bomber MACRs with their detailed crew interrogations end up to be the only narratives as to what happened. The fighter
groups, however, were very narrative and represented the composite of the
interrogations of the pilots after the missions. I was able to copy off more
of our 1st FG and 71st FS mission reports. I now have the complete set
from Jan. 1, 1943, through the end of the war in May 1945. The copies
almost made my baggage exceed the weight limit."

He wished us a happy Easter and hoped the bracelet would arrive that
week. What an outstanding man, I thought. I couldn't believe how lucky I
was to have him as a resource.

The next day Paolo wrote that he would be in New York from April
26th through May 5. I wanted to go meet him, as I would Inga in Seattle,
but logistics kept me away. Of course, Paolo wouldn't have expected me to
go, but I felt I had short-changed him.

I caught him up on where we were with the packet of materials for
the Roath team and told him I was waiting for the CIL file to arrive with
the bracelet. I also wrote my thank-you to Martin Selling and took him up
on his offer to help with the translation of Inga's article. I told him the

manuscript was on its way and he'd have it in a few days.

Meanwhile, Jim e-mailed Mark Baldwin to say the package should be in their hands by now and asked if they would confirm its receipt.

The CILHI packet arrived on April 25. In it was a letter, a folder with photographs of the bracelet and its packaging, and an Evidence/Custody Document for me to sign. But there was no bracelet and no copy of Billy's CIL file 5034, as the letter said there would be.

I called Rachel Phillips to find out why, but a young man in her office answered and told me she had gone on vacation. My throat tightened and I felt anger rising as I envisioned waiting two weeks before she could get back and send the file and the bracelet. I tried to keep my voice from quavering as I explained my problem, but the gentleman was way ahead of me. He said mine wasn't the first call he'd received that required follow-through on something Ms. Phillips had neglected to do before she left, and he promised to send the file by Federal Express the next day. At least someone was on the ball.

I read what was in the package I did have. Johnie Webb's cover letter answered the questions I had asked in my letter to him almost a year before, after the bracelet's existence had come to light in Billy's personnel file.

According to documents in the file, the following answers are provided in response to your questions.

Where and when was the I.D. bracelet found?
On a translation document dated July 26, 1952 the Territorial Legion of the Carabinieri at Bolzano Italy notified the Ministry of Foreign Affairs in Rome that on July 9, 1952 they had recovered the remains and the identification "tag" with the inscription "Lt. William O. Wisner, 0 708778". The Ministry of Foreign Affairs in turn notified the U.S. Embassy of this finding.

Where are the remains associated with my uncle now?
According to the document titled Record of CIL Remains, the remains assigned CIL #5034 are placed in above ground storage at Griesheim/Main Mausoleum.

Is there the remotest possibility, given the advances of science and DNA testing, that these remains can be positively identified?
Remains are sampled for mitochondrial DNA analysis only when

traditional forensic anthropological and odontological techniques and circumstantial evidence are not strong enough to support a positive identification. Mitochondrial DNA is a viable tool in the identification of human remains, but only when used in conjunction with other corroborating evidence.

Based on the anatomical chart in the file and the amount of remains recovered, there is a possibility of sampling the remains for mitochondrial DNA. The final decision will be based on the actual remains upon disinterment, if that should occur.

If it is found, can we get the bracelet back?
The bracelet is enclosed herein. Please sign and date the DA Form 4137 and return it to Ms. Rae Phillips, Senior WWII Analyst in the Casualty Data Section at the address above. A self-addressed stamped envelope is enclosed for your convenience.

If the official story is that he went down over Italy, why were remains and the I.D. bracelet transferred from a mausoleum in Griesheim, Germany?
The American Graves Registration Service Mausoleum Griesheim/Main (Mediterranean) Germany was the operating mortuary with the responsibility of processing cases from that area in Europe.

The letter said the CIL file was enclosed which, of course, it wasn't. But the young man I had spoken to was as good as his word, and the Fed Ex package came on the 27th, one year to the day after I had first written to Webb.

This time the file was complete. I pulled out the brown packet. Typed on the outer envelope was "Identification bracelet engraved 'William O. Wisner 0708770' CIL #5043, Griesheim/Main (formerly Unknown X-70035, AGRS Mausoleum Grieshiem/Main (MED) Germany, S&R 721)." Inside that was a corrugated folder that had been fastened shut with brown paper tape, and inside that was a small brown envelope marked "One (1) I.D. bracelet for: Lt. William O. Wisner 0-708 770 Recovered with Case SR 722 Designated Unknown X-70035 (Med Zone) Re-designated C.I.L. #5034." Inside that was a small card onto which the bracelet had been taped. I tipped the envelope, and the bracelet slid into my hand.

It was a little tarnished, but it wasn't burned black, as I had expected. In fact, the part covered by tape had been even shinier back in 1952 when it was affixed to the card and sealed in the envelope. I wondered who had polished it before wrapping it up.

It had no clasp, and only half the chain was intact, but there it was, in my hand at last. I breathed a sigh of relief and gave in to the tears.

Once I composed myself, I read the file. This one was much shorter than the last one I had. The first document, dated 20 August 1954, was the same as the last memo in Billy's Individual Deceased Personnel File. It asked that the bracelet be retained with CIL file 5034 until such time as the case was resolved and stated that once the case was identified, the file and bracelet were to be forwarded to the Memorial Division for further action. The next 12 pages were more copies of letters I had already seen and more forms with the same information about the bracelet and the remains.

The next page was a Record of CIL Remains for file 5034 describing remains removed from grave X-70035 as "Distal _ L/Humerus; proximal _ L/Ulna and proximal 2/3 L/radius." Under "Disposition of Remains," it said, "Placed in above ground storage at Griesheim/Main Mausoleum,...Unknown X-70035 Griesheim/Main Maus (Med Zone), Subj: 'Identification of World War II Deceased', dtd 1 December 1952." Added at the bottom was "Note: One (1) I.D. Bracelet for Lt William O. Wisner 0-708 778 forwarded to OQMG with this report." That form was dated 12 December 1952.

The skeletal chart showed the extent of the remains they found. As described on the previous form, the blacked out portions were segments of the three left arm bones just above and below the elbow—not enough in those days to make a positive identification. The Dental Comparison Chart indicated no teeth were recovered. At the bottom of that form was a notation that the remains were recovered "5-10 miles NE of Bolzano."

Wrong. We now knew that Billy's crash site was due north of Bolzano.

The next document was intriguing. It was from Headquarters, 7770 USAREUR QM Mortuary Service Detachment and said, "The only recoverable remains of: William O. Wisner...previously buried as Unknown X-70035...Identification is approved...by the following members of the board of Review,...dated 12 September 1952." It was signed by three members of the Quartermaster Corps but had been stamped CAN-CELLED five times. A hand-written note added later and signed by someone at the Identification Branch approved the CIL designation.

Following that was a Report of Burial, stamped CANCELLED four times.

The next form was the "Identification Check List" that weighed pros and cons for identification. The only items marked "favorable" for identification were date and place of death, cause of death, estimated weight and age, identification bracelet. Under Remarks it said, "2/Lt William O. WISNER, 0-708 778 was the pilot and sole occupant of P-38 A/C #43-28379 which crashed approximately five (5) miles N.E. of Bolzano, Italy on 20 October 1944. Unknown X-70035 was recovered from the crash site on the mountain near SARENTINO 5 to 10 miles N.E. of Bolzano, Italy. Torrential streams passing the area of crash site have washed away most of the plane wreckage and the remains. Identification media listed above plus anthropological findings prove the case Unknown X-70035 to be the only recoverable remains of 2/Lt William O. Wisner." At last, an official indentification. But that form was stamped CANCELLED in two places.

In other words, Billy had been "officially identified" three times, but someone had changed his mind and canceled the forms.

After that, there were more forms, another skeletal chart, copies of the mission report, and a copy of Jack Anderson's eyewitness report of the crash.

The next page revealed that the government was pretty sure whose remains they had. It was dated about a month before my fifth birthday, when we were living in San Antonio. Idy and Papa were still on Melbourne Street. They never heard a word.

```
                    HEADQUARTERS
       7770 USAREUR QM MORTUARY SERVICE DETACHMENT
       APO 757                                 US ARMY


                              14 October 1952


   NARRATIVE OF INVESTIGATION


   AUTHORITY:


   In accordance with the instructions contained in
   ID # 986, dated 7 August 1952, a visit was made to
   SARENTINO (Sheet 5/A 9887), Italy to recover the
   remains of 2/Lt WILLIAM O. WISNER, 0-708778.
```

FACTS AND CIRCUMSTANCES:

Records indicated that 2/Lt WISNER was the pilot of
P-38 A/C #43-2837 which was last seen in a spin 5
miles northeast of BOLZANO, Italy. Subject casualty
was reported KIA 20 October 1944. A letter from the
Italian Ministry of Foreign Affairs, dated 26 July
1952, stated that human bones and an ID bracelet
bearing the name WILLIAM O. WISNER, 0-708778 had
been found near SARENTINO, Italy.

FINDINGS:

A visit was made to the Carabinieri at SARENTINO,
Italy. A small box containing the remains and the
ID bracelet for WISNER were received from the
police. The crash site, located on a mountain near
SARENTINO was then visited. A thorough search of
the crash site failed to reveal additional
remains. The crash site is located in a rocky
stream bed of a type know as a "Torrente". It is,
in other words, a rather small stream except when
there is a heavy rainfall or melting snow. It then
becomes a channel to carry off this water, and has
a very strong current, which is quite capable of
carrying away a crashed aircraft. Practically all
of the wreckage has disappeared, either taken away
by scrap hunters, or washed away by the stream. It
is the opinion of this investigator that most of
the aircraft and certainly the remains have been
carried away by this stream. These remains were
assigned SR #722.

CONCLUSION:

It is concluded from the above that the remains
recovered are the only recoverable remains of 2/Lt
WILLIAM O. WISNER, 0-708778.

RECOMMENDATION:

It is recommended that the remains recovered be
declared the only recoverable remains of 2/Lt
WILLIAM O. WISNER, O-708778. [emphasis added]

> THEODORE R. PETERSON
> 1st Lt   QMC
> Investigator

The U.S. government knew whose remains they had found. My heart
bled for my grandmother. She should have been told.

The next document was a translation of a letter in Italian that followed, written to the U.S. Embassy in Rome from the Ministry of Foreign
Affairs in Rome and dated 26 July 1952. They, too, knew whose body had
been found.

VERBAL NOTICE

The Minister of Foreign Affairs has the
pleasure to inform the U.S. Embassy of the
following: The Territorial Legion of the
Carabinieri at Bolzano has notified us that on 9
July, at location Heissbraum, were recovered human
bones together with an identification tag with the
inscription "Lt. William O. Wisner, O 708778".

The remains of Lt. Wisner were found not far
from the place where the wreckage of an American
Fighter plane was hit during an air battle.

The remains have been placed in a sealed box
and handed to the Sarentino townhall charnel-house
and the tag is being held in suspense by the
Carabinieri of Sarentino.

The Minister of Foreign Affairs sends his
best regards to the U.S. Embassy.

Seal of the Ministry of Foreign Affairs

Heissbraum—another location name. Would we ever learn where Billy was?

One more translation followed, but this one was not accompanied by the original Italian document.

ITALIAN REPUBLIC

TERRITORIAL LEGION of CARABINIERI
(Italian gendarme) of BOLZANO

Section of Sarentino

Sarentino, July 12, 1952

TO: Attorney of the Republic   B o l z a n o
TO: Superior Office of the Carabinieri   B o l z a n o

SUBJECT: Finding of pieces of mortal remains
pertaining to an allied pilote.

Reference is made to our letter with
same number and subject, dated July 9, 1952. We
herewith beg to inform you that from the
examination executed by Dr. Planger Giorgio of
this community results that the three human bones,
pertaining without doubt to the deceased pilote
Lt. William O. Wisner, are to be:

two thirds of the ulna
one piece of the radius
one piece of the humerus (see report of the
doctor).

July 10 and 11 other excavating works
have been made but no other mortal remains could
be found.

From investigations made, results that
the allied authorities at this time have been
informed of the place where the remains of the
pilote have been discovered and that after the
liberation an american official has been present
for recovery.

It could not be established, however,
if said allied official has succeeded to find out
the place because O. Wisner has been buried at the
shore of a torrent where the airplane probably has
dropped and in time of full stream a great part of
the bones may have been carried away by the water.

The three bones found were put into a
little case which, closed and sealed, has been
given in custody to Mr. Aichner Giuseppe,
sacristan of the local parish to be put into the
ossuary of the community (see receipt joined).

The plate of recognition, however, is
kept from this command at the disposal of your
office.

Signature: Maresciallo Palaia Artemio

I assumed the "plate of recognition" meant the I.D. bracelet. A transmittal letter for that translation and another copy of the Burial Report
came next.

And that was the end of the file. But in that last letter, the Italian
authorities had said the bones were "without doubt" Billy's. If only the
U.S. investigators had been as sure. But I guess there just weren't enough
remains to fit U.S. requirements for identification.

Instead of being elated about finding Billy, I was depressed. We had
worked so hard, and this file indicated most of his body had been washed
away. I held on to a faint hope there might be more at the site for the
investigators to uncover, but it didn't look promising. How could I tell
Mother the only thing left of Billy was his bracelet and three bone fragments? And where were those bones now?

I copied the file and mailed it to Jim. In my e-mail saying it was on its way, I wailed, "Why the hell didn't anyone tell the family?" But I knew we'd never know the answer.

I showed the file to Jack and choked back my tears as I told him how frustrating it was that everyone had worked so hard with so little to show for it. "It didn't end up the way I hoped it would," I cried.

He held me close. "But, Honey," he said, "that's real life."

He was right, of course. And no one ever said life is fair.

24

WHAT NOW?

From: Jim Graham
Sent: Thursday, April 27, 2000
To: Dale, Diana
Subject: Re: The File

I sure can understand your deflated feeling after this long saga.
It's like finding the Pharoah's tomb and then discovering it's been
looted. It does your soul no good, though, to vent wrath on a
bunch of unknown bureaucrats from the past. Bill's bracelet is a
real tangible reward for your pursuit.
I still think the location of the crash site is meaningful. The notation
that the Territorial Legion of the Carabinieri at Bolzano notified the
Ministry of Foreign Affairs in Rome that on July 9, 1952 they had
recovered the remains and the bracelet, leaves a possibility that
the Carabinieri or the Foreign Ministry records may be archived
somewhere. They might contain the specific location information. I
tried a couple shots in the Internet to see if I could raise someone
in the Bolzano Carabinieri, but haven't hit paydirt. Maybe when
Paolo gets home, he might be just the guy to dig that one out.
I still haven't heard anything from Mark Baldwin, so don't know if
they are on the case or not.
Have a good weekend, and thanks very much for the copy of the
file.
Jim

* * *

Jim was more optimistic than I. But I sent the investigating team a copy of the CIL file, anyway. My disappointment in its contents was apparent in my cover letter. I wrote, "It appears, at my first reading of the file, that an investigation of the crash and burial site by you may not be warranted for my uncle. However, I'm not fully convinced that's the case. I do hope that a DNA test is a possibility, though so that a definitive identification may be established, in light of the fact that my family was never notified that his remains were recovered." I said they shouldn't allow this latest development in the Wisner case to preclude them from pursuing the Twedt investigation.

I tried to be philosophical and wrote Jim, "After all is said and done, I don't regret a moment of our journey. I met some wonderful people, and no matter what, it's still closure." I meant it. If it had stopped there, I would have been happy.

But it didn't stop there. Jim picked up the ball and ran with it once again, even though he fumbled it along the way. He wrote, "I was preparing a DRAFT of a message I thought you might want to send to Christoph and Inga and was trying to get it into position to FORWARD the draft to you, and I screwed up and it was SENT!!! Dang it!"

His intentions were apparent when he explained himself. "For one thing I was wondering if you felt it might be a pre-empt of the more authoritative contact from Roath/Baldwin and secondly whether or not Paolo should be tied in—and thirdly, what are Christoph and Inga going to think receiving a message from me with your by-line?"

He apologized for the foul-up and told me to issue any disclaimers or correction I thought might be needed, then said, "You just can't trust an old guy with bad eyesight, hearing, memory, and judgment!" I wasn't sure about his eyesight and hearing, but I could attest to the soundness of his memory and judgment.

His e-mail to Inga and Christoph recapped what was in the missing CIL file. He told them the bracelet and remains had been found at "the location Heissbraum," that the remains had been given to the Sarentino town hall, and that the bracelet had been held by the Sarentino Carabinieri. From there, the U.S. Army mortuary service had taken over. He told them about the flooding stream that had taken away most of the evidence and remains.

Given that information, Jim asked them if they could contact the Sarentino police or town archives to see if there is any more information on the precise location of the crash site, which would help the Army team who now has our search data.

That same day I heard from Inga, who had written before she got Jim's e-mail masquerading as mine. Her e-mail, entitled "After Easter Egg," was chatty and informal but had little to do with the search. We were writing as friends, and I loved hearing about her life.

She told me she hadn't heard from the American investigators yet, but would be available to them when she got back from Vienna.

We were in a holding pattern on Billy's case, but Inga's involvement in the Ritten crash began to gain altitude. Jim had connected with Vance McDonald, one of the survivors of the bomber crash, who lived in Marysville, Washington. He told Inga that Vance would be in Europe in September to re-visit the crash site. Inga was thrilled to arrange a meeting.

She then came through with new information on our crash. She was happy to stop by the Sarentino Carabinieri (Sarnthein in German), "and I am sure, Christoph will also try to join me, if he is not too busy with school.

"But let me tell you what I did in the meantime: There is a weekly Sarntal newspaper that comes into almost every house, made by a guy I know: Toni Hofer at Sarnthein. I called him up and asked him for assistance and so he published an article about our research, not forgetting to encourage readers to help. This has caused the following reactions:

- a new eye witness who possesses a large metal thing from the Plunerbach crash. I will soon get pictures from the object and the numbers on it, then look for someone to scan it and to send it to you (or draw it and fax it to you, as I did with the turbo charger part);
- a Sarntal lady who has moved to Trento in the meantime but reads the weekly to keep contact to her home valley: She knew that after the Aberstückler Nock-crash (the one opposite Plunerbach; Twedt?) a corpse was buried in Sarnthein, and was excavated soon after and brought away. (Could it have been brought to the Florence graveyard?)
- another witness who possesses a camera, found at the Nock-crashsite."

Inga said she and Toni Hofer would check out those leads during the next few weeks. The snow was melting, but it would take some time before anything would be accessible. Then she cleared something up for us. "I confronted Toni with the location 'Heissbraum.' No coincidence, except Heiss is a rather common name for a farm. The crash site 'near Sarentino, located in a rocky stream, type Torrente' fits perfectly for the Plunerbach (Bach=stream=torrente). I was told, too that the crashsite was in or very near to the stream bed."

Like me, Jim wasn't convinced there was enough evidence to bring the investigators to the site, and he wrote Inga, "The story of the lady who moved to Trento is very significant. I checked the listing of the names on the wall at the Florence cemetery and both Wisner and Twedt are in the list. We'll have to do some further investigation to determine if there is a specific burial site there for Lowell Twedt. We have thought that the listing at Florence was only a memorial honor for them as there are quite a few of the names that we know did NOT have any remains buried there. If it is true that Lowell Twedt's remains are reburied at the Florence cemetery, there might not be any reason for the Army team to come to the Sarntal. For Diana's family and for the Twedt family, it is desirable that we try to identify each of the crash sites so that they know specifically where Bill Wisner and Lowell Twedt came down."

Jim faxed Inga copies of the Carabinieri letters so she could use them in her research, although I doubted there would be much more to discover. The mystery now was what happened to the remains found in 1952, not what happened to the bracelet. That was on my wrist. I'd had a jeweler add the missing chain and a clasp, and I picked it up May 4. When I put it on, it felt natural against my skin, as if it had found a comfortable new home.

But that only deepened my depression at not having the story turn out the way I'd hoped. With fewer e-mails coming in, I had less to look forward to. I knew how post-partum depression must feel, and in my case the baby had died. We were near the end of our search, and we hadn't found what I had hoped for.

Paolo got back from New York and had the same reaction to the contents of the CIL file. "Oh God, a lot has happened while I was abroad. I feel sad, I don't know if this is the 'right' feeling, but that is. I can't imagine why all this happened, but I don't understand one thing: why were the remains not buried with all the military honours? It's a matter of 'number'? Are these maybe not sufficient for a "positive identification"? As far as I'm concerned, it means that the possibility to bury Bill's corpse are now next to zero. But don't worry, we all will try to do our best—with or without CIL—to look after other remains at the area.

He said he had taken a day trip to Washington, D.C., to visit the Air and Space museum, and then to Arlington National Cemetery. "I wanted to see in advance the sacred place where I was hoping to come back, for the official ceremony…" I hadn't given a thought to where Billy might be re-buried, if we found him. But I was sure it wouldn't be Arlington. His mother would have wanted him home in Texas.

Paolo closed by saying he had already checked the archives of the Carabinieri "some months ago," and there's nothing there. It was sad, he agreed, but he still looked forward to discovering more.

A diversion came in the form of the translation of Inga's article from Martin Selling. It was long—13 pages single-spaced in the original—and I could tell he had worked hard on it. I was sure I had abused the favor, and I hoped whatever I could do for him in return would measure up. The translation had been complicated, but Selling was from southern Germany, so at least he understood the regionalisms in Inga's writing. I pored over every word.

She called her story "About Forgetting and Remembering." Her opening paragraph states: "Some people who could recall the past but refuse to do so say that it is time that the past should be put to rest. They say that forgetfulness is a blessing and will cite experts to back them up. However, when may the 55 million dead of World War II be forgotten? Fifty-five million is a number of dangerous, self-destructive proportions. It is the entire population of Great Britain."

She tells of the inquiry that had come to her through the local tourist office asking if she would look into a plane crash in her neighborhood. She knew it well, because, "I have lived near the crash site for 25 years. When our son was of the same age as his father was at the time of the crash, he showed him the spot, when since then the firs grew again and the ground is covered with heather and cranberry bushes. Here was the wreckage, and there was a body in a leather jacket and his eyes wide open. According to my older in-laws, it was a treasure-trove for the wartime children of Ritten. Lots of rubber for sling shots to hunt squirrels; yellow leather upholstery, strong enough to last for years. And the emergency rations for the crew: cookies and cans and chocolate and chewing gum, unknown delicacies dur-ing the war years. The dead man was soon removed, and much of the wreckage was taken by the farmers who put the metal parts to good use. There was enough left for imaginative boys. And there were still eyewitnesses around, as I was told."

She visits all the eyewitnesses, getting conflicting testimony as to how many crew members survived and how many were captured. She checks her son's books about airplanes and discovers that the P-38 Lightning we are looking for is different from the bomber that crashed near her home. Now she must look elsewhere.

She gets my fax and my note with the photo of Billy. "He squats before a light wood wall, beaming in his Air Corps uniform, the cap with the emblem a little askew over his almost-laughing eyes, Bill from Texas. Also a cowboy hat would become him, it seems. Between his knees, a small, pensive dog sits with bat-ears, the left hand of the lad hangs loosely over his left knee and over the back of the dog, as if it has only for the moment only stopped petting it for the photo. A signet ring is on the ring finger, but of a bracelet nothing is to be seen under the pushed-up cuff. Does he perhaps wear it on the other arm? The slender right hand lies loosely rolled up on the right knee.

"Bill from Texas, as old as my own son, of whom I have a quite similar photo, with our cat. But instead of the war uniform, he's wearing a T-shirt."

Her research takes her to the state archives and the state library; but there is nothing in the newspapers about a crash on that day. But an interesting story from July 1944 tells of a soldier who had parachuted from a bomber and had to be rescued from a steep mountainside by Hubert Mumelter "in a masterstroke of alpine climbing." That must have been the crash on the Sciliar that Paolo told us about early in his research.

Inga's story tells how she is led to Keith Bullock, but his specialty is bombers, not Lightnings. He wants to know more about the crash near her home, but no one seems to remember anything specific about that one.

Then she tells of Hans Grimminger in Augsburg, Germany, another historian. He faxes her copies of the German flak reports for that day, which lists the sites of the successfully downed aircraft. "I take out my old hiking map of the Sarntaler Alps, and the names can be easily interpreted phonetically. There is the Kirchberg; the 'Messner Basai' is the Pazzei Alm and belongs to the Messner Farm in Aberstückl; Blunabach is the brook belonging to the Pluner Farm; Kesselberg is west of the Talfer [river] between Astfeld and Aberstückl."

She enlists the help of her friend, Florian Murr, who lives in the area of the crashes and learns that "[o]ne of the pilots of the [P 38] Lightning pilots parachuted into the Antran Alm below the Hirzer and walked down to the Aberstückler Nock. Ander Gams and Barl Kofler, both with rifles, stopped the American but let him go. Then he went down the road to Abner and was taken prisoner. Both men are no longer alive. Another pilot was found dead at the crash site and buried at the Aberstückler Nock. It is late for inquiries, but Florian Murr thinks that Luis Gramm at the Messner farm in Aberstückl may know something."

At this point in her story, Inga learns that Christoph Mair has gotten involved through Jim Graham, and the two agree to meet. She describes their visit to the Weger farm. "Aberstückl lies isolated on the left cliff. Right above on sunny mild field is a *Häusergruppe*, an old house and bar, and a *Stadel*, a new house. That is the Pluner, Christoph says, and I am already past the entrance. Therefore, I back up, into the lane and up to the new house. The entrance is a dirt road to the new house. There is a bell, and an old woman opens the door. Strangers. What do they want? Christoph introduces himself, he comes from Barth. She relaxes. About the downed pilot? Jakob is in the cow barn. The barn is low and dark, a wooden structure. Cows look around, nosily. We and Jakob go outside and I show him the photo. The time machine starts.

"He was outside, it was a pleasant afternoon, said Jakob. He heard the drone of aircraft and then he saw them as they were going down. Bang! Behind the Nock. One [plane] was also behind him. He saw the plane spiraling from the sky and towards the trees, smoking and then a crash in the middle of the woods.

"Of course he went there. Pieces were all over the place [by the stream] that they call the Krössbach—not Pluner—after the nearby farm. And a charred body on the ground. He could recognize only one toe with the skin on it. Near the body was a bracelet on the ground, all black with two 'W's in the name. The farm hand from Huber, a nearby farm, buried the dead man right at the place and erected a cross from two fence slats. This man is no longer alive.

"Much later, after the war, an Italian junk dealer and a Carabiniere came. The dealer took away the old iron. The bracelet? One man could still know something about it, Franz Mader, who has the gas station in Sarnthein. Now comes the farmer's wife and takes a look at the photo of the pilot…neither she nor Jakob thinks that he was exhumed."

Inga relates how Jakob points out the piece of metal from the crash near the edge of the woods. "Christoph climbs up and scratches away some snow with his foot. There is something and he scratches some more. Numbers are there, but the way the piece is lying there, not much can be seen. I fetch a shovel from the manure pile. Now, Christoph clears the piece, pulls and pushes until the frozen snow breaks away, sets it upright and lowers it along the almost vertical grass and drags it into the yard. There it stands at the corner of the house in the sun. Now, all the numbers can be read.

"On first sight it looks like a piece of an auto. But it must be part of a motor. Pipes are sticking out from the hollow center, and I make note of the numbers. Nothing on the piece is rusted. There is only some moss where a stud sticks out. And Jakob comes with a box of bright sheet metal. This is from the airplane, and from a pipe he fashioned an ashtray which he likes. He will not give it up. We assure him that nothing will be taken from him. Then he goes away again and brings a hacksaw. He had made the bow from a part of the wreck. The saw blade is rusted, but not the bow. He had often wondered about it. The name on the six-sided screw is easily readable. It is Rockford S.P. Co."

Inga goes on to interview more eyewitnesses, among them Alois Gramm from the Messner farm. "He remembers vividly the parachuting pilot who was escorted past the farm to the valley below. He also knows that the airplane that crashed on the Kesselberg had exploded in mid air. Pieces were strewn around in a wide area. There was even a shoe among it."

She goes back to the Weger farm to take photos. "I ask Jakob again to tell me once more the story of the crash near the Plunerbach. He confirms everything. The burial by the farm hand, the bracelet, the visit after the war by the junk dealer, the fruitless search for the grave, the shape of the airplane. He had also found a piece of the cockpit, some form of glass. He had made a knife handle from it. He placed under it a photo of the mine in Rabenstein. This was a nice souvenir."

Inga continues her narrative, leaving no stone unturned. "I drive down on the other side of the valley…to take a picture of the crash site for Diana Dale. An old man goes for a walk with a little girl. I think that he is about the right age and I talk to him. Josef Thaler, who lived at the Hamann-Bauer farm in Muls in 1942, observed the crash above the Pluner and pointed out to me how I can locate the crash site by looking upwards along the riverbed, just below the forest line where there is a small depression in the wooded area. He saw the charred body. A foot, not burned, was sticking up. He knows nothing else."

She sends her son Matthias the story, because his book helped her learn the difference between a bomber and a Lightning. He writes back, "I once flew in such a P-38 (but only on the computer), a really robust airplane with powerful armament, very manageable and with acceptable maneuverability. Important: big gas tanks with long-range capability, up to 3000 km…"

Her research uncovers a bomber crash at Garmesegg, nearby, and an unfortunate incident that happened in April 1945. "White Sunday. Five girls from Bozen take a trip, actually a pilgrimage, to see the Madonna. They want to go to Maria Saal, but just in front of the tunnel bombs fall. Three girls were killed. They were buried at the Lengsteiner graveyard, with great care and with all honors. The dead enemy soldiers, if something was left of them to bury, were put in the unsanctified part of the graveyards, and after the war they were exhumed. No American should remain in hostile earth."

She recalls an article she had written about two old men from the former East Germany, who were familiar with the Ritten area. "I received their long letters with descriptions of old airplanes. [They wrote me] because I published several times a year, on an honorary basis, the 'Rittner Bötl.' [In the articles they shared their] reminiscences about their service in the Ritten flak station, which was housed in the elegant Hotel Holzner in Oberbozen. In addition there were photos, small, formatted in pale sepia with serrated borders. Many men in pleasant poses on the balcony. One had even saved tickets from the Rittner [Ritten's] cog-wheel railroad and, naturally, his pay book. Herr Timpe made his sentimental trip as soon as possible and was heartily welcomed by the hotelier. Since then he was able to spend some days on the house and liked nothing better than to talk about old times.

"I wrote to both and received from one a typewritten letter with other recollections. His 29th birthday was on the 19th October 1944 for which he had organized a round of drinks. (He remembers very well that it was a day later that he received the message that downings were reported. Two, he thinks. His involvement with the battery involved only re-adjusting the guns every time.)…

"The other, Herr Strumpf, also writes for magazines about the local history of Gotha and answered immediately by e-mail after I appealed to him to use his extraordinary long-term memory."

Herr Strumpf's e-mail was lengthy. He wrote, "My long-term memory consists largely of my diary of 1945. (I am not so sure about my statements involving 1944.) In late autumn of 1944 we succeeded in downing nine Lightnings out of 11. The airplanes were visible from Ritten in the direction NW, therefore probably above the Sarn Valley. The downings were investigated for a long time and we were allowed to paint nine more rings on our gun barrels to the two already there. The downing of the two bombers was on 16 February 1945, one crashed nearby. Our search unit retrieved two dead and two wounded who were brought temporarily to the hotel. The dead were handed over there, and the prisoners were attended to. I have no idea what happened afterwards. Both hits were confirmed and we were allowed two more rings, but these were the last ones."

Inga rechecks each man's story with the other. "Herr Strumpf refers to his diary, and Herr Timpe, cogitates again on his typewriter. In his opinion, it would have been unlikely the nine downings would have been credited to the flak unit 548 at the Hotel Holzner. It was an ongoing custom that, after a proved downing, the neighboring staffs of two flak units would exchange information, 'and as duty officer I would have been informed first. However, the quarters were quiet. I surmise, rather, that the neighboring unit was awarded the bulk of the hits.' ...Mr. Timpe will think some more about it."

Inga's research verifies at least part of the two men's stories. "Anyway, the Rittner flak battery has the number 548, and it is mentioned in the Grimminger reports on Flak hits in the Sarn district. Therefore, my research, which started at Ritten by mistake,...came back with more information on Ritten. But meanwhile, so to speak, it has turned from passive into active, from the end to the beginning, from effect to cause. From the victims to the perpetrators? However, I have to note that I cannot accept, now that I'm personally involved, that Herr Timpe or Herr Strumpf could have killed the pilots Wisner and Twedt. And one shouldn't permit sentiment to intrude...."

Inga ends her article with Bob Cardin's confirmation that the turbocharger they found on Jakob Weger's farm was from a P-38. She concludes that her research into Billy's crash is a success, but she still must solve the mystery of the bomber crash on the Ritten plateau.

I was intrigued that, even though she refused to believe it, Inga had very probably met the men who were partly responsible for Billy's death. But, strangely, I felt no animosity toward them. Firing an anti-aircraft gun is as far removed from face-to-face combat as flying bomber escort. It wasn't personal; it was their job.

I just wished they hadn't been so accurate.

25

WE WAIT

From: Dale, Diana
Sent: Friday, May 12, 2000
To: David Roath
Subject: Wisner and Twedt Investigation

Dear Mr. Roath,
This is Diana Dale, niece of William O. Wisner 0-708778, just checking in. I refer to the sizable packet of information sent by Mr. Jim Graham of Seattle, as well as the copy of Wisner's CIL file, recently found by CILHI, that I forwarded to you last month.
After all of our (read: Jim Graham's) hard work and the flurry of e-mails and research information that have traveled back and forth over the past few months, the current silence is disconcerting. Would it be possible to get a progress report from you or Mark Baldwin? I'm writing on behalf of my family as well as that of Lowell Twedt and all the people who helped us in our search. My parents are coming to Colorado early next month, and I would love to have something to report.
If you haven't had a chance to address our cases yet, I certainly understand; I realize we're in a long line of hopeful families. But it would be comforting to know that the paperwork has reached your offices and to hear your initial reaction.
Thank you for your time.
Sincerely,
Diana T. Dale

* * *

It was the middle of May, and the silence from the Mortuary Affairs team was deafening. They hadn't even acknowledged receipt of Jim's 100-plus-page information package, and I was getting impatient. I knew they were probably off investigating another case, but I didn't care. I wanted something to happen.

I shared Paolo's anguish and disappointment about the contents of the CIL file. There was so little left of Billy in 1952, how could they possibly find anything else? But I couldn't stop hoping.

Inga was having computer problems again and sent me a fax to thank me for a book I had sent her. The photograph of her garden in springtime reminded me of the Rocky Mountains, so I thought she would enjoy a book a friend of mine had collaborated on, a nice coffee-table book that would give her a glimpse of Colorado and its gardens. Nothing I could do would repay her adequately for what she had given us, but I had to do something. Inga's reaction was self-effacing: "What I did to help searching your uncle—I liked doing it—and I am curious myself."

And her curiosity had paid off. Her Ritten crash investigation had developed into another international collaboration involving Keith Bullock in Austria, Jim Graham and Vance McDonald in Washington and others in Italy. So even if my search for Billy had been disappointing so far, at least some other good would come out of Inga's efforts.

Then, as if to give me something to think about while we waited for a response from the investigative team, on May 17 I heard from a professor in Munich, Univ. Prof. Dr. Med. Bernd Gansbacher. "I have read with interest the story of William Wisner. The newspaper in Südtirol described that you are trying to clarify the circumstances of his unfortunate death as pilot. It happens that I am a native of this valley and know [a] few details of the story from my mother, who is the daughter of the only physician working in the valley during the war." He asked to meet me in early June while he was in Denver for the American Society of Gene Therapy conference.

I readily agreed. I hoped he could add something to our story, if only a little "local color." He would call me when he got to Denver to arrange a time and place.

Inga wrote that our case was still turning up evidence. "Since I involved Toni Hofer, the Sarntal journalist, in the search I have another strong local helper—and local does mean very much in this things: more confidence, more contacts, less misunderstandings. Toni Hofer sent me some pictures of the propeller wing which was taken away from the Plunerbach crash site (by the way: 'Heissbraum' from the CIL file is nothing else than 'Heiss-Brunn' and means the Plunerbach site! So you see, we have not to be so much in despair about the CIL-file. At least we have another confirmation that we found your uncle's crash site and not Twedt's)...At the end of May I'll go up to the Plunerbach site with Toni Hofer and Jakob Weger and Christoph (if he is able to join us). I'll take pictures and I hope very much to make clear the contradiction between the 1952 investigation and Jakob's remarks concerning the burial."

Jim Graham was off in Riverside, California, attending the 1st Fighter Group Association reunion and kept in touch by e-mail. He tried to find someone in the squadron who remembered Billy, but most of the men at the reunion had been overseas from mid-'43 to mid-'44, too early to know Billy or Jim.

Inga set her trip to Sarntal for the end of May. She e-mailed Jim and me, "This Wednesday we'll make our Sarntal excursion and hopefully get up to the Plunerbach (Heissbrunn) crash site. In the meantime you both are experts in South Tryolean toponomastics. It is not unusual that there are several names for almost the same place: one farmer called it this way, the other that way. And those very old micro-names of this type have not even been translated by the Italian Fascists (as they did in the '20s with most of the names). So they exist only in the indigenous form. Let's wait and see if Jakob is able to find the location."

She added that Vance MacDonald would visit his Ritten crash site during the last four days of September. "In the meantime I want him to write down his memories about the B-17 crash he was involved [in], otherwise new impressions could cover the old ones. And Ritten is changed very much now."

Wednesday came, but Inga couldn't get to the site. It was rainy, there was a bad bike accident on the road from Ritten to the Sarn Valley, and two members of their group had other commitments, so they postponed to the following Friday. She wished me a nice visit with Prof. Gansbacher.

I was too shy to meet Dr. Gansbacher alone, and I knew Jack could help us keep the conversation going if I got stuck, so we all met at the Denver Athletic Club for lunch on June 2. Bernd said it was Inga's article in the local Sarntal paper (Toni Hofer's newsletter), that had caught his attention. He told me I wasn't mentioned in it by name, just "a woman from Denver, Colorado," but my quest had caught the whole valley's attention. He had tracked me down through Toni and then Inga.

As he said in his e-mail, his grandfather was the only physician in the valley during the war, and Bernd's mother would assist him on his rounds. Bernd was not yet born, but October 20, 1944, was a big day in the valley, "the only time the war came to Sarnthein," he said, with three planes coming down at once. He knew the crash site well, because Jakob Weger's farm is near the family home of Bernd's friend Hans, whose mother still lives there, and the crash site is just "an hour's walk from her house." Of course, there was nothing his grandfather could have done for Billy, and because of the many turns our conversation took, I forgot to ask him if his grandfather had treated Olson after he was captured.

It was a pleasant lunch but not as enlightening as I had hoped. I did get a kick out of knowing I was a celebrity somewhere, though, even if no one knew my name.

Inga sent Jim a photograph of the propeller blade found at Plunerbach, and Jim scanned it for Bob Cardin. The numbers were still legible, and Jim hoped Bob might be able to tie it to a specific engine. No such luck. The best Bob could do was confirm that it was a left-hand blade from a P-38. "We can't connect it absolutely with the Wisner A/C because the only records would be in the specific A/C log book —now long gone." Only half the blade was left, because a local farmer had been cutting off pieces of it for farm equipment turbines. Jim said that if I wanted it, I should speak up before it was all gone. I told him to leave it where it was, happy it was being put to good use.

Jim couldn't stand the silence any more than I could, so on June 7 he e-mailed Mark Baldwin to ask for "some indication of the status of the subject within your offices." The next day he wrote Bill Jordan to see if he had any insight into what we could do to get a response from Mortuary Affairs.

In the meantime, I got a letter from Bill Ward with copies of the photos taken of their groups when they were at Moses Lake, the same photos Idy had in Billy's scrapbook. Bill Ward pointed himself out, at the left end of the middle row, four men down from Billy. He included a photo/specification sheet for the P-39, the plane they flew at Moses Lake, and told me that was also the plane Lowell Twedt was exiting in the photo I had sent him.

He added that his story about his time with the 71st had expanded beyond the short time Billy was there into full-blown wartime memoirs, so it was taking him longer to write than he'd originally planned. I was pleased he'd been inspired to put his experiences on paper. It would be a fine legacy for his grandchildren.

On June 9 Jim finally heard from Baldwin. The message was short and sweet: "We are researching the case and waiting for guidance from Washington and Frankfurt on the status of information contained in the report. Once we receive the information we will coordinate a response."

Thank goodness. I now had something concrete to tell Mama, and it wasn't a moment too soon. She and Daddy arrived from St. Louis the following day to stay with us before heading to their mountain cabin for the summer.

That night after dinner, as we sipped our wine I gave Mama a small box and told her it wasn't a gift, but something that belonged to her. She had a sense of what she was opening, and her hands trembled. When she read the engraving on the bracelet, she burst into tears. She was amazed I had gotten it back and was a little confused about how it all had come about. I reminded her and Daddy about the lost file and related how it had finally resurfaced. I caught them up on where the investigation was now, and once she gained her composure, Mama called her best friend back in St. Louis to tell her about it. I didn't eavesdrop, but I could tell she was proud of me.

But I hadn't done it to make her proud. I did it because we needed to find Billy.

June 11 brought Inga's report of her trip to the Plunerbach. "Friday afternoon gave us ideal conditions for our Plunerbach expedition. And an expedition it was, really! My stiff leg muscles are telling me still that I was there. Jakob guided us (Toni Hofer = the local journalist, Christoph and me) well and found the suspected point without searching. It's about 1-1/2 hours above his farm, to reach only by foot, climbing up a steep path and then without a footpath through the thicket. And then you can hear the strong rush of the Plunerbach which comes down in a hurry over the mountain flank. It had still enough water but the thaw was already over. There can be much more water in spring and after heavy rainfall. Nevertheless: while Jakob went to and fro to look after the exact crash place, Christoph, looking into the clear water, stooped and grasped a rusty piece of iron. I took pictures of the scenery, the persons, and of the iron. Then we went down where Jakob's cows would wait for him...

"And this is my résumé, Diana: it's the most beautiful place to be buried – high up in a clean, green mountain wilderness near the crystal stream, and covered by nothing else than plants which have grown, wilted and pressed by snow, 55 times. After having seen the place in all its peace and quietness I wouldn't be too eager to make any more researching or exhumation there. And to find what? After being sure (from the CIL file's mentioning 'Heißbrunn' as your uncle's crash site) that it is the exact place. And Jakob confirmed that Heißbrunn is just another name for exactly this part of Plunerbach. (Heißbrunn means 'water reservoir belonging to Heiß farm' which is neighboured to Jakob's farm.)

"After leaving Jakob and Christoph, Toni and I proceeded some miles north to Außerpens where we met Robert Aster. He is the one holding the propeller wing on Toni's pictures. And he is a very skillful mechanic who is able to produce small power stations for the farmers which they use additional to the normal electric power, to save money. For the small turbine vanes (looking like silver spoons) he used the Aluminum of the propeller wing because it's a very strong and pure material. And Robert Aster is also the one to hold the huge camera from the Kirchnock Lightning, Twedt's. I took pictures of all of this which I'll send to both of you. And I noted the numbers on the camera...If the factory still exists, could it be possible to get a confirmation, if it was Twedt's Lightning where it had been installed? By the way: Did you ever get contact with Twedt's relatives or with Olson, himself or relatives? Maybe you mentioned, but I forgot."

It sounded like a lovely site. I understood why Inga thought we should leave it alone, but I didn't agree. We had come so far, and I still hoped there was something left at the site besides bits of wreckage. I couldn't wait to see her pictures.

The information about the camera intrigued me, and I thought that might be yet another piece of evidence that would speed up the investigation, so I searched the Internet to see what I could find out. One collector responded to my e-mail, but he was a little perplexed as to why I wanted to know about this particular camera, since we already knew it came from a P-38. I told him why we were hoping to tie it to a specific P-38. He was intrigued and said he'd post a message on his bulletin board but nothing ever came of it, and I doubt if anything will. If a propeller blade can't be traced to a specific plane, it's doubtful a camera could.

I couldn't wait to get to the cabin for the weekend and share Inga's discoveries with my folks. It was a relief that they knew about the search and pending investigation, because now I could tell them everything as it was happening.

But something else happened first.

26

CLOSE CALL

From:	Dale, Diana
Sent:	Monday, June 19, 2000
To:	Jim Graham, Inga Hosp, Bill Ward
Subject:	(none)

Dear Inga, Jim, and Bill,
I'll send this to all of you at the same time, so I don't have to tell the same story three times. It's been a very tough week, but all is well now.
Thursday I got a phone call from my father saying my mother had had a stroke and he was taking her to the hospital in Fort Collins. […] That's the bad news. The good news is that over an 18-hour period she recovered 100%—a little weak, but there is no permanent damage. […] What a relief! […]
Inga, thank you for your lovely description of the Plunerbach site. I shared it with my parents, and Dad and I agree that it would be nice to have some sort of memorial placed there, but we're not sure what yet. The investigators may want to visit the site again to see if there's anything they missed, but I'll leave that decision to them. I still want to visit it and see it for myself. I will be in touch with all of you once I get back on track. Thank you all for everything.
Love,
Diana

* * *

Mama seemed tired when she and Daddy were with us in Denver, but I chalked it up to the two-day drive from St. Louis, which gets harder for them every year. My blood ran cold when I got the call from Daddy saying he was taking her to the hospital. He told me she had a similar episode in May but refused to go to the doctor because it was over in a couple of hours. But this time was different. She'd been unable to answer questions since 10:00 that morning, and when he asked her what her dog's name was, she replied, "I don't know." That dog, Pepe, was her life. This was serious.

I offered to leave for Fort Collins right away, but he said to wait until they got to the hospital. I thought about the strokes my grandmother had had, and it crossed my mind that I may have given Mama Billy's bracelet just in time. But I wasn't ready to let her go. This couldn't be the end for her, because we still needed to know the end of Billy's story.

The follow-up call came from Bob Way, our mountain neighbor who, with his wife Lou, had accompanied Mom and Dad down to the hospital. Bob said Mama was going in for a CT-scan and he would call again after that. I knew I should be there, so I started out for Fort Collins at 8:00 with my suitcase packed. As I drove, I prepared myself for the worst.

Daddy had just finished walking Pepe and was getting Mama's overnight bag out of the car when I pulled into the parking lot at 9:00. He said she'd been moved to a private room, and Bob and Lou had stayed with her while he was at the car.

Mama was surprised to see me. I don't think she remembered she was in Colorado and thought I had come to see her in St. Louis. All she could say was "Oh, Baby," and ask open-ended questions, like "How did you…?" and "Why did you…?" and "Where's…?" She would gesture with her hand, prompting us to finish her questions for her. Most of the time we guessed wrong, and she'd get frustrated. Because her short-term memory was gone, even if we answered correctly she'd forget what we'd said, and we would go through the litany over and over.

The CT-scan showed a blockage but no bleeding. That meant she had a chance of recovery. They gave her a blood thinner and told us they would keep her overnight to monitor her blood pressure, which was dangerously high. The nurse told me to put her jewelry in a safe place, and as I was taking off Billy's I.D. bracelet, I thought again how glad I was that she knew we might have found her brother.

The hospital social worker brought a cot into the room for me and found a motel for Daddy that allowed pets. He left at 11:00, exhausted, and I went down the hall to read for a while, too wired up to sleep. Mama drifted off immediately, blissfully unaware that she was scaring the daylights out of everyone.

I went to bed around midnight, and at 1:00 a.m. the nurse came in to wake Mama, take her blood pressure, and ask questions to monitor her progress. That routine jangled us awake every two hours. Each time I would get up, pull on my jeans, and go stand where Mama could see a familiar face while the nurse quizzed her.

Mama's confused responses to the nurse's questions were interesting and, in retrospect, quite funny. When the nurse asked at 3:00 who was president, she turned up her nose and said, "Oh, it's that old, um, Clinton." The nurse would ask her who I was, and she'd say, "That's my baby—um—my baby." I wasn't sure how to feel about that. She knew the president's name, a man she didn't like, but it took her until 5:00 a.m. to remember the name of a child she'd given birth to and presumably loved. And she had a hard time getting her age right. First she was "two-ty-two," then 32, but by 8 a.m. she finally got 82 right. At first she couldn't come up with her last name, then she said it was Wisner. It wasn't until half an hour before her husband of 60 years arrived that she came up with her married name.

At each wake-up call, she would ask me what had happened. I'd tell her she'd had a stroke, and she'd say, "I don't want to have a strake," mispronouncing the word. I'd tell her it was too late, she'd already had one, and I'd remind her about her mother's strokes. It wasn't sinking in, and by morning, even though she was lucid, she still didn't grasp the seriousness of what had happened to her.

Even though Mama had been steadily improving through the night, I resisted calling Daddy too early, in the hope he was getting some rest. I was all set to phone him at 8:30 when he walked in, obviously resigned to the worst possible outcome, his face taut and pale. But by that time Mama was sitting up, and I had combed her hair and put some lipstick on her. When she saw Daddy, she smiled and waved, and I'll never forget his reaction. A flood of relief swept over his face, his color came back, and he giggled like a little boy as he rushed over, grabbed her hand, and kissed her. He exclaimed over and over how remarkable and wonderful the difference was as I related Mama's progress through the night.

Bob and Lou stopped in, and they, too, were impressed by her improvement. Mama called them by name and was incredulous when I told her she hadn't been able to, just 12 hours before. After the Ways left, Daddy and I settled in to spend the day while doctors and nurses conducted more tests to determine if there was permanent damage.

Mother started to worry about Pepe, who would spend the day in the car. It was cool and overcast, so he wouldn't be in any danger of heatstroke, but when I announced I was going downstairs to take him for a walk, the nurse suggested I bring him inside.

"A dog in a hospital! Isn't that against regulations?" I asked.

"Of course it is, but we care more about what's good for the patient," she said. "I'll show you a back way, so you don't attract attention." She told me I didn't have to hide him, but I shouldn't flaunt him, either.

When I put Pepe on the bed, he snuggled up against Mama's leg. Her blood pressure had been going down, and by noon it was normal. The doctor told us the tests results looked good and that her high blood pressure had probably saved her from permanent damage, because it had forced blood past the blockage to nourish the brain.

Mother was released at 3:30, and we drove up to the cabin for a quiet weekend. In spite of some physical weakness and serious fatigue, she was fine.

I was even more determined to finish the search for Billy, and soon.

About this time Michal Mucha, my Polish friend who was first to respond to my bulletin board message about Billy, sent me an e-mail. His research, the "Aircraft M.I.A. Project," now had a Web site, www.samoloty.ip.pl/amiap/. I checked it out, passed it on to Jim, and suggested to Michal that he and Jim get in touch for further research. Michal told me some P-38s of the 1st Fighter Group were lost on October 14, 1944, on an escort mission to Blackheimer, and he wanted to know if we had any information on them. Billy had flown on that mission; in fact, it's what had caught Michal's eye in the bulletin board message and prompted him to e-mail me. Billy had written home about strafing three locomotives on the way home from that mission, but he neglected to mention there had been any losses.

Jim checked his mission reports for that date and reported to Michal that one P-38 from the 94th Fighter Squadron went down in Hungary during the strafing. "The pilot bailed out and was captured and sent to Dulag Luft West.* He returned home later." Jim's Missing Aircrew

---

*A Dulag is a German interrogation center; a Stalag is a German POW camp; add the word Luft, and it specifies the camp or center as a Luftwaffe (Air Force) facility.

Reports showed only one P-38 lost that day.

Once again, using the Internet had delivered the goods, and I was glad to be able to help someone else, for a change.

Jim made himself even more useful by helping Inga plan her vacation to the Pacific Northwest. Our trip to Seattle was becoming a reality, and I allowed myself the luxury of looking forward to it. We would arrive by the afternoon of August 23rd, in time to join Jim in meeting the Hosps' ferry from Vancouver. I felt I knew these people pretty well, but still we'd never met. There was a possibility it could be awkward. Jim and I hadn't met, either, but we sensed we could support each other when we met our foreign friends.

Inga's photos of her trip to the Plunerbach site arrived June 13th. The first was of Christoph, Toni, and Jakob standing at a fence with the Sarn Valley stretching out below. On the back Inga wrote, "At this point Jakob was working on Oct. 20, 1944, when he saw the plane spiraling down towards the crash place which is situated outside the picture, right, and higher up in the forest." The next two photos were close-ups, one of Toni and Christoph together, and one of Jakob alone, each with the Plunerbach cascading down the steep, rocky stream bed behind them. I could see how the word "torrente" applied. It looked more like a waterfall than a stream.

The next photo showed Christoph, with Jakob and Toni, looking at the piece of metal he had just found in the streambed. Another photo was of Jakob, pointing his walking stick at "the place where he found the corpse, 55 years ago." The last photo showed Jakob, Inga, and Christoph, with the Plunerbach behind them. At last I had a lovely face to put with Inga's equally lovely e-mail voice.

Now that I knew what Inga looked like, I sent Jim and her a digital photo of me, taken recently at my office. I was a media specialist for a local newspaper, and there were some strange items in my workstation that showed up in the picture: a stuffed alligator on my monitor in the foreground, and a clutter of maps and papers in the background. In response, Inga and I both received an e-mail from Jim with a photo attachment. He thanked me for the photo and said I looked just about as he imagined, adding, "E-mail correspondence certainly reveals a lot about a person." He told us that in his photo, "I'm the one on the left." Finally, I would see what Jim looked like, and I was excited. As I opened the attachment entitled "Jim and Albert," I wondered who Albert would be.

Jakob Weger, Inga Hosp, and Christoph Mair near crash site

The "photo" turned out to be a silly cartoon of a man drinking coffee with his dog. I told Jim I didn't have the heart to tell him he looked exactly as I had imagined him, too. We laughed about it later, when he told me that only a portion of my photo—the stuffed alligator—had come through on his computer. He thought I was being a smart-ass and had responded in kind.

Inga received both pictures just fine, and replied to both of us, "Now I know how you look: Diana looks like a zone map, and Jim—well, like 'Jim' with 'Albert,' cup of tea and stars-and-stripe-ball. Thanks to you both! I'll post both of your pictures on my fridge to 'learn' them and have a drink whenever I look at you."

The weather in her part of the world had turned warm, she said. "Our 2000 summer is a 100's summer (down at Bozen) and a 75's summer up here. I try to avoid Bozen. Otherwise I get grouchy too." She was arranging the ferry ride down to Seattle from Vancouver and would tell us when it arrived so Jim and I could be there. "And thanks for your telephone #, Jim. And thanks to both of you for all your kindness, pictures included. My daughter Julia at Vienna has a scanner; I'll ask her to scan a family photo for you – after tomorrow, for she'll have an [important] examination tomorrow.

By the way: we are 4 = one family – father Bruno (61), mother Inga (57), daughter Julia (23), son Matthias (20)."

She closed by saying that Vance McDonald and Keith Bullock had gotten in touch with the daughter of the co-pilot KIA in the Ritten bomber crash. She was born three months before her father's death.

Daughter Julia was as good as Inga's word. Her e-mail began with "Hello Mrs. Dale, hello Mr. Graham," then she introduced herself. "My mom told me a lot about you two and I know all about the tragic story of your uncle Bill, Mrs. Dale. I'm happy that my mom was able to help you to reveal some details about his disappearing. She wrote me that we (my family) are gonna meet you during our trip to America. I'm studying in Vienna and I own a scanner and she asked me to send you some pictures of us and it is a pleasure for me to do that. You can see my mom, my brother and me, unfortunately I don't have a picture where my dad is on, too. I send one separately. I hope you will have a lovely summer!"

Now the Hosps were no longer strangers. I could tell from their pictures that I was going to like these people.

Jim must have felt guilty for having sent a cartoon, so on July 10 he sent a photo of himself with his late wife Becky. "The attached photo of me with my dear wife Becky was taken in 1998 shortly before she died of cancer," he said. "My looks haven't changed much, but my life sure has." My heart went out to him. She was lovely.

Our plans to meet in Seattle were coming together nicely, but my professional life had taken a different turn. Because of a company reorganization I was informed on a Thursday that I would be given a new position the following Monday. It was a step backward, and I wasn't sure I wanted to take it. Jack and I had been talking about the possibility of my retiring soon, and I didn't feel comfortable starting a new job knowing I would be a short-timer. So we agreed, even though it was premature, it was time for me to move on. Hooray! For the first time in 30 years I could take a trip and not worry about using up vacation time. I gave notice and looked forward to being a lady of leisure.

On July 20 I heard from Mark Baldwin, one of the investigators. He was continuing to research the case and trying to locate information on the closure of the Griesheim Mausoleum in 1952. He asked that we keep them "updated with any site recoveries that your team makes and any discoveries that have been made in the past couple of months."

Any site recoveries *we've* made? We had scrupulously avoided contaminating the sites for fear we'd disturb things we shouldn't, and we were making sure Baldwin and his group had the same information we had. It was up to them now, so what were they waiting for? I forwarded Baldwin's e-mail to Jim and Inga, and Jim suggested we ask Inga to summarize her visit to the Plunerbach and tell Baldwin what Jakob knew about the specific crash location. Jim would send Baldwin the photos and tell him about the propeller blade. Once Inga did her part, there would be nothing for us to do but wait—again.

I re-read Baldwin's note and noticed the phrase "closure of the Griesheim Mausoleum." No wonder Jim's contact in Germany, Roland Geiger, couldn't find it. I pointed the phrase out to Jim, and he replied, "I don't have any background on the mortuary operations of the time, but I had heard that the government was working hard to situate all remains at U.S. military cemeteries or Stateside." Maybe Billy's remains from 1952 had been buried at Florence, after all. I might have seen his grave without even knowing it.

Our Seattle trip was taking shape. Jack and I wanted to treat everyone to dinner as thanks for their hard work. But after much "to-ing and fro-ing" about which restaurant and what kind of food would be best, Jim suggested having a catered dinner at his house. He reasoned we could talk much more easily in a private home, and his had a great view. I thought that was a good idea, but I decided to go one better and fix the meal myself. I had a good, foolproof menu that was informal and very American. Jim agreed to the idea.

About this time Jim heard from his friend Dick Kahler, who had kicked off our search back in December. Dick had dropped out of the project because he was busy retiring from the banking business. But he wanted to tell Jim that he had received an interesting note from David Roath. David had come across the Carl Hoenshell Web site Dick had designed, and he and wanted to correct a technical error. In the Hoenshell story Dick had said that Roath's group was part of the CIL in Hawaii. Roath wrote, "I just wanted to clarify that I am not part of CILHI. I am the director of the United States Army Memorial Affairs Activity-Europe. Our office is located in Landstuhl, Germany. Our office took the lead to get the [Hoenshell] P-38 site surveyed and based on our assessment this allowed our office in coordination with team members from CILHI to complete the search and recovery mission. I just wanted to add that for historical accuracy. By the way, I found your story while working on a new investigation in Italy.

I enjoyed reading it. Keep up the good work and who knows maybe our paths will cross again. David Roath."

Dick thought Jim might want to use Roath as a contact, but we were way ahead of him. The Italian investigation Roath had referred to in his e-mail was ours. Roath no doubt had gotten the Hoenshell Web site from our research package, and his e-mail to Dick was the result. We had come full-circle.

On July 23rd Inga did as Jim requested and sent a letter to Baldwin summarizing what she and Christoph had found at the Plunerbach site. If Roath's team was paying attention, that should be the last bit of information they would need to get started.

And we were just a month away from our Seattle rendezvous.

27

COMING TOGETHER THERE

From:	Baldwin, Mark, 21TSC SptOps
Sent:	Friday, July 28, 2000
To:	Paolo Cagnan, Christoph Mair, Chad Twedt,
	Inga Hosp, Diana Dale, Jim Graham
Subject:	Lt. Wisner Search

Greetings all,

I have been trying for the past few days to make contact with the searchers in Italy for assistance, but have been unsuccessful.
Mr. Roath and myself are coming to Italy on Tuesday – 01 AUG to examine the crash site. We need confirmation that someone associated with the search and knows the crash area will be able to meet with us and lead us to the site.
Any assistance and e-mail confirmation is greatly appreciated.
Mark Baldwin
USAMAA-E

* * *

O nce again, one of us was out of touch when something exciting was happening. This time it was my turn. I didn't get Baldwin's e-mail because I was setting up a new computer system at home. Jim had to call me to let me know they were going to be at the site. This was the first time I'd heard his voice, and I liked his easy manner and sense of humor. He told me he had sent Christoph's and Inga's phone numbers to Baldwin and e-mailed the two of them to ask if they could be there to help.

August 1st would have been Billy's 76th birthday, so I took it as a good omen they would arrive that day. On August 2nd Inga reported in. I finally had my e-mail up and running and was relieved to be back in communication at such a crucial time.

It was late when Inga was writing. "Soon midnight, but I must tell you! The expedition had been postponed by the investigators for one day, so we missed the birthday (but without a confirmation, if they would be at the place I suggested), so for me it began with calling the members (and hoping they would be able to come together today instead of yesterday). Anyway, my son Matthias and me went down (and up) to Muls, and there they were at the Hotel Feldrand which I had suggested to them (100 m away from Jakob's farm).

"David Roath, Mark Baldwin, a young lady, and an interpreter (Italian-English! who would never understand one single word in Jakob's or the others' dialect, so we left these two down at the Hotel) - and a car, built more for highways than for high ways like ours. But they were very pleased with the Hotel.

"One by one our company dropped in: Christoph on his scooter, coming from his job in a laundry (having changed his shift to be with us), Toni Hofer with his huge Toyota Jeep, spending half a day of his last vacation week. First we sat down and discussed the object and the mysterious non-matching of serial numbers and the open end of the Where-are-the-Wisner's-remains-story (you know, the three-bones-file etc). Then we drove over to Jakob's, while a thunderstorm was beginning to come up. So I tried to get them on the way.

"Toni got five of them in his big car, Matthias and I took Jakob's handicapped son, who was so eager to come with us, aboard my tiny Suzuki Vitara, and then up we went, up the slope with a gradient of about 35% (which we hiked last time), up to the point where Jakob saw the Wisner plane (and where I made the picture I sent you), then hiking the last 30 minutes through the thicket. Jakob was the smartest, finding his way just to the same point we were for the first time. Mark had the metal detector and the GPS, David had a digital camera, and I had nothing [other] than an umbrella used as a stick (because I didn't want to go up there again, you know: my knee!).

"With the first raindrops we reached the site. AND THEN THEY DISCOVERED THAT THEY LEFT THE BATTERY FOR THE METAL DETECTOR IN THE CAR!

"Well, Jakob explained everything, made a little sketch how he found the plane beside the creek (its water was a wonderful drink after hurrying up!), Toni made a hole where Jakob pointed out the situation of the grave, but of course with no result without the detector. Then the rain came down more and more, thunder grumbled, and we had to hurry down to the cars. After creeping down we 'visited' the turbo generator near Jakob's farm, Hans carried all the pieces I mentioned (the ashtray, the metal saw, and some more), they made pictures, we admired Mrs. Weger's beautiful garden, and had a look to the cowshed, while the rain poured.

"Then we said Goodbye. Toni was kind enough to guide them to Mr. Aster (which has the propeller blade, and the camera). So they would make it back right for dinner. Matthias and I had to hurry back to Ritten. You know: the summer-theatre, which I am part of the organization staff, very probably spoiled by the same thunderstorm. And we returned with thunder and lightning. But when the show began (Shakespeare: 'The Taming of the Shrew'), it was over - and everything was fine.

"Tomorrow, Aug. 3, they will have to hike up to the place (without cars), the whole 1-1/2 hour's way with detector (and, hopefully, the battery), guided by their GPS. They will try to find something to convince themselves starting a more intensive investigation next week. They hope to return with a larger group and two trucks and materials. But that will not be before Wednesday—and so I won't be able to join them because of our depart[ure] to Montreal. And then they will hike up to the other two crash sites, too. Christoph will care, Toni will care, and they know best where to go for information (and to get information, because they are known to the local people).

"By the way: Paolo Cagnan called me yesterday evening, but then I didn't know if they really would come today, and I think, he's also busy at work. And certainly he will be informed, too, by the researchers, and can join them next week."

She said Mark and David promised to keep them informed about the invstigation. "They are nice and eager guys, although not very familiar with our local or even regional reality (which is not simply Italian, you know, but I tried to teach them a little bit...).

"And, Diana, it was nice for all of us, heading up just round Bill's

birthday. Just as if he knew. And, shortly before parting, we talked with
Mrs. Weger in front of the cowshed, and she asked me, where they come
from, and David did a little drawing on a sheet of paper, showing where is
Minnesota (he is from Fargo, and my children and I love the 'Fargo
movie!) and where Oklahoma, Mark's native country. And then she asked
which religion David and Mark would cling to (because here about 95% are
Catholics). And they said, glancing at me, they trusted in God, and that
there would be something after dead. And Mrs. Weger was very pleased by
this answer, and mentioned, she was convinced, for otherwise they would
not try so hard to find your uncle's remains! Isn't that touching?"

I was as excited as Inga was. She had really taken this to heart. And she
was thrilled with the idea of my cooking for them in Seattle. "Your home-
cooking idea is as gentle as tempting. My daughter Julia and I, having been
once in Santa Fe NM, like Mexican style cooking very much, and the others
have their experiences with hot cooking, too, because we had, years ago, a
Singaporean sailor as our guest, and he was a very skilled cook—hot hot
hot! So don't worry at all! And if you are going to cook, I can do the dishes
afterward. Okay?" She closed her e-mail with "Until soon at Seattle! Or
until the next e-mail!" and signed with love and kindest regards.

Things were falling into place for us, but once again Paolo had been
left out. He wrote Jim on August 4, "All right Jim. I'm very glad to hear
your voice, again. There was an article, today, printed in the German speaking local newspaper. While I was explaining to my editor that we'd better
wait for the US team to know if we can write something about them, Inga
Hosp 'interviewed herself,' stating that the US team already came here,
visit the places and will come again next week. I don't know what to think
about it. I talked to her some days ago and she seemed to be cooperative…Baldwin wrote me that they absolutely want to meet me, so that I
don't think that they could be already here without letting me know about
their presence. But you never know…Ciao"

You never know, indeed. Paolo was completely in the dark, and the
tone of his e-mail revealed his disappointment. If the investigators had tried
to call him, they were unsuccessful. He labeled his next e-mail "Bad Surprise." It was short and curt. "The US team came last Wednesday and
stayed here for two days: I was told about it by Christoph, today. Sincerely,
just to let you know, I'm disgusted.

I felt terrible about the oversight and apologized as soon as I got his
message. I had assumed he knew, because his name was on Mark Baldwin's

July 28 e-mail announcing they'd be there August 1. Jim told Paolo he had given the investigators addresses and phone numbers for everyone who had worked on the search. He then advised him to stay in touch with Christoph, who was in the loop. But Jim and I weren't much help. Ironically, much of what we knew about the investigators' plans was after the fact and second-hand.

Paolo continued to check in with Jim, and Jim kept forwarding his messages to me. I was at the cabin, missing everything as it happened, and the e-mails that greeted me when I got home were disturbing. There was still no resolving the Inga-Paolo conflict.*

But it wasn't long before Paolo bounced back. "In fact, the problem was not the US team...It's always the same old story: Inga Hosp. I talked to her three or four times during the last week. I was quite surprised, because she seemed to be very gently and cooperative...for the first time. She promised to let me know about every news. I trusted her. Why not??? In fact, what happened was that she knew perfectly everything and, instead of informing and/or contacting me, she decided to organise everything with her son and with the reporter of the 'village newsletter'. 'Village newsletter'...what a shame for me!!! Eventually, only to show (to me and to the rest of the world) how brave and clever she is, she let herself being interviewed by the German newspaper, so that I was the only one in the whole South Tyrol who didn't know that the US team was already arrived. Christoph is a nice guy, never had any problem with him."

Paolo went on, "Yesterday, I received the following message from Baldwin:

> We went to the site on Wed evening (02 Aug.) and on Thursday
> morning (03 Aug.).
> We were taken to the site at the creek by Dr. Inga Hosp,
> Christoph Mair, Toni Hofer and Jacob Weger.
> I wanted to set up a meeting with you on Friday, but we had to
> depart for a return trip to Germany first thing on Friday.

---

*A year later Inga told me that when she was arranging the hotel accommodations for the U.S. team, they requested that a reporter not be involved in the investigation. They must have changed their minds after meeting Paolo. When I related Inga's message to Jack, I said, "Y'know, this whole conflict would have been avoided if Inga and Paolo had just sat down and talked to each other." Jack replied, "Well, Baby, you could say the same thing about WWII."

We plan a return trip to Sarntal on Wednesday 09 Aug, to begin
work on Thursday, with an expected stay of 5 - 10 days.
We will be staying at the Feldrand Inn. This will all be confirmed
after Monday afternoon.
I apologize that things did not work out for our meeting on this
trip, but on our return trip I do need to meet with you and see the
information you have. We came away with as many questions as
we did answers. At this time, a lot of information and numbers do
not add up.
Thanks for your assistance and I look forward to meeting with you.
Mark Baldwin, USAMAA-E

"So, as I told you," Paolo concluded, "I won't have any problem
with the US-team. In the next days, you will [be] immediately informed by
me of any kind of news, bad or good. If I can join the team…"

That was a relief. Inga may have shut him out, but the U.S. team was
working with him. I didn't question Inga's motives; I knew she had my
interests at heart, and in her mind they just didn't include Paolo.

On August 7th Mark Baldwin wrote to tell me of their preliminary
investigation. I already had the details from Inga, but Mark said they would
return with the complete search and recovery team on Wednesday, August
9. "I'm not sure at this point that we will be able to make a recovery of any
additional remains at the site near Mr. Weger's house. We will conduct as
thorough a search as possible." He would let me know more later.

At last, a direct communication from the team—the only first-hand,
"official" word to me that an investigation would take place. I was beside
myself, stuck here in the States when I desperately wanted to be there to
witness the excavation. But they hadn't invited me, hadn't even given me
fair warning.

Everything was happening at once, and the timing couldn't have
been worse. My sister and her family were in Colorado for their annual stay
at the cabin, the only time I get to see them. Pack to School, my charity for
homeless children, was gearing up for its big push, and with only three of
us spearheading the project I had to be there to help. Jack's new business
was barely getting started and now that I was retired, which in my case was
just a fancy word for unemployed, money was tight. What's more, I would
have been in Italy when Inga and her family were in America. It just wasn't
happening the way I'd hoped.

On August 8 Paolo e-mailed Baldwin a thorough report of the three crash sites, documenting which parts of the wreckage were found at which sites. He then wrote follow-up articles for the paper as the investigation progressed and e-mailed Jim a re-cap. "Let's talk about: a) Olson, b) Twedt, c) Wisner.

a. We could find a lot of evidence regarding Olson's plane. We could find two machine guns Browning .50—one of which almost intact—with the ID serial numbers, part of the nose and many other wreckages. Now we are absolutely sure that Olson's plane crashed at about 2.300 meter high in the mountain, next to the Pazzei Alm, or Messner Basai. Alois Gramm was a very good eyewitness in this sense.

b. It's very difficult to determine what happened with the Twedt's plane. According to some testimonies, there must have been an explosion into the air: this reconstruction fits with the Anderson report which refers of debris. If Twedt's plane exploded into the air, as you know, there isn't a lot to do. But we are not sure about it. Gramm remembers of a wooden cross, next to the Kirchnock at Kirchberg. But he wasn't able to find it again, and all the excavations were unsuccessful. We scanned again the Church documentation, but with no result. Roath says that there are only speculations and that the cross could have been a normal cross, not a burial site actually. I don't think so, but there isn't a lot to do, unless we want to dig up the whole mountain.

c. David Roath believes we are next to the truth. Today, Monday, the excavations gave some good evidence. The place— which was indicated by Jakob Weger—it's called 'Heissbrunn' and it's located at about 1650 meter, next to a stream called Krössbach. It's the same place mentioned by the CIL-file you sent to me. The excavation it's becoming bigger and deeper. The area it's about 6x4 meter and one meter in deepness. This morning the team found some glass pieces of the 'cover' of the pilot cabin and a small pieces of iron or metal which is supposed to be part of a boot. This shows that that's the impact point. Roath believes that the burial site should be right here and says that they will [be] going on 'til they can find some pieces. He's optimistic."

I couldn't believe how much had happened while I was away. Jim for-warded Paolo copies of the MACRs, and I sent Paolo the Italian docu-ments that were in Billy's CIL file and wondered why I hadn't done that sooner. Roath wasn't allowed to give Paolo any information out of the files, but they did ask him to track down the Italian who had found Billy's remains in 1952. It was up to me to fill him in on who that was.

Paolo wasn't sure there would be anything left to find at the site, but his research discovered, "There was a man who found out the bracelet and the few bones in July 1952, but he died 20 years ago. I've already checked it, but I still have some other investigations to do. The carabiniere-report does-n't say if both the bracelet and the remains were founded during an excava-tion or just in the wood. Question: is there still a burial site? Has ever been a burial site? We still don't know, but we are on the right spot for sure."

Paolo also asked about the searches in 1947, and wondered what happened to the remains found in 1952. He asked Jim to use his intuition on what else might be important and send it along.

Now that Inga was on her way to America, Paolo was the team's main source of information. I was at the cabin unable to get e-mail so he report-ed the progress to Jim, and Jim forwarded it to me at home. Every trans-mission was duplicated when I got back to check e-mail, but better two than none. This was too important to miss.

Paolo's August 11 e-mail to Jim said, "I'm completely exhausted, staying with the US-team from 8 am 'til 6.30 p.m.," he wrote. "And they started at 5.30 a.m...I'm trying to summarise the results: no corpses, actu-ally; two machine guns, one from Olson's plane."

He went on, "Starting very early in the morning, the team went back to the Plunerbachtal, supposed to be Wisner's burial site. They started to dig up the place indicated by Jakob Weger, even if there's still something strange: the turbo-charger serial I.D. doesn't match with the I.D. complete list of the three planes, in possession of David Roath, a very nice guy as all the rest of the group. They also could find a camera for the aerial picture, but it's not possible to determine where it comes from. After 5-6 hours of excavating, we could find quite a big piece of fibreglass, under a huge stone. They will go back there tomorrow to make further excavations.

"In the afternoon we went to Mr Gramm at Aberstückl. He still remembered of my visit and was very gently. We went to the Pazzeialm. We dig out one place, supposed to be the burial site, but weren't able to find anything. Then we went next to a hut where—as I was told in March—was supposed to be a machine-gun. In fact...the serial numbers match with the Olson's plane, which matches with my geographical reconstruction. There was part of another machine-gun, but I didn't see it and I can't tell you now if it was worth or not.

"We are still quite far away from the truth: to discover the two burial places. It's not so easy, but I can assure you that the guys will do their best."

He came back with another update on the excavation, this time very excited. "I WANNA THANK YOU FOR EVERYTHING...Talking about the Griesheim mystery: David Roath told me that the Mausoleum doesn't exist anymore, so that we are not able to know what happened with those remains. But David, a very tough guy—he is only 39, but very experienced—is still working on this task. As I understood, there is a sort of stupid competition between CILHI and National Archives, so that they're hiding each other the documents and the Roath team is just in the middle, trying to find out what's going on with this offices. I talked to Mr. Mark Baldwin and expressed all your gratitude to them. He asked me for telling you—unofficially—that they understand the situation and they're doing all their best to help you.

"Many TV-news from both Italy and Austria, including the Italian national TV RAI, covered the story. You will receive the copies of the news with the US-team final report. I have a lot of beautiful pictures of the US team at work, of the excavations, of the recovered wreckage and so on...My editor asked me this morning to interview you...At first I said: 'Are you joking???' But then I realised he was right! In fact you're the most important person in this story: If you hadn't start trying to know what happened, we all wouldn't have this incredible experience, both emotionally and professionally for me.

"The editor said to me: why don't you try to interview this lady and let our readers know why is she trying to know what happened, looking for the remains and so on? And why don't you try to let our readers know who was William Wisner? I have to admit, he was right. That's why I'm asking you if you want to let yourself being interviewed by me. Diplomatically speaking, in my opinion it could also be a good way to show the US-team your appreciation for what they're doing: they have an Italian/American translator so that they are reading all of my articles.

"You know, to interview you sounds a little bit strange for me, because I already know 80% of your answer, according to our long and friendly personal correspondence...I'll try to forget everything and figure out that I don't know much about the story. You're not obliged to answer, that must be absolutely clear: if you want to do it, just do it; if you don't, don't worry. I'll tell my editor you prefer to 'remain in the shadow.' You could also answer only to some questions, not to all. It's up to you, but again, you're not obliged, really."

He added a P.S.: "The team is trying to find out where the remains were sent (a national cemetery or a university with anthropological studies) after they were declared unknown at Griesheim."

The interview was long, but it gave Paolo some background he had missed: who I am, what started the search in the first place, some family history. He also asked what kind of person Billy was, which was gratifying. Without Billy's personality, it's just a report.

One interview question took me by surprise, though: "Some people could not understand which is the sense of this 'operation,' which costs a lot of time and money. How is your feeling towards the possibility to find out what happened with the remains of your uncle and the possibility to recover them and have a 'proper burial site' in the US?"

The cost of the investigation had never crossed my mind. I replied, "My uncle and so many other men like him made the ultimate sacrifice for their country. I would expect no less from my government than to do what's right. A government that would treat its most precious resource as something to be tossed away and forgotten is not one I could respect. I am proud that my country takes this seriously; it's their job. My uncle was called to do a job, and he took it seriously, too."

I told him I hoped Billy, or at least what was left of him, could be brought home. He was a Texas boy, and I felt he would want to be buried in Texas. I was certain his mother and father would have wanted him there.

On August 16 Mortuary Affairs left me an e-mail and a phone message. I had a feeling this would be important. The e-mail said:

> Mrs. Dale, my name is Liz Tate. I am a Mortuary Affairs Specialist with the Department of the Army, Mortuary Affairs and Casualty Support Division, in Alexandria, VA. Although I left a message for you on your home phone, I decided to also send you an e-mail.
> I am contacting you on the advice of Mr. Dave Roath, our Mortuary Officer in Europe who I know has been assisting you in your attempts to locate the remains of your uncle, Lt. Wisner. Mr.

> Roath called me this morning to let me know that he is currently
> in Sarentino, Italy, and that he has located what is believed to be
> you uncle's crash site. An identification (ID) tag with your uncle's
> name on it, and portions of what are believed to be human
> remains have also been recovered. The ID media and remains
> have also been turned over to the Italian authorities as required by
> their laws. Mr. Roath will obtain custody of the remains after all of
> the required procedures are followed. Also, Mr. Roath and his
> team will continue to search the site to see if there are any
> additional remains or items to be recovered. Once his
> investigation is complete, the remains and items will be
> forwarded to the U.S. Army Central Identification Laboratory,
> Hawaii, for identification processing.

She gave a phone number, which I couldn't dial fast enough. Liz answered on the first ring. She said they had found two incomplete (or partial) teeth, a complete tibia, a partial fibula, and various other bone fragments. There was lots of wreckage at the site, too, and they also found buttons, an I.D. tag with his name on it (no doubt his dog tag, because we had his bracelet), and what they thought was a portion of a necklace.

She said they were excavating a three-meter by six-meter area and would continue digging until they reached sterile soil. After that, everything they recovered would be forwarded to the CIL in Hawaii for testing and further identification. The results from their tests would take quite a while. "It won't be this year," she warned, then asked me to remind her to give us a copy of the full report once the investigation was complete.

I told her how relieved I was the investigation had not been a waste of their time and resources. She countered with a point I hadn't considered. "Actually, you made our job easy," she said. "You came to us with good information, and usually it's the other way around. In most cases we get notification of uncovered remains, and it becomes our job to try to identify them and locate the next of kin. After more than 50 years, that's not easy."

I hurried back up to the cabin to tell the family about the discoveries, and I forwarded Liz's e-mail to Jim before I left. I didn't include Paolo, because I assumed he knew what they had recovered. After all, he was right there at the site and had been telling us what was happening.

But when Jim referred to the findings in an e-mail to him, Paolo's response was frantic. "What the hell is happening? I talked to David Roath some minutes ago and it was a very strange phone call. In this sense: it seems that they could find some remains, but he's not authorised to tell me anything; he says I have to get every piece of information from you or Diana because she is the first person who will have some good news. As you write, it seems that something has changed in the last 24 hours. So, now I'm asking you: What do you know exactly? What does the Virginia report says? You're speaking about the success of the search…Please, tell me what's happening!!!!! As soon as possible!!!"

Poor Paolo. Baldwin's discretion overrode the inquisitiveness of the reporter on the scene, and he had told Paolo nothing about what they had found. They needed my permission and wouldn't tell him anything without it. But since they never asked for my permission Paolo was left out, once again.

Jim came to the rescue and explained it to Paolo diplomatically: "I can understand that David Roath won't tell you anything. When government people are dealing with personal lives, they will only inform the direct family of the person involved. The information I received had been given to Diana by the people at the headquarters of the Mortuary Affairs organization that David works for. Diana was thrilled to know they had some success in finding things at the site, so she sent me a message before she left for her cabin in the mountains. I, too, have to respect Diana's privacy, so I must let her send you information when she returns. I believe the search has produced satisfying results for her. Be patient—Diana will fill you in."

It was thoughtless of me not to share the news with Paolo, but before I had a chance to fix the problem he found out through other means, testament to his skill as a reporter. "After some phone calls around the world, now I know something more: the day before yesterday, the team was able to find out some human remains (bones) and a plaque, which shouldn't be the I.D. one—of course, because it is in Diana's possession—but something else, still important. They will continue digging up until Monday, when they are supposed to leave. All the remains were given to the Carabinieri. Then, they will be given back at your Government and eventually sent to CILHI.

"There won't be the final solution until the remains are DNA-tested, but I'm absolutely sure that we got it and I can't express how glad am I. Jim, Diana, believe me: this is a very beautiful day in my life, like a child birth or something similar. That's the reward for all the efforts we spent during the last eight months. The US-team was absolutely brilliant, but they were also expressing their appreciation for what I've done and—as I told David—I'm very proud of having been part of the team.

"If I will get some more information, I'll let you know. If not, I'm thrilled to read the report sent to Diana: it seems that my today's 'whole-page interview' with her was a lucky sign of success…"

As they say in Texas, bless his heart. He really did care. His next e-mail was to me only.

CIAO DIANA
We got it!!!
Thanks God we got it
Your interview was lucky!!!
I won't be able to catch information directly by the US-team:
you're the only one who has the right to be informed
Please, let me know the official information as soon as you're back
And, then, get ready for the champagne!!!
I'm really glad.
I won't forget it, be sure….
ciao Princess
Paolo

His enthusiasm was endearing. He had attached his article with my interview. The lead paragraph starts, "They did it. The seven Americans have found what they were looking for: the remains of William O. Wisner, pilot of the fighter plane downed by the Germans in the skies over Sarentino on October 20, 1944." Now that was in print, it had to be true.

He wrote again on August 19. "If you are back (you were right: when something happens, someone is always absent or far away…) I'm sure you'll have a lot of e-mails to read. This is my latest message, but I hope you will answer as soon as possible. First of all, let me say again: THAT'S GREAT!!!!!!!!!"

He had three requests. One was from Roath, and the other two were from him. Roath wanted to know if I had received a bracelet or an I.D. tag from the government, "because he still doesn't know and he says that's quite important for him. He says that some documents are referring to a bracelet, some others to an I.D.-Tag. As you must already know, he was able to find either the bracelet or the I.D.-tag (I'm not allowed to get this information…) but I assume he wants to be sure about what you have got the 1952's researches. I will meet him this morning (Saturday) at 10 am, but will check the e-mail every hour..."

His information was, as he put it, "only unofficial." He knew they had found some bone fragments, some form of I.D., parts of uniform, etc. But he wanted the whole report, "or perhaps just giving me some details of the findings, if it doesn't hurt you. It's up to you to decide how much my desire to know more is in contrast with your right of privacy. Again, do as you prefer, you know that I've always respected you."

His next request was for his readers who, after his interview, would like to know what I was thinking. "and how did you react about the positive solution of the case, which wasn't 100% sure at the beginning, as you know. You could say, for instance: 'Sono molto contenta!!!' Or, in German: 'Das ist wunderbar!!!!'

"Hey Diana, I'm really enthusiastic about what happened. The US team is completing the excavation and waiting for the authorisation to send the remains to CILHI. In every case, I'll let you know."

I set Roath straight about the bracelet/I.D. and told Paolo I was elated about the findings and so was Mother. I told him, "We spent Thursday morning in tears together as we went over the findings. I was able to share the news with my entire family, because my sister, Billie, and her husband, Harold Fischer, and their children are at our mountain cabin (they live in Michigan). Their children's names are Katherine Diana Fischer and William Thompson Fischer. Katie is 19 and Bill is 16. They were all very excited and pleased with the results." Paolo didn't really need to know everyone's names, but I hoped he would see that Katie was named for me and that both my sister and Bill were named for Billy.

I also told him I was relieved the efforts of the investigators were rewarded; I knew how hard they must have worked. I asked Paolo if they were going to investigate Lowell Twedt's site next.

His reply was empathetic. "I'm very glad to know that everyone in your family was emotionally involved in the good news. I would have liked to share the tears with you: tears of emotion, of joy, of satisfaction..." He went on to give me more information about the team. "Yesterday the Medical Forensic Examiner came to Sarntal from Landstuhl, Germany. As far as I'm concerned, the 'Memorial Affairs Activity Europe'—David Roath is the director—will also run all the DNA examination. They are working together with CILHI, but in fact they are independent and, as I could understand—they don't want to be mixed or be confused with CILHI. They are proud of being a very successful investigation team with almost 100% of positive I.D.. All the team will leave tomorrow morning, Monday, to Land-stuhl. David Roath has to write lots of reports. Eventually, everyone involved in the story was very happy. You can imagine, I suppose."

He didn't have any information on Twedt. "There are two 'negative' speculations: either Twedt's plane exploded in the air (Anderson report) and there's nothing to looking for, or the corpse was discovered by the foxes—after having buried—and eaten. But David still would like to find out the true, even if it seems to be quite difficult. I will also do my own investigation, but I'm not optimistic about it."

The next step, he said, was to wait for the DNA tests and official reports, which could take from three to six months. He was going to enter his diary of the search in a literary competition.

Then he related another factor that had affected the outcome, one that turned out to have been a turning point in the investigation. "Just to let you know, Jakob Weger was wrong. The burial site he indicated to David was the wrong one. The 'right man' was Konrad Rungger, the owner of Feldrand which is—paradoxically—the hotel which guested the US-team. He indicated another burial site, around 50 meters up in the wood along the stream compared with Weger's. And this second one was the right one."

Who was this Rungger fellow, I wondered. I asked Paolo for clarifica-tion and told him at last we were finally getting more answers than ques-tions. I wished he could join Inga, Jim, and me in Seattle and tell us all about it. He replied quickly. "More answers than questions, yes. As you know, David Roath came the first time to Sarntal with three other members of the team and went to the wood with Christoph, Inga and Toni Hofer. They decided that there was sufficient evidence to come back.

"The next week they came again—eight people—and on Wednesday they went on the wood with Jakob Weger. He indicated the location of the burial site. They started to dig up, with no positive result. They came back to the Feldrand, the hotel which is not more than 50 meters from Jakob's house. Someone told David that the owner of the hotel, Konrad Rungger, must have known something. Rungger was asked about it and he said he knew exactly the location of the burial site.

"The next day, Thursday, they went back to the wood with Rungger, who indicated another spot, which is approximately 50 meters up along the same stream. You know, a difference in 50 meters (it's a very steep wood) it's quite a big difference for making a precise excavation. The US-team started to dig up on the Rungger's site and could find some small pieces of iron and so on. The next day they went on and were convinced: that was the right spot. The further excavations, as you know, confirmed that Rungger was right.

"Now, how is the story with him? I tell you, even if you don't buy my newspaper...Rungger, born 1939, was only 5 years old in 1944, but his uncle—who lived at the Huberhof, which is the nearest hut/cabin next to the crash-site—knew exactly the crash-site. He went there immediately after the explosion and the fire. Some days after, he went back and noticed that the corpse was still there, next to some [wreckage], not more than two meters away from the stream called Kroessbach. He decided to bury the corpse, took a white sheet, collected all the remains and buried it at the same spot, putting a cross on the ground.

"Konrad was told many times about this episode. Two or three years after, he started to go along the wood with the sheep, stopping every day next to the wooden cross. He thinks that the cross disappeared—for unknown reasons—at the beginning of the Sixties, but he has always been able to remember where's the place: next to a big rock. He knows very well the spot also because it is not far away from the water-tube which Konrad constructed next to the stream, to let his hotel have drinkable water. It eventually seems that the US-team found also some remains of the cross and Konrad recognized them. So, that's the story."

Paolo must have wished he could be with us in Seattle, too. His P.S. said, "I wanna have a picture of you all together!!!!"

I resolved to write Konrad Rungger and thank him for helping the investigators pinpoint the site.

But first it was time to go to Seattle to meet Jim and Inga.

28

GETTING TOGETHER HERE

From:	Jeanne Simonds
Sent:	Monday, August 28, 2000
To:	Diana Dale
Subject:	Here's to you!

Hey Jack and Diana! (as you say in the South).
We are still talking of the fine visit that left ten people talking and
hugging as they left. It was all good stuff.
I think of standing at the pier wondering if we would recognize
four strangers who had only one voice and then knowing
instantly that the Hosps had arrived.
Jim's house was just the right setting with the best weather, and
the thing he wanted was that we could all be together and not
divided into groups. Anything he wants. That's the way it was.[...]
I was so privileged to be a part of your group and allowed to
follow the hunt. I am partloularly impressed with your
compassion for your grandmother and mother that started this
whole scenario. Some of us might have the opportunity to
perform a grand deed but don't even see the gold ring, let alone
try to catch it. You are really to be saluted. And I do.
Love from Bellevue,
Jeanne

* * *

J ack and I arrived in Seattle on August 22nd, rented a car and drove to the home of our friends Dick and Julie Hamann. The weather was beautiful—70s and sunny. After we got settled and visited with our hosts for a while, I called Jim to let him know we'd arrived and find out the order of the next day.

He said he was ready for us, and the table was set for eight. I quickly did the math and counted only seven of us, so I asked him who the eighth was. He said he had a "lady friend," who had been following our story with him all along. Once I knew there would be an "outsider" there, I asked if it would be all right to include Dick and Julie, because they helped make it possible for us to be there. He said he was happy to comply and would rearrange the table to accommodate them.

He said Jack and I should be at his house by 11:00 to give us plenty of time to start dinner and then meet the Hosps' ferry from Vancouver at 2:30. The directions to his house sounded confusing. Thank goodness Jack had his cell phone; if we got lost Jim could "talk us in."

We bought wine and the ingredients for carnitas, a New Mexican dish of pork, slow-cooked in spices until it's falling-apart tender, eaten on flour tortillas with sautéed onions, guacamole and pico de gallo salsa. I had hoped an unusual menu would help break the ice, and eating with the fingers would make it more fun. For dessert, I had my brother-in-law's recipe for a simple chocolate ganache. Jim would provide the salad and the ambience.

In spite of my trepidation, Jim's directions were perfect. We never missed a turn and arrived promptly at 11:00. Jim greeted us at the door and introduced us to Jeanne Simonds, a charming and gracious lady, who immediately put us at ease. Jim was exactly as I imagined him—tall and lean, wry and easy-going.

The table was elegantly appointed with a lace tablecloth, silver, and crystal, and the dining room afforded a spectacular panorama of Lake Washington. I understood why Jim wanted to have the dinner there; the setting was homey and scenic—just perfect for our plans.

Jeanne and Jack sat down in the living room to get acquainted, hitting it off immediately, and I set to work in Jim's well-equipped kitchen. With Jim as my able sous-chef we had dinner organized in no time, so while the dessert was chilling and the pork was simmering, we ate a light lunch on the deck and chatted until it was time to leave for the pier. Jack had to take a conference call that afternoon, so he stayed at Jim's while I followed Jim and Jeanne to the pier in our rental car.

The ferry was on time, but the Hosps were nowhere to be found. We hadn't anticipated how long it would take them to clear customs, and an hour after the boat had docked there was still no sign of them. Jim, Jeanne and I filled the time with chit-chat, and just as we were beginning to worry that the Hosps had changed their minds about coming, I caught sight of Inga's blond hair in the last crowd of people to disembark. After introductions, hugs, and photographs, we arranged the logistics of hotel check-in, car rental, and getting back to Jim's. Jim took Inga, Bruno, and Matthias to rent their car so they could follow him home, and I drove Julia and Jeanne back to Jim's house in my rental.

Jeanne pointed out landmarks along the way, and as we passed the Boeing plant she said that was where her late husband, Ralph, had worked with Jim. Now I understood the easy nature of Jim and Jeanne's relationship. Jim, Becky, Jeanne, and Ralph had been friends for 35 years.

I'm sure Julia Hosp was uncomfortable, stuck alone in a car with two much-older strangers, but she soon opened up. Her English was excellent, after only two years of study. She told us she was getting an advanced degree in microbiology at the University of Vienna, and that she loved the United States.

It was good we got to know her before the rest of the family arrived at Jim's, because once they did, everyone started talking at once. We sat on the deck, admired the view, exchanged gifts, drank Mexican beer, and talked about our lives, the investigation, the Hosps' trip through western Canada, the Ritten bomber crash, and Billy.

Matthias, a tall, affable, charming 20-year-old, had a great sense of humor. He was a veterinary student, also at the University of Vienna, and shared an apartment there with Julia. Bruno was open and friendly, not stern at all, as I had assumed he would be as minister of cultural affairs for the province of Südtirol. And even though Bruno's second language was Italian, not English, he understood almost everything we said. But if an unusual phrase or a joke didn't compute, he would look quizzically at Inga, and she would translate for him. The punchlines may have come to him a little late, but he got them, and the rest of us enjoyed the instant replays.

Inga, with her Nordic features, was tall and beautiful. Her gracious smile and confident demeanor inspired my best behavior, and as I got to know her better I felt sure I had made a wonderful new friend. In fact, I wanted to adopt all of them. As we exchanged gifts (a scarf for me, and for some reason a blue apron for Jack), I relaxed and savored the prospect of spending the next day with them touring Seattle.

Julie and Dick arrived right on time for dinner, and after introductions and more conversation, I finished getting dinner ready. We all moved into the dining room, and once we were seated and the wine was poured, Jim raised his glass. "Here's to Bill," he said.

"To Bill," we echoed. If he only knew.

29

FINDING FRIENDS

I think, nowadays, friendships are absolutely the best
result from yesterday wars, aren't they?

Inga Hosp

* * *

After Seattle, more waiting. The results of the excavation were mini-
mal, because there was so little left of Billy to find, but they were
anything but disappointing.

In his e-mailed "unofficial report" in October 2000, Mark Baldwin
asked me not to repeat the results until I received the complete recap from
the Central Identification Laboratory, at least six months away. He did say
that when they completed their work they had held a brief prayer service and
marked the burial site with a cross. I know that would have made Idy happy.

To his e-mail Baldwin had attached a front page article that ran in the
Ramstein Air Force Base newspaper, *The American*, on September 1, 2000.
The article couldn't mention Billy by name until after the investigation was
completed, but it was about him. Accompanying the article was a color
photo showing a flag-draped casket being carried off an airplane by eight
soldiers. The cut line read: "A combined honor guard from the 86th Airlift
Wing and the 1st Armored Division carry the casket of a recovered World
War II pilot." I burst into tears when I read Billy had been given full military honors, but this time they were tears of joy. Billy was on his way home
at last.

We didn't know it at the time, but the day Billy was being honored at Ramstein, Jim, the Hosps, and Jack and I were sightseeing in Seattle. We had a wonderful time getting to know each other while we toured Jim's beautiful city and the campus of his alma mater, the University of Washington. When we dropped the Hosps back at their hotel, we gathered for one last drink to celebrate our success in finding Billy and each other. It was hard to say good-bye, but we vowed to see each other again as soon as time and circumstances permitted.

Bruno and Matthias Hosp (back row);
Inga Hosp, Diana Dale, Julia Hosp and Jim Graham (front row)

The next month, Katie Fischer, my niece, left for Florence, Italy, for a college language, culture, and art history program. At 20, Katie had matured into a lovely young woman with more confidence and poise than her mother and I combined had at that age. When I e-mailed Inga about Katie's trip, she insisted Katie get in touch with her as soon as she was settled. They found a weekend late in October that would work for everyone's schedule, and Katie described it in a two-page letter. I was jealous she had gotten to see Inga's world before I did.

October 30th, 2000

Dear Diana and Jack,

Here I am in Verona, writing to you on Florence paper, having just left Bozen. So it goes...

The weekend with Inga and Bruno was as wonderful as it could possibly have been. I'll try to describe it. By the time I arrived Friday evening, it was very dark, and there was nothing to tell me that I was among the mountains. It certainly seemed, however, that I wasn't in Italy any more. I had a couple of hours until Inga could meet me, so I wandered some of the cobblestone streets of Bozen. The buildings were pastel-colored, the roofs were pointy, the restaurants sold speck and Knoëdl. It was very quiet and safe-seeming. Inga was instantly warm and welcoming, of course.

It was about a 20-minute drive up winding, steep, and for me, confusing roads. We left the lights of the city below us and passed a series of turn-offs to villages. Finally, we turned onto what looked like a road through the woods, which is what it was, but it is also where they live.

Inga gave me some tea and introduced me to Thai, who had recently been bitten by a dog (or something) and was full of stitches and had to wear a collar. Since his whiskers were obscured, he would occasionally walk into walls and door frames. He is very sweet, 17, and apparently will go for walks with the family through the woods. Some cat.

I slept in Matthias' room, which is full of model ships and planes and boy stuff. The house is large and very nice, very comfortable. In the basement is the largest, albeit not quite "finished," model railroad I have seen in a private house. There are two large wood-burning stoves, which kept the whole place toasty.

Saturday was perfect fall weather. After breakfast, at which point I met Bruno, who is molto simpatico (we spoke Italian), I went for a walk up the road through the woods. Then, I saw the mountains. Did I ever! The peaks are rocky and stunning, extremely high. All of the hillsides were green, dotted with lots of yellow, orange and red. I hadn't realized I missed the turning leaves until I saw them again (Florence is grey and green only). I passed several picturesque farms with sheep, horses and cows. The *cows were great – they had bells. The sound carried through the trees, and other than that it was perfectly quiet.*

I met lots of friendly German-speaking hikers—trails run all over the region. I climbed a hill and saw mountains for almost 360 degrees. Very Julie Andrews. That afternoon I went with Inga and her neighbor Marena to another part of the valley to try a brand-new cable car. We rode in a little compartment up a very high hill. At the top, of course, the view was amazing. We took a nice walk, stopped at an inn for some food, and then again at another inn on the way back. Everywhere we went, Inga knew someone.

I got a very strong sense of community throughout the region. We stopped at the cemetery in the village of Klobenstein/Lengmoos (they share a parish and are right next to each other). Marena's husband is there, as are Bruno's parents. I was impressed that every grave had flowers and was well tended. It was a lovely place and showed how old the region is, how people who were born there have stayed there. At least in past generations.

That night we went to a dinner for members of a village band—each village has a band. Bruno went in an official capacity, which was kind of neat. No one sat down until we got there, and we sat at the "reserved" table and were served first. Everything was in German, or the Tirolean dialect, which meant that I would have been completely lost, except that I sat next to Inga who explained things to me. I also sat next to a nice man named Hans, who had studied in Padova and spoke Italian with me. When Bruno made a speech, I sat still and tried not to attract attention, which went out the window when I heard him say my name. He gave an abbreviated explanation of why I was there. It was a very long, very social, very good dinner. Very non-Italian— they kept bringing big platters of MEAT. There was the new wine/juice of the season, roasted chestnuts, and a guitar/accordion combo. The two men came and went often, playing funny folk songs. One of them told lots of jokes, which were funny even if I didn't understand them. Lots of fun.

Sunday morning I took the same walk, but it was foggy and all I could see of the mountains were the tops sticking through the clouds, which was also very cool. Then, another celebration. The parish priest has been there for 50 years, so there was a big turn-out at the small, old church. On the lawn out front a band played, wearing traditional costumes, a choir sang, speeches were made, gifts were given. Bruno was also dressed up, and spoke. Little kids ran around, bored, adults greeted each other, horses grazed in the background. Everyone knew everyone and had known them for a long time. Very enjoyable.

All of this is meant to lead up to my point. Ritten, and the Sarn Valley, are wonderful, wonderful places. Inga and I drove as near to the crash site as we could that afternoon. Didn't go up, because it does seem hard to get to, but she pointed it out in the treeline. I am glad to have seen it in October, when the conditions are just as they were on Oct. 20th, 1944. The trees, the rockiness— as terrible as it is to say—this would have been a good place to take a last view of the land. I can't imagine it anything but tranquil, however. The signs of war are gone; it is easy to think that it never happened.

But we have a reminder that it did, and I am so glad, Diana, that you figured everything out and made my going there possible. I'll never forget my time there, or Inga and Bruno. Of course, I intend to see them again. They were so much fun. Inga called me her "weekend daughter." Inga wants me to get in touch with Julia, which I will, and says I should go to Vienna. I would love to go to Vienna, but it won't happen this time. But in any case, I am so glad our family has new friends. It's worth a lot.

We also saw the Iceman! The museum is brand-new, very interesting.

Tomorrow, I go to all the museum-like places in Verona that were closed today, Monday, which meant that today I did churches. All nice, nothing spectacular. Then I go to Bologna for two days, then Lucca with Dad. Looking forward to seeing him a lot.

Miss both of you, and thought about you a lot this weekend. Give my love to the zoo. I'm going to talk to all of our cats in Italian when I get back!

Love,
Katie

About the time Katie was writing her letter, I got a call from Mary Chopelas Johnson. Mary is John Chopelas's older sister, and her friendship with Mama has lasted more than 65 years, just as John's friendship with Billy would have lasted, had Billy lived. Mary asked me if I had thought about giving the story of my search to either the *Oak Cliff Tribune* or the *Dallas Morning News*. I told her I had contacted the *News* back when I started the search, but they had never responded. At Mary's suggestion I e-mailed the story to her favorite columnist, Steve Blow.

Steve called me as soon as he got my e-mail, and wrote a column about it right away. It was entitled, "Time, miles no match for family ties," and he told the story in a charming, succinct writing style.

That bit of publicity generated a few responses, one of which came all the way from Ft. Lee, Virginia. While the writer didn't leave his or her name (probably because the official results of the investigation hadn't yet been released), the sentiment was gratifying. "I worked on this recovery mission for the family of William Wisner. It was the BEST feeling to walk out of those mountains knowing that this family actually had closure. The members (military) of the team never got to speak to her, but I personally would like to thank her for pushing. Because of people like her we get to bring home family members to this day. I tell people I work with every day that I love my job and this is one reason why.

"So, if you can, please tell her that the mission we did was a great feeling of accomplishment, closure and heartfelt sympathy and happiness for her and her family, and she gives hope to others that are in similar situations. It lets them know that we do hear them."

If I'd had any guilt about having caused U.S. tax dollars to be spent on my family's case, that reaffirming message erased every trace.

And Paolo got his wish. His articles in the *Alto Adige* were so well received he won a literary prize heralding his future as a writer. I asked him for details, and he replied, "The literary prize I won was called 'Autori da scoprire' which means 'Authors to be discovered.' It was the first edition of the prize, which is organized by the [provincial council of Italian culture in the] Autonomous Province of Bolzano. I won 3 million lire (less than 2,000 Usd...) plus the publication of the book by the Italian publisher Sperling & Kupfer, which is a branch of Mondadori, the biggest Italian publishing company. My book should be published in September 2001."

It wasn't the Pulitzer, but it was a fitting tribute to a promising and diligent writer.

Besides furthering Paolo's literary career, our search for Billy indirectly helped launch my nephew's college career. As part of his application to Carleton College, a private liberal arts college in Northfield, Minnesota, Bill Fischer, Katie's younger brother, had to write an essay. The topic he chose was "If you could have lunch with anyone, who would it be, and why?"

His reply, along with his straight A's and natural talent, helped gain his admission acceptance.

There is a photograph I've looked at nearly every day in my life that has had a bigger impact on me than any book, movie, or song. This old black and white picture practically tells its own story. The three people you see in it have all played a major part in my life, despite the fact that one of them has been dead for 56 years.

It is a picture of my grandfather, my grandmother, and her brother Lt. William O. Wisner. It was taken in 1944, when Lt. Wisner, my great-uncle, was only twenty years old. The smile on his face shows genuine love for the two people next to him, and extreme pride in the uniform he's wearing. He would die, crashing to the earth in a fireball, only a few months later.

My college application reflects my passionate interest in history. More than simply learning the stories of nations and cultures of the past, I love trying to feel what the ordinary people of the past felt as they went through culture changes, revolutions, and wars. Despite my liberalism, the study of war has fascinated me beyond most other things. I hate war, but I yearn to understand it and feel what it meant to people. We must appreciate the fact that wars are carried out by innocent young people, just like my great-uncle. If I could have lunch with anybody, it would be with Lt. William O. Wisner.

I can't believe that he was only three years older than me when he died. He flew P-38's from an airbase in [Foggia], Italy, and had only been in the war five weeks when he was killed. On a combat patrol over North Italy, two planes in his group collided, and the debris hit a third plane, causing it to crash. The third plane was Wisner's; only two parachutes were seen after the accident. That is all his family ever knew.

If I were sitting at a table with him, the first thing I'd look for would be his youthful enthusiasm. Why was he anxious to leave college, in favor of risking his life overseas? Was there pressure by his peers to join the war? I have to believe that he must have been scared, despite the fact that most twenty year olds feel a certain invincibility. I've never had the chance to ask someone who was in WWII about their experiences. If I could ask Bill Wisner, it would be incredible: I would get the story directly from a boy in the thick of it. I would, of course, have to satisfy the basic questions: what was it like to fly a P-38? I'm sure he would say, "It was swell!" How was the waiting in between missions? What did you do to amuse yourself during downtime? Who were your buddies, and how did you get along? I wonder how a young man from Texas dealt with the death that he surely came into contact with every day.

Most importantly, I would have to answer his questions. Let's assume he knew who I was, he knew he had died, and he knew it was now the year 2000. He would love to hear of his sister's happy life with my grandfather, and of their two daughters. I would tell him what has happened since his world ended in 1944. I would want to gauge his reactions to news of space flight, of the following wars, and of my life in this crazy era.

I think that Billy deserves, more than anything, a thank-you. The easiest thing not to realize is this: all the men who died in WWII don't even know who won. Billy deserves to know that he died not in vain, and his country went on to prosper and succeed. He deserves thanks for paying the ultimate price for something I believe was a very noble cause. He deserves to know that his mother sent 350 letters looking for him after he was filed "MIA," and what happened to his family. If only I could have lunch with him. He was so loved by his family, and my grandmother has never gotten over his death. I must tell him he was not forgotten. I was named for him.

Over the past year, my aunt, Billy's niece, has researched the incident of his death, and for the first time has confirmed that he was not taken prisoner but died when the plane crashed. She has made contact with the Italians that buried his charred body on a wooded slope 56 years ago. The remains of his plane, and an I.D. bracelet, were recovered by the Army after the war, but my family was never informed. A few weeks ago, he finally had a military memorial service, and his bracelet is now on my aunt's wrist.

William Thompson Fischer

Fannon and Maxine Thompson with Billy, 1944
(the photo that inspired the college essay)

Once the Sarn Valley investigation was complete, our lives went back to normal, so Inga, Jim, Paolo, and I corresponded just for fun. While I loved the chatty e-mails, I missed the thrill of the chase. There were no surprises when I opened my e-mail, no clues to follow, only the wait for the official report.

But Jim and I remained connected to the Sarn Valley. On the Internet Jim discovered an elder-hostel tour of the Lake Garda region, an area not far from Bolzano and the Hosps' home, and he and Jeanne signed up for it. The two-week tour in May 2001 would include seminars on the culture and history of the region, and Jim decided to extend their trip another two weeks so they could tour the Südtirol and visit the crash site. They thought it would be great if Jack and I could join them, but with Jack's fledgling business in the balance and with me still retired, we knew we couldn't afford to go so soon. Fall 2001 was the earliest we figured we could swing it, and so we stuck to our plans.

But it wasn't long before something would change our minds.

30

UNSPEAKABLE SADNESS

To:	Diana Dale, Jim Graham, Vance &
	Barbara McDonald, Keith Bullock, Billie Fischer
From:	Inga Hosp
Date:	April 18, 2001

Dear Diana, Jim & Jeanne, Vance & Barbara, Keith, Billie,
Sorry, I cannot reply with "Happy Easter": On Good Friday, April
13, our dear son Matthias has died.
Inga, Bruno, Julia

* * *

I was stunned when I read Inga's e-mail. I couldn't believe that charming, handsome young man was gone. Matthias had inspired Inga to help with the search for Billy because he was the same age Billy was when he crashed. He had ridden with Jack and me the day we were sightseeing in Seattle. He had been so full of fun and so interested in everything we saw.

I couldn't imagine what had happened, so I went to the Web site for the Alto Adige newspaper, and there was a short cover story about him. All it said was that his body had been found in a ravine. I tried to piece together a scenario that made sense. I knew Matthias was going home early for the Easter holiday, so perhaps he'd lost control of his car or fallen during a hike. No matter what the circumstance, I couldn't wrap my mind around the fact that he was gone. The wait for an answer was agony.

We sent condolences to Inga and her family, certain no words could help their grief. I regretted not going to Italy with Jim and Jeanne, but we had already made up our minds. But Jim had another idea. He wrote, "Jeanne and I are beginning to get serious about getting ready to go on our grand trek to Italy. We feel that this culmination to the search for your Uncle Bill should definitely include you. I recognize that the timing isn't the greatest for you and Jack, but I would like to throw a rock down the well and see what reverberations I get.

"I would like to ante up a $5,000 no interest, no term loan to you to entice you to join us in Milan on May 29 after our elder hostel and spend the two weeks til June 12 with us in the Tyrol. If you can make that fit the case for both you and Jack, the better it would be, even if he could only risk a few days from his business. In any case, we would be delighted to have you as our 'point person' in contacting all the friends made during our search.

"We feel that you and Inga have a special simpatico and that your presence and involvement would be comforting to her. She needs all she can get. In any case, the meeting will be heart-rending for all of us, but maybe we can make it a satisfying emotional memorial to both Bill and Matthias.

"Please give it some serious consideration before responding—but don't lolligag either—the reservations clerks are waiting! We're listening for the echo!"

I couldn't believe Jim's generosity. Jack and I talked it over, and we agreed that if Jim could make such an offer, we could figure out some way to make the trip. Jim was right: We should all be there to support the Hosps in their grief.

Three days later, Inga wrote to tell us that Matthias's death was not an accident. The day after Matthias's funeral she wrote and said, "We all are rather exhausted. The torture for all of us was six days long, until now, finally, Matthias can take his rest. I am sorry to tell you that he committed suicide on Good Friday afternoon, throwing himself over the edge of a vertical rock about 200 m down into a precipice. The rock is called Johanniskofel, situated near the Ritten village Wangen (on the Sarntal-directed slope of the Ritten). It was always a favourite place of the whole family because of the great sight from there, and we visited it with the children several times, years ago. But it is about 2-1/2 hours walking distance from our house, and nobody ever thought that he would walk this far when he left home on Good Friday late morning. So 200 men, dogs, helicopter never did search after him there.

"During the morning he was with his books, preparing for a pathology examination and waiting for the veterinary to call him to join him for practising. And during those perhaps two hours—or better in the last moment because he answered calmly at least two phone calls and reported them from the 1st floor balcony to Bruno sitting down in the garden with some papers and letters (I was down at Bozen with Julia for a doctor's appointment)—the idea of killing himself must have come over him and must have occupied his brain immediately. So he wrote down two lines of Farewell, covered them with a postcard showing a small cat, and left the house. When Bruno came in, calling him everywhere, he was already away (and Julia and I returned by noon, perhaps half an hour after he left). We wondered why he had not informed his father about going away, but we had no doubt that the veterinary must have come in the meantime and had taken Matthias with him to, perhaps, an urgent case which occurred sometimes before. But at 3 p.m. the veterinary phoned that he now would come and take Matthias with him. And it was then that we ran through all the house, and it was Julia who found his last message.

"But we had absolutely no idea where he could have gone: So they searched first all the vicinities and found nothing until late night, and they couldn't find anything the whole Saturday, too. Then, about 3.30 p.m., a tourist from Austria called us communicating that he had found a purse of a certain Matthias Hosp, and that we should come down to a farmhouse near the Johanniskofel to get it. In that second I knew everything. And we told this to the searchers, and they went down and found him immediately. Before jumping he had put his purse, keys, glasses, and his watch on a bench near to the chapel on top of the rock, had stopped the watch himself—and then...

"The pathologist doing the autopsy (who is a friend and knew Matthias himself) told us that he must have been dead immediately, and I also called a friend who is a physician to question him about the forces working in such an event. And we were glad (glad?) to hear from all of them that he did not suffer at all, not even for a second. And of course I interviewed another friend who is a psychiatrist about what's going on during an unplanned suicide like this (because there was not the slightest signal or clue that he had planned killing himself, nor the slightest reason like love affair, drugs and so on, and we asked every single friend, school mate..., only that during the last months he was terribly busy with a calendar like his father, hurrying from one examination to the next one, and beyond this, as president of a students' league for this spring and summer, he had to plan, organize and realize many activities; the psychiatrist told me that this kind of permanent stress situation can cause suicide when a phase of relaxation—like holidays—is taking place, and that it comes to one's brain in a sudden, like a shadow, cancelling everything except the idea of killing oneself). It must have been this way...

"For Bruno, Julia, her boyfriend Thomas and for me—as well as for his many friends—it is unbelievable but true. And you can imagine: we walked through hell several times, between hope and despair, and hundreds of attempts to get an idea where he could have moved after leaving home.

"Now he is buried with Bruno's parents, his grave a hill of flowers, accompanied yesterday afternoon by more than 1500 people, missed by everyone who knew him and by so many people who know only Bruno, or Julia, or me.

"Dear friends, I want to thank you all for your condolences, also on behalf of Bruno and Julia. And I hope that we once will be able to see the world and our lives in brighter colors. For now and for a long long period we will be in the grip of darkness, grief and sorrow. We loved Matthias so very much, and he was such a gentle, helpful son with many gifts and talents. We never had to complain about what he did. And he always gave us the impression that his world was alright, that he had dreams and relied on visions for his future, and that he was in perfect shape. Now we will have to learn living again—with another concept of life, reduced, diminished, loaded with an everlasting shadow. Please stay near to us!"

I couldn't stop crying. A parent should never have to bury a child. That family had been through hell, and there was no way to console them.

Now my odyssey included questions about not one, but two handsome and promising young men. With one of them we knew why he died but not where, and with the other we knew where but not why. I was torn between leaving the Hosps in peace and wanting desperately to be there with Jim and Jeanne to provide whatever solace we could.

Jack and I decided to go. There was no alternative.

31

THE PILGRIMAGE

To: Christoph Mair
From: Jim Graham
Date: May 5, 2001
Subject: June 2001

Hi Christoph—
Diana Dale, the niece of Lt. Bill Wisner whose P-38 crashed near your area in the Sarntal in 1944, and I are traveling to Italy in the first week in June and would sure like to meet you in person. We will be staying at the Gasthof Kematen in the Ritten area and visiting Inga Hosp whom you worked with last year in finding the crash site.
Is it possible for us to meet you on some day between May 31 and June 3? We may also be in the area a few days later if those days are not OK. We will ask Inga Hosp to check with you to see if we can all meet near your home in the Muls area or somewhere convenient for you.
We certainly appreciate your efforts in support of our search for the Wisner crash site and want to thank you in person. As you know, the U.S. Army team did excavate the site and did find Bill Wisner's remains which are now being verified by scientific DNA means at the Central Identification Laboratories (CIL) in Hawaii.
Hoping you are doing well and that we can meet in June.

* * *

Getting ready for a trip to Europe isn't easy, and once we decided to go there didn't seem to be enough time. I did manage to e-mail Liz Tate at Mortuary Affairs to find out the status of Billy's case, and she replied, "According to the anthropologist, the remains were sampled on 26 March and the samples sent to the DNA laboratory that week. We are now waiting for the comparisons to be made which, unfortunately, takes a while (I'm not sure how long but believe it's 60 days). The DNA laboratory will then write up their report of the results and send it back to CILHI for incorporation into the identification case file."

That didn't make sense, so I had to ask her, "Sorry to be so dumb, but what will they compare the sample to? We have not been asked for DNA samples from either my mother or me, which I assume they would need for a positive I.D.. Is that the next step?" Her answer was contrite.

"Diana, your question was not dumb—my response to you was! You are right to question what the samples will be compared to because we have not yet received your blood sample! I'm sorry—I jumped the gun a little. I will send you a DNA kit today." She said I should take it to my physician to draw the blood and return it as the package instructed.

She went on to clarify what she had told me before. "The samples that were sent to AFDIL (the DNA lab) were bone samples that the CILHI anthropologists cut which appear to have good potential for extracting the DNA. Once the DNA has been extracted THEN it is compared to the blood. The extraction process is what has been happening over the last month. I am not an expert on the particulars of the extraction process, but I do know from my visit to the lab last year that it is a very involved process. Once DNA has been successfully extracted from the bone samples, AFDIL reports that to CILHI and CILHI then asks me to get the blood sample from the maternal donor. CILHI normally waits until AFDIL reports back that they were able to extract the DNA before they ask me to obtain the blood sample. Hopefully, the extraction process is near completion by now. I hope this explanation clears up your questions."

The kit arrived about two weeks before we were to leave for Italy. The nurse at the blood bank where I donate plasma every month was happy to draw the sample for me, and I packaged the vials with the ice pack the lab provided and shipped it to the DNA lab in Rockville, Maryland. No wonder identification takes so long. The samples have to be shipped halfway around the world and then back again.

Before long we were off on our own trip halfway around the world.

As arranged we met Jim and Jeanne at the Hertz counter at Milan's Malpensa Airport as soon as we cleared passport control. They had arrived just five minutes before us, having come by bus with their elder hostel group, the rest of whom would fly home that day. It was great to see them, and Jack and I were giddy with excitement and jet lag. We stuffed every inch of the rental car with suitcases and tote bags and headed east toward the Ritten plateau, Jim doing the driving and Jack helping him navigate the treacherous freeways around Milan.

After we stopped for lunch on the eastern shore of Lake Garda, Jack took over the driving and I navigated. Jim and Jeanne took catnaps as we headed north along the Adige River. Jack remarked that the picturesque castles perched high on the hillsides above the valley were the small kingdoms that inspired our fairy tales. Each castle maintained vigil over its own domain, and its strategic vantage point over the valley afforded early warning of approaching travelers. By highway they seemed close together, but on horseback it would have taken a day or more to travel from one realm to another.

It was only 2:00 p.m. in Italy, but Jack's body clock insisted it was 6:00 a.m. after a hard night with no sleep. He felt fine when he took the wheel, but by the time we approached Bolzano I was slapping his thigh regularly to keep him alert.

He rallied with a second wind, though, once we got to the confusing streets of Bolzano and the steep, winding road up to the Ritten plateau. The beauty of the vineyards on the near-vertical hillsides and the breathtaking glimpses of the valley as it receded below had us all rubbernecking, and it was difficult to keep our eyes on the road. After a few wrong turns we realized the hotel tourist map I was navigating from bore little resemblance to the road we were traveling, so we simply followed the signs to the Hotel Kematen and pulled into the lot at 3:30, just as we had estimated.

The proprietor of the Hotel Kematen, Alois Untermarzoner, greeted us graciously. His deferential treatment made sense later when we learned that he had been a student of both Inga and Bruno at one time. As we toured his 800-year-old hotel, he pointed out the woodwork, saying Bruno's grandfather had crafted it all. When he came to a small, arched wooden doorway about five feet tall and barely two feet wide, I thought it was a special closet, but when he opened it, I realized it was the entrance to our suite. For the next week, every time Jack had to duck down and rotate his shoulders to squeeze through the tiny door, it was as if a fairy-tale giant were disappearing into his lair. Several hotel guests made similar comments.

We could see part of the Dolomites out our window, so it didn't take us long to make our way down to the terrace to take in the whole breath-taking panorama. On the left was the Schlern/Sciliar, the stunning massif formation where the pilot Paolo spoke of had been stranded when he bailed out. It's no wonder a skilled climber had to rescue him. The sheer walls were almost vertical, and we could watch their color change from lavender to amber to rich, deep russet as the sun moved across the sky. Next, the Rosengarten, a jagged formation shaped more like stalagmites than mountains; after that, more snow-covered peaks, then a deep green forest. Alois pointed toward the Hosp home, hidden among the trees above the meadow on the far right.

The field being mowed in front of the hotel filled the cool, clear air with the intoxicating scent of fresh-cut hay. Stupefied by jet lag and the beauty of it all, I sat down on a bench to absorb the view. The steady drone of the DC-10 that had enveloped us for six hours had been replaced by the high-pitched whine of sportscars whizzing past us on the *autostrasse*. Now, as I sat in front of the hotel in peaceful silence, my ears picked up the dis-tant buzz of a bumblebee as he made his way through the wildflowers along the fence line. I couldn't believe I was finally there.

Jim called Inga, who told him we were expected for dinner at her house at 7:30 that evening. She said it was within walking distance, and there was a trail that connected the hotel to her house. We all agreed it would be good to stretch our legs.

Back in the room I called Paolo, nervous about meeting him over the phone. But his phone personality matched the one in his e-mails, and his friendly eagerness put me at ease. He said everything had been arranged for Friday's trip to the crash site. Inga wouldn't join us because of her bad knee, and I knew that meant she would never meet Paolo and find out for herself what a kind person he is.

When Inga's name came up, Paolo made one request: If Inga planned to write an article for the German-language paper, he would very much like to get his story published first. I told him I would do what I could to make that happen.

After a couple of hours of rest and some wine and cheese in Jim and Jeanne's room, we started out. Satiny brown cows chewed thoughtfully and followed our progress with big, liquid eyes as we skirted their pasture and disappeared into the woods beyond. The sun was still high, but the dense trees blocked the light, and I had a sense of why the forest inspired so much fear in so many fairy tales.

The path delivered us onto the Gebrack road, and as we climbed the hill toward the Hosp house, there was Inga, arms outstretched, walking down to greet us. We took turns hugging her, and it was as if no time had passed since our meeting in Seattle nine months before. But we all knew Inga's world had changed completely, and sadness weighed down the joy of our greeting.

Bruno met us at the house, and before going inside we toured the grounds. The meadow that served as the Hosp yard was in bloom, and the daisies were just beginning to open. Inga told us she wouldn't allow the yard to be cut until after they had dropped their blossoms. Deep burgundy lilac bushes 30 feet tall filled the air with their sweet fragrance, and I caught my first sight of a cuckoo methodically inspecting a flowerbed for grubs.

Earlier I had heard a cuckoo calling in the forest behind our hotel. When I asked Jim if he'd heard it, too, he said, "Yes, but I thought it was a clock somewhere and wondered why it was chiming at such an odd time." Funny how tuned we are to artificial sounds. It hadn't occurred to Jim that we were in "real" cuckoo country.

Dinner was ready, so Inga seated us around the large wooden table in their cozy *stube*. I learned later that this multi-purpose room has for centuries formed the heart of every Tyrolean home. A *stube's* walls, floors, and beamed or coffered ceilings are all made of wood to retain heat. A large table fills one corner of the room, and benches provide convenient, space-efficient seating around it and around the large ceramic oven that fills another corner. Back when people baked bread in the farmhouses, the oven door would open into the kitchen, adjacent to the *stube*. That way, the smoke and soot would be confined to the cooking area while the closed end of the oven, which projected into the *stube*, kept it toasty warm on even the coldest days, a simple, efficient, and brilliant design.

But the Hosp home was built in the '70s, so their *stube* oven door opens into the living room near the back door for easy access to the firewood outside. There were at least two cords of perfectly-cut firewood neatly stacked along the wall that Inga told me Matthias had cut the previous fall. The Hosp *stube* was adjacent to a modern kitchen opposite the oven, but it had the same cozy atmosphere of an ancient room. The walls and shelves held native folk art and items from local costumes. A rack of pewter plates that had been in Bruno's family for 400 years decorated one side of the room and on the opposite side a heavy chest held a photo of Matthias surrounded by burning candles. In the ceiling above, pointing north, was the *heilige geist*, a sculpted white dove symbolizing the Holy Ghost, which can be found in every home and *gasthof* in the region.

We feasted on a dinner of pasta with tomato and peppers, bread, and fresh fruit for dessert. We toasted our gathering with the local beer in season and a lovely red wine, also of local vintage. Our conversation followed many paths, and we laughed and talked easily. We often spoke of Matthias and took turns shedding tears as we shared our memories of him. Bruno brought out the photos from the funeral, and it was heartbreaking to see Inga, Bruno, and Julia walking at the head of the solemn procession. Nearly two thousand people had followed the casket as it was borne to the Klobenstein/Lengmoos cemetery, the same one Katie had described in her letter seven months before.

As the dinner dishes were cleared and conversation began to lag, we realized it was time to go. Jack and I had managed 35 hours with no sleep and were beginning to get punchy. Jim and Jeanne were also starting to fade, so before we all nodded off in our plates Bruno took pity on us and drove us back to the hotel.

We slept hard and awoke refreshed, ready for a morning of sightseeing with Inga. At breakfast on the hotel terrace in the brilliant sunshine, Jeanne asked Jim if he had remembered to put sunscreen on his nose. He said he had, in fact, put it all over his face. Jack put in, "Maybe you should have used it as hair oil, too." That set the tenor of our week from then on—good-natured ribbing and easy laughter.

Inga picked us up at 10:00, and we headed for the Rittner Horn, the highest point on the Ritten Plateau. The cable car ride to the top was thrilling, and Inga pointed out the sights, including Billy's crash site on the back of one of the lower mountains, and the small community where Mussolini would have retired. Thanks to boys like Billy, things turned out differently for him. We walked up to a *gusthof* near the summit to drink some of the local beer and take in the panorama of the surrounding Alps. When Jack offered to pay for the drinks, Inga narrowed her eyes, set her jaw, and said, "I don't understand your accent." We learned later the word "hospitality" comes from the same root meaning as her last name. No wonder nothing we tried to do could stay ahead of the Hosp generosity.

That evening Inga took us to the cemetery to view Matthias's grave. Like Katie, I was struck by beauty of the place. Each grave had an elaborate iron cross, photos of its inhabitants, and a raised bed with blooming flowers. As I wandered along the gravel paths separating the neat rows, I noticed that even the oldest graves were still being tended. The cemetery was small and intimate, nothing like the sterile "memorial parks" in America, where all the headstones look alike and only cut flowers are allowed.

Bruno and his brother, Josef, met us at a nearby restaurant for pizza. Over dinner, they told us about their lives in Klobenstein during the war and afterwards. With Inga translating, Bruno recalled seeing the bombers as they flew up the valley, below his sightline on the Ritten Plateau. He said Klobenstein was so remote back then, he was six the first time he had ever seen an automobile. That was when the Americans came. He seemed wistful as he told how the G.I.'s would take the village children for rides in their jeeps.

The next day's itinerary included a trip to Bolzano for shopping and a tour of the museum for "Frozen Fritz," better known as Ötzi, The Iceman.* Bruno, president of the museum, gave us an informative guided tour, then treated us to a delicious lunch on the terrace of the Hotel Laurin. Just as we sat down to eat, the skies opened up in a spectacular downpour, while we stayed warm and dry under the terrace's elaborate canopy.

The rain stopped as quickly as it started, and the sun was coming out just as we finished lunch. Next stop was the Sarn Valley to meet Jakob Weger, the man who had seen Billy's crash when he was 15 and on whose farm Inga and Christoph had found the turbocharger. I rode with Inga, and the others followed in the rental car.

Inga was my kind of driver: skillful, confident, and aggressive. As she negotiated the tight curves, she told me the road had been built by the Fascists in the '30s to make use of the hydroelectric potential of the region. Before that time, the valley was essentially cut off from the city below. That explains its charm. There are no tourist attractions, and the few commercial buildings blend in with the traditional architecture. There is nothing to

---

*Discovered in 1991 by some hikers in the Ötztal Alps near the Italian-Austrian border, this 5,300-year-old mummified remnant of the Bronze Age is the most complete specimen of its kind in the world. And it may be the world's oldest murder-mystery, because it was later determined by a Bolzano physician that the man had an arrowhead lodged in his back. The whole story can be found at www.iceman.it.

spoil the beauty and rural ambience.

Inga had warned us we would have to go by the Johanniskofel, the promotory where Matthias had ended his life. I didn't want to be the reason she had to drive past it for the first time since his death, but Inga said she would have to do it sooner or later. At least she wasn't by herself. She showed me where it was, then slowed slightly and pointed back at the spot for the others to see. I followed her gesture toward a sheer rock face, 600 feet high, above the valley floor. When I looked back at Inga, tears were streaming down her face.

"Oh, Inga, what was he thinking?" I asked, not knowing what else to say.

She negotiated a sharp turn through the narrow gorge and cried, "We'll never know," then recounted the theories she'd been given by the experts. "I can only hope he is at peace now," she added. I reached over and patted her arm in a feeble attempt to provide comfort. We rode on in silence.

Higher up the valley, she pointed out two mountains on the left. First was the Kirchnock, the low, wooded foothill where the pieces of Lowell Twedt's plane had come down. Above and behind that was the Pazzei Alm, much higher and rockier, where Olson's plane crashed. I tried to visualize Olson's disabled P-38 heading straight for the mountain as his parachute drifted down above the little town of Aberstückl/Sonvigo as what was left of Twedt's plane fell on the low hill below.

But before I could take it all in, we had come to a stop in Jakob Weger's driveway. I looked up at the house and saw the word *Plunerhof* painted on the side, no doubt where the Plunerbach had gotten its name (or maybe it was the other way around). Jakob and his wife, Maria, came out to greet us. Maria wore a dress covered by an apron and had a pink kerchief on her head and floppy galoshes on her feet. Jakob was dressed in the uniform of the region, a Tyrolean hat, work clothes, and a blue apron. A friendly little cat and some rather aloof ducks followed behind him. I heard the dull, rhythmical clanking of a cowbell and looked up to see its owner carefully picking her way down the steep path from a pasture above. Inga introduced everyone and translated as we stood in the farmyard and chatted.

Jakob beckoned to Jim and me and led us around to the back of the house. There, propped against the wall, was the turbocharger from Billy's plane, the one Christoph and Inga had dug out of the snow just a year before. We stood and stared at it, and at last Jim broke the silence as he reached for me. "Did you ever think we'd get here?" he asked.

"It doesn't seem real," I said, returning his hug. His eyes, like mine, were full of tears. We took turns photographing each other with the turbocharger and with Jakob, who seemed pleased to have us there, even though we didn't understand a word he said.

By the time we got back to the farmyard, Christoph Mair and a female reporter from the *Dolomiten*, the German-language newspaper, had arrived. The reporter took notes as Inga related the story and identified all the players. I was wearing Billy's bracelet, and at what I thought was the appropriate time, I showed it to Jakob and the reporter. Jakob took a good look at it, and Inga translated as he said, "That's the same one I saw." It was good to get a confirmation, even though there was no doubt.

I had remembered that Jakob still used items made from the wreckage from Billy's plane, two of which were an ashtray and a hacksaw. As a joke and a gesture of good will, I had brought along a souvenir ashtray from Colorado and a new hacksaw as gifts. When Jakob unwrapped the saw, he insisted on giving me his old one. I tried to refuse, but he just smiled and said, "I only need one." I accepted, thinking it might be rude not to. The reporter photographed the exchange. You'd think we had just awarded each other the Nobel Peace Prize. I noticed Jakob didn't show me his ashtray, much less offer it to me. Inga had said it was one of his favorite things, and although I was curious to see what it looked like, I didn't want to put him in an awkward position by asking to see it.

I had told Inga about Paolo's request that he be allowed to publish first and hoped it had gotten to the reporter. But she was asking lots of questions, and seemed in a hurry. I was afraid Paolo would be "scooped" by the *Dolomiten* once again. Paolo's articles had been more in-depth than the *Dolomiten's*, but he still was under pressure to get this story printed first.

The Wegers invited us into the house for *apfelzaft* [apple juice], and their youngest son joined us. Hans, who has Down syndrome, had accompanied Inga on the exploratory trip to the crash site with the U.S. team. Jim asked Hans if those were his trophies on the shelf, and he replied that he had won them in the equivalent of the U.S. Special Olympics and proudly showed us his medals, too. It was a charming afternoon, made more so by the warmth and hospitality of these wonderful Tyrolean people.

The next day would be Paolo's, and I didn't want anything to spoil it. As soon as we got back to our hotel I called to tell him about the Dolomiten reporter and assured him I had done what I could to get them to hold the story for a couple of days.

But the next morning, there was our visit to the Weger farm, complete with photos, in the weekend edition of the *Dolomiten*. (Inga later apologized and told me she didn't realize it would be published so soon.) The article was short, less than half a page, but still it unsettled me. As we waited for Paolo on the hotel veranda, I started to worry. What if we didn't get along? What if he was angry about the *Dolomiten* article? What if he was an aggressive, callous reporter, who only wanted the story? What if...?

But before I could think of the next What if, I heard Jim say, "This must be our man, now." I looked up, and there was Paolo, beaming, as he came to greet us, arms outstretched. After hugs and handshakes, all my fears vanished. He was open, friendly, warm, and sweet. He brushed off my apologies about the article with a shrug, saying he had expected as much and assuring us his story would be much better.

I rode with Paolo while the three J's followed in the rental car. This time we took a shortcut across the plateau. The steep, winding road afforded glimpses of the Sarn Valley as we inched our way down the steep slope and around dicey curves made more treacherous by the occasional oncoming car or truck. As he approached each blind turn, Paolo would honk his horn. At one point he apologized, "This is the way we drive in Italy." From what I could tell, he was right: Italians drive with one foot on the gas and one hand on the horn at all times. But in spite of their aggressiveness and love for speed, they are highly skilled. They have to be. In Italy, it's pay attention or die.

First stop, the Carabinieri office in the village of Sarentino, where they were holding the two machine guns found at Olson's crash site. Paolo said no photographs would be allowed inside, and we had to be "buzzed" in at the gate—very dramatic.

The Carabinieri are Italy's military police. In an effort to reduce corruption, each officer is assigned to a jurisdiction away from home. I assumed the young Carabiniere with the intense blue eyes who greeted us was new to the area, because he gave no sign of recognition as Paolo explained why we were there. He then led us to a back hall and unlocked a vault where the machine guns were held. The lights were out in that part of the building, so he and Paolo carried the guns into a sunlit room where we could get a good look at them.

Under Italian law, war artillery must be destroyed as soon it is found, but Paolo had convinced the authorities to hold these guns until we could see them. How those twisted, rusty, empty metal shells could be considered a threat now is beyond me, but the law is the law. Jim recorded the serial numbers for his records, just in case that would be the last evidence that they ever existed. Paolo felt they had historical significance for Italy, and even though the U.S. authorities had no interest in them, he was trying to place them in a museum somewhere.

Next stop, Garmesegg. Paolo wanted us to see the story from his perspective and to introduce to us the people who had been so helpful, even though the bomber wreckage he found at this site had little to do with our search.

When we pulled up Florian Innerebner, the Garmesegg farmer, was mending a fence, sporting a Tyrolean hat and a blue apron, just like the one Jakob Weger wore. Now I understood the significance of the aprons the Hosps had given Jack and Jim back in Seattle, and why they were suitable gifts for men. They aren't kitchen aprons at all. In Südtirol, the farmers wear them to protect their clothing, because an apron is easier to wash than dungarees and work shirts. Now, every time Jack wears his, I think of Jakob and Florian.

We toured Florian's workshop, and he demonstrated how he had adapted the various pieces of bomber wreckage for his work. Most useful was the oxygen cylinder he had cut in half for a water tank. The tank hangs above the milling saw and drips water on the blade to keep it from overheating.

Just before we left, Jim asked Florian (with Paolo translating from English into German) if he had been in the war, too. Florian replied that he had been sent to Russia with the Wehrmacht. When the war was over he walked home, all the way from St. Petersburg. I can't imagine the hardships he must have endured traveling through strange countries devastated by years of war. I wanted to hear more, but Paolo was on a timetable so we had to move on.

Next stop, the Hotel Feldrand, just beyond Jakob Weger's farm. This was the place where Inga had suggested the U.S. investigators stay because it was closest to the crash site. Paolo had us gather around an empty table while he told us the story of his search. Using the 10 editions of the *Alto Adige* with his stories about finding Billy, he proudly explained the articles and photos. I realized how important this story was to him, and that it was not just journalism. His attention to detail and the friendly way people treated him revealed an emotional attachment to our story. He had been diligent and circumspect, and I was proud to know him.

Christoph Mair joined us for a lunch of salad and grilled trout, caught that morning in the Talavera River just across the road. Then, just as we were finishing our wine, Konrad Rungger, the proprietor of the Hotel Feldrand, pulled up a chair. With Paolo translating, Konrad told us how he had sneaked up to the crash when he was just five years old. One hundred square meters of forest were ablaze, and it took several people to put the fire out. When Konrad's uncle saw him so close to the danger, he grabbed him, gave him a stern warning, and sent him home. As he related the memory, Konrad pantomimed picking up a child by the collar, and setting him down, shaking his finger at the imaginary boy.

He went on to say that two days later his uncle, Stanislaus Reichsiegel,* had gone back to the site, wrapped Billy in a sheet and buried him, marking the spot with a cross. And even though the cross had disappeared in the '60s, Konrad still knew the spot, because for years he had passed by it every time he took his father's sheep up to higher pasture.

But the U.S. team had begun excavating at the site Jakob Weger identified, because that was the first location they knew about. At Jakob's site they had found some evidence of a crash, but they could tell it was not the point of impact and, therefore, not the burial site. Back at the Hotel Feldrand, they were discussing abandoning the expedition when someone told them Konrad might be able to help.

At first the team didn't take him seriously. After all, the cross was no longer there, and how good could the memory of a five-year-old child be, anyway? But when Konrad insisted he knew the exact site because of a big rock that also marked the spot, they decided to try once more. Fifty meters farther up the mountain, they found a piece of plexiglass from the cockpit canopy, indication they had found the point of impact.

The rest is history, and now it was time to see the place for ourselves. Konrad would drive us to the site—or as close as he could get—in the hotel van. I was thrilled, because now Jeanne could come up with us. She had been in on the story with Jim from the beginning, but because of a brace she wore on one foot that wouldn't allow her to walk up a steep slope, she was resigned to the fact she would have to wait for us in the hotel lobby. Now she could witness the end, first-hand, with the rest of us.

Before we started out, Paolo, with Italian flair, presented me with two items. The first was a jagged piece of wreckage. This was the definitive piece linking the crash site to a P-38, he told me, because it bore traceable part

---

*Back in March 2000 Inga had referred to Stanislaus Reichsiegel as "a Huber-farm cowboy" when she related Jakob's version of the story.

numbers. While the turbocharger on Jakob's farm was able to bring the investigators to the right neighborhood, it wasn't direct evidence, because it wasn't at the crash site. The piece Paolo gave me had been found during the excavation, and he had convinced the investigators to let him give it to me.

The second gift was a bundle of fresh flowers to put on the site. I hugged Paolo and thanked him for his thoughtfulness. He had brought a jar for their water, but Konrad said he had something better and disappeared into the hotel. He came back with a blue and white syrup container designed to look like an elegant Delft vase. Such thoughtful cooperation and attention to detail, I was beginning to feel unworthy. But I told myself this was being done for Billy, not me.

Holding the flowers and vase, I climbed into the van with our troupe. We drove up the valley to Weissenbach and turned off onto a steep, narrow logging road that scaled the hill behind the village. Just as we started to gain altitude on the road, we met a logging truck coming down, and Konrad had to back down about 100 feet to make room for it to pass. Backing down such a steep, narrow trail was harrowing to me, but when Christoph said Konrad used to drive a tour bus all over Europe, I relaxed. European bus drivers are among the best in the world.

We stopped to open a locked gate and reached the point where we had to proceed on foot. Konrad led the way. Paolo had pulled Jack aside earlier and told him he needed to stay ahead of me and be ready with the camera, so I stumbled along behind, still clutching my flowers and vase. The hillside was steep, 45 degrees in places, and even though we were traversing it, I had a hard time keeping my footing on the slippery pine needles and uneven ground. Behind me, Jim held on to Jeanne from above, and Christoph placed himself strategically downhill from both of them, in case of a mis-step. I couldn't look back to see how they were faring, but I didn't hear any screams, so I knew they were all right.

As I picked my way along the last few feet, I was able to look ahead and see Konrad and Paolo beaming up at me and Jack ready with the camera. Then I saw the covered wooden cross that marked what had been Billy's home for 56 years, and I burst into tears.

At the base of the cross was a raised bed planted with blooming flowers. Konrad took two candles in holders from the arms of the cross, and I helped shield them from the wind as he lit them. Then he filled the vase with water from the turbulent stream and cleared a place for it at the foot of the cross. I put Paolo's cut flowers in the water and set the vase, careful not to tip it over.

Konrad had turned the bare hole left after the excavation into a lovely memorial, and he clearly was proud of his handiwork. He had even tacked a photocopy of my favorite picture of Billy inside a plastic sleeve to the cross. On the page he had written:

> *Pilot aus Amerika.*
> *William O. Wisner.*
> *Abgestürzt um 1130 Uhr*
> *am 20 Oktober 1944.*
> *Wir wollen deinen Weg gehn dass wir dich glüklich wiedersehn.*
> *Her gib Ihn die Ervige Ruhe.*

> (American pilot,
> William O.Wisner,
> crashed at 11:30 a.m.
> on 20 October 1944.
> We follow your path, so that one day we may meet again.
> O Lord, give him eternal peace.)

It was almost more than I could bear, and I couldn't stop crying. But I couldn't stop smiling, either, because this was the end of a lifetime of mystery. This is where Billy had been all along, and it was beautiful. I wished Idy and Papa could see it, and I couldn't wait to share the photos with Mother and Daddy.

Paolo pointed across the valley to Olson's and Twedt's crash site. The pale purple-grey of the Pazzei Alm above was speckled with patches of snow and cut by dramatic waterfalls. Sunlight on the pastures above the Kirchnock glowed in soft yellows and pale greens. Words can't begin to describe its beauty, and no photo will do it justice.

And it was made more beautiful by the strangers who had shown so much love and respect. Paolo had carefully staged the day, but even he didn't know the lengths Konrad had gone to. Besides building the cross out of larch, the traditional wood for a warrior's grave, Konrad had set it a meter deep into the ground to be sure it would stay for a long, long time. He had staked out the path, moved rocks and soil, remembered to bring candles, and planted flowers he had brought up from the valley. All for someone he had never met.

Paolo showed us where he sat during the investigation. He wasn't

Paolo Cagnan, Diana Dale, Jim Graham, Jeanne Simonds, Christoph Mair,
Konrad Rungger at crash site

allowed to help, so he recorded the activity at a distance, from early morning until 6:30 in the evening, every day for a week. Then he would e-mail
Jim and me, and write his stories.

We stood and talked, raising our voices to be heard above the pounding roar of the Krössbach (here, the official name of the stream called
Plunerbach down below). *Torrente* described it perfectly. As fast moving
and full as it was that first day of June, I couldn't imagine what early spring
run-off would be like. And there had been 55 springs since Billy crashed on
its bank. It's a wonder there had been anything left to find.

But Christoph, who had pulled a piece of wreckage from the stream
just a year before at Jakob's site, found another piece of metal at this one.
Then, a few feet away, Paolo found a piece of fabric about six inches square.
He handed it to me and said it was fiberglass upholstery from the cockpit
seat. I showed it to Jim.

"This is the last thing Billy touched before he died," I blubbered.

Jim chuckled and said, "He was sittin' on it," and I laughed, too.
This was a happy occasion, and I shared it with people who cared about me
and about Billy.

View across the valley, where Lowell Twedt and Virgil Olson crashed

I got up the courage to speak a little Italian to Konrad and pointed to the ring Billy was wearing in the photo tacked to the cross. I told him the only thing we hadn't found was that ring, the one he never took off. Mother had asked me about it when I reported what the investigators had found, but it wasn't among the items they mentioned. I told Jack I wanted to come back one day and hike up from the valley along the stream bed, just to see what else I might be able to find. I envisioned the ring stuck under a rock somewhere along the way, waiting to be discovered.

I wanted a souvenir for Mother, so I picked some blossoms off the flowers Konrad had planted. They looked familiar, but I didn't know their name. Jeanne was our flower expert, so I turned to ask her what they were.

She had been watching me and smiled. The look on her face told me she had been anticipating my question.

"They're Sweet William," she replied.

32

HOME AGAIN

To:	Diana Dale, Jim Graham, Jeanne Simonds
From:	Inga Hosp
Date:	June 22, 2001
Subject:	Back to Reality

Dear Diana & Jack,

Dear Jim & Jeanne,

So glad I am to know you all safely at home! Thanks a lot for your reports about the last week of your stay to Italy (and Austria and Switzerland). And, yes, it's always a mess returning back home and getting reorganized. [...]

Days are wonderful now: long and (finally) warm and almost cloudless. Tomorrow (!) the first rosebud will open, but Daisies and Lilacs are (almost) finished now. The smells outside the house change rapidly between the perfume of haymaking and that of liquid manure – which follows haymaking immediately. Yesterday it was hay...

I spend my days with... well, I spend them somehow. And I am also trying to get back to my writing, but in my head there is still the (un)merry-go-round spinning on and on.

Oh, and I forgot to tell you why I didn't want to join you [...] during that Friday with Cagnan: I am still upset with his newspaper and don't want to make contacts with it for a certain reason. Imagine: half an hour after we learnt what happened to Matthias a reporter and a photographer of Alto Adige rang at our

door, started to make pictures round the house and wanted to
speak about my emotions. I could only say "Vergognatevi!"
[shame on you] and send them away.
I wish you splendid summer days, too, and every success you
need (or even like)!
Love to all of you
Inga

* * *

In spite of all hopes, I now knew there would never be a friendship
between two of the people who meant so much to me in this investigation. After Inga's e-mail I could understand why Inga was so reluctant
to have anything to do with Paolo or his newspaper. It was as if they were
trying to prove her right; reporters were not to be trusted, and Inga tarred
Paolo with the same brush. Of course, I knew better.

But even though Inga and Paolo never joined forces in the search, or
maybe it was because they didn't, the outcome was a success. And it was
crowned by our perfect day at the crash site. There was no way Konrad
could have known the English name of the flowers he had planted on
Billy's former grave, or that Sweet William symbolizes gallantry. When I
translated it into the Italian equivalent, *Dolce Guglielmo*, Konrad was surprised. *"Non sapevo questo* [I didn't know that]," he said.

I could barely pull myself away from the place where Billy had waited
56 years to be found, but we had accomplished what we'd gone there to
do. Everyone needed to get back, so I declined when Paolo asked if I wanted some time there alone. This was their place as much as it was mine, and
it was time to move on.

We went back to the Hotel Feldrand for beer and interviews, and
once again Paolo took the role of serious investigative reporter, asking
questions he already knew the answers to. But the story had to be done
right. Afterwards, we scouted the hotel grounds for a suitable place for a
memorial. I envisioned a little park with a plaque and a bench where people
could sit in the shade, enjoy the stream, and think peaceful thoughts. Now
that I saw the area for myself, I knew it could be done. Konrad took us to a
spot under some trees behind the hotel, next to a small bridge over the
Plunerbach connecting Jakob's farm to a meadow filled with wildflowers.
He said three hiking trails come together at that point, so there would be a

lot of foot traffic. It was a perfect spot for a weary traveler to sit and rest, and think about peace.

Konrad had work to do and Paolo wasn't quite finished with us, so after the interviews, we struck out for the farm of Alois Gramm, just below Olson's crash site. His daughter-in-law greeted us and said Alois was out walking. She jumped in her Jeep to bring him back, and Paolo introduced us when they got back. He invited us inside, and I was grateful to get out of the wind, which by now had the bite of the glaciers it had just passed over. We gathered around the table in the corner of their warm *stube* so Alois and Paolo could tell us about how they searched for Twedt's grave. They had torn up much of the hillside in the process, but found little more than small bits of scattered wreckage.

Conversation was difficult, and more than once Paolo would start translating in the wrong language. I'd stop him and say, "No Paolo, in English (or German), please." Smiling, but through gritted teeth, Paolo would reply, "It's not so easy." I don't know how he did it at all. He was processing information in three languages at once, two were not his own, and one was in a dialect difficult for him to understand.

It was a lovely visit. Jim exchanged e-mail addresses with Alois's grandson, and we moved on. Paolo joined us for dinner back at our hotel. Good conversation, good food, good wine—the end to a perfect day. We hated to say goodbye to Paolo, but it was late, he had a long drive home, and we were all exhausted.

Jack and I were in bed by 11:30 and Jack fell asleep immediately, as he usually does. He says it's because of a clear conscience, but I've always teased him about having no conscience at all. I tried to drift off, but I was just too excited by the events of the day to sleep. After tossing and turning, I got up at 2:00 and wrote in my journal until after 3. I was afraid I would forget something, so I chronicled every single detail of the day. When I finished and finally did fall asleep, my dreams were a jumble of Billy, airplanes, mountains, and my new friends.

We spent our next three days in the Ritten area sightseeing and getting to know our friends better. Julia Hosp came home for the weekend and joined us for a hike to the Earth Pyramids and a train ride to Oberbozen for coffee in the lobby of the Hotel Holzner, where the German anti-aircraft officers had been billeted during the war. Inga pointed out the spot on the hotel lawn where the big guns had command of the valleys flanking the plateau. Seeing it in person, I realized it was a miracle more planes hadn't been shot down on October 20, 1944. They would have been easy targets.

On Sunday morning Jim, Jeanne, Jack and I drove to Bolzano for a tour of the *Alto Adige*, Paolo's newspaper. Except for the guard at the front desk, Paolo was the only person working that day, and I apologized for his having to come in just to show us around. But he told us that now that he was a manager he worked most weekends. He gave us copies of that day's paper with our story in it. The headline read, *"Dopo 56 anni, una tomba per Bill il pilote* [After 56 years, a memorial for Bill the pilot]". The article filled a page, and one of the photo cut lines read, "Rungger with 'his' cross."

Paolo Cagnan at his desk at the *Alto Adige* in Bolzano

We took our leave of Paolo, then headed up another valley to Marien-berg for a tour Inga and Bruno had arranged of the highest monastery in Europe. As we drove, I did my best to translate the article for my fellow travelers. Paolo had written another good story.

The day was cool and overcast, and as we approached the monastery, we couldn't tell where the mist stopped and the clouds began. Bruno arrived just after we did and introduced us to the abbot, Herr Prelate Bruno, and one of his former teachers, Father Matthias, who would give us a private tour. Fr. Matthias didn't speak English, so it was up to me to translate his Italian, and I kicked myself for not having studied more before we left. Using my inadequate Italian to translate what I could understand and my rusty art history to interpret what I couldn't, I paraphrased his commentary on the crypt's 12th Century frescoes. I know I missed a lot, but Jack, Jeanne, and Jim seemed satisfied with the results. Bruno and Fr. Matthias were none the wiser.

Bruno invited me to ride back with him in his chauffered car, and I readily accepted. As minister of culture for the province, he was the best imaginable tour guide, and he answered a lot of the questions we'd had about the points of interest we passed on our way up. When Bruno pointed out a tiny church dating from between 500 and 600 A.D., he told me Christianity had arrived about that time and was brought by St. Boniface from Ireland, not Rome. There was a lot more I wanted to know, but by the time I could look up the Italian words I needed to form the question, I would forget what it was I wanted to ask.

That evening Inga cooked us a delicious dinner of local cuisine, and the next day we toured Klobenstein and paid our respects to Matthias one last time. Bruno and Julia were on their way back to Vienna, so Inga joined us for our final dinner at the hotel. We said our good-byes, and Inga picked Jack up at 3:00 the next morning to take him to Bolzano for his too-early train back to Milan. As one who values her sleep, I see that as friendship above all price. Of course, Inga insisted it was no trouble, because "I don't sleep much these days, anyway." But still…

Jim, Jeanne, and I made the best of our last week in Europe. We drove over the Brenner Pass into Austria to meet Keith Bullock at his home in Mils bin Imst. Keith was the good-natured former RAF pilot and air war historian who had helped us early in our search and was instrumental in solving the riddle of the Ritten crash that had first brought us together with Inga.

Sadly, a severe stroke in January had left Keith paralyzed on his left side, and although it hadn't dampened his wit or sense of humor, he was confined to a wheelchair and could only see a little out of his right eye. He couldn't use his computer yet, but with the loving and stern encouragement of his wife Helene (a 1968 Olympic bronze medal winner for the luge) and daughters Becky and Sarah, there's hope he'll recover and be able to get back to his bomber research. I hope so. His contribution is irreplaceable.

We spent the rest of our week in the Lake Como and Lake Garda areas, taking day trips into Milan, Verona, and Venice. The trip was lovely, but after our pilgrimage to the crash site, it was anticlimactic. I think we all looked forward to going home.

Waiting for me when I arrived back in Denver was a letter from the Department of Defense Armed Forces Institute of Pathology in Washington, D.C., acknowledging receipt of my blood sample. It said, "the request for your whole blood sample does not imply there are recovered remains associated with your loved one." I called the service casualty officer who was filling in while Liz Tate was on medical leave to find out what that meant. He said it was standard wording in their form letter, but he would check on it. He ascertained that Billy's bone sample was in the process of being compared to my blood sample at their lab in Rockville, Maryland, and called back to say it might be a long time before we had the results.

I managed to hold off a couple of weeks before I e-mailed Liz Tate on July 11 to ask her how soon after the comparison was made and the identification was positive would we be able to get Billy home. I had to start thinking about arranging a burial plot in the military section of the family cemetery in Dallas. I wanted to know if we had to pay for it.

She told me it takes at least 60 days before CILHI gets the results of the DNA processing, and there seemed to be a big backlog. Once the results were received at CILHI, she said, the forensic specialists would have to write up their final case reports and submit them to the scientific director for his review. After that, the case would be sent to her office for final review. That's when they would schedule time with the family for a final briefing and to arrange the burial. She said Mother would be the person to sign the authorization for disposition, and the funeral could take place about two weeks after the signing.

The government provides the burial allowance, which includes the cost of the plot, she added, and they would bury him anywhere we wanted, even Arlington National Cemetery.

Then she said something that filled me with dread. "Now, please don't get too excited for completion because I am checking further with CILHI regarding a possible hold-up in completion of the case. My boss...said that...since the crash site was not closed by a CILHI anthropologist, they may need to do either a further excavation of the site (to ensure that Dave Roath and his team got everything) or after reviewing Dave Roath's Search and Recovery Report, they may decide to send an anthropologist to the site to conduct a final survey and then close the site. It is standard procedure for all excavation sites to be 'closed' by a forensic anthropologist. I will let you know what or if a decision has been made on that issue."

Here we go again, I thought, remembering that early in our search Paolo and Bill Mays had commented on the "rivalry" between Mortuary Affairs and CILHI. It was not so much a rivalry as one entity being the watchdog for the other, or perhaps the two in competition to get the evidence first. But it seemed that a forensic anthropologist's visit the site was unnecessary, to say the least. I wrote Liz back, saying I hoped they wouldn't have to send an anthropologist. "Frankly, it's such a beautiful site with such a lovely memorial, if anything is left there, that's okay. I can't think of a better place to spend eternity. Besides, the original remains found in 1952 are God-knows-where now (possibly in an 'unknown' grave at Florence Am. Cemetery, but as far as they've been able to determine no records reveal what happened to them after they left Griesheim mausoleum). In addition, the parts they didn't find last August are probably somewhere in the Adriatic by now, and the parts they did find are now divided between Hawaii and Maryland. So what's the difference? He's a well-traveled kid, and as long as some of him comes home to Dallas the family will be happy."

I meant it. And Mother and Daddy, who were back in Colorado for the summer, agreed. That summer flew by—no strokes or other mishaps, thank goodness. We all got back to our routines, and life was pretty good until the September 11th terrorist attacks. I hadn't contacted Liz Tate for quite a while and was just getting ready to when our world turned upside-down. I felt guilty when I finally did touch base with her on September 19, because I feared the same DNA lab that was testing our samples would be identifying the remains of the victims of the attack on the Pentagon. I told Liz I would understand if that caused a delay in our case, but I wanted to know what, if any, progress had been made.

Liz answered me on September 27, apologizing for the delay, but it was worth the wait. "I have good news for you—they have a match for the DNA! The case will now be written up and forwarded to this office for final review and then the presentation to your family. I don't know how long it will be but I would guess no more than approx. 3-4 weeks for the forensic specialists to write up their final reports. Thank you for being patient with us—I know it has been a long process!"

I forwarded Liz's e-mail to Jim, Jeanne, Inga, Julia, Paolo, my sister, and Katie and Bill, now off at college. Then I called Mother and Daddy to give them the news. When I called Jack at work and told him, he said, "I don't know why, but that brought tears to my eyes. Thanks for calling to cheer me up," he said, dripping irony with his tears.

But at last it was real. This was incontrovertible proof we had found Billy.

I was depressed for the next two days. Our journey was over.

About two weeks later Jim and I received e-mails from Paolo announcing the release of his book. The photos he attached were of him speaking at a press conference, of the book's cover, and of the Bolzano bookstore window display complete with a huge model of a P-38 suspended above. His book, *Trov@te il Pilota Wisner* [Find the Pilot Wisner], should do well.

I waited as long as I could to contact Liz Tate again, hoping she would e-mail me first. But by October 25, I could hold back no longer. Her reply on October 29 said the case was being forwarded to her office for review. I asked if she thought we might be able to have a funeral before Thanksgiving. She wasn't optimistic.

But we arranged it, anyway, and the funeral was set for November 21, the day before Thanksgiving, in Dallas. Billy would be back home, 57 years and eight months after his last furlough in March 1944.

Two representatives from Mortuary Affairs, one of whom flew in from Washington, met with Mama and Daddy in St. Louis on November 13 and went over the report with them and had Mother sign the papers. Daddy told me, "They told me a whole lot more about DNA than I needed to know, but they were very nice guys and very thorough." The report was extremely detailed. Photos of the excavation revealed bits of fabric and rubber, small pieces of metal fasteners, lots of debris, and what was left of the cross Stanislaus Reichsiegel had erected 56 years before. The package of personal effects found at the site came a few days later. In it were Billy's dog tag, its broken silver chain, a small gold arrow charm, and his collar emblem. There wasn't much.

But it was enough.

As soon as I had a date for the funeral, I e-mailed everyone who'd had any role or interest in the story. Sister couldn't be there, and I was sure none of my helpers would be able to come. For the foreign searchers it was short notice; for the domestic ones, it was too close to Thanksgiving, and they all had family plans. But we had been together at the crash site, and that was just as important. We wanted to schedule the service then, because what was left of our small family in Dallas would be in town for the long holiday weekend.

Billy was eligible to be buried at Arlington National Cemetery, but the purpose of our search had always been to bring him home to Dallas. He would be buried in the military section of Laurel Land Cemetery, not far from his parents.

Shortly after arrangements were finalized I received a call from Jim Goad with the Confederate Air Force.* The funeral home staff had told him about Billy's story, and he called to ask my permission to do a fly-over at the service. I told him that would be wonderful. When he said it would include a missing-man formation in honor of Billy, I started to cry. Jim said he and his friends do this often in honor of WWII vets, and his voice broke as he explained why: "It's because we are so lucky to live in this free country, and we have those boys to thank for it." He said the planes would be WWII-era, but only trainers, no P-38. I wondered if Billy might have flown one of them at Perrin Field or Eagle Pass.

The more I thought about the plans, the more I worried about the details. We would stay with my aunt, Margie Thompson, widow of Daddy's brother, Morris. Although Margie had known Billy, he wasn't her blood relative, and I feared all the excitement would overwhelm her. But when I asked if it would be all right if some of the family and friends came to her house after the funeral, she was her usual calm, gracious self and said they would be welcome.

I didn't sleep much in the days before the funeral. I woke up in the middle of the night with a million thoughts, and couldn't get to sleep again for hours. When I did, I had weird dreams and strange songs running through my head. My left eye started to twitch, and my face broke out. I'd been working toward this day for three years, and the stress of wanting it to be perfect was taking its toll. All I could do was cross my fingers and hope the rain in Texas would stop in time.

---

*On December 7, 2001, the Confederate Air Force changed its name to the Commemorative Air Force (www.confederateairforce.org). It is an all-volunteer, nonprofit, 501(c)(3) organization incorporated under Texas laws for charitable and educational purposes. Its purpose is "1) to preserve in flying condition a complete collection of combat aircraft flown by all military services of the United States in World War II; 2) to provide museums for permanent protection and display of these aircraft as a tribute to the thousands of men and women who built, serviced, and flew them; 3) to perpetuate in the memory and hearts of all Americans the spirit in which these great planes were flown for the defense of our nation; 4) to establish an organization having the dedication, enthusiasm and esprit de corps necessary to operate, maintain and preserve these aircraft as symbols of our American military aviation heritage."

Jim Goad told a media friend about our story, and before I knew it, I was talking to a reporter for the ABC affiliate in Dallas. He was a kindred spirit who loved stories like these, and I was pleased there would be video coverage. Maybe the day wouldn't have to end, after all; I could play the tape any time I wanted to.

Jack couldn't make the trip with me, but maybe it was just as well. This would be a ceremony he'd have trouble getting through, too much like his fighter-pilot dad's, 11 years before.

Our first order of business in Dallas was to meet with the Army liaison, 1st Sgt. Rita Burks. Sgt. Burks, a 27-year Army veteran, was there to answer questions, get the paperwork done, and coordinate the honor guard. Even though she had never coordinated a funeral quite like this one, Rita had everything under control and by the time it was over I felt I was saying goodbye to another dear friend.

The next day we met with the funeral home. Steve Blow had recently mentioned Billy's homecoming in his *Dallas Morning News* column, and as a result the Laurel Land funeral director had spent two days fielding questions from reporters. I agreed to be available to them, but I appreciated his help in keeping things understated at the funeral. Reporters from three television stations and three newspapers, one of whom had flown in from Denver, covered the story.

The director informed us Ellison Vault Company had donated a stainless-steel vault for Billy's casket, and as special tribute they had engraved a P-38 and the Air Force insignia on the lid. He added that Laurel Land would donate all costs above the $4,325 government allotment. The vault company and the cemetery each absorbed about $2,000, as a tribute to Billy's sacrifice and his unusual story.

We were ushered into the visitation room where Billy's silver, flag-draped casket lay in quiet dignity. A U.S. flag, a Texas flag, and a large spray of red, white and blue flowers stood sentinel. I put my hand under the flag and touched the casket to make sure it was finally real. I wasn't sure what to feel, and a flood of relief and grief washed over me.

In the military section of the cemetery they had flagged two lots closest to where Daddy's brother was buried.* We chose one about six rows over and three up from Morris, in the shade of an oak tree. Of course, Billy would-

---

*And, we learned later from Lucy and Paul Tarver, not far from both Dalton and Jack Tarver. The high school buddies were together again, at last.

n't know the difference, but it made me feel better that he'd be close to someone he'd known. I joked that he and Morris could catch up on old times.

At last the day arrived.

Laurel Land delivered flowers, and Daddy and I picked up the food trays for the reception. I spoke with reporters on the phone, and the morning flew by. Before any of us was emotionally ready, it was time to go. I filled a tote bag with Billy's photos and memorabilia for the reporters and family to see, and we set out for Laurel Land.

I told the reporters we would say a few words at 1:30, before the visitation, but when we arrived at 1:00 a couple of them were already waiting for us. We set up the room with Billy's photos and yearbooks; the reporters set up their cameras and microphones. Mother, Daddy, and I sat on a sofa, and they filmed while I told them the story of our search. They asked questions, photographed Billy's things, and cleared the room by 2:00 as family and friends arrived. I was in a fog; it was all happening too fast.

Fifty people came. Some knew Billy in grade school and had come because they saw the announcement in the paper; others knew Billy's buddies and wanted to honor him on their behalf. Mother's cousin Jean, whom she hadn't seen in more than 30 years, was there, and so was Cousin Peggy and Cousin Marshall's daughter Lynne Russell. There were other cousins with children I'd never met, and some I wish I'd had more time to talk to. They told me Billy's disappearance had been as much a mystery and loss to them as it had been for me.

John Chopelas's sister, Mary Johnson, came with her son Byron; Jack's baby brother Keith Dale, who lives in nearby Coppell, brought his whole family and presented me with a carved replica of a P-38. The last of the Tarver boys, Paul and Bobby Joe, came with Paul's wife, Lucy. Bobby told me he was only 13 or 14 when Billy left, but he, too, looked up to him as another older brother.

The visitation was too short, and before I could talk to everyone we were being moved out for the service. The pilots were waiting for the funeral director's signal to start the fly-over, and we couldn't hold them up.

Billy's closest relatives climbed into the limousine, and we followed the funeral coach to the canopy-covered gravesite. The string of cars behind us stretched as far as I could see. As the coach slowed to a stop in front of us, I could see the leader of the honor guard giving a slow, solemn salute as they removed the casket. I couldn't swallow for the lump in my throat, as we moved to our seats.

In complete silence, except for the leader's quiet commands, the honor guard placed the casket on the bier and moved away. The chaplain read Billy's funeral notice and a few verses from John 14 and gave a short prayer. Then it was Daddy's turn to speak. He recalled how Billy had favored Mother's other beau, who drove a motorcycle, while Daddy had to court her on the bus. He said Billy was always smiling and laughing, that he had many friends who admired and loved him, and that his devotion to family and country was unsurpassed. He added that if Billy was watching, he'd be tickled, but would wonder why all that "hoopla" was about him.

Then it was my turn to speak. I couldn't let the day go by without telling about the many people who were responsible for that special gathering, specifically Jim Graham, Inga Hosp, Paolo Cagnan, Jakob Weger, Konrad Rungger (and his uncle who buried Billy), and the people of the Sarn Valley.

I thanked everyone for coming.

As I sat down, we heard the drone of the planes as they approached the cemetery. They flew from south to north in formation. I knew they would circle over the VA hospital north of Laurel Land for the benefit of the patients, then they would come back. I moved out from under the canopy so I could see the formation better, and Jack's brother, Keith, came up next to me and put his arm around my waist. As we waited for what seemed like ages in the deafening silence, I whispered to him, "Maybe it's the missing *men* formation," and he chuckled. But it wasn't long before we could hear them coming back.

As they entered the skies above the gravesite, the plane in the center made a slow right turn away from the formation, toward the setting sun, signifying the missing man. The lump in my throat got bigger.

As the drone of the planes faded in the distance, the honor guard lined up on either side of the casket and folded the flag. With tears in his eyes, Sgt. Beavers, a tough-looking former tank commander, knelt in front of Mother with the flag clutched to his chest. As he presented it to her, he whispered, "On behalf of the president and a grateful nation, please accept this token as symbol of your loved one's dedicated service." I could barely hear what he'd said and knew Mother hadn't caught any of it, but she thanked him, anyway, then passed the flag to me and said, "This is for you, for all you've done."

Then seven members of the honor guard formed a line and fired three rounds, and stood at attention as the bugler played Taps.

The chaplain read the 23rd Psalm and closed by saying, "In a time when so many are leaving for overseas, it is fitting that one should be coming home."

And then it was over.

We stayed behind to talk to reporters and take some pictures of the P-38 on the vault before we got back into the limousine. As we pulled away I looked back at the casket, shining in the late afternoon sun. I said my last goodbye to Billy. I knew I would miss his presence in my life, and my heart ached.

By the time we got back to the funeral home everyone had left for the reception. The honor guard had changed clothes and were getting ready to leave, so I caught up with one of them to ask him if he'd had a chance to see a picture of the man they honored that day. "No, ma'am," came the reply, "we never do." I pulled Billy's photos out of my bag, and the rest of the guard gathered around to see. They listened intently, some with tears in their eyes, as I told them the story of finding Billy 56 years after he was lost.

I thanked them all for honoring him so beautifully.

Then, as one voice, they thanked me for bringing him home.

EPILOGUE

FINDING BILLY

* * *

As I write this, it strikes me that I'm 35 years older than Billy will ever be. But whenever I think of him, I'm still a little girl looking up to a man I always thought of as handsome, loving, fun, thoughtful, capable. My quest proved I didn't make that up.

But besides confirming what I'd hoped to be true about Billy, it also gave me gifts I never expected—new friends, people I never would have met had I not started this journey.

Jack and I met John Chopelas, Billy's boyhood friend, in October 2000, when he came to Colorado Springs for a gathering of his 452nd Bomb Group. We joined him for the reunion dinner-dance, and even though I had corresponded with John over the years, meeting him face to face was a treat. It was his first outing since his wife Emilie had died, and I think it helped boost his morale. We shared memories of Billy, and John made us honorary members of the 452nd Bomb Group, a wonderful bunch of guys.

Steve Blow's first column in the Dallas paper caused another new friendship to form. A few days after it appeared, Steve gave me the phone number of a man named Charles Leak, who had read the column and wanted to talk to me. Before I called, on a hunch I looked him up in Billy's high school yearbook. There he was. When Charles answered the phone, I told him my name, then said, "You went to high school with my uncle." He said he had, but didn't know Billy then, "Although I suspect we played football together." He had another reason for wanting to talk to me. He had been at

Perrin Field at the same time Billy was, and Hicks Field with Bill Karstetter, who was at both Eagle Pass and Salinas with Billy. Since Charles was in the L's and Billy was in the W's, they didn't know each other at Perrin.

But, coincidentally, just a few months before the column appeared, Charles was updating information on his military unit, and Bill Karstetter had sent along a copy of a letter my grandmother had written him, thinking it might be of interest in his research. Charles added it to his records but didn't think about it again until he saw the column and recognized the name. He sent me a copy of the letter, and it proved to be important.

Bill Karstetter was one of the boys who answered Idy's 1946 mass mailing to Billy's Eagle Pass classmates. He told of the trip from Salinas to Moses Lake with Billy, Paul Summer, and Eddy Steffani in 1944, including an anecdote about being stopped for speeding, then getting a police escort when the patrolmen learned they were late for their assignment. Then he filled in more gaps on the last few months of their training together. The letter Charles sent me was Idy's grateful reply. Unless her letters had been returned undeliverable, I could only guess at what she had written to Billy's friends. This one described Billy's relationship with his parents, and it broke my heart when Idy wrote, "Mr. Wisner cries nearly all the time." Papa's voice is silent through most of Billy's story, but this letter reveals the depth of his grief.

Another result of Steve Blow's column was a memorial to Billy in Oshkosh, Wisconsin. A member of an aviation enthusiasts' group saw the column and contacted David C. Lau of the Experimental Aircraft Association (www.eaa.org), saying he thought Billy's name should be added to their memorial wall. David e-mailed me, "I was so impressed with the work you did in tracking down the remains of your uncle. It would be a small token of our appreciation for that effort and a tribute to all airmen who were lost and their remains never recovered."

Billy's name was read, along with 50 others added that year, at their national convention and air show in Oshkosh on July 29, 2001. The wall is "Dedicated to those who have loved and supported aviation. Individuals honored…made aviation special in the lives of those they touched. We will remember them with love and appreciation." Because Billy loved flying so, he would be proud to be included.

My original intent was to find Billy's buddies from overseas, who could help me know Billy better. But of all the people I met during my research, only one knew him in Italy, Bill Ward, and they were just getting to be friends when Billy disappeared. Sadly, about a year after he helped me with this book by writing his memories of their time together at Foggia, Bill Ward passed away from ALS. His memoirs will be a family treasure.

In researching this book, I did get to know some of Billy's friends through letters. I learned that Eddy Steffani died in the war and Paul Summer died in the '80s. But others who figured prominently through old letters disappeared as the narrative followed the search for Billy, so I would like to finish their stories here.

Clarke Wiseley, Billy's best friend from Eagle Pass who adopted Billy's family as his own, stayed in close touch with my grandparents after the war, but Idy didn't keep his letters after 1945. Mother remembered he had been killed after the war but didn't remember the details. I turned to the Internet to find the answer. I found one Clarke Wiseley listed on www.qwestdex.com; that had to be Clarke's son the "lil' redhead." I wrote him a letter, and he passed it on to his mother, Avis, who called me as soon as she received it.

Avis told me Clarke had remained in the service after the war as a flight instructor, assigned to Perrin Field, where he and Billy (and Bill Karstetter and Charles Leak) had taken basic training just five years earlier. On June 16, 1950, Clarke was checking out a student on his last flight before graduation when their T-6 trainer spun in and crashed, killing them both. The cause was never known. Avis said the shock was more than she could bear, and Clarke's sister and brother-in-law, Evelyn and John Croft, had to fly to Dallas to make the funeral arrangements. I'm sure my grandparents attended the service.

Evelyn Croft died of cancer in the 1960s; her husband has also passed away. They were friendly with Billy at Moses Lake, but their memories of him died with them. Avis never met Billy, because she married Clarke after Billy left for final training. Avis sent me some photos, among them two my mother also has of toddlers Clarke III and my sister, Billie Gene, playing in the Wisner living room in 1947. Clarke visited often and wanted his family to know and love the Wisners as much as he did, but after he died Avis left Texas and lost touch. Clarke's friendship with Billy had been the glue that held the families together.

Billy and Maxine's cousins, Marshall Hill Russell, and Cecil "Brother" Hill, have passed on, but the twins, Peggy Hill Wangler and Betty Hill Meitzler, still live in the Dallas area, as does their other cousin Jean Wencker Petree and most of their offspring.

The Tarver boys were prominent in Billy's teen years, and there are two photos of them in Billy's scrapbook, one of Dalton, Jack, and little brother Paul mugging for the camera, and the other of handsome Jack in his Marine uniform. Dalton was killed before being shipped overseas, and Jack came back from the war but didn't keep up with our family. Dalton had been the correspondent, and so we lost touch with the Tarvers, too.

Looking for Tarvers in the Dallas area, again through the Internet, I found a Dalton Tarver. Figuring this had to be a relative, I wrote him a letter and got an e-mail response from the grandson of Paul Tarver, named after his great-uncle. Dalton gave my letter to his grandfather, and Paul called me the next day. He told me about playing football and tennis with Billy and the time Billy borrowed their car for a date during his last furlough. Jack Tarver died of cancer in 1984, so even though Billy's story was filling out, my first-hand sources were dwindling.

Each time I came across a letter from a friend of Billy's, I tried to find him. Most of the last names were unusual, so my search wasn't too hard, but there were several John Zebrowskis listed. John had trained with Billy, but they had gone separate ways after cadet training. Letters in Idy's file show "Zeb" kept in touch with the Wisners until 1947. I wrote 10 letters, hoping one of them was the right one, and again I received a reply by e-mail, this time from John, himself. He sent photos and shared memories and caught me up on his life. After multi-engine school, he stayed Stateside for a while as an instructor before being shipped to Bari, Italy. His bomber was shot down on his 11th mission over the railroad yards of Vienna on December 7, 1944. He and his crew avoided capture until February 27, 1945, thanks to some Slovakians who risked their lives to hide them. He kept in touch with his saviors and went back to visit them in 1998. After the war John worked for American Airlines until he retired in 1980.

There were no letters in the files from Eva Summer or Gertrude Twedt after 1946. Contemporaries of my grandparents, they've also passed away. I have no way of finding Rosemary Steffani or her two daughters. Idy had written in Billy's Eagle Pass yearbook that Rosemary remarried, but she didn't say to whom. With no last name, a search is impossible.

Through the Web I located a Louis W. Wust, the boy who had spent a weekend with the Wisners in Dallas during training at Perrin Field. An e-mail came back from his son, who told me Louis, Sr., passed away in 1991. There are some disappointments.

Charles Leak, whom I met through Steve Blow's column, knew Walter "Pat" Patton, Billy's buddy in California. Charles had no luck tracking Walter down through his alumni association, so on a hunch, I called Edna

Summer, Paul's widow. She gave me an address for Robert Stinson, who had been at Eagle Pass with Billy and Walter and had stayed in touch with Paul through the years. He told me Walter had become a doctor, had four sons, and was still living in the Dallas area at least until the late '70s, when they lost touch. Charles did some checking in Dallas, found Walter's son Jeff, also a doctor, who told me Pat passed away in 1996.

That was a bigger disappointment for me. Pat Patton was the only person who could have shed some light on the mystery girl or girls in the photos taken with Billy in California before he shipped out. Billy was serious about a girl in California, and if Idy had just known her name, she would have tried to reach her. Keeping in touch with Billy's friends was a way to keep their memories of him alive. That way, so was he.

Ruth Peck, Billy's ice-skating companion and co-worker at Sears, stayed close to the family after Billy left for California, and Idy and Mama gave her a wedding shower when she married Robert Orsburn (or Osburn) in June 1944. Newspaper items about her shower and wedding were pasted in Billy's scrapbook, but locating Ruth has been fruitless.

Our other uncle, Daddy's brother Morris, came back safely from the war in the Pacific. He and his wife Margie had three children, my only first cousins, Carole, Ken, and Kathi. Morris died of a heart attack in 1992, and in 1996 Ken succumbed at age 47 to non-Hodgkins lymphoma. Our little family seems so much smaller now.

Besides the friendships, some more good things came out of our search. Paolo Cagnan got his wish for a literary prize from the *Alto Adige Cultura e Territorio*, "Autori da Scoprire," when his diary of the search, *Trov@te il Pilota Wisner*,* came out in October 2001. When I translated it, each time he told of being in the dark or following a dead end, I relived the guilt I had felt every time it happened.

But there was one bit of information Paolo had that I didn't learn about until I read his book. The Mortuary Affairs team had shown him a document dated July 9, 1952, that wasn't included in any of my files. In it was the name of the man who had discovered the bracelet and Billy's remains. According to Paolo's book, Ettore Coruzzi had come across the bracelet and remains while working on a project for a Bolzano architect and had notified the Carabinieri in Sarentino.

---

*Cagnan, Paolo, *Trov@te il Pilota Wisner*, Sperling & Kupfer Editori, Milano: 2000.

Paolo learned that Coruzzi died in a car accident several years ago, and his family couldn't contribute anything to his research, an interesting highlight but a dead end. *Trov@te il Pilota Wisner* ends with the successful closing of the excavation in August 2000.

But even though his book stopped there, Paolo's interest in the story didn't. In a n e-mail dated January 10, 2002, he added a cryptic paragraph. "The last thing. Maybe, I'll have something new for you in the next week. Are you curious? Please, let me know exactly which Billy's objects (wrist[watch], bracelet, ring etc.) you think have disappeared in those days. Maybe, I know who stole something…"

I immediately thought of Billy's ring, something of value that could easily have been stolen. Then Paolo added another teaser in a follow-up e-mail. "Talking about my latest discoveries about Bill, I wanted to make you a surprise, because two weeks ago a friend of mine found an article of the *Alto Adige*, I think of 1945, talking about a trial against a local who was charged of having stolen some items from the body of a US-pilot, not mentioned where. I went to the Court to look for the documents, but they were transferred to another Archive and I have to wait. As you can see, is always the same story with the missing files. Be patient, I'll let you know."

But once again the complicated location names had played a trick on us. A gold ring had been stolen from the body of an American serviceman, but this one died in April 1945. "You know what happened?" Paolo asked. "I read Mules, which is 'our' place next to the Feldrand [Hotel], but [there is] another small village north of South Tyrol, that's Mauls and not Muls, in German. Oh, God, so many difficulties with the names!!! I'm so sorry."

It was a disappointment, but I knew recovering Billy's ring would have been a miracle, and I've had more than my allotment of those. But it was sweet of Paolo to try.

Just as I thought this story was finished, I learned that the Internet is a two-way street. All along I had been the one trying to find people, but on March 29, 2002, someone we'd been looking for found me. An e-mail from a man named Jack Svela had the words "Virgil Olson" in the subject line. Olson was the pilot who had been hit by the flak that started the events of October 20, 1944, and Jim had exhausted all his resources trying to find him back when we started our search. Svela said he and Olson had been surfing the Internet to try to locate information on the commanding officer at Foggia. Olson's records had been destroyed in the fire at the St. Louis Army Personnel Records office, and he was hoping to reconstruct them through other means. In so doing, they ran across Jim Graham's story about our search for Billy on the 1st Fighter Group Association Web site, and found my e-mail address. I sent Svela my phone number, and Olson called me the next day.

Olson said we couldn't find him in the phone book because he was listed under his wife's name. He seemed surprised we'd been looking for him, but he was happy to answer my questions about the events of October 20, 1944. Over the years he had forgotten the names of the other pilots involved in the accident, but when I refreshed his memory about Billy, his wingman, Olson said, "I was very fond of him. He was a likable young guy and took his position as instructed and maintained it well during several other missions. He did an excellent job of protecting my butt. It was sad when we got into this fracas."

He said on that day Billy was behind him and slightly low, exactly where he should have been, when Olson was hit by the flak. "I was going to take Bill and return to base. When I saw the other plane [Twedt] coming toward me, I called him twice to 'clear me low.' I got only one garbled reply, then he pulled up suddenly and hit me on my good side. When I saw him coming, I realized I had to get out. I couldn't get rid of my canopy, because it was warped, so I had to get down low in the seat to kick it off." Twedt's collision with him had caused him to go into a flat spin. He doesn't remember pulling his ripcord and thinks it must have caught on something as he bailed out, because he hit his head on the horizontal stabilizer. When he came to he was lying on an incline so steep he was almost standing up.

"A man came up to get me and was pointing his gun as he approached. He escorted me down the mountainside." Because of the near-vertical incline, it was difficult going, and one misstep could cause a rockslide. He assumed that the man was a member of the local civil defense organization, because he was not in uniform. "The man took a handkerchief out of his pocket and dipped it in the stream to put cold water on my head and face and to try to stop the bleeding. I remember he also carried a pint bottle with a piece of wadded-up waxed paper he used as a cork. He shared the contents with me, and it tasted like grain alcohol and burned my cut tongue.

"He took me to a hut at timberline, a two-level building where the animals stayed below and a Catholic priest lived above. The priest was going to hide me until the end of the war. I could speak a little Italian and he could speak a little English. I remember he kept sending a young girl down to the cellar to get wine. After my second glass, I was happy to hear that the priest was going to hide me. I was telling him I was unarmed except for my sidearm and just about had him snowed, when a young unarmed villager came in with a belt of [my] ammunition around his neck, which shot my story to the Catholic priest. That prompted him to call for a one-horse cart to take me down to the town [where] I was lodged in jail and told to lie down on the cot. A well-educated Luftwaffe officer came in and terrorized me in very good English, waving his arms and threatening me with the P-82 he had in his holster, saying the U.S. had no business being involved in the war. I wasn't sure if he was going to shoot me or not.

"After the local jail, I was taken to another jail, probably in Bolzano, where I was kept in solitary in a room with no furniture, just a wooden plank, and a peephole in the door. The prisoner across the hallway from my cell was a German soldier who had been caught going AWOL. He would be sent to a work detail every morning, and once he slipped me a piece of newspaper under the door with a piece of hard candy on it; another time it was newspaper with loose tobacco. Presumably I was to roll a cigarette using the newspaper, but I didn't have anything to light it with. When we did see each other, he tried to speak with me in limited English and managed to tell me he had competed as a runner in the 1936 Olympics. He was proud to say he ran against Jesse Owens.

"The only food they gave me in that jail was three or four boiled potatoes soaked in vinegar. I stayed there four or five days. Every day I was

Virgil Olson's POW I.D. card

taken to the hospital for treatment, and every night I was taken to the train station to meet the train for Frankfurt, because they never knew which night it would arrive. I was first taken to Frankfurt for interrogation, then to the Sagan prison camp [Stalag Luft III], then Moosburg [Stalag VIIA]."

Olson's account confirmed what I had hoped, that Billy was doing everything right on that mission. I asked Olson if Twedt may have been hit by the flak, too, causing him to fall backward and pull back on the stick and run into Olson. He said it was possible, but there's no way to know. Olson told me the same thing he'd told my grandmother: until he received her letters after the war, he didn't know Billy was involved in the accident. I realized that if she had just asked Olson where he'd been captured, her search might have had a different outcome. But I'm sure it never crossed her mind.

And while Idy's hopes of finding Billy never diminished, her efforts eventually did. She and Papa turned their attention to what was left of their family. Mother, Daddy, and my sister lived the post-war American dream. I was born in November 1947. I'm the one with Billy's coloring and dimples, as Idy so often reminded me. She and I were close, and I know it was bittersweet for her to see him in my face.

In 1952 Daddy was transferred from Dallas to San Antonio, the first of many promotions throughout his 42-year career with Southwestern Bell. We left Texas in 1954, but until the late '50s spent many of Daddy's summer vacations in Dallas, and we celebrated Christmas there with both sides of the family through 1975, even after Sister was married and we were both out of college. Idy and Papa lived for those visits, and Christmases were never the same after we stopped going.

We stopped because one summer evening in 1976 Idy complained to Papa about a terrible headache. She had suffered from migraines all her life, so Papa knew what to do. He gave her two aspirin and helped her lie down on the sofa. But when he checked on her later, she wouldn't wake up, so he called an ambulance. An aneurism had burst causing a cerebral hemorrhage, and she never regained consciousness. Ten days later she died. She was 88.

Her funeral was a tribute to a wonderful woman, well attended by friends and family. The chapel overflowed with flowers, children, and babies, three of the things Idy loved most. It was a beautiful, sunny day. The bluebonnets were in bloom, and the cemetery was lush and green.

As I watched them lay my sweet grandmother to rest, I remember hoping she had found her Billy, at last.

WILLIAM O. WISNER

AMERICAN PILOT
US-PILOT
PILOTA AMERICANO

MY BROTHER–MY HERO–MY FRIEND

Crashed above this site October 20, 1944

He fought against tyranny so the world might live in peace

We are grateful to our South Tyrolean friends who helped us bring him home after 56 years

MEIN BRUDER-MEIN HELD-MEIN FREUND	MIO FRATELLO-MIO EROE-MIO AMICO
Er starb, wo dieser Bach entspringt	Precipitato sopra questo luogo
Abgestürzt am 20 10 1944	il 20 ottobre del 1944
gefallen im Kampf gegen Tyrannei,	Ha combattuto contro la tirannia
damit auf Erden Friede sei	affinché il mondo potesse vivere in pace
In Dankbarkeit unseren Südtiroler Freunden, die	Siamo grati ai nostri amici sudtirolesi che ci hanno
geholfen haben, ihn heimzubringen nach 56 Jahren	aiutato a riportarlo a casa 56 anni dopo

AFTERWORD

Inga Hosp, Paolo Cagnan, and Konrad Rungger have helped establish a memorial to Billy behind Konrad's *gasthof*, the Hotel Feldrand. Inga installed a bench a few months after we got back from Italy, and Paolo and Konrad saw to it that the memorial plaque my parents commissioned in 2002 was installed behind the bench, next to the stream that flows down from Billy's crash site. The plaque pays tribute to Billy and thanks our friends in the South Tyrol, without whose help he would never have been found.

The most important friendship, though, is one that never had a chance to form. Had Billy made it back from that mission on October 20th, I know he would have crossed paths with a young flyer from Seattle named Jim Graham. Knowing Jim, and with a pretty good understanding of Billy, I'm positive they would be buddies to this day.

But since Billy didn't get to be Jim's friend, I guess I'll have to do.

ACKNOWLEDGEMENTS

Telling this story was a labor of love I couldn't have done alone.

Jim Graham made it possible. His network of friends, Dick Kahler, Bill Mays, Steve Duncan, Bill Jordan, Roland Geiger, got us started, and his steady hand and cool head kept the search on track. I have no doubt his helpmate, Jeanne Simonds, kept Jim on track.

My gratitude to Inga Hosp and Paolo Cagnan can never be expressed adequately. I am blessed to be counted among their friends and to have been included with Bruno and Julia as part of the Hosp family. They enrich my life.

I thank Christoph Mair for acting as diplomatic liaison.

John Chopelas and his love for Billy and interest in "things WWII" kept my curiosity strong. His support and encouragement assured me Billy was worth finding.

Billy's old friends allowed themselves to be re-discovered so I could fill in the gaps: Bill Ward, Eva Summer, Avis Wiseley, Paul Tarver, Dalton Tarver, John Zebrowski, Bill Karstetter, Louis Wust, and Virgil Olson. Charles Leak, who never knew Billy but was willing to help, anyway, inspired me to keep looking for the hard-to-find ones.

Martin I. Selling's translation of Inga Hosp's article brought a different perspective to the search. I don't know of any way to repay him, except to say thank you.

Friends who provided everything from lodging to criticism to editing include Dick and Julie Hamann, Kathryn Warren, Nora MacIntyre, Susan Rutherford, Becky Barry, Bob and Lou Way, Anne McGihon, Denny McGihon, Sue Sheridan, Cindy and Ed Fern, and Emilie Leman. Carol Trotter got me started on the right foot; Jan Marino said I could do it. They and my friends Joy Dugan, Jane Cantine, Carol Duncan, Diane Deschanel, Patty Gysin, Wendy Sime, Lee Ellis, Felicia Duvall, Mary Jones, Gaylynn Long, kept me from getting discouraged.

I thank U.S. Mortuary Affairs for the good work they do every day, especially David Roath and Mark Baldwin, their team members, and Liz Tate. They never lose sight of the importance of their jobs; they keep honor alive.

Steve Blow of the *Dallas Morning News* appreciated the story of a hometown boy, David C. Lau added Billy's name to the EAA Memorial Wall, and Edwin Baquet added his story to the P-38 museum at Riverside, California. Howard Pankratz of the *Denver Post*, through his well-written articles, gave me confidence this story was worthy of attention.

My appearance on *Hollywood Squares* won me a new car, and Bud Wells and Linda Cabral of the *Rocky Mountain News* made it easy to sell it so I could finance the initial publication of this book.

Gil Asakawa's gentle editing and Scott Johnson's creative design gave the book life. Thanks to Judy Joseph for bringing them my way and guiding me through publication.

Thanks to my parents, Maxine and Fannon Thompson, for their love and pride; to my sister and her family, Billie, Harold, Katie (my proofreader), and Bill Fischer, for providing perspective; to Margie Thompson for opening her home to "no blood kin"; and to the entire Dale family, who gave me me an appreciation for military life and the honor therein.

And to my husband Jack, who never doubted my ability and who will always have my love, respect, and gratitude. Honey, you can put away the tissues now. I promise I won't ask you to read this book again.

AUTHOR'S NOTE: In most instances, grammatical and spelling errors in the letters and e-mails have been left uncorrected in order to preserve the personality of their writers. However, corrections were made where the errors might misrepresent the writers' intended meaning or confuse the reader.

APPENDIX A

MISSION REPORT

Mullins' Note: Pet Dog is the 27th Sqd, Cragmore is the 71st Sqd [Billy's], Springcap is the 94th Sqd

71st FIGHTER SQUADRON
1st FIGHTER GROUP
APO   520

20 October 1944.

1. <u>MISSION AND TARGET:</u> To provide close escort on penetration, target cover and withdrawal for two groups of B-17's of the 5th Wing hitting oil storage tanks at Regensburg, Germany.

2. <u>AIRCRAFT AND CHRONOLOGY:</u> 17 P-38's of which one was spare, Lts Olson, Wisner, Captain Elliott, Lts Anderson, Jones, Ferguson, Lambert, Brewer, Janacek, Dunne, Decker, Twedt, Burns, Summer, Hutchins, Knapp and Hurley up from base, Salsola L/G at 0855 hours. There were two early returns. Lt Brewer was down at base at 1045 hours as he was unable to obtain gas from left belly tank. Lt Burns had his left engine cut out at altitude, turned back about 30 miles south of Venice and was down at base at 1100 hours. 15 P-38's did not make rendezvous with bombers. Lts Olson and

Twedt collided in mid-air near Bolzano, Italy and Lt Wisner
spun in at Bolzano, Captain Elliott crashlanded at Duress,
Italy; pilot ok. All this was due to intense, accurate
heavy flak over Bolzano at 1115 to 1120 hours. 11 P-38's
down base at 1320 hours.

3. <u>ROUTE:</u> Base up Adriatic making landfall on Italian
coast 10 miles east of Venice and continuing on course to
Bolzano then reciprocal headings back to base going west of
Venice.

4. <u>RENDEZVOUS, FORMATION AND ASSAULT:</u> Escort with Pet Dog
leading, Cragmore high, right, and Springcap low, left in
good formation until arriving in vicinity of Bolzana [sic],
Italy. At about 1115 hours Cragmore was 7-8 miles south of
Bologna [sic] when intense, accurate heavy flak was
encountered, so Red, White and Green flights broke right
and Blue flight left to skirt flat, then broke right again
and passed south of Bolzano to catch other three flights
who were about 5 miles east of town. When Red Flight was
about 5 miles northeast of town, Red #1 and 3 were hit and
#1 called Pet Dog and told him he had two men on single
engine and that he was going to take squadron back to base.
About this time over "B" channel came the words: "Go
down", repeated several times and then Red #1 and white #4
collided in mid-air. The flying debris from this collision
apparently hit Red #2 and in a few seconds he went into a
spin and went in. No chutes were observed. Blue leader
began to escort Red #3 back to base as he was on single
engine and called White leader and as he was alone with his
flight suggested Cragmore returned to base. Green flight
was not in sight and was not seen till 10 minutes later on
course home. Blue leader took over Squadron and crossed
weaved over crippled Red #3 until he crashlanded at
"Duress"; pilot o.k. Cragmore did not continue on mission
because by the time this situation at Bolzano was
straightened out, Pet Dog and Springcap squadrons were out
of sight and would have been impossible to overtake.

<u>RESULTS OF BOMBING:</u> 71st was not in target area.

6. <u>RESULTS OF STRAFING:</u> None attempted.

7. ENEMY AIR RESISTANCE AND ACTIVITY: None.

8. FLAK: Intense, accurate heavy at fighters from
vicinity south and north northwest of Bolzano, Italy.
Scant, inaccurate heavy at Venice.

9. SIGNIFICANT OBSERVATIONS: None.

10. WEATHER: CAVU

11. AIR SEA RESCUE: None.

12. RADIO SECURITY: Broken by Springcap at 1050 hours
when a "bogie" was called in.

13. FRIENDLY AIRCRAFT SEEN LOST OR IN DIFFICULTY: None.

14. ENEMY AIRCRAFT SEEN DESTROYED BY OTHER GROUPS: None.

15. VICTORIES AND LOSSES: 4 P-38's, 3 pilots, Lts Olson,
Wisner and Twedt were lost in vicinity of Bolzano, Italy.
Lts Olson and Twedt collided in mid-air after being
crippled by flak and Lt Wisner was apparently hit by debris
from colliding aircraft and spun in. Captain Elliott crash
landed at "Duress" on way home; pilot o.k.

16. SORTIES: 15

17. SQUADRON LEADER: Lt Jones, Flight leaders, Lts
Janacek and Hutchins.

18. COMMENTS: Radio contact was not attempted with
bombers. Captain Elliott returned safely to base at 2000
hours, this date.

                              [Signed]
                              EDGAR P. CHRISTIAN,
                              2d Lt., Air Corps,
                              Ass't S-2 Officer

The *Golden Slipper* as it might have appeared,
giving credit for the three locomotives Billy strafed
(drawing by Don Moore, commissioned by John Chopelas)

Appendix B

Search Report

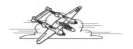

S & S DETACHMENT MIRANDOLA
AMERICAN GRAVES REGISTRATION SERVICE
MEDITERRANEAN THEATER SEPARATE ZONE COMMAND-MTOUSA
APO 782   US ARMY

PO 360.33   22 August 1947

SUBJECT: Transmittal of Completed Cases.

TO   : Commanding Officer
         American Graves Registration Service
         Mediterranean Theater Separate Zone Command
         APO 794 US Army   Attention S-3

   1. Transmitted herewith is Completed Case pertaining
to crew member of aircraft P-38 J, AAF Serial Number 43-
28379, reported as Killed in Action 20 October 1944.

   2. An investigation was conducted by this
Headquarters in the Bolzano, Fortezza, Trento area in an
attempt to recover the remains of American deceased. No
remains of American deceased personnel were recovered.

   3. No parts of the wrecked aircraft could be

located. Inquires at the general disclosed that all
American deceased that were recovered from any aircraft
that crashed in the area, during the course of the war, had
been interred at the local Civilian Cemeteries and at a
later date removed to an established US Military Cemetery
by American AGRS personnel.

4. Investigation at this headquarters reveals that a
total of 14, (Fourteen) deceased American personnel have
been recovered from the above-mentioned areas previously
and interred at the US Military Cemetery, Mirandola, as
Unknown American Soldiers.

5. Inasmuch as complete and thorough ground search
has been conducted in the area where subject plane is
reported to have been last sighted, and no remains
recovered, it is recommended by the undersigned that this
case be declared closed to further searching and swooping
activities and that a possible association be attempted
with the casualties listed on the attached case and the
Unknown American Soldiers recovered previously from the
same area.

6. In the event association proves negative, it is
then recommended that this case be declared closed and the
remains of subject personnel be declared non-recoverable.

                        Robert W. Campbell
                        Captain   Inf
                        Commanding

APPENDIX C

RESOURCES

The Internet is a fluid tool that changes constantly. Some of the Web sites listed may no longer be viable, so using a search engine will reveal new resources. The following is by no means a complete list of resources, but they are good places to start. Every search will take on a life of its own as archives are read, witnesses are located, and facts are uncovered. Follow each lead to its end, because "with the Internet, a dead end is just a fork in the road that is easily corrected."

Active-Duty Records (80 percent of which were destroyed by fire in 1973):

> National Personnel Records Center (a division of the National Archives and Records Administration)
> Military Personnel Records
> 9700 Page Avenue
> St. Louis, MO 63132-5100
> Phone: 314-538-2050

U.S. Battlefield Cemeteries:

> American Battle Monuments Commission Operations
> Court House Plaza 2, Suite 500
> 2300 Clarendon Blvd.
> Arlington, VA 22201
> Phone: 703-696-6897
> Fax: 703-696-6666

Individual Deceased Personnel File (IDPF) (Include pertinent information on the MIA, such as name, rank, service number, where he was last stationed, and the date of his disappearance when making the request):

Army (includes Army Air Corps):
Commander
U.S. Total Army Personnel Command
ATTN: TAPC-PAO (FOIA)
200 Stoval Street
Alexandria, Virginia 22331-0482
Phone: 703-325-5300
By e-mail, tapcper@hoffman.army.mil

NOTE: If you are not a family member or if you need the file on another serviceman for your research, be sure to state that *you are making the request under the Freedom of Information Act.* Under this legislation, you are entitled by law to this information, even if you are not related to the MIA.

Navy:
Officer In Charge
Naval Medical and Dental Affairs
Mortuary Affairs Branch
PO Box 886999
Great Lakes, IL 60088-6999
Phone: 800-876-1311, ext. 621, 627, 628
Fax: 847-688-3964

Marine Corps:
Marine Corps Historical Center
1254 Charles Morris St. SE
Attn: Reference Section
Washington, DC 20374-5040
Phone: 202-433-3483
Fax: 202-433-4691

Merchant Marines:
Old Military Civilian Records
National Archives
7th and Pennsylvania Ave NW
Washington, DC 20408
Phone: 202-501-5385

Related Organizations or Web Sites (by no means a complete list):

American WWII Orphans Network (AWON)
    5745 Lee Rd.
    Indianapolis, IN 46216
    Web site: www.awon.org
    E-mail: awon@aol.com

U.S. Army Personnel: www-perscom.army.mil/tagd/cmaoc/
rfad-web-geninq.htm
U.S. Army Mortuary Affairs: www.quartermaster.army.mil/MAC/
Embassies: www.usembassy.state.gov
National Personnel Records Center: www.nara.gov/regional/
mpr.html
Military memorabilia and bulletin board: www.wae.com
Search story of interest: www.behindbarbedwire.com/carlh.htm
MIA hunters: www.pro5.com/mia
Central Identification Laboratory: www.cilhi.army.mil/
WFI Research Group: www.cntn.net/wfirg/
Aircraft MIA Project: www.samoloty.ip.pl/amiap/

Search engines: Using more than one search engine and typing in more than one combination or permutation of the subject's unit (or key words) will maximize results (e.g., searching for 1st Fighter Group, then trying 1st FG).

Bulletin boards: Many military unit alumni associations have Web sites with bulletin boards. Posting messages where appropriate can get the attention of someone who may know something important or have access to records containing leads.

INDEX

Page numbers in **bold** indicate photographs.

Photos & Illustrations